Standard Biology

GRAHAM MOFFAT
and
IAIN STEWART

F H S Science Dept

Aug 1991

UNWIN HYMAN

Published by
UNWIN HYMAN LIMITED
15/17 Broadwick Street
London W1V 1FP

© Graham Moffat and Iain Stewart

First published 1990. Reprinted 1991

All rights reserved. No part of this publication
may be reproduced, stored in a retrieval system,
or transmitted in any form or by any means,
electronic, mechanical, photocopying or otherwise,
without the prior permission of Unwin Hyman Limited

British Library Cataloguing in Publication Data

Stewart, Iain
  Standard biology.
  1. Biology
  I. Title II. Moffat, Graham
  574

ISBN 0-04-448116-0

Designed by Geoff Wadsley
Artwork by RDL Artset Ltd
Typeset by MS Filmsetting Ltd, Frome, Somerset
Printed and bound in Great Britain by
Butler and Tanner Ltd, Frome, Somerset

Contents

Teacher's Preface — iv
Student's Introduction — v
Acknowledgements — vi

The Biosphere — 1
1 Ecosystems
2 Studying an Ecosystem – Abiotic Factors
3 Studying an Ecosystem – Biotic Factors
4 Identifying Organisms
5 Chains and Webs
6 Energy Flow
7 Populations
8 Nutrient Cycles
9 Pollution – Cause and Control
10 Water Pollution
11 Resource Management

The World of Plants — 32
1 Plant Varieties
2 Uses of Plants
3 Seeds and Germination
4 Flower Structure and Pollination
5 Pollen Tubes and Fruit Formation
6 Seed Dispersal
7 Asexual Reproduction
8 Artificial Propagation
9 Photosynthesis
10 Plant Leaves
11 Plant Transport

Animal Survival — 61
1 Food
2 Feeding
3 Digestion
4 Digestive Enzymes
5 Absorption
6 Sexual Reproduction
7 Reproductive Organs
8 Development
9 Development and Care
10 Water Balance
11 Waste Removal
12 Kidneys – Real or Artificial
13 Responding to the Environment
14 Biorhythms

Investigating Cells — 90
1 Microscopes and Cells
2 Cell Division
3 Cells and Diffusion
4 Cells and Water
5 Chemical Reactions in Cells
6 More About Enzymes
7 Cells and Energy
8 Aerobic Respiration in Cells

The Body in Action — 119
1 Food and Energy
2 Breathing
3 The Lungs
4 The Heart and Circulation
5 The Structure of Blood
6 Support and Movement – The Skeleton
7 Bones and Joints
8 Muscles and Movement
9 Levels of Performance
10 Senses and Reactions
11 The Eye and Sight
12 Hearing and Balance
13 The Nervous System

Inheritance — 149
1 Variation
2 A Visit to the Zoo
3 A Visit to the Botanic Gardens
4 Inheritance of Characteristics
5 Gametes, Chromosomes and Genes
6 Monohybrid Crosses
7 Sex Determination in Humans
8 Chromosome Mutations
9 Improving Domestic Animals and Plants

Biotechnology — 179
1 Introducing Biotechnology
2 Yeast, Baking and Brewing
3 Dairy Products
4 Growing Microorganisms
5 Pollution
6 Food and Fuel from Microbes
7 Genetic Engineering
8 Genetic Engineering in Medicine
9 Antibiotics
10 Biological Detergents
11 Immobilised Enzymes

Glossary — 208
Index — 215

Teacher's Preface

Standard Biology is a core textbook providing a complete coverage of the Learning Outcomes of the Scottish Standard Grade Biology syllabus. The book is divided into the seven topics covered by Standard Grade Biology.

Each topic is further sub-divided into short chapters designed to provide flexibility and ease of use. An introductory panel called 'Key Ideas' aims to set the scene for the content of each of these chapters. The chapters are clearly differentiated into general and credit level text; but throughout the book we have tried to keep the text as simple as the subject matter would allow. The credit level sections always follow the general level material in the chapter and they are indicated by pairs of arrows.

At the end of each chapter there is an 'Activities' panel: the activities cover both knowledge and understanding and problem solving, and they are graded into three broad levels, indicated as follows:

- ○ general level
- ◑ general/credit level
- ● credit level

There is a comprehensive glossary of terms at the end of the book and most of these terms appear in bold print in the text.

Student's Introduction

How to use this book:

1. If you want to find out about a main topic, look it up in the **Contents** page at the front of the book.

2. If you cannot find the topic in the Contents page, you should look it up in the alphabetical **Index** at the back of the book.

3. The **Key Ideas** section introduces each chapter and summarises the main points which you will be able to read about in the chapter.

4. If a word is printed in **bold** it means that it is especially important.

5. The main text covers general level material and the credit text is marked with arrows like this:

6. The **Activities** box at the end of each chapter allows you to check that you have remembered and understood what you have read. Some of the activities give you practice at solving problems.

7. If you want to find the meaning of a biological word you can look it up in the **Glossary** which is at the end of the book.

Acknowledgements

We would like to thank Walter Whitelaw for his writing contribution to 'The Biosphere' topic and his editorial comments on the entire text. Special thanks should also go to our wives and families for their tolerance during the production of the book.

The authors and publisher would like to thank the following for permission to reproduce photographs:

Aberdeen-Angus Cattle Society (Louis Flood Photographers) 175; Dr. R. J. Aitken, Medical Research Council, Edinburgh 87; Heather Angel (Biofotos) 1 (top, bottom and middle left, middle right), 3 (top right), 76, 88 (middle); Ardea 3 (bottom right), 14, 30 (top left), 80, 149 (top right); Associated Press 26 (middle); Ayrshire Cattle Society (Douglas Law Photography) 175; A-Z Botanical Collection Ltd 39; Bass Brewery 197; Dr. Alan Beaumont 1 (bottom right), 3 (bottom left), 7, 46 (left); Biophoto Associates 34, 42 (middle and right), 50, 87 (top), 88 (left), 91, 92 (top and bottom), 95 (top and bottom), 98, 131, 182; Rex Brinkworth 172; British Diabetic Association 199; British Petroleum Company PLC 105; Camera Press 26 (right), 38; City of Portsmouth, Planning Department 24 (bottom right); Bruce Coleman Ltd 3 (bottom middle), 24 (bottom left), 31, 32; The Donkey Sanctuary 149 (top left); Friends of the Earth Trust 26 (top); Geoscience Features Picture Library 3 (top left); Griffin and George 6 (top); Tony Harris 108; Adam Hart Davis 42 (left), 46 (right), 78; Marc Henrie 88 (right), 149 (bottom right); Hereford Herd Book Society 175; Highlands and Islands Development Board 3 (middle right); James Howden Group Ltd 26 (left); ICCE 27; Jersey Cattle Society 175; Kidney Research Unit for Wales 84; The Ministry of Agriculture, Fisheries and Food 30 (top right); The National Canine Defence League 149 (bottom left); National Rivers Authority 190; Natural History Photographic Agency 12; Oxford Scientific films 59; Popperfoto 201; Royal Botanic Gardens, Edinburgh 155; Safeway PLC 25; Science Photo Library (David Scharf) 170; Scottish and Newcastle Beer Production Ltd, Edinburgh 37 (four pictures); Slazenger 134, 147; Tesco Stores Ltd 24 (middle left); Unicef (UK) 120; US Department of Agriculture, Soil Conservation Service 30 (bottom); Water Research Centre 46 (middle).

1 Ecosystems

Key Ideas

In *ecology* the basic unit of study is the *ecosystem*. An ecosystem is made up of all the living things present, and their surroundings. Differences between ecosystems are caused by biological and physical factors.

Every ecosystem is made up of the non-living *environment*, or *habitat*, and a *community* of living things. This community is made up of a unique group of animals and plants.

Think of a journey you make – to and from school, on a field trip or on your holidays. On any journey you pass through many different **ecosystems**.

Between the ecosystems, there are no *exact* boundaries. *Within* an ecosystem there will be a common **community** of plants and animals.

Between one ecosystem and the next, there will be clear differences in the **habitat** – the surroundings – and in the kinds of animals and plants found there.

Ecosystems vary greatly in size. A mouse in a cage could be an ecosystem. On a bigger scale, a pond and a small island are ecosystems. Larger still are the main British ecosystems shown below.

All ecosystems together form the largest ecological unit of all – the Earth itself. Scientists call this the **BIOSPHERE**.

The Biosphere

2 THE BIOSPHERE

Whatever the size, every ecosystem can be described by its **abiotic** factors – its climate and habitat – and its **biotic** factors – the plants and animals present.

Let's look more closely at what is meant by abiotic and biotic factors.

Abiotic Factors

Climate 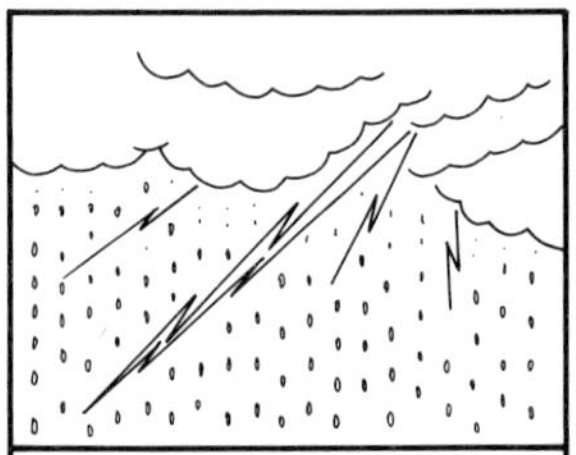
- Rainfall and humidity 
- Temperature and day length 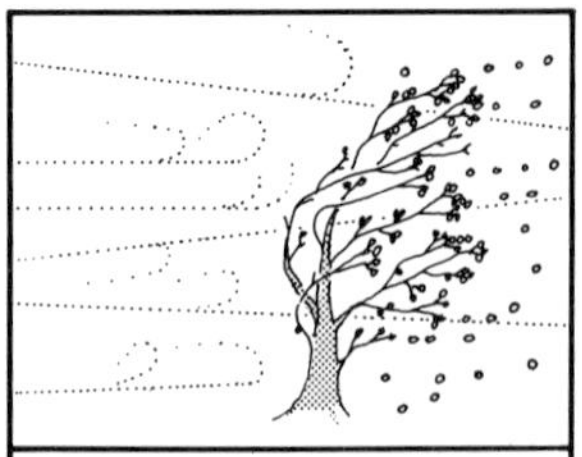
- Wind

Geography 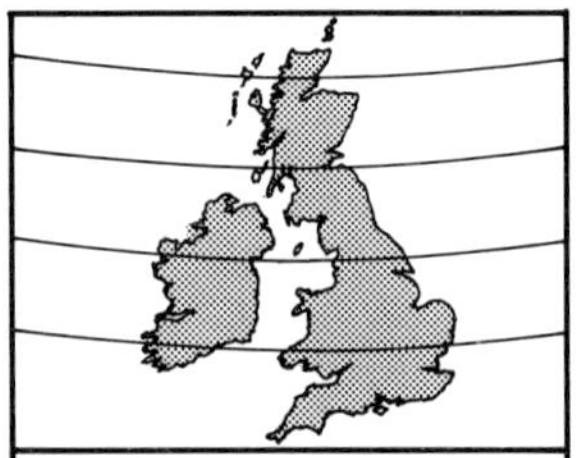
- Latitude 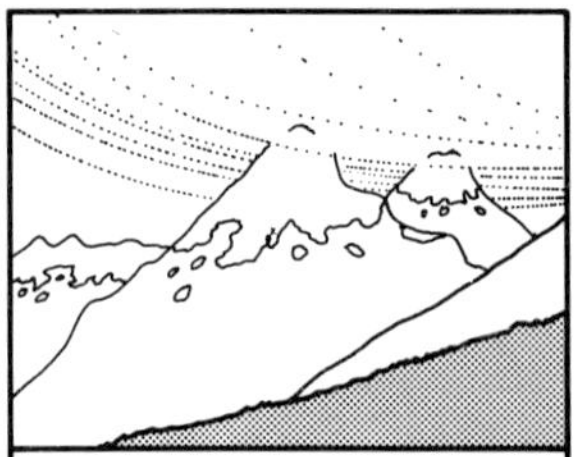
- Altitude and slope 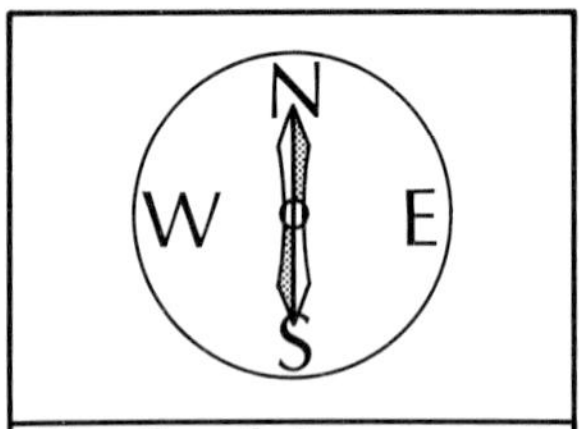
- Direction of slope compass bearing

Soil 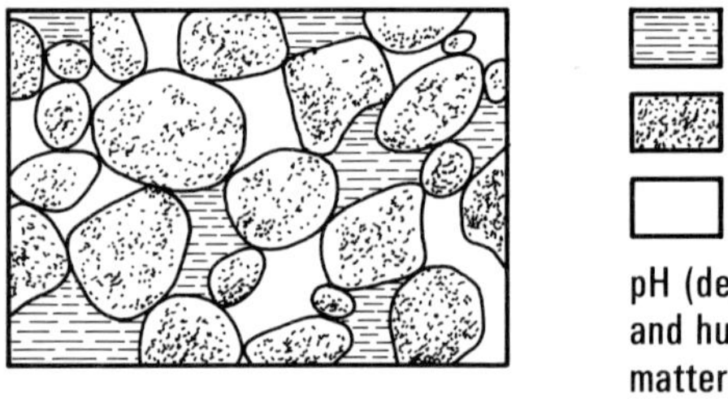
- Soil water
- Soil particle
- Air space

pH (degree of acidity) and humus (decayed matter) are also important

Biotic Factors

- Competition (between species)
- Food supply
- Effect of humans
- Predation

Just think of the number of possible combinations of abiotic and biotic factors in even a small area like Britain. Only plants and animals well suited to the habitat will survive. They make up the community of an ecosystem.

THE BIOSPHERE 3

It is amazing that even the most severe habitats can support life. Look at the examples below.

Bacteria are found in boiling hot springs known as geysers in Yellowstone Park, USA. No other living things could survive such heat

Small alpine plants, lichens and mosses can survive the cold, windswept conditions on the high summits of mountains

Humans Alter Habitats

Humans have a major effect on their surroundings. There are many examples to show how we have spoiled natural habitats. For example, in Britain this century, we have had to produce more food and timber for an increasing population. Native trees were cut down and any suitable land was used for farming.

The only space left for new trees was on wild mountainous uplands. Quick-growing trees, such as Norway spruce, were imported from abroad and planted in huge numbers. They replaced the original natural communities of different kinds of trees and changed the habitat of plants and animals in these areas.

Crops used to be grown in smaller fields on smaller farms than we have today. It is more profitable to grow cereal crops like wheat and barley in large fields, which can be ploughed and harvested using large farm machinery. Combine harvesters cannot be used in small fields, nor can small farms afford them. To make larger fields, farmers have removed many hedgerows and small woods. This has destroyed many plant and animal communities.

Conifers provide a less varied habitat, with fewer plants growing on the forest floor

A mixed woodland contains different kinds of trees which provide a varied habitat

Small fields have hedges and banks providing homes for many creatures, and contain a variety of shrubs and small plants

Prairie-style fields have no plant variety and shelter few animals

Many native species have become **extinct** through human selfishness.

4 THE BIOSPHERE

Activities

1. What is meant by the term ecosystem?
2. State the meaning of the term community.
3. Copy and complete the table below. You will need about 10 lines. Give an example for each factor.

Factors that affect the characteristics of an ecosystem

Biotic Factors	Examples	Abiotic Factors	Examples
Effect of humans	cutting down forests	Climate	rainfall

4. Name three of your *local* ecosystems, and for each one, describe the habitat and its community of living things.

2 Studying an Ecosystem – Abiotic Factors

Key Ideas

To study an ecosystem, it is essential to take measurements of the relevant abiotic factors of a habitat. A number of tests and measuring instruments can be used. Care must be taken to avoid *errors*. Abiotic factors can affect the number and types of organisms found in an ecosystem. The abiotic and biotic factors in an ecosystem affect each other.

It is important to have accurate ways of describing the main types of abiotic factors. Some of the techniques used are described below.

Geography

An **Ordnance Survey** map supplies useful information about *physical* characteristics which will not tend to change.

Physical characteristics affecting the type of organism found include:

slope, the direction the slope faces, height of land, presence of rivers or towns.

Reading physical characteristics from a map

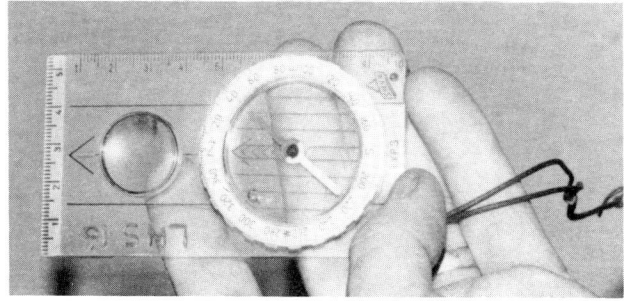

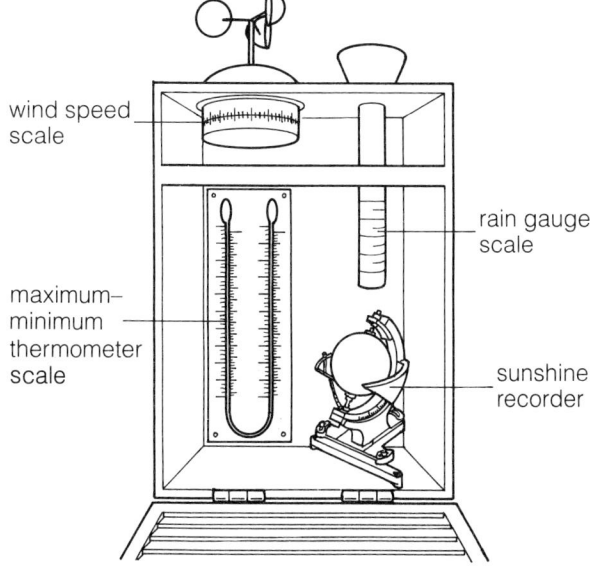

- wind speed scale
- rain gauge scale
- maximum–minimum thermometer scale
- sunshine recorder

A compass can be used to check the direction in which a slope faces. This can affect plant growth: for example, south facing slopes are warmer and get more light than north facing slopes, increasing plant growth rate.

Climate

A mini-weather station collects valuable data. The climate will change from day to day. To get an overall picture, many readings need to be taken over a period of time of such things as:

rainfall, light intensity, air temperature, wind speed.

6 THE BIOSPHERE

Geographical and climatic factors affect both land and water environments. On the land, soil types can affect the organisms present.

Soil

We tend to think of soil as one kind of substance, but there are several different types of soils. The plants growing in an ecosystem are good indicators of the type of soil. Some plants have special requirements: heathers will grow well only in acid soil for instance.

Knowing the type of soil can help you to predict what plants should be able to grow well in it. You can also alter that area of soil to enable other plants to grow in it.

Tests on soil may include finding out the following characteristics:

  particle size – affecting air content and drainage.
  pH – how acidic or alkaline the soil is
  water content and drainage of the soil
  mineral content of the soil
  humus content – the amount of dead plant and animal remains

Chemical tests on small samples of soil can identify the amount and type of minerals needed for plant growth, such as nitrates and phosphates.

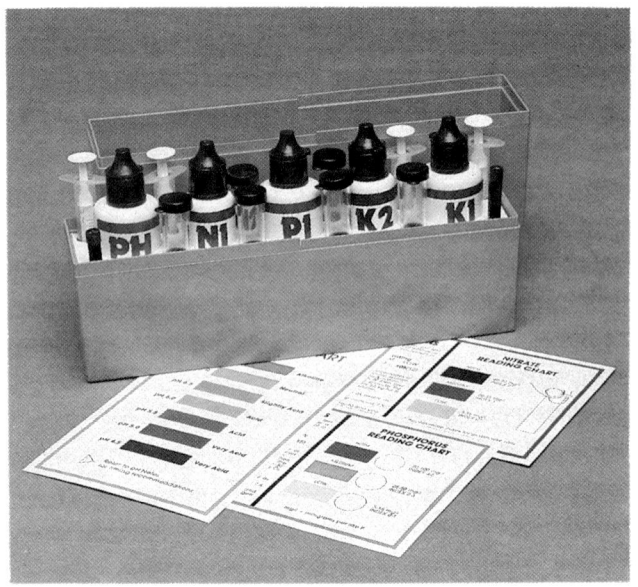

Water

Watery ecosystems vary in their characteristics.

Oceans of sea water are quite stable ecosystems. They are vast in size, they have similar characteristics, and they do not tend to change very much.

However, fresh-water habitats can be very varied. Rivers and streams are of running water, while ponds and canals tend to have still water.

Water temperature, speed of flow, dissolved oxygen content of the water and pH can also vary widely.

All these characteristics can affect the type of organisms found. For example, animals in fast flowing water are often adapted to allow them to attach firmly to rocks.

The speed of flow in a river can be measured as shown below.

An object such as a small boat or table tennis ball is released on the river; the time it takes to travel over a known distance allows the speed of flow to be calculated.

Errors in Measurement

Errors can happen in measuring an abiotic factor. For example, in measuring the flow rate of water in the river, the small boat, timed as it moves downstream. However, if it is trapped, even for a short time, behind a rock or branch, then the measurement of flow rate would be inaccurate.

Minimising Errors

Errors can be reduced by obtaining as much data as possible, and by taking care over the reading of instruments and recording of results.

Averaging out the results of many measurements is likely to make data more reliable.

In addition, obvious errors in measurement should be ignored. An example of this would be in the flow rate experiment, page 6. If the small boat became trapped, then that result should be ignored.

Distribution of Organisms

There are many ways in which abiotic factors can affect the community of living organisms in an ecosystem. A few examples are given here.

1. The amount of light affects the rate of photosynthesis in green plants. Therefore within a given area, the amount of shade from walls, buildings or cliffs will affect the types of plants growing there.

The amount of light also varies with the seasons and the part of the world studied.

2. High winds may damage or even uproot some plants. Therefore in very open, exposed areas very few plants may be able to grow.

3. Soils which have a low **pH** are not suitable for some plants. One reason is that many of the bacteria responsible for recycling nutrients cannot survive in a very acidic soil. For example the bacteria involved in the nitrogen cycle (see Chapter 8).

4. In a watery habitat the amount of dissolved oxygen present in the water can vary. In areas of low oxygen content, the only animals which may survive are those which can best use the little oxygen available, for example bloodworms.

5. A major abiotic factor in today's environment is **pollution**. This is dealt with in more detail in Chapter 10.

Activities

○ 1 Copy and complete the following table to show the different groups of abiotic factors, and the types of factors which can be measured within each group.

Group	Factors
geographic	

○ 2 From the table of results in the speed of flow experiment on page 6, calculate the average time taken for the boat to travel 10 metres downstream.

○ 3 Describe how an abiotic factor could limit the growth of plants on the floor of a coniferous woodland.

3 Studying an Ecosystem – Biotic Factors

Key Ideas

To study an ecosystem, it is necessary to find out what kind of organisms live there. Various methods of sampling are used. It is important that the *samples* give a true picture of the kinds of organisms in the ecosystem.

Taking Samples

It would be impossible to catch and record every organism from an ecosystem. Instead, an ecologist takes **samples** of the organisms present. The samples should represent, fairly, the number and the variety of organisms present. This is very difficult to do, and many different methods of sampling have been devised to help ecologists with this task.

Sampling Techniques

The technique used in sampling will depend on the type of habitat and kinds of organisms expected. In general, plants are easier to sample than animals because they do not move around.

Here are some ways to sample an ecosystem such as a woodland with a small stream running through it.

Sampling Plants

To sample ground cover plants like grasses, we can use a simple piece of apparatus called a **quadrat**. This is a square wooden or metal frame, usually with sides 0.5 metres long. It is placed at random on the ground in the study area and the plants inside the quadrat are identified and counted.

Sampling Small Mammals

You can sample small mammals like mice and voles using a **Longworth mammal trap**. This type of trap does not kill the animals. The traps are placed evenly around the area of study in places where small mammals are likely to be found. Around the base of a big tree would be a good place for wood mice.

The trap should be baited by scattering a little food around its entrance, and it should contain bedding and food for any animal likely to be caught. Any animal entering the trap will trigger a trip wire which closes the door behind it.

Sampling Water Invertebrates

Invertebrate animals living in the stream can be sampled by catching in a net. You should disturb the mud or pebbles on the stream bed with a kicking action of your feet. Then you can draw a net through the disturbed water to catch the animals. They are tipped into a tray for examination.

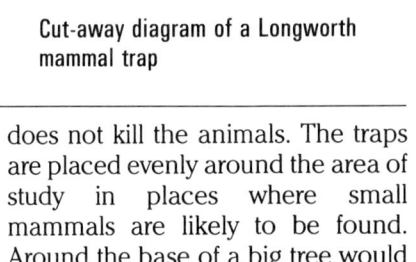

Cut-away diagram of a Longworth mammal trap

This pupil is sampling the invertebrates in a stream by *kick sampling*

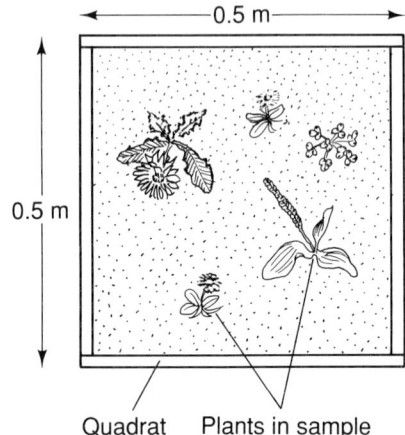

A quadrat like this one can be used to sample ground cover plants

THE BIOSPHERE

Sampling Errors

An ecologist might easily get the wrong impression about the organisms present in an ecosystem if he uses faulty sampling methods. For example, he might fail to take random samples. Again, he may simply not take enough samples to suit the area of study. Look at the drawing.

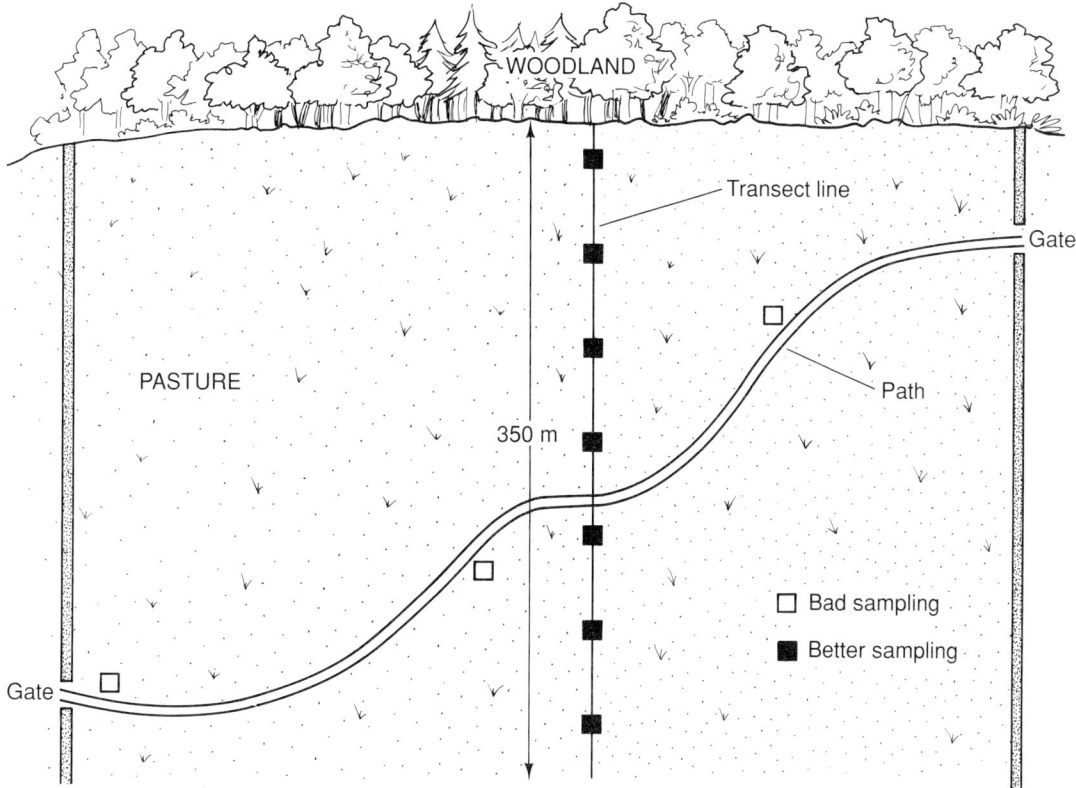

An ecologist who wants to sample the grasses in this pasture might walk along the path and lay a quadrat every so often, as shown. He has not sampled at random in the pasture because all the areas he has selected are near to the path. Also he has taken too few samples for such a large area.

There are better ways of finding sample sites. One way is to use a line called a **transect** which crosses the field as shown, and to take quadrat samples, say, every 50 metres. At the sample sites the ecologist drops the quadrat over his shoulder. This method results in a much more realistic idea of the range of grasses present.

Activities

1 What is meant by the term "sample"?
2 Why do organisms need to be sampled?
3 Describe the apparatus used to sample ground-cover plants.
4 Why should mammal traps be checked regularly?
5 Describe how to net small fresh-water invertebrates.
6 Why are the sites marked □ on the map likely to give a wrong picture of the grasses in the pasture in general?
7 What are the advantages of the transect method described in the passage?
8 Describe an even better way to sample this pasture.

4 Identifying Organisms

Key Ideas

After samples have been taken, each organism found must be identified. This is done using a *biological key*. The key is often in the form of a series of questions about the organism and the questions are answered by looking closely at it. The questions lead finally to the name of the organism being identified.

Using a Biological Key

Organisms caught in a net sample from a fresh-water stream are shown in the diagram on the next page. Below is part of a simple key for identifying the organisms. The lines of dots across the key mean "if the answer is Yes".

Key of Some Fresh-water Invertebrates

1. Does it have legs?......................go to 2
   Does it have NO legs?...............go to 7

2. Does it have 3 pairs of legs?.....................go to 3
   Does it have more than 3 pairs of legs?.....go to 5

3. Has it a case of stones or sticks? ....**Caddisfly larva**
   Does it have no case?..................................go to 4

4. Does it have 2 tails? ....**Stonefly larva**
   Does it have 3 tails? ....**Mayfly larva**

5. Does it have 4 pairs of legs?......................**Water mite**
   Does it have more than 4 pairs of legs?.....go to 6

6. Does it have a curved back?......................**Fresh-water shrimp**
   Does it have a straight back? ....**Water louse**

7. Does it have a shell? ....**Fresh-water snail**
   Does it have NO shell?.................go to 8

8. Does its body have NO segments?............**Flatworm**
   Is its body divided into segments?............go to 9

9. Does it have suckers? ....**Leech**
   Is it thin and red-coloured? ....**Tubifex**

THE BIOSPHERE 11

The following is a **checklist** of all the organisms mentioned in the key. Copies of checklists are used when sampling, so that when an organism is identified in the sample the correct box can be ticked.

Caddisfly larva	☐	Water louse	☐
Fresh-water shrimp	☐	Water snail	☐
Stonefly larva	☐	Leech	☐
Mayfly larva	☐	Flatworm	☐
Water mite	☐	Bloodworm	☐

The checklist might also be used to record the numbers of the different organisms in a sample.

Activities

This diagram shows a tray of organisms caught in a net sample in a fresh-water stream running through a piece of woodland. Look closely at the drawing of the different species.

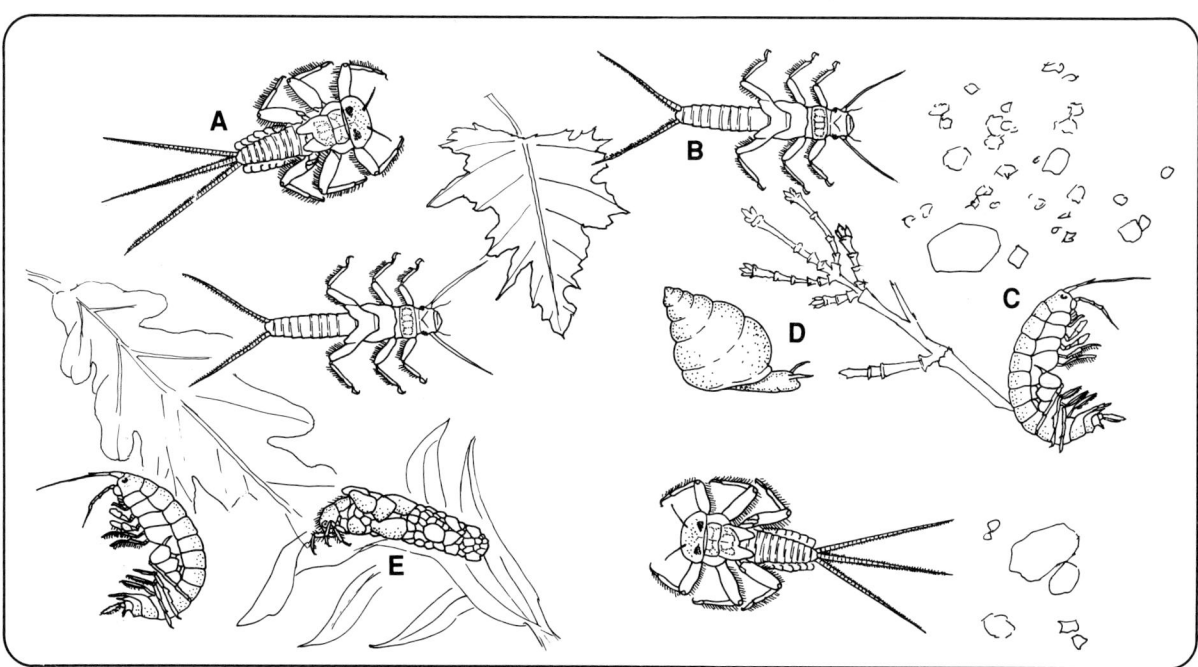

○ 1 Identify the organisms **A–H** using the key on the facing page.
○ 2 Copy out the checklist.
○ 3 Use your checklist to record the number of each kind of organism present in the sample.
○ 4 Copy the pie chart and fill it in from your checklist to compare the numbers of different organisms in the tray.

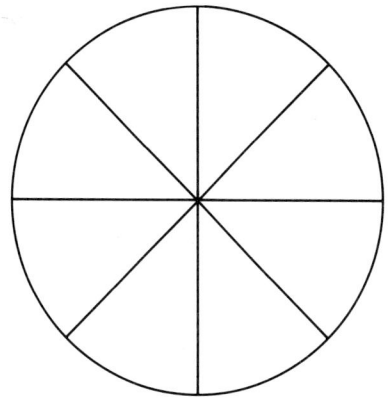

12 THE BIOSPHERE

5 Chains and Webs

Key Ideas

Ecosystems use the Sun as the source of energy. Organisms can be grouped as *producers* or *consumers*. Producers can make their own food directly, using light energy. Consumers obtain their energy by eating other organisms. *Food chains* and *food webs* show the feeding relationships in an ecosystem.

Owl pellets contain the bones of many small mammals. These can be identified from their jawbones

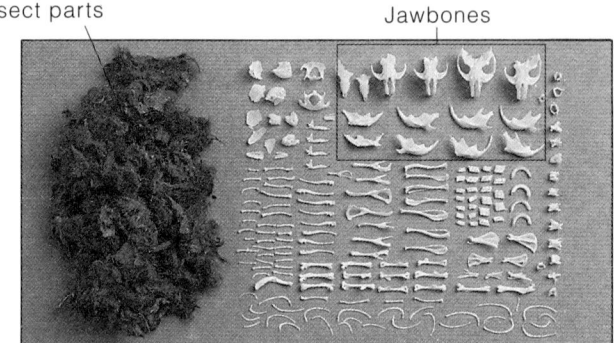

If you go for a walk in a wood you may find strange furry things on the ground. These are owl pellets. Owls are predators, often feeding on small mammals as their prey. These are usually eaten whole and the owl spits out all the undigested bits as a pellet. A careful study of the bones in the pellet allows the prey to be identified, as shown in the picture.

So an owl pellet can tell us a lot about what goes on in the woodland. It gives us a snapshot of feeding relationships in the ecosystem. From this and similar information we might be able to produce a **food chain**:

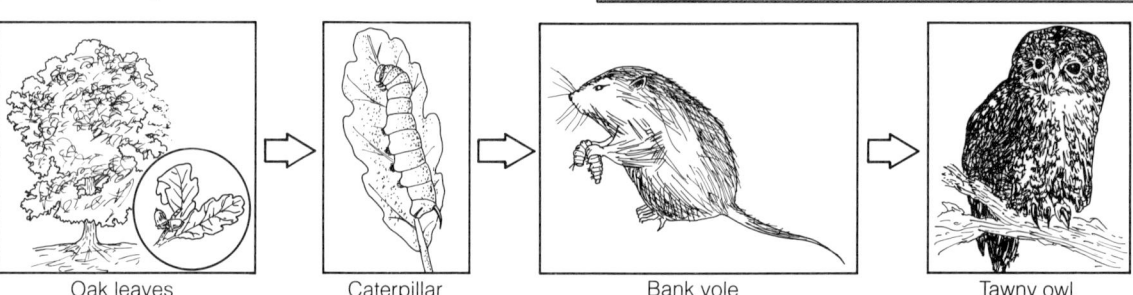

Oak leaves → Caterpillar → Bank vole → Tawny owl

A food chain describes the movement of energy through the community. Each arrow leads from the organism being eaten to its consumer. There has to be an energy source at the start of the food chain, and this is usually light energy from the Sun.

Green plants are the only organisms which can use sunlight directly. They are able to produce their own food by the process of **photosynthesis**. For this reason these plants are called **producers.**

All other organisms obtain their energy by eating plants or other animals and are called **consumers**.

These consumers can be described from their position in the food chain as **primary, secondary** and **tertiary consumers.**

Consumers can also be described by what they eat. **Herbivores** eat plants, **carnivores** are meat eaters, and **omnivores** eat both plant and animal foods.

The different ways of naming organisms in a food chain are summarised below.

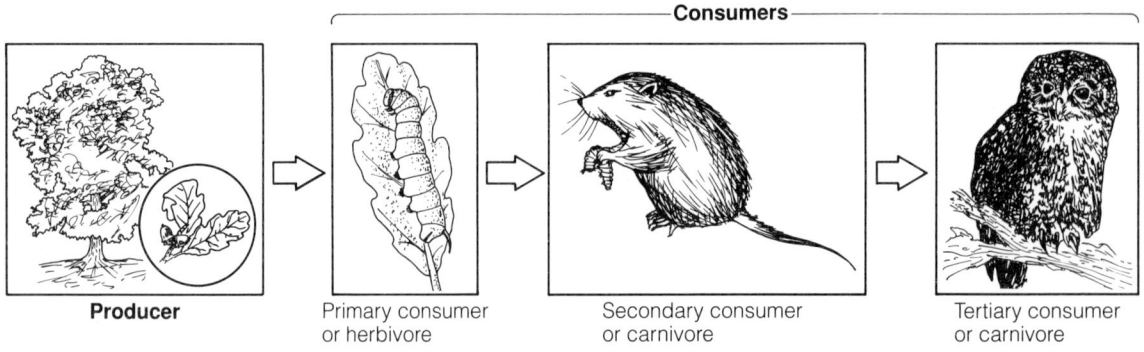

Producer — Primary consumer or herbivore — Secondary consumer or carnivore — Tertiary consumer or carnivore

THE BIOSPHERE 13

Food Webs

In the wild, an owl does not live on bank voles alone. It may also eat small birds and shrews, for example. This cannot be shown on a simple food chain diagram. Nor can the omnivores which eat both plants and animals. A **food web** provides a much more complete picture. Look at the woodland scene.

A Woodland Scene

Members of an important group of consumers can be seen on the ground in the woodland. Mushrooms and toadstools – fungi – are **decomposers**. These organisms obtain their energy by consuming dead plants and animals. Without them there would be no decay. The countryside would be littered with dead material and a lot of energy and raw materials would be lost from the ecosystem.

From this woodland picture, we can make up a food web diagram which gives the possible feeding relationships between the organisms shown.

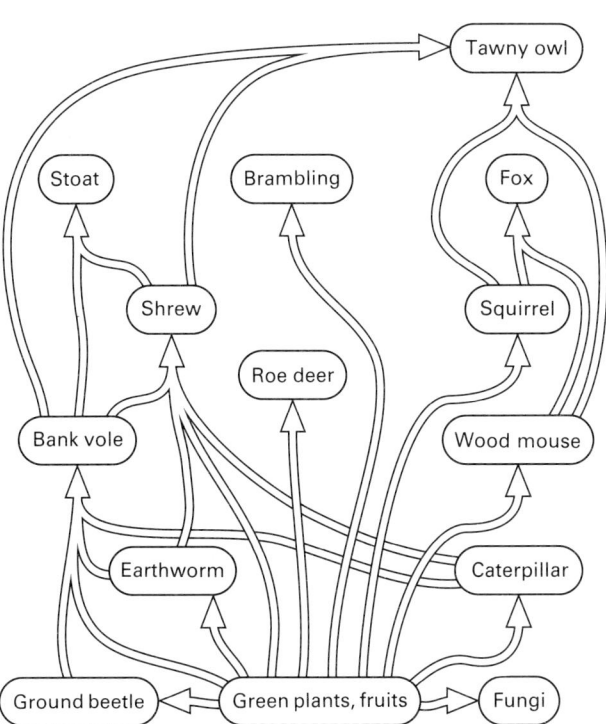

A Woodland Food Web Diagram

A food web is made up of many linked food chains. Anything that disturbs one of the members of the food web can have serious effects on the whole ecosystem. For example, if the caterpillar population was destroyed by a disease or chemical sprays, an immediate effect would be less food for the bank voles. This, in turn, could cause shortages for the tawny owl and fox, threatening their existence as well.

For an ecosystem to remain in balance, the food web must not be disturbed. Humans cause great damage to ecosystems, and sometimes themselves, by ignoring the importance of the local food webs, as we shall see in the Activities.

14 THE BIOSPHERE

Activities

○ 1 Construct a food chain using the following organisms: human, grass, sheep.

○ 2 On your food chain, label the producer, primary consumer and secondary consumer.

◑ 3 From the food web diagram on page 13, make up a food chain involving five organisms named in the food web.

◑ 4 Label the organisms in your food chain using the terms: producer, herbivore, and carnivore.

● 5 Read the following case study and answer the questions which follow it.

Crocodile Handbags – A Case Study

Crocodiles are hunted for their skins which can be used to make attractive handbags and shoes. There is a danger that overhunting could have serious effects. The food chain below can be found in Central Africa.

Food chain diagram

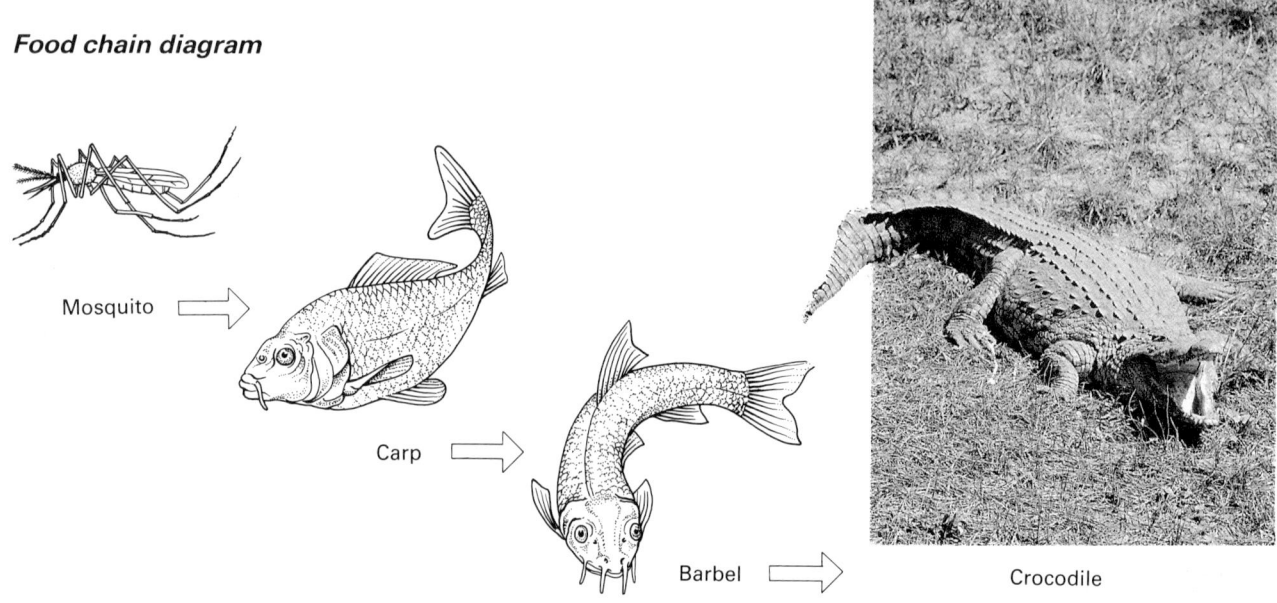

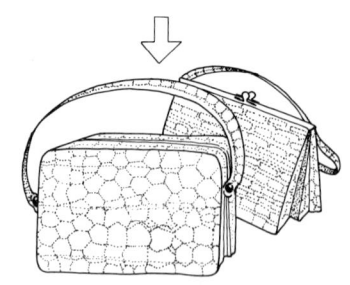

Crocodile hand bags

If too many crocodiles are removed, the number of barbels may increase, causing a decrease in the number of carp. This in turn results in a large increase in mosquito numbers. The natural balance has been destroyed.

The problem is that certain types of mosquito carry the disease *malaria*. In the Tropics some 350 million people suffer from malaria each year. Can we afford the consequences of producing crocodile handbags?

(a) If crocodiles became a protected species and were no longer hunted, what might happen to the number of people suffering from malaria? Explain your answer.

(b) Explain why the food chain diagram in the case study does not give a true picture of the effect of crocodiles and humans in this ecosystem.

6 Energy Flow

Key Ideas

***Energy* is required by all living organisms.**
In an ecosystem there is a flow of energy from the Sun through producers to the consumers. There is a loss of energy at each link of a food chain.

Energy flow through a leaf

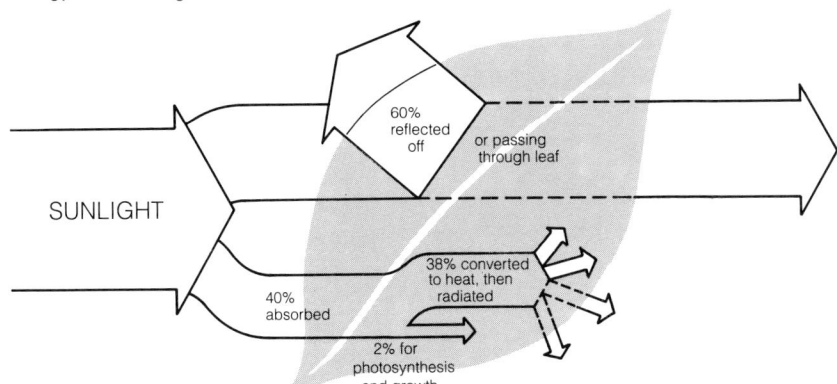

Plants can use the sunlight that flows into an ecosystem; but how well do they use it? Of all the light hitting the surface of a leaf, about 60% is reflected off the leaf or passes through it. The leaf absorbs 40%, and of this, only about 2% is used for photosynthesis. The rest of the absorbed light is converted to heat in the leaf. This heat is then lost from the leaf by radiation.

The **light energy** used for photosynthesis is changed to **chemical energy**. About half of this is used in the plant's living processes and some for growth. Growth of the plant increases the food supply for consumers in the ecosystem.

In the end, only about 1% of the sunlight energy available to that leaf has been used in plant growth.

Animals can convert about 10% of their food into new **tissue** by growing. The remainder of the food eaten is used for the other life functions of the animal, as the diagram shows. These activities use energy which is lost from the food chain.

If another animal were to eat voles, it would need to eat *ten* voles to increase its size by the weight of *one* vole.

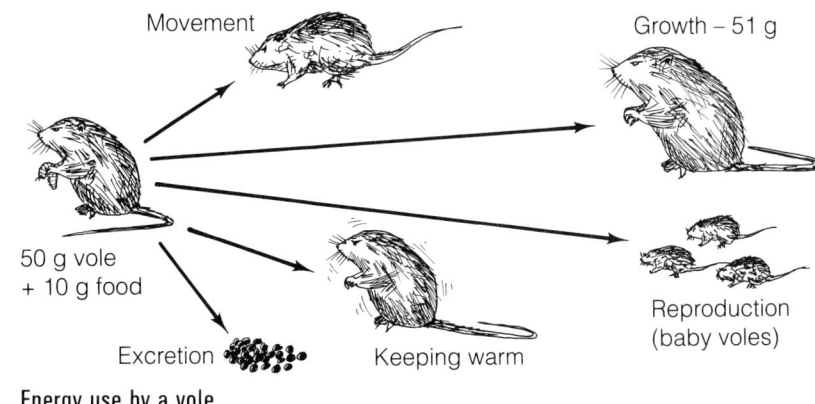

Energy use by a vole

Food chains are usually short because so much energy is lost by the activities of the animals. Most food chains have only three or four links, as the diagram shows.

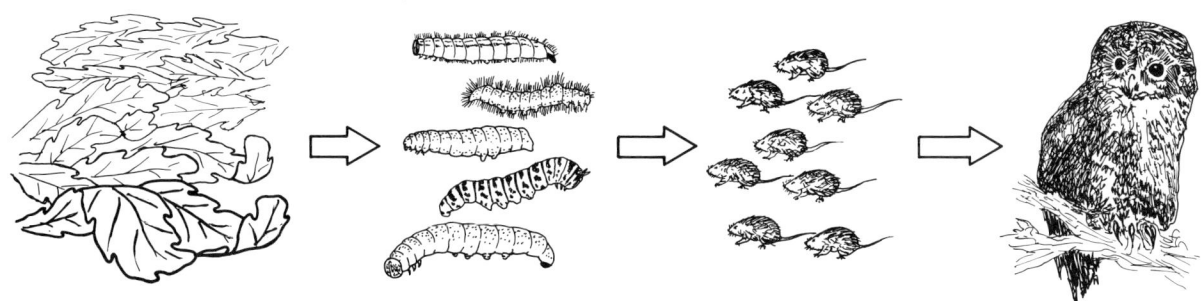

16 THE BIOSPHERE

The idea of the reduction of energy along a food chain can be shown by using diagrams called **pyramids of number** and **pyramids of biomass**.

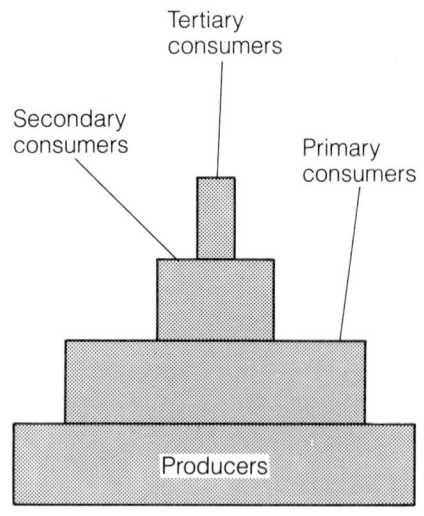

Pyramids of Number

To draw a pyramid of number for a food chain, the number of organisms is counted for each feeding level: producers, primary consumers, secondary consumers, tertiary consumers etc. This is done for a given area, say 1 hectare (10 000 square metres).

Horizontal blocks, representing the numbers of organisms, are drawn to scale on graph paper. The block representing the producers is placed at the bottom of the diagram. Placing the blocks for the other feeding levels one on top of the other, as shown, gives a pyramid shape.

You will notice as you look higher on the pyramid of numbers that the population size decreases for each type of organism. Also, the *size of the individuals* tends to increase higher up on the pyramid.

There is a problem with counting the *number* of organisms. Oak leaves were the producers in the pyramid shown. But the entire oak *tree* might have been called the producer.

In this case, one oak tree counts the same as one caterpillar, although they are obviously very different sizes. This effect can produce misleading diagrams.

Therefore it is better to measure the ecosystem by constructing a pyramid of biomass.

Pyramids of Biomass

Biomass is a measure of the mass of living tissue of an organism or of a population of organisms. A pyramid of biomass gives a better diagram. It shows the *loss of mass* from producers to consumers in a food chain.

Activities

○ 1 Draw a pie chart showing the "fate" of sunlight energy reaching a leaf, giving the energy as percentages.

○ 2 State what happens to the energy contained in the food of an animal.

◑ 3 From the following data of a food chain, produce a scale drawing of a pyramid of numbers.

Organism:	Producers	Primary consumers	Secondary consumers	Owl
Numbers:	2900	350	80	0.5
Mass of organisms:	800 kg	67 kg	11 kg	0.8 kg

● 4 From the data in the food chain above, produce a pyramid of biomass drawn to scale.

● 5 Describe 2 ways in which a pyramid of biomass gives a clearer picture of energy flow in a food chain than a pyramid of numbers.

● 6 Explain why the number of owls is only 0.5.

7 Populations

Key Ideas

The growth rate of a *population* of organisms depends on the number of births and deaths in the population.
The size of the population will depend on factors which affect birth or death rates, like disease, predators, *competition* for requirements, and pollution.
In real populations these *natural checks* usually produce a *stable* population.

If a population had no natural checks, it would show a huge increase in numbers.
Look at what could happen to a shrew population.

The shrew has a breeding season from May to September.

It has an average litter size of four young.

It can produce young every four weeks.

It is able to reproduce after four weeks.

It lives for about 18 months.

If a pair of shrews were able to breed under ideal conditions with all of the young reproducing and with no deaths, then at the end of the first breeding season there would be 110 shrews in the population.
If this population growth continued unchecked, and no shrews died, then after 5 full breeding seasons the number of shrews would have increased to over **400 million**!

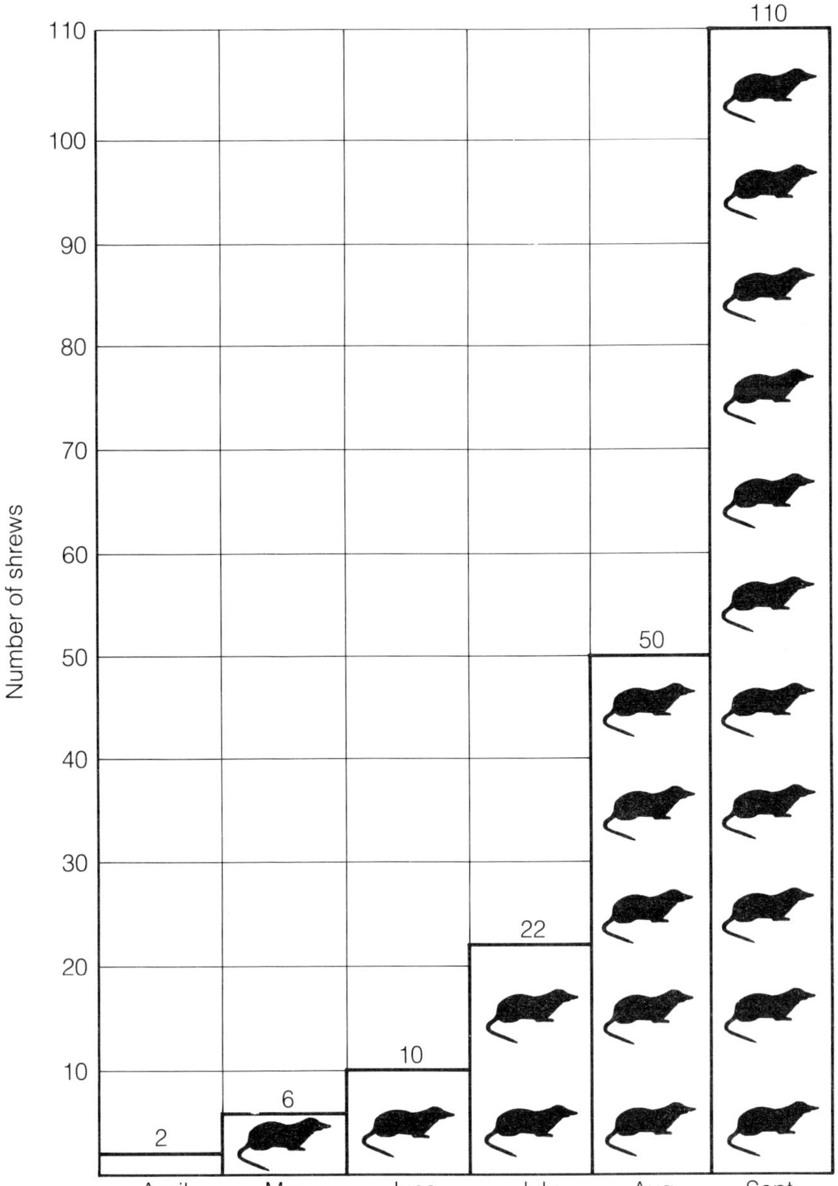

Graph of changes in the size of a shrew population during the breeding season

18 THE BIOSPHERE

However, this population living in ideal conditions is unlikely to occur in nature. After an initial increase in population, natural checks will limit the numbers of individuals that survive.

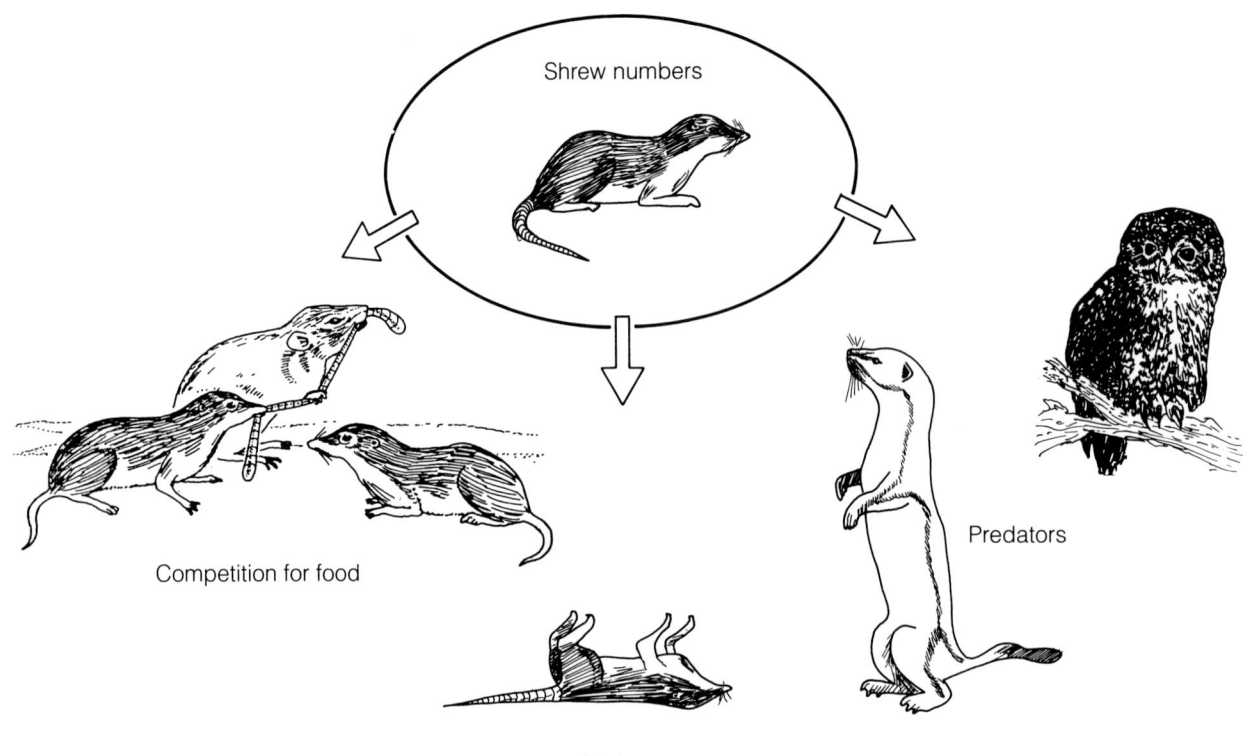

Predation, competition and disease control the size of animal populations

Within a stable ecosystem, the numbers of individuals of any species do not change very much from year to year. One of the main causes of stability in a community is **competition**.

Competition Within a Species

Food is a limited resource. If a population increases, food will become short and some individuals will die of starvation. Extreme overcrowding causes some females of the species to become **infertile**, and so fewer young are produced.

Territorial behaviour in some animals ensures that enough food is available for them. Territorial animals compete with others to obtain defined breeding areas. The "losers" in the competition for territory are forced to **migrate** to find a less crowded habitat.

Competition Between Species

There may be competition for food between different species in a community. Predators may have the same prey: owls and stoats will both feed on shrews, although they can take other prey as well.

Plants, too, may compete with each other for light, water or minerals from the soil.

Competition may end with the weaker species being eliminated, or with both species being able to live together in smaller numbers.

In nature, competition between species is limited because two species do not usually have identical requirements. Each species has its own **niche** in the ecosystem. The niche of a species refers to its exact "job" in the ecosystem.

No two species share exactly the same niche.

Activities

1. Which two factors affect the growth of a population?
2. Give three examples of factors which prevent unchecked growth of a population.
3. Explain what is meant by the term "competition".
4. Look at this graph of the growth of a population of yeast cells.
   (a) Why does the population rise quite slowly between points **A** and **B** on the graph?
   (b) Why does the rise become steep between points **B** and **C**?

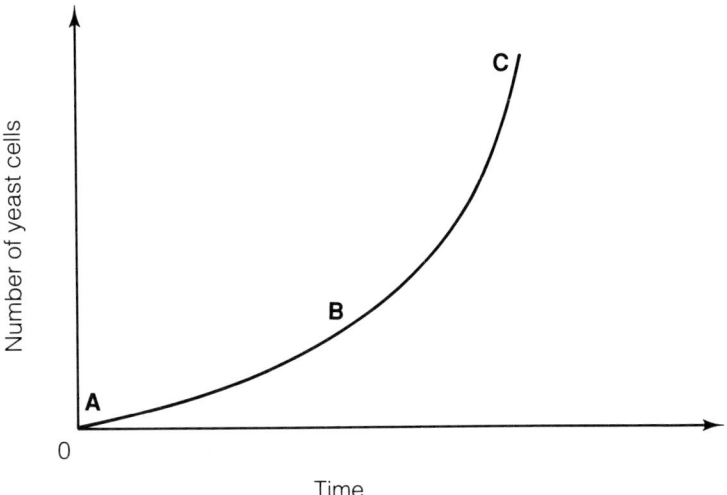

5. A graph showing the growth of the human population looks very like this one, with a steep upward curve for the last 150 years. What factors have lowered the death rate of the human population in recent years?

20 THE BIOSPHERE

8 Nutrient Cycles

> ### Key Ideas
>
> The food which passes along food chains is made mainly from *carbon*, hydrogen, oxygen and *nitrogen*. These are taken in from the air and the soil by the producers of the food chain, the green plants.
> At the same time as these substances are absorbed by the producers, they are being replaced by natural processes like *photosynthesis, respiration* and *decay*.
> The circulation of substances in the ecosystem by absorption and replacement is called *recycling*.

Two of the main cycles in nature are the **carbon cycle** and the **nitrogen cycle**.

The Carbon Cycle

We can use a woodland food chain to show how the carbon cycle works.

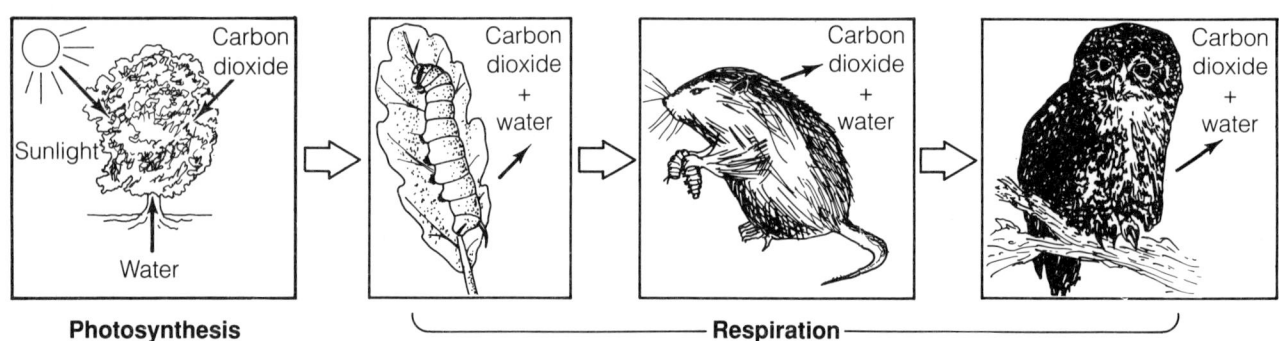

Photosynthesis — **Respiration**

Carbohydrates contain carbon, hydrogen and oxygen. The oak tree makes its carbohydrate food by photosynthesis using carbon dioxide gas from the air and water from the soil. Light energy is used to make this process work.

The consumers in the chain eat the food made in the tissues of the oak tree. All of the organisms release the energy from the food in another process called respiration. This releases carbon dioxide and water vapour into the air. In this way the cycle continues again and again.

Death and Decay

Death happens continually in the biosphere. All living things eventually die, and when they do, their remains will be **decomposed** by bacteria and fungi in the soil. These decomposer organisms release the carbon from the remains of organisms as carbon dioxide through respiration.

Fossil Fuels

Millions of years ago, large forests existed on Earth, and the seas were alive with animal and plant life. As these plants and animals died, their remains were turned into **fossil fuels** which were preserved and are used today. The fuels contain carbon originally present in the bodies of the organisms. When we burn these fuels the carbon is released in carbon dioxide, and hydrogen in water vapour. This is not a natural process and is endangering the natural balance by releasing too much carbon dioxide into the air.

THE BIOSPHERE 21

This drawing shows some of the processes which take place in the carbon cycle for the woodland food web.

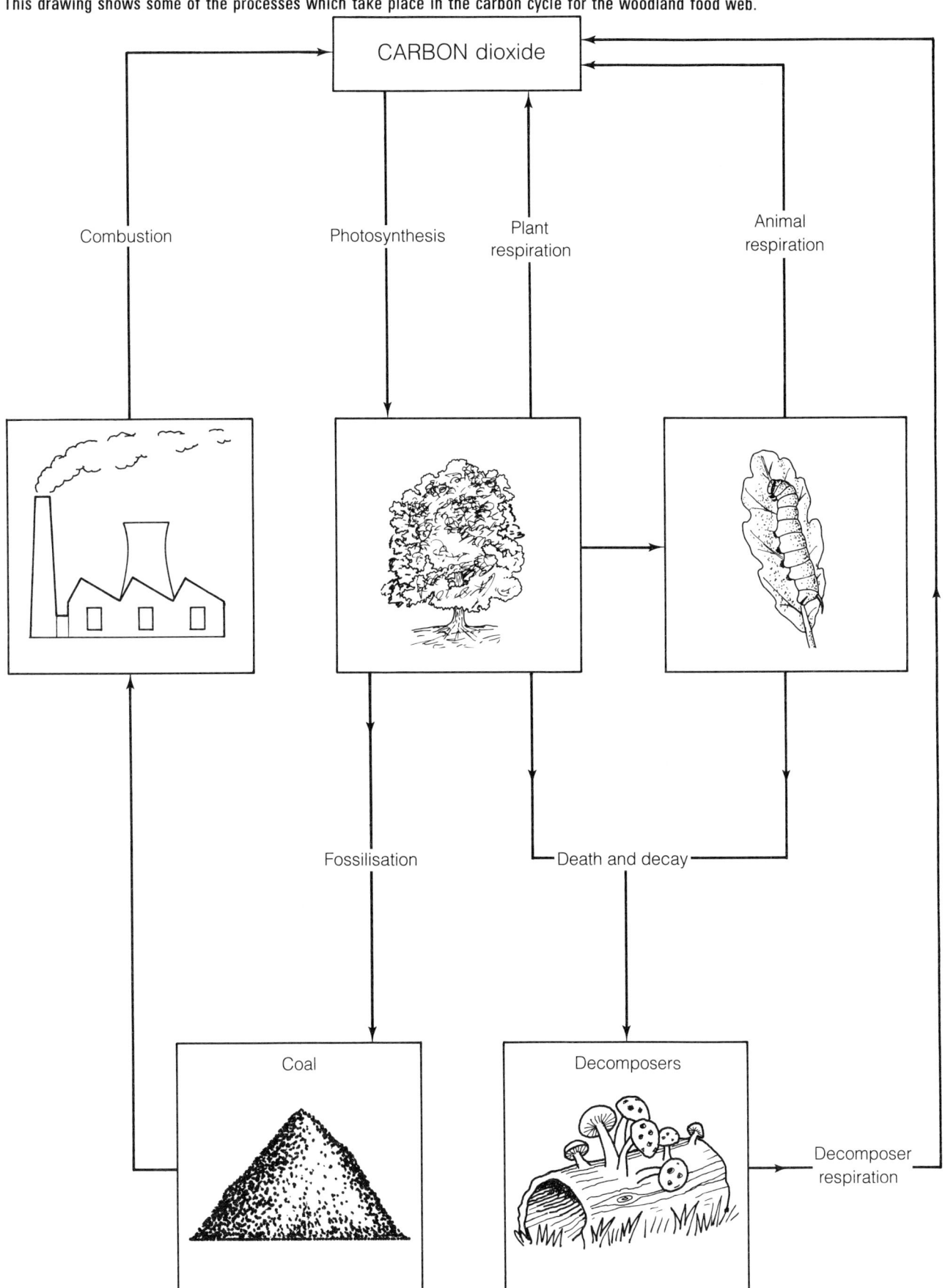

22 THE BIOSPHERE

The Nitrogen Cycle

Plants and animals need a supply of nitrogen to make proteins. Proteins are essential for growth and other life processes.

The atmosphere of Earth contains huge quantities of nitrogen gas. However plants can obtain their nitrogen only from the soil, in the form of **nitrates**. Animals can get their nitrogen only by eating plants or other animals.

The nitrogen in the air can be converted into nitrates in a variety of ways:

(a) **Lightning** can convert nitrogen and oxygen in the air into nitrates.
(b) Some bacteria in the soil, called **nitrifying bacteria**, can convert nitrogen and oxygen to nitrates.
(c) Some plants, called **legumes**, which include peas and beans have **nodules** on their roots. These nodules contain bacteria which can convert nitrogen and oxygen into nitrates.
(d) **Nitrate bacteria** can convert **nitrites** in the soil into nitrates.

Any excess nitrates in the soil can be converted into nitrogen by a group of bacteria called **denitrifying bacteria**.

This drawing shows the nitrogen cycle for the woodland food web.

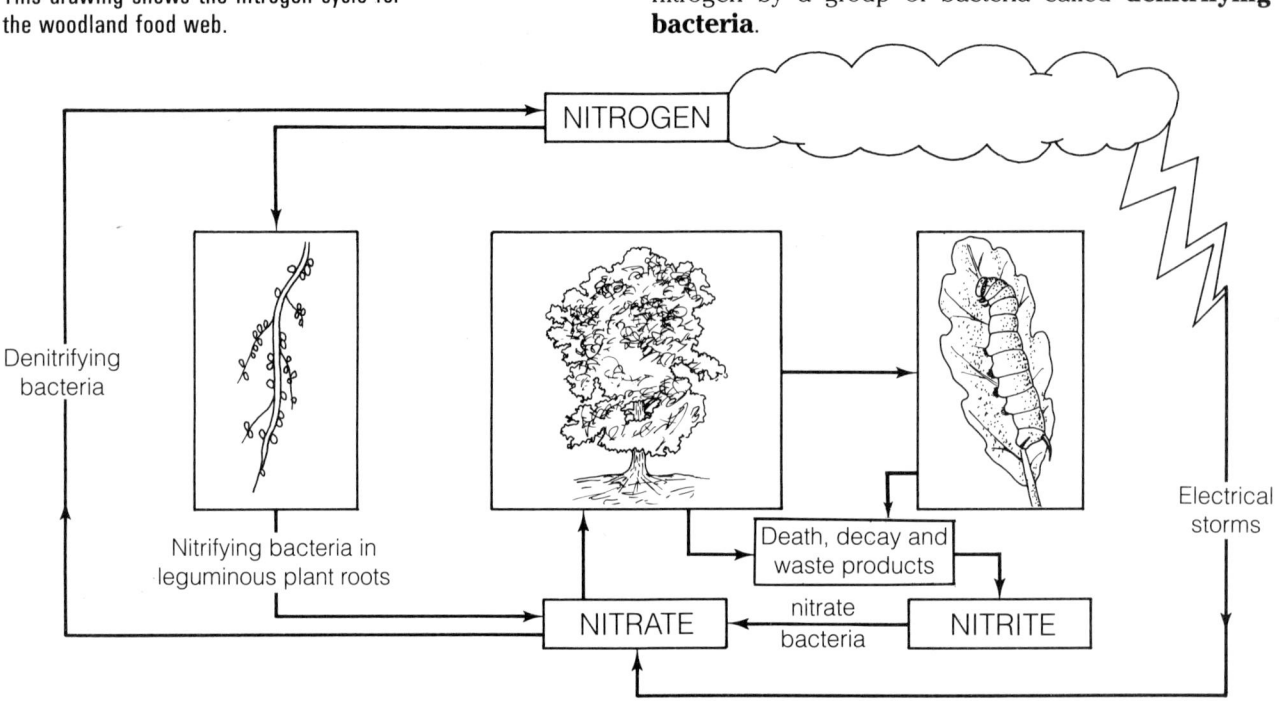

Activities

1. Why is it important for carbon to be cycled in nature?
2. Draw a very simple version of the carbon cycle using the words in this word bank:
   photosynthesis, respiration, decay, fossil fuels, carbon dioxide, carbohydrate.
3. Where do plants get their nitrogen?
4. Where do animals get their nitrogen?
5. List the ways in which nitrogen can get into the soil.
6. Make a simple drawing of the nitrogen cycle using this word bank:
   nitrogen, nitrates, nitrites, legume, plant protein, animal protein, nitrifying bacteria, denitrifying bacteria.

9 Pollution – Cause and Control

Key Ideas

Pollution can take many forms. It can affect water, land and air. Our homes, our farms and our industries all add to the pollution of the environment. It must be controlled.

Places Change

The plants and animals in ecosystems are usually well adapted to their particular habitats. Everything fits together like a well-made jigsaw puzzle. However, most ecosystems are constantly changing as they adjust to variations in climate and to new organisms entering the habitat.

If humans pollute the environment, some ecosystems may not be able to adjust to the effects of the pollution. As a result, some of the animals and plants may not be able to survive and will become extinct.

Sources of Pollution

The first humans are often described as hunter/gatherers. A tribe might have moved from place to place, preying on animals and eating available plant material such as fruit. Humans were a part of the natural food web, and any effect they had on the environment was small.

In time, humans became settlers. People made their homes in one place. In order to survive, people made major changes to the environment. Animals were **domesticated** and the land was **farmed**. They developed simple industry to make tools, weapons and household goods. These activities led to increased pollution of the environment.

Today, there are more humans than ever before. We therefore produce much more waste from our homes and industries. We need more food, so our farms use chemicals and machines to try to improve the success of crops and livestock. We want a more luxurious lifestyle, so we build more factories to produce more goods – and waste products. We use more energy and so build more power stations – these produce waste as well.

The three main sources of pollution are **domestic, agricultural** and **industrial**. Each source produces wastes which pollute fresh and sea water, the air and the land.

It is vitally important to fight pollution *now*! We all have a part to play, by making other people aware of the dangers to the biosphere and by taking direct action wherever possible.

24 THE BIOSPHERE

Domestic Pollution

The sewage which we flush away every day can kill the plants and animals in our rivers and seas if it is not treated properly

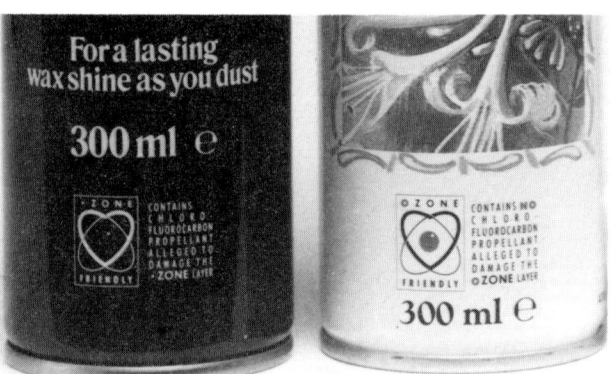

You can now buy aerosols which contain no CFCs. They are called "ozone friendly".

Water

In Britain we each use about 140 litres of water every day. The 50 litres we flush down the toilet probably go to a sewage works for treatment. If you live on the coast, your sewage might be pumped directly into the sea. Untreated sewage can kill water plants and animals. To control this pollution, we need to improve our sewage treatment works.

Air

About 500 million **aerosol cans** are made in Britain each year. They use a type of gas called **CFCs** (chlorinated fluorocarbons) to force liquids, such as hairspray, out as an aerosol. These gases destroy part of the Earth's upper atmosphere called the **ozone layer**. This layer prevents too much harmful **ultra-violet radiation** from reaching us. If the ozone layer is damaged there may be an increase in skin cancers and other disorders.

The only way to control CFCs is to stop making and using them. In 1987 a number of countries agreed to cut CFC production by two-thirds by the year 2000. We can all help by not buying aerosol cans which contain CFCs.

Land

An average household produces 1000 kg of rubbish in a year. About 85% of this is packaging. If it is not dealt with carefully, it can become a breeding ground for disease and pests like rats. Dangerous chemicals and bacteria can drain into nearby streams and rivers.

There are several ways of controlling this type of pollution. The various kinds of rubbish, for example glass, metals and paper, can be recycled. We can help too: do not drop litter; put glass in bottle banks; avoid buying packaged goods where possible.

Rubbish can also be used to reclaim land.

Much of the rubbish in this photograph could be recycled.

In the largest land reclamation scheme outside the Netherlands 190 hectares of land has been reclaimed in Portsmouth Harbour, much of it with local rubbish.

Agricultural Pollution

Water

Modern farming tries to produce more and better quality crops by using **fertilisers** and pest-control chemicals. These substances are usually able to dissolve in rain-water. As a result, they find their way into streams and rivers. **Weedkillers** and **pesticides** can therefore be carried long distances and kill a wide range of harmless plants and animals.

Water pollution could be controlled by reducing the use of these chemicals. Organic farming uses no artificial chemicals. However, the crops are more expensive because more people are employed on such farms. You can choose what to buy, though, and as more people buy organically grown produce, so the price will come down.

Organic produce like this is available in most supermarkets. It is often more expensive than food produced by modern farming methods.

Air

Farming activities pollute the air with chemical sprays and by the burning of stubble after harvest. Chemicals can be transported to other ecosystems in the wind or in the bodies of animals. In this way, food webs many miles away can be damaged. Smoke ash from fires may reduce the ability of trees and shrubs to absorb sunlight for photosynthesis.

If spraying and burning *have* to be carried out, careful timing can reduce the effects of airborne pollution from farms.

Land

The over-use of chemicals can damage the soil and make it less fertile. Any unsold produce or waste material that is dumped attracts rats and flies, which may carry disease. The control of land pollution requires good management to minimise the amounts of chemicals used on the land, and to make sure that everything produced can be sold.

Industrial Pollution

Water

Most industrial waste is treated in factories. Some goes straight into rivers. There are several different types of pollutants.

Some chemical industries produce **heavy metals**, like lead and mercury. These can kill living things and are known to cause brain damage in humans.

One solution is to limit, by law, the amount of waste which factories are allowed to release. Another is to treat the waste to make it harmless.

Air

Industrial air pollution comes from factories and power stations. Smoke reduces the amount of light available to plants for photosynthesis. It can also combine with fog to make **smog**. Smog damages the breathing systems of animals. Chemicals in smoke can cause the formation of **acid rain** which can kill vegetation on land and a wide range of water life.

Air pollution can be controlled by using smokeless fuels and by **scrubbing** – washing the gases – as they leave the chimneys. However, this can be expensive.

Land

Industries produce a variety of wastes which are transported to tips. Some of this waste can be poisonous. Poisonous waste must, by law, be tipped at sites where there appears to be little chance of drainage water carrying the waste away. However, there is much illegal tipping of waste at unsuitable sites.

In addition, we now face the problem of the disposal of **radioactive waste** from nuclear power stations. This includes nuclear waste imported into Britain to be processed.

26 THE BIOSPHERE

Pollution from Power

To maintain our present lifestyle and to make sure that our most basic needs for survival are met, we risk endangering the ecology of our planet. In earlier times pollution was local. Any waste produced by a community stayed in the immediate environment. Today, the huge scale of pollution makes it a global problem.

A good illustration of this is the problems created by power stations. A world without electricity is hard to imagine, but the world can do without the pollution its production causes. This includes waste from the nuclear fuels like uranium and plutonium, and from burning fossil fuels like coal, oil and gas.

However, to reduce pollution from power we need to develop alternative sources of energy. Some examples are shown below.

Dead trees above a Phurnacite plant

Wind power

Solar panels

Chernobyl as seen on TV after the disaster

Buildings near Chernobyl being washed of radioactive dust

Wave power: Salter's ducks. Electricity is generated as they rock in the waves

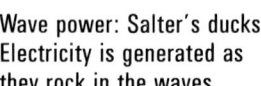

Activities

1. Draw a table to summarise the different types of pollution. Give an example of each, and state its effect(s) on water, air and land.

2. Imagine that you are a pollution inspector who is called out to inspect a house, a farm and a factory.
   (a) For each one, write a short report describing the pollution you might see. Describe the effects each is having on the local ecosystem.
   (b) Make some suggestions for controlling each type of pollution.

3. Describe the main reasons why fish are not able to live in heavily polluted water.

4. Explain how you *personally* can help to reduce pollution.

5. Give an example of an alternative energy source. Describe the advantages of using it and suggest three areas in the world where you think it would be most effective.

10 Water Pollution

Key Ideas

Human waste from toilets and sinks is called *sewage* and is often passed into rivers and seas. The release of this sewage affects the plant and animal life because it reduces the amount of oxygen in the water. Fewer organisms are able to survive near sewage outflows. The number and type of organisms found in an area of water are useful *indicators* of the level of pollution by sewage.

Human organic waste is the sewage which is sometimes pumped into our rivers and seas. It contains large amounts of nitrogen-rich compounds and bacteria. The bacteria feed on the organic waste and use oxygen from the water to **respire**. This leads to a massive increase in numbers of bacteria which means that there is less oxygen available for other organisms. The result is that there is a smaller variety of organisms near sewage outflows.

Biological Indicator Species

Certain species are known as **indicators** because their presence shows that the water is fully oxygenated and is unpolluted. The absence of these organisms might indicate that the water *is* polluted. This could be confirmed by the presence of other organisms which do very well in water that is low in oxygen. **Stoneflies** and **mayflies** are characteristic of unpolluted water, whereas **bloodworms** are usually very common in water which is polluted with sewage because they can live in low-oxygen conditions.

Case Study (continued on page 28)

Imagine that a small town pumps sewage into a river which runs through a woodland. The level of pollution that this causes is investigated by taking samples of bacteria from the water and also by measuring the amount of dissolved oxygen. The information on this graph shows the results obtained:

28 THE BIOSPHERE

This drawing shows three sites where samples of the invertebrate animals in the river were taken. The numbers and types of invertebrates present are also given.

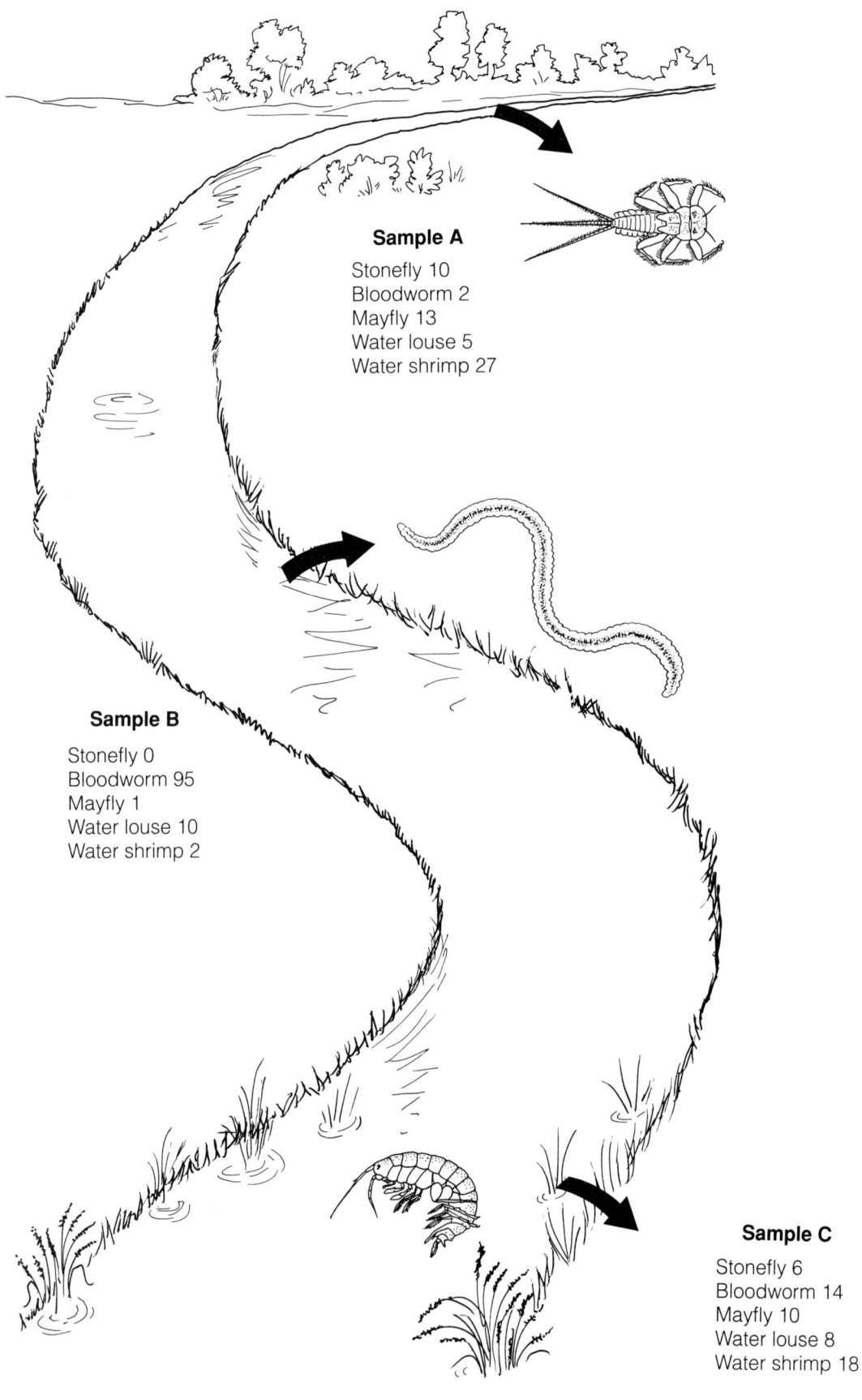

Sample A
Stonefly 10
Bloodworm 2
Mayfly 13
Water louse 5
Water shrimp 27

Sample B
Stonefly 0
Bloodworm 95
Mayfly 1
Water louse 10
Water shrimp 2

Sample C
Stonefly 6
Bloodworm 14
Mayfly 10
Water louse 8
Water shrimp 18

THE BIOSPHERE 29

This graph shows the results of a study on another river. The lines on the graph refer to oxygen, microbes, and several indicator species.

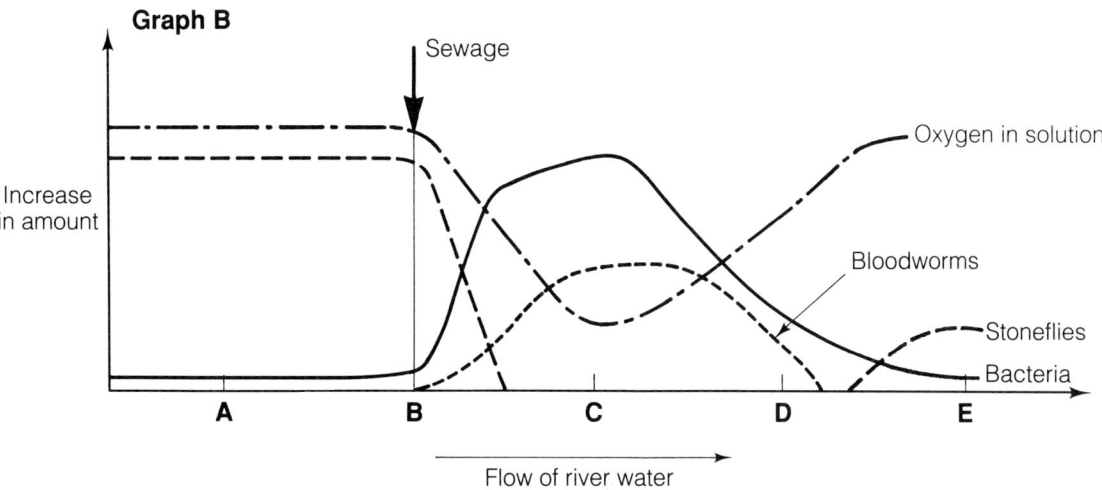

Activities

Read the case study before answering these questions.

○ 1 Describe how samples of the organisms at **A**, **B** and **C** would be taken.

○ 2 Identify the three organisms in the pictures. Use the key on page 10 to help you.

○ 3 Draw three bar charts to show the number of each species at each sample site.

◐ 4 Describe where you think the sewage pipes join the river. Explain your choice.

◐ 5 Describe exactly what is meant by an indicator species.

● 6 The river in graph B flows from **A** to **E**. Explain how the lines on the graph support this statement.

● 7 What evidence is there that the river is able to recover from the effects of the sewage discharge?

● 8 Which type of organism shown on the graph could be used as an indicator of pollution?

● 9 Which organism *not* shown on the graph might be used as an indicator of unpolluted water?

● 10 Fishermen reported dead fish floating in the water at a point on the river. Which of the points A to E might this be?

11 Resource Management

Key Ideas

As human populations grow, the natural resources of the Earth become used up. Ecosystems like forests and oceans are used more and more to meet human needs. We must manage these resources carefully, as mistakes made now could cause problems for generations to come. New ecosystems which we have created, such as farms and forest plantations, must also be managed with care.

Bad Resource Management

Monoculture

Increasing populations have forced humans into trying to grow more food. One way of doing this is to clear areas of natural vegetation and plant huge fields of the same crop.

This method of growing food is known as **monoculture** and it can have bad side effects. If natural vegetation, such as trees and other plants, is cleared, the shelter it provided from wind and rain is lost. The topsoil may be gradually blown and washed away, turning the area into a desert. This is exactly what happened in the USA in the 1930s when bad management led to the creation of a desert known as the Dust Bowl. This stretched from Kansas in the west through Oklahoma, Colorado and Texas, into New Mexico.

Monoculture also encourages the pests of the crop being grown to spread. If the pest gets a hold, the entire crop can be lost. In Ireland in 1845 a fungus known as potato blight destroyed the entire potato crop. Since the potato was about the only crop being grown, many people died of the resulting famine, and many more were forced to emigrate to the USA. The result was a drop in the population of Ireland from $8\frac{1}{2}$ million to $6\frac{1}{2}$ million people in the years following the famine.

Cereal monoculture

Potato leaves showing blight

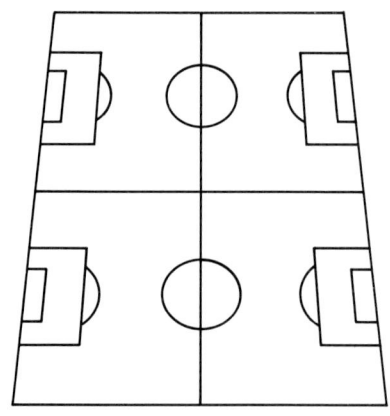
The size of two football pitches is about one hectare.

Destruction of the Rainforests

There are about 800 million hectares of tropical rainforest in the world today, but it is being felled at the rate of about 50 million hectares per year. This represents an annual loss of a piece of forest about the size of the British Isles. In the Amazon basin of South America, the rainforest is felled for timber and to make way for agriculture. There are massive problems caused by this method of management.

Since the trees are harvested instead of dying naturally and rotting back into the soil, huge quantities of minerals are removed from the ecosystem. This means that the soil under the felled area is less fertile and will only support crops for a few years. The people therefore have to cut down more forest each year, abandoning old fields as they become useless.

The trees in the rainforest use much of the water which falls as rain and cycle it back into the atmosphere. If they are cut down flooding can occur. This can wash the topsoil away into the rivers, making it impossible to grow crops.

Perhaps the problem that should concern us most about the loss of rainforest is that we are losing many species of the plants and animals which live there. The ancestors of many of our present crop plants, including the tomato, came from the forests, and scientists now know that these ancestors of our food crops can be used to breed new crop varieties. If the ancestors are made extinct along with the forest, this will become impossible.

Tropical rainforests contain more species of plants and animals than any other ecosystem in the world

Timber Harvest

The modern forester controls the ecosystem carefully. Timber production is balanced with the needs of wildlife. Land unsuitable for farming, like uplands, can be used to plant new forest. Young trees of a variety of species are grown in nurseries for about three years. They are then planted out in the selected area to blend in with the landscape.

Every effort is made to merge the forest into the surroundings. Features of the environment such as crags and waterfalls are left visible. Fertilisers and pesticides may have to be used, but with care, so that they will not produce harmful side effects such as pollution. Trees are harvested by thinning out the forests rather than clearing huge areas.

Felling is carefully controlled so that it does not greatly change the appearance of the environment. Open areas are cut through mature forest to act as fire-breaks. These also allow other plant species to grow, and may attract animals such as deer.

Branches and foliage are left on the site after thinning to become breeding sites for insects and birds. Dead and dying trees are left to rot and the vegetation will eventually decay back into the soil. In this way, the natural cycle by which nutrients are returned to the soil is maintained.

Activities

1. Give two examples of bad management of natural resources.
2. For each example, give the consequences of the bad management.
3. For each example, try to think of ways in which the management might be improved.
4. List the ways in which modern foresters control the ecosystem when they plan and manage a new forest.

The World of Plants

1 Plant Varieties

Key Ideas

There are many different *varieties* of plants; we know of over half a million species. We group plants into two main types: flowering and non-flowering.

With so many varieties, each with its own special properties, plants can provide nearly all of humanity's needs.

Plant sizes range from microscopic to enormous: *Wolffia* is a tiny pond plant 0.5 mm in diameter; the giant redwood can grow to a height of 117 metres.

The first simple plants appeared on Earth over two thousand million years ago. Then they were only small single-celled organisms. Today there are still plants less than 0.5 mm across, but there are also plant "giants" over 80 metres high, and many thousands of different forms in between.

There is an enormous range of characteristics in plants – different colours, different shapes, with or without flowers. Each type of plant has its own special group of characteristics.

Types of Plant

Algae
Algae are often single-celled and live in wet habitats.

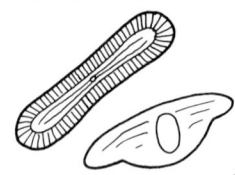

Fungi
We usually think of fungi as being mushrooms and toadstools, but there are also microscopic fungi like yeast, which are especially useful to us (see page 181).

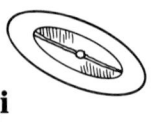

Conifers
Conifers are woody plants which produce seeds, although they do not have petals or fruits.

Monocotyledons
These are flowering, seed-producing plants. The veins in their leaves run parallel to each other. The embryo plant has one seed leaf (cotyledon).

Mosses and Ferns
Like the algae and fungi, these plants do not produce flowers or seeds.

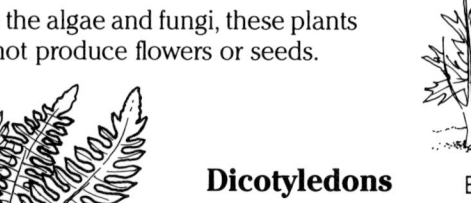

Dicotyledons
These have two seed leaves and have leaves with a branching network of veins.

THE WORLD OF PLANTS

Plants are Important

Green plants make their own food, and all animals, including ourselves, obtain their food from plants or from organisms which eat plants. The first living organism in any food chain or web is usually a green plant.

When making food, green plants use carbon dioxide from the air and release oxygen. Most living things need oxygen to help them obtain energy from the food they eat.

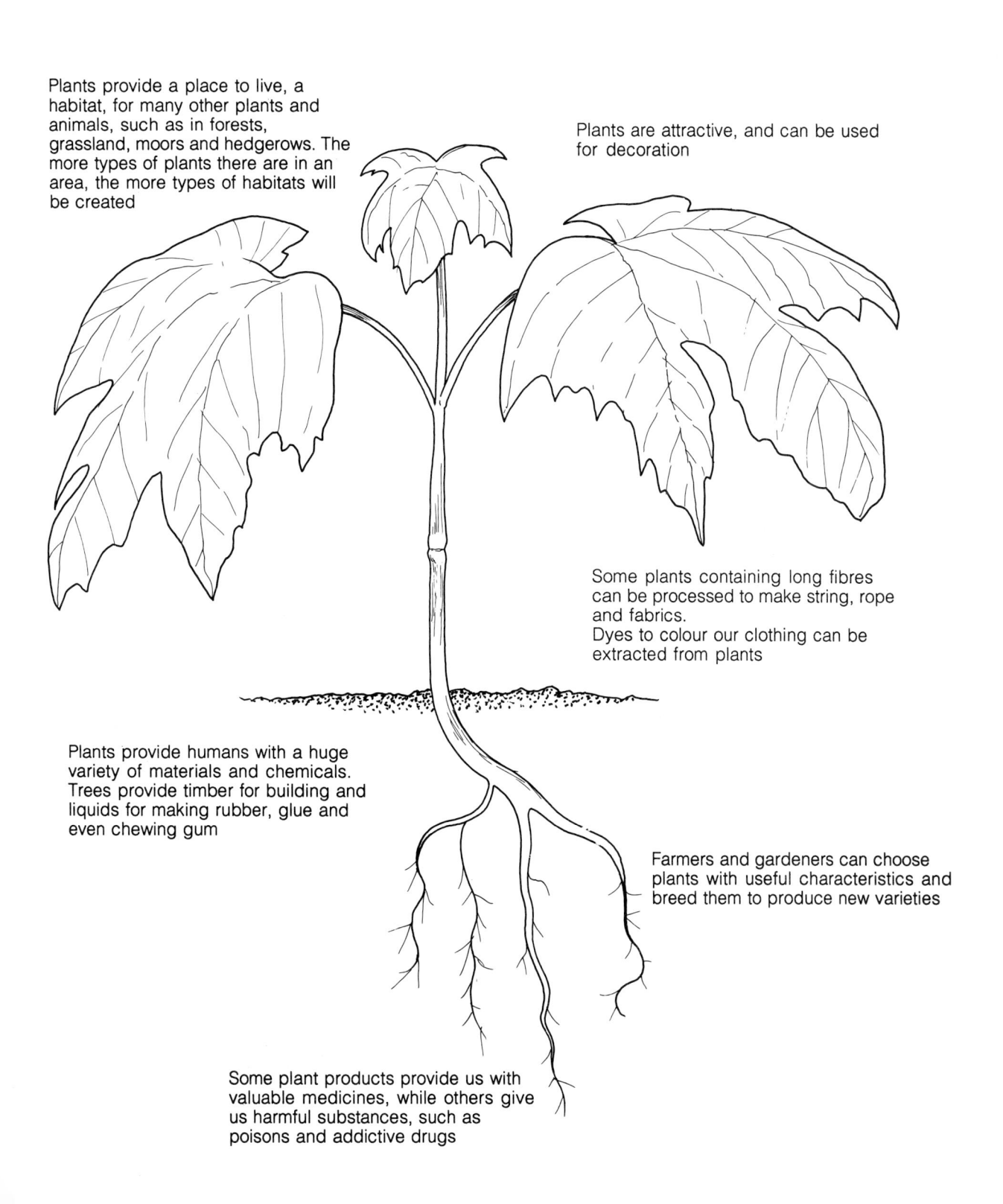

Plants provide a place to live, a habitat, for many other plants and animals, such as in forests, grassland, moors and hedgerows. The more types of plants there are in an area, the more types of habitats will be created

Plants are attractive, and can be used for decoration

Some plants containing long fibres can be processed to make string, rope and fabrics.
Dyes to colour our clothing can be extracted from plants

Plants provide humans with a huge variety of materials and chemicals. Trees provide timber for building and liquids for making rubber, glue and even chewing gum

Farmers and gardeners can choose plants with useful characteristics and breed them to produce new varieties

Some plant products provide us with valuable medicines, while others give us harmful substances, such as poisons and addictive drugs

34 THE WORLD OF PLANTS

Humans, as well as other animals, depend upon the wide variety of plants that exists in the world. In photosynthesis, green plants use up carbon dioxide and produce oxygen.

You can read more about photosynthesis on page 52.

If the numbers of green plants were reduced greatly, less carbon dioxide would be used up and less oxygen produced. In the atmosphere, there would be more carbon dioxide and less oxygen. These effects would be harmful to animal life on Earth.

As the amount of carbon dioxide in the air increases, less heat is able to escape from the Earth. This could result in the *average* surface temperature of the planet increasing by 2 or 3 degrees Celsius over the next 50 years. This in turn *could* cause the ice at the Poles to melt and the sea level to rise by over 50 metres!

Heating of the Earth's atmosphere is called the Greenhouse Effect: a greenhouse gets much hotter than the air outside it because more heat from the Sun stays inside it than can escape through the glass.

Every year, an area of the world's rainforest equal to the size of Britain is being destroyed. Burning the tropical rainforests reduces the number of plants; it also reduces the **variety** of plants left on Earth. Many different plant species are being destroyed all the time. This leaves fewer types of habitat for the animals that are able to survive fires. So the numbers and types of animals are reduced too.

Many animal species have already become extinct because their natural habitats have been destroyed.

Many farmers grow only one type of crop, e.g. wheat. To make harvesting easier, the farmers create huge fields by digging up hedgerows and small areas of woodland. This reduces the variety of species and habitats, and in the long term exposes the fields to wind and rain. The topsoil is gradually blown or washed away and the land becomes infertile. In some parts of the world this process has created large areas of desert.

Plant breeders are continually making new varieties of crops. Stocks of the old varieties need to be kept because if the total number of varieties decreased, there would be fewer types of parent plant to crossbreed from. For this reason, we need to maintain as many varieties of plants as possible. For instance, assume there was only one variety of a major food crop, such as rice. If it were attacked by a new disease the whole crop could be wiped out, and there would be no other varieties (which are resistant to the disease) to replace it.

You can read more about this on page 30.

Rust disease on barley

THE WORLD OF PLANTS 35

Activities

1. Describe, in sentences, at least three results of plant life suddenly dying out across the world.

2. Make up a table listing at least six advantages of having as many varieties of plants as possible. Give a named plant as an example for each advantage. The table will have two headings as shown below.

Advantage	Example

3. Look at the diagram below.
   If there is no replanting, and if deforestation continues at its present rate, how long will it take for the world's rainforests to be totally destroyed?

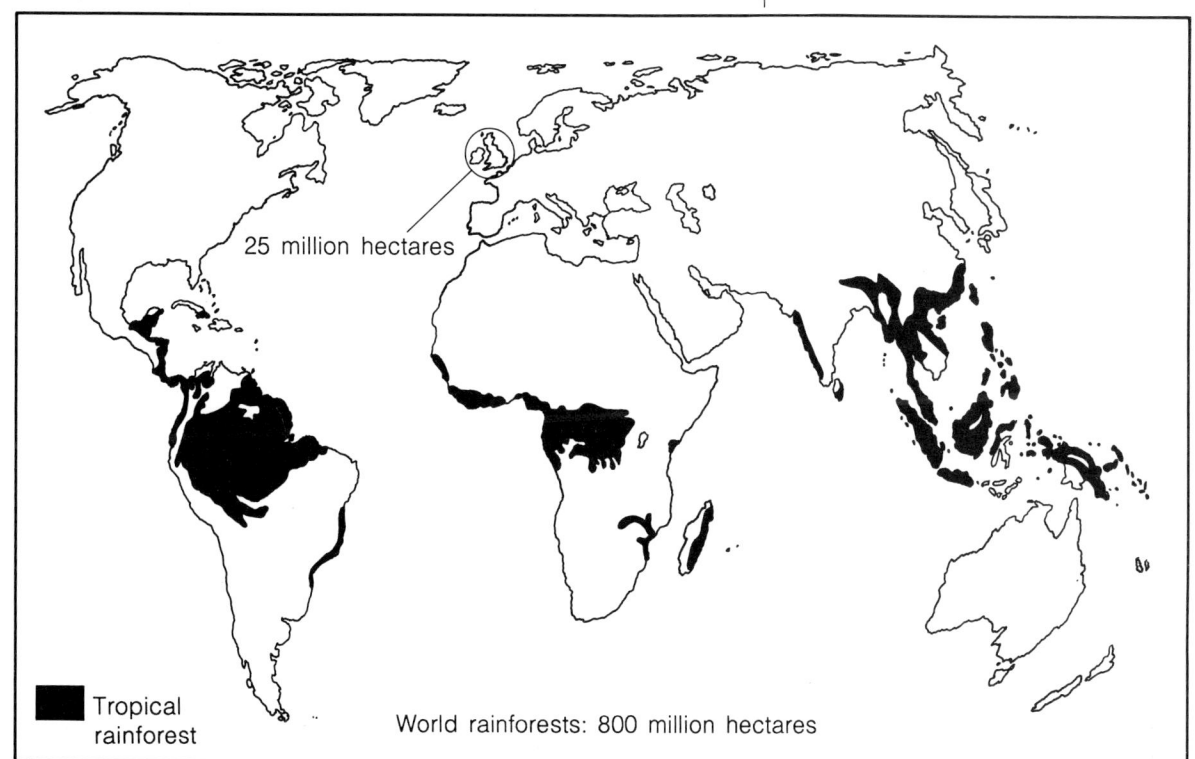

25 million hectares

■ Tropical rainforest

World rainforests: 800 million hectares

4. Use the following word bank to write a letter to persuade the government of a country to stop cutting down its forests.

   green plants, carbon dioxide, variety, temperature, habitat, extinct.

2 Uses of Plants

Key Ideas

Plants provide animals with *food* and *oxygen*. Plants and plant products also provide humans with *medicines*, *fuels* and raw materials such as *wood*. Often these raw materials are refined by factory processes to make specialised products such as *beer*.

Plants and Humans

Since prehistoric times humans have used plant products to help them survive. We have learned to use and adapt all the different parts of plants.

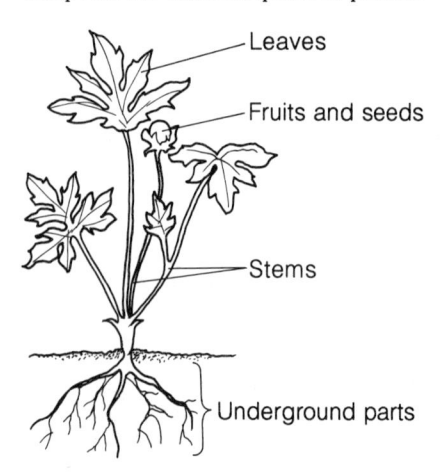

- Leaves
- Fruits and seeds
- Stems
- Underground parts

Using Leaves

Plant leaves can provide food. Although humans are unable to digest the cellulose in leaf cell walls, other animals like cows and sheep can. These animals therefore process the food into a form which we can digest. The leaves which humans do eat, like cabbage, provide us with nutrients and **roughage**, and to make them more digestible we often cook them first.

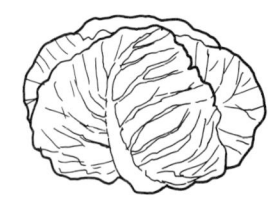

We use the leaves of some plants, like parsley and other herbs, as flavourings.

Leaves can provide us with useful (and harmful) drugs. For a long time, plant products have been used to treat disease. These herbal remedies can work very well, although it is not always understood *why* they work.

Foxgloves are poisonous. Extracts from the leaves affect the heart and other muscles and can kill. However, if used in the correct quantities they can be of benefit. Scientists have been able to purify these extracts to produce a drug called digitalis which is used to treat certain heart diseases.

Foxgloves

Some plant leaves produce **stimulant** drugs which can have harmful effects on humans. For example, tobacco contains nicotine and tea contains caffeine.

Using Stems

Plant stems can be very tough. They need to be strong to support the plant's leaves and flowers and to prevent the plant from being bent or broken. This strength can come from being hard and woody like an oak tree, or by being tough and fibrous like rhubarb.

Timber from the trunks of trees is used as a furniture and building material. Much of the timber cut in the world today is processed to make paper, by pulping the wood fibres with water.

The fibres from the stems of other plants can be used to make rope and string, and fabrics. For example, linen is made from flax, and rope and string from jute and hemp fibres.

Using Underground Parts

The underground parts of plants – usually the roots, but sometimes adapted stems or leaves – can provide food. Food, in the form of starch, is stored in them during the growing season.

A potato is a swollen underground stem

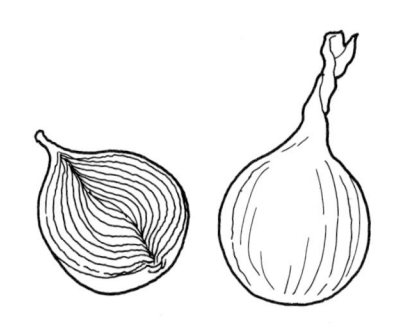

An onion is made up of swollen leaves

THE WORLD OF PLANTS 37

Using Fruits and Seeds
Many fruits and seeds are sources of food for humans and animals.

Seeds contain a store of food which is usually starch. This provides energy for the growth of new roots and shoots. Perhaps the most important seeds we use are those from cereal crops like wheat and barley. These seeds, and many others, are usually processed in some way before being consumed. For example wheat is ground and sifted to make flour.

Harvesting barley

Barley grains

Beer Production – A Case Study

Beer is made by a process called **brewing**. When a fungus called **yeast** is fed on **sugar** in the absence of oxygen, it produces **carbon dioxide** gas and **alcohol**.

Traditionally, the sugar used by brewers comes from **malt**. Malt is germinated **barley**, a cereal crop. Barley seeds contain stored **starch**. As the seeds begin to germinate and grow, the starch is broken down to form sugars. This process is controlled to produce the malt for brewing.

Malting
The barley is first soaked with water and then warm air is blown through it to start off germination. The barley is turned regularly to keep a constant temperature throughout the grain. It takes about 5 or 6 days for the seeds to release special chemicals, called **enzymes**, which will convert the starch to usable sugars.

The malting is stopped by drying the grain with hot air. This stops the seeds from developing further.

Germinating barley

Floor malting

Plants and Energy

In the modern world, energy is a precious commodity. Recent research has shown that plants *could* be one answer to our future energy needs. Fuel is one of the main sources of energy for humans, and new ways of using plants as fuels have been suggested. Some examples are described below.

1. In South America, the fuel for many cars is **alcohol**, not petrol. The alcohol is produced from sugar cane plants. Around 5 billion litres of this fuel is produced per year by Brazil alone.

Unfortunately, there are several problems with using sugar cane in this way. Some people say that the cane should be used for food and not as fuel. There are also technical problems which need to be solved before the cane alcohol is able to compete in the market place with alcohol produced in ways which do not use plants.

2. A second possibility is to make **methane** gas using algae such as seaweeds. Seaweeds could be grown on a huge scale on "floating farms" on the oceans. The growth of the seaweeds could be encouraged by using human sewage as a fertiliser. The seaweed could then be harvested and fed into a land-based tank where bacteria would digest it and produce the methane as a waste product.

Problems with this idea are mainly practical ones such as how to harvest and transport the seaweed back to land.

3. A third possibility is to use plants to produce **hydrogen** gas which is an ideal fuel. Hydrogen is produced by plants at a certain stage in photosynthesis. When hydrogen burns it produces no pollutants because the only waste product is water.

Unfortunately we have not yet developed the technology needed for this process.

Activities

○ 1 Make a summary table to show how humans use various parts of plants. The headings could be:

Plant Part	Plant Example	Use to Humans

○ 2 Describe, in your own words, the process of malting. You could do this by making a flow chart.

● 3 Summarise the potential uses of plants to produce fuels. What are the main problems connected with the exploitation of plants in this way?

3 Seeds and Germination

Key Ideas

Flowering plants produce *fruit* at the end of the summer. If a fruit is opened, seeds are seen inside. Each seed contains an embryo plant along with a food supply, wrapped up in a tough protective coat. When the conditions are right, the seed will start to grow into a new plant and thus continue the species.

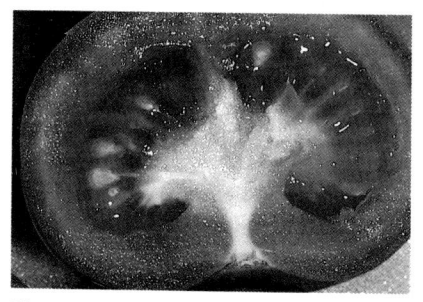

The tomato is a fruit – the yellow "pips" inside are the seeds.

The Structure of Seeds

The broad bean is a good example of a seed coming from a flowering plant. This seed is large, and the parts of the seed are easy to see and identify. The seed is surrounded by a tough coat called the **testa**. This protects the seed contents from damage and infection. Inside the seed is a young **embryo plant**. The young plant has a shoot called a **plumule** and a root called a **radicle**. The food store for the young plant is in the fleshy leaves called **cotyledons**.

External view

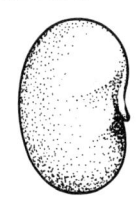

Internal view
- Plumule
- Radicle
- Micropyle
- Cotyledon

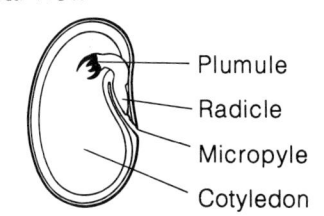

Testa removed
- Cotyledons
- Plumule
- Radicle

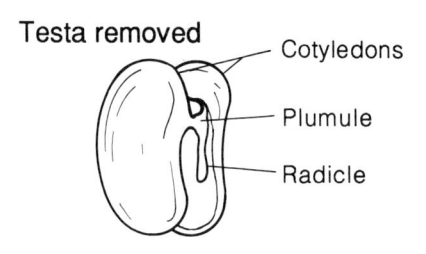

The broad bean seed

Dormancy

A seed will usually stay **dormant** for some time after release from the parent plant. This means that for this period of time its life processes are "shut down". The dormant seed is triggered into life by exposure to certain conditions.

Seeds from the Arctic lupin thought to be over 10 000 years old have been found in frozen soil in Canada. In spite of their age, when given the right conditions in the laboratory, some of them germinated.

Germination

Germination is the term which describes the early growth of a seed. When the embryo plant starts to break through the testa, the seed is said to be germinating. Certain basic conditions are needed to allow a seed to germinate. These are:

1. **Water** – to swell and soften the seed and to move substances around within the seed;
2. **Oxygen** – from the air which allows the seed to release energy from its stored food;
3. **Warmth** – a certain range of temperature, usually between about 5 and 45 degrees Celsius for British plants.

In order to germinate, a seed needs all of these conditions.

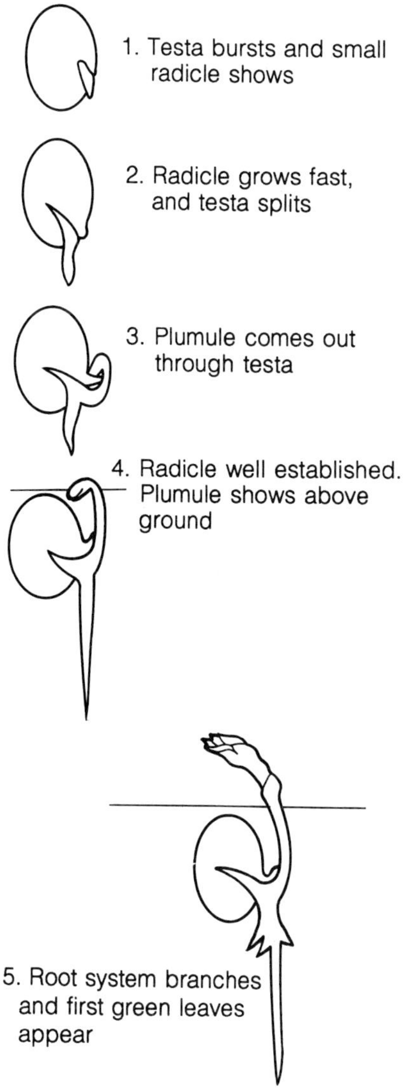

1. Testa bursts and small radicle shows

2. Radicle grows fast, and testa splits

3. Plumule comes out through testa

4. Radicle well established. Plumule shows above ground

5. Root system branches and first green leaves appear

Stages in the germination of a broad bean seed

40 THE WORLD OF PLANTS

Stages in Germination

As water is drawn into the seed, the seed swells and the seed coat bursts. The young root and shoot start to grow and emerge from the seed coat. The root grows downwards into the soil and the shoot grows upwards into the air. The food for this growth is starch stored in the cotyledons. When the shoot reaches the air and has grown its first green leaves, it can start to produce its own food and no longer relies on the cotyledons.

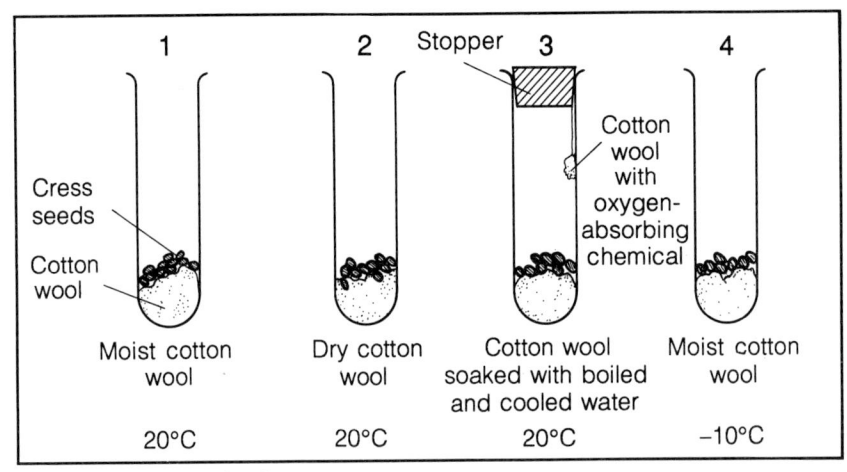

An experiment on germination

Temperature and Germination

Temperature affects the number of seeds in a batch that will germinate in a certain time. Usually seeds will only germinate between temperatures of 5 and 45 °C. The graph below shows the percentage of cress seeds which germinated within 48 hours over a range of temperatures.

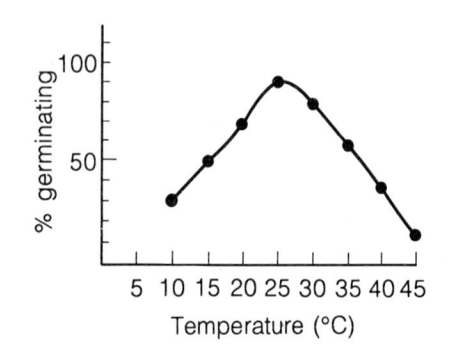

Eight batches of cress seeds were germinated in ideal conditions but at different temperatures. The graph shows the percentage of seeds in each batch which had germinated after 48 hours

Activities

1. Copy and complete this table:

Seed Part	Simple Name	Function
radicle		
plumule		
cotyledon		
testa		

2. List the conditions required for germination.

3. Study the drawing of the tubes containing cress seeds.
   (a) In which tube(s) will germination *not* occur?
   (b) For each one say why germination does not occur.

4. Study the graph for germinating cress seeds.
   (a) What seems to be the best temperature for germination?
   (b) What percentage of seeds germinated after 48 hours at 10 °C?
   (c) Describe the changes in the percentage germinating between 10 and 45 °C.
   (d) What range of temperatures gives better than 50% germination?

4 Flower Structure & Pollination

Key Ideas

After germination and a period of growth, the new plant produces special stems carrying *flowers*. These special stems are for sexual reproduction. After a flower is *pollinated* and *fertilised*, the petals die back and a fruit forms. The fruit contains the seed which will develop into the next generation.

Flower Structure

Diagram **A** shows the basic structure of a flower, and details of the male and female parts are shown in **B** and **C**. All of the many different shapes and sizes of flower are only variations on this basic structure.

Flower Parts

Flowers have four main parts:

1. A ring of **sepals** which protect the flower in bud.
2. A ring of **petals** which attract insects to the flower.
3. A set of male parts or **stamens** which make the male sex cells called **pollen**.
4. A set of female parts called the **carpels** which make the female sex cells or **ovules**. A flower may have more than one carpel.

Pollination

When the stamens of a flower are ripe, the **anthers** burst open and shed pollen. This pollen must be carried to a female **stigma** for **fertilisation** to happen.

In **self-pollination**, pollen from one flower lands on the stigma of the same flower. This is not so good for the plants since it reduces the amount of variation within the species, making the species less able to adapt to change and to resist disease.

Most plants have **cross-pollination**: the pollen from one flower lands on the stigma of a different flower. There are various ways to ensure cross-pollination. Some plants have different ripening times for the male and female parts of the same flower. In others there are separate male and female flowers. Some species even have male-only and female-only plants.

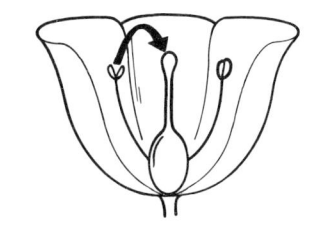

Self-pollination

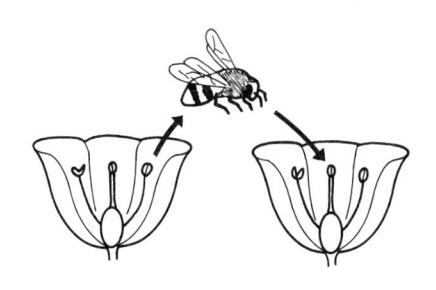

Cross-pollination

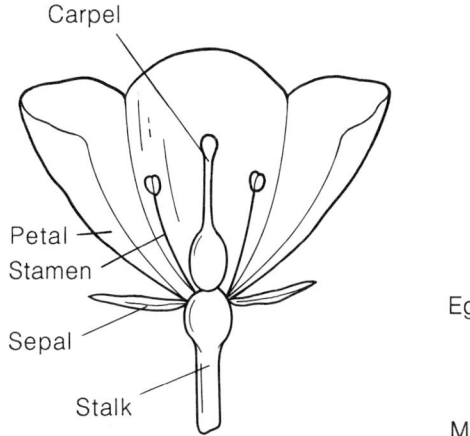

A
Basic structure of a flower
(labels: Carpel, Petal, Stamen, Sepal, Stalk)

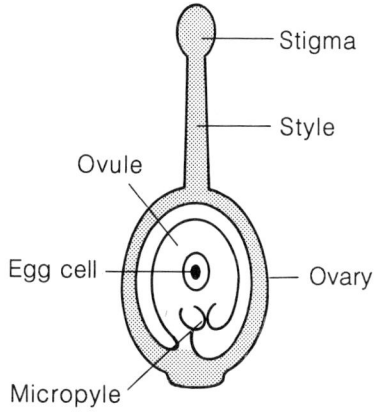

B
The carpel is the female part of the flower
(labels: Stigma, Style, Ovule, Egg cell, Ovary, Micropyle)

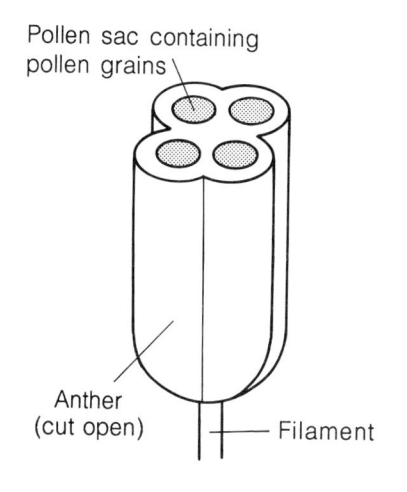

C
The stamen is the male part of the flower
(labels: Pollen sac containing pollen grains, Anther (cut open), Filament)

42 THE WORLD OF PLANTS

Methods of Pollination

Plants can be pollinated by the wind or by insects. The structure of the flower suggests the pollination method.

1 Insect Pollinated Flowers

Some flowers are insect pollinated. These flowers have large attractive petals, usually coloured and scented. They often produce **nectar** for the insects to feed on. Their pollen grains are large and sticky to attach easily to insects' bodies. The male and female parts of these flowers tend to be stiff and enclosed within the petals.

A common insect pollinator is the honey bee which has specialised back legs to hold pollen. The leg joint which holds the pollen is called the **pollen basket**.

2 Wind Pollinated Flowers

Wind pollinated flowers, like those of grasses, are held on tall, rigid stalks, so that their pollen can be caught by the wind. The flowers are usually inconspicuous, small and either green or white. They have no scent or nectar and tend to hang droopily from the plant. The sex organs hang outside the flower and the stigmas have a large surface area to catch the pollen.

The pollen grains themselves are very numerous and light like dust. The pollen of some wind pollinated plants such as pine trees have little air sacs. These make the pollen buoyant and easily carried by the wind.

Honey bee with pollen basket

A hollyhock pollen grain, × 260

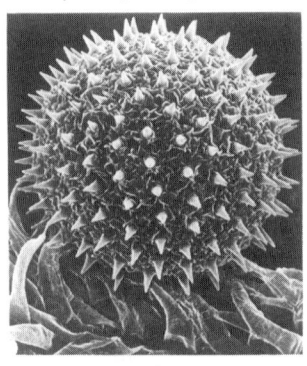

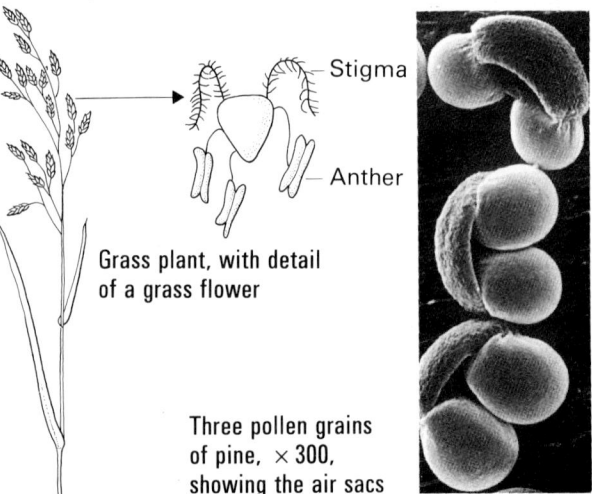

Grass plant, with detail of a grass flower

Three pollen grains of pine, × 300, showing the air sacs

Insect and Wind Pollinated Flowers Compared

Insect
large, conspicuous
coloured petals
scent, nectar
enclosed sex organs
large sticky pollen
held upright on plant

Wind
small, inconspicuous
green or white petals
no scent or nectar
dangling sex organs
dusty pollen
hang droopily on plant

Activities

1 Match the following structures to their functions:

Structures	Functions
sepal	male organ
petal	catches pollen
stamen	produces sugary liquid
anther	protects buds
stigma	contains egg cells
ovary	attracts insects
nectary	makes pollen

2 List the features of the drawing of a grass flower which make it suitable for wind pollination.

3 How is the structure of the pollen basket of the honey bee suited to its job?

4 Describe a typical insect pollinated flower.

5 How is the pollen grain of hollyhock suited to insect pollination?

THE WORLD OF PLANTS 43

5 Pollen Tubes & Fruit Formation

Key Ideas

After pollination, the pollen must reach the ovary and join with *ovules* to produce the seeds. The flower parts must die back and the flower structure must change into a fruit. The fruit design has to allow for the dispersal of the seeds.

Pollen Tube Growth

When pollen grains reach the stigma they are stimulated to grow by a sugary substance made by the stigma cells.

A pollen grain grows a **tube** down through the **style** tissue and into the ovary. The tube is nourished by the style tissue. The pollen tube carries the male nucleus, and when the tube tip reaches the ovary, it enters the ovary through a tiny pore called the **micropyle**.

Fertilisation

The male nucleus from the pollen tube fertilises a female nucleus in an **ovule** and the ovule then becomes a seed.

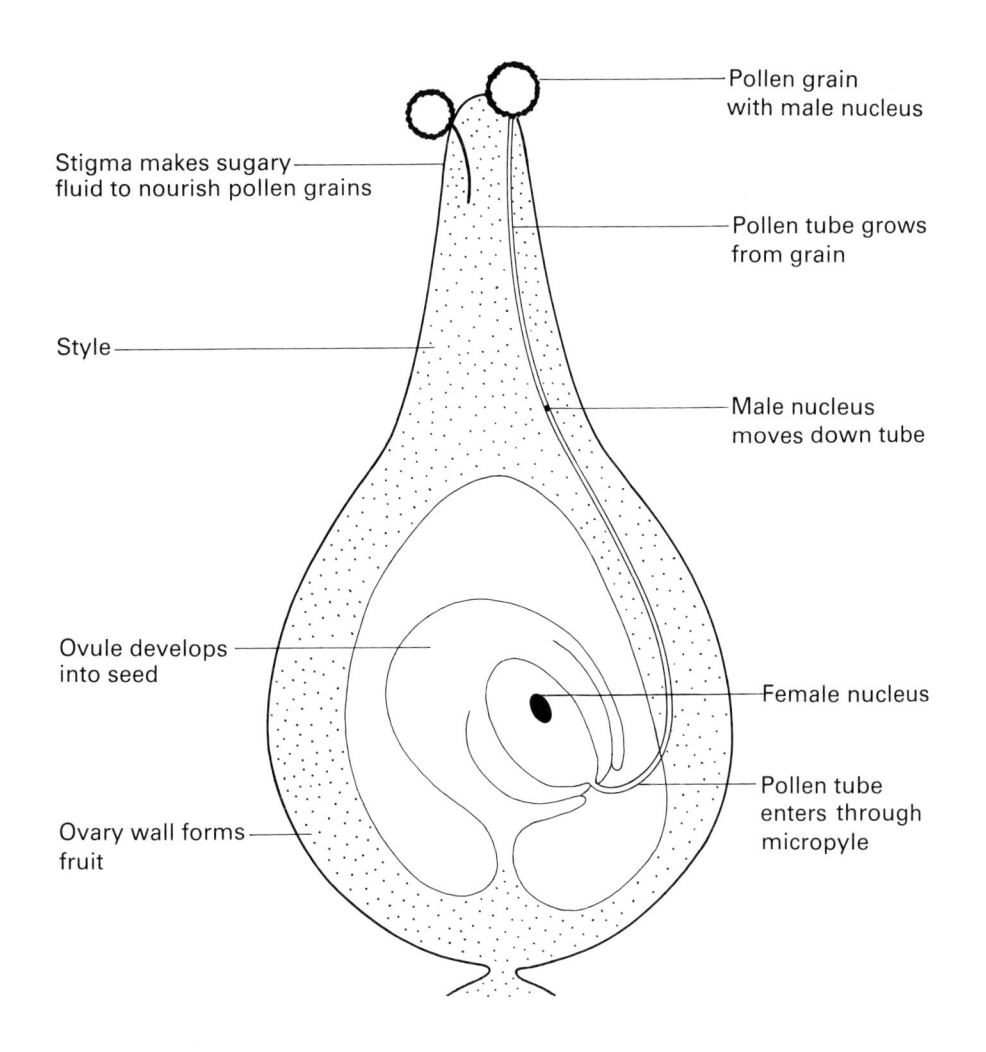

Labels on diagram:
- Pollen grain with male nucleus
- Stigma makes sugary fluid to nourish pollen grains
- Pollen tube grows from grain
- Style
- Male nucleus moves down tube
- Ovule develops into seed
- Female nucleus
- Pollen tube enters through micropyle
- Ovary wall forms fruit

44 THE WORLD OF PLANTS

Fruit Formation

After fertilisation the ovules become seeds. The whole ovary develops into a **fruit**. The drawings below show the formation of the fruits of tomato and poppy plants.

Tomato

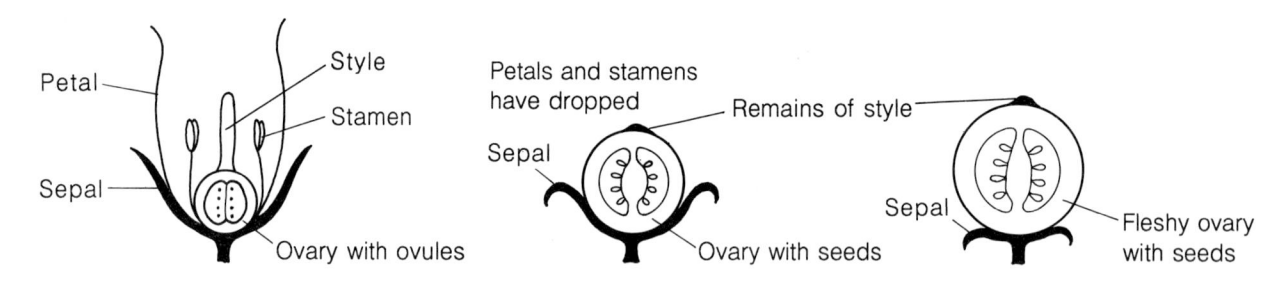

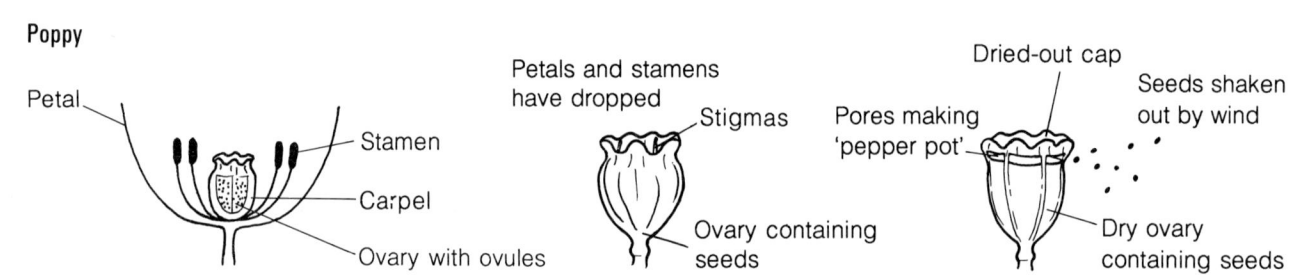

Poppy

1. Flower before fertilisation   2. Developing fruit just after fertilisation   3. Fully developed fruit

Activities

○ 1 Write one or two sentences describing how a pollen grain gets from the anther of one flower to the ovary of a second flower. Use this word bank:

insect, wind, ripe, anther, stigma, style, micropyle, pollen tube, ovary.

● 2 After fertilisation, what happens to:
  (a) the ovule?
  (b) the ovary?

● 3 During the formation of the tomato fruit what happens to the following structures?
  (a) stigma and style
  (b) ovary wall
  (c) ovules
  (d) petals and sepals

6 Seed Dispersal

Key Ideas

Mature fruits and seeds must be *dispersed* away from the parent plant. This prevents *crowding* and hence *competition* between offspring and parent. Dispersal also allows the species to colonise new areas.

The particular methods of dispersal of fruits and seeds are determined by their structure. In some plants the seeds alone are dispersed and in others the fruits containing the seeds are dispersed.

Wind Dispersal

Some fruits and seeds have a structure such as a wing or a parachute to catch the wind and help them disperse. Sycamore and dandelion are two good examples.

In others, such as the poppy, the fruit is like a pepper pot filled with tiny, light seeds which are shaken out by the wind.

In all of these plants the structures involved are very light to aid **dispersal**.

Sycamore fruit — Wing, Ovary containing seed

Dandelion fruit — Parachute, Seed

Poppy fruit — Remains of stigmas, Pores through which seeds are scattered, Ovary containing seeds

External Animal Dispersal

Many plants have fruits or seeds designed to catch on to the fur or feathers of animals. These fruits and seeds may then be carried by the animal until they are brushed off at some distance from the parent plant. The structures often have hooks or spikes, as in burdock or goosegrass.

Burdock fruit — Hooks

Goosegrass fruit

Internal Animal Dispersal

Some fruits are eaten by animals. These fruits are often juicy and brightly coloured. The seeds inside are protected from the digestive juices of the animal by their seed coat. After a while the seeds are passed out of the gut of the animal in its droppings. This means that the seeds can be dispersed some distance from the parent plant. It also means they are deposited along with a ready-made fertiliser.

Gooseberry and rose hip are examples of fruits dispersed in this way.

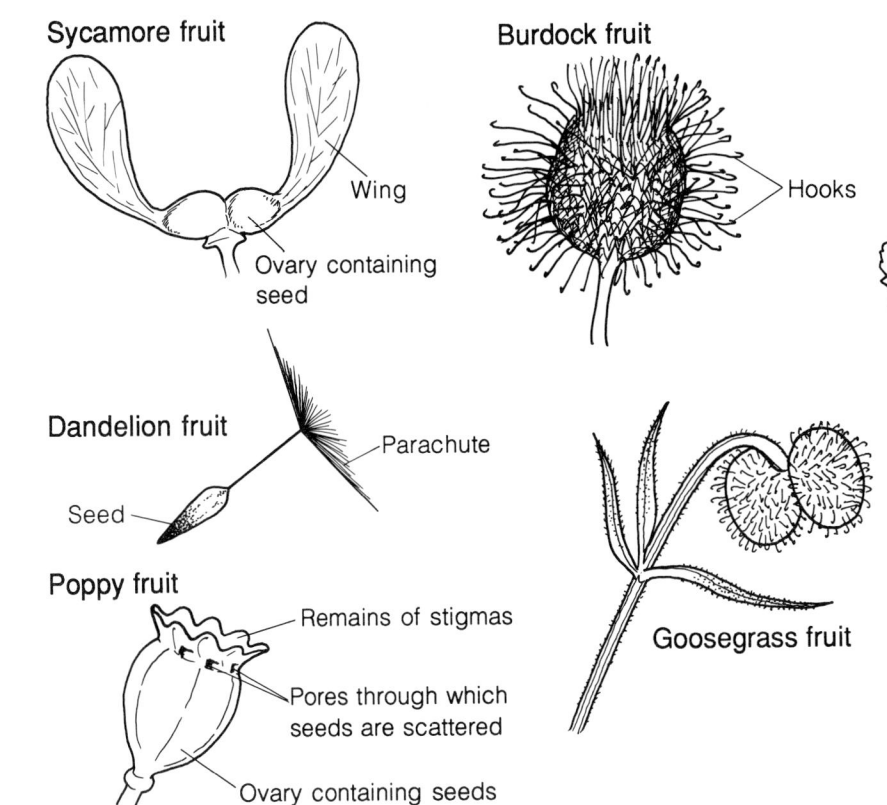

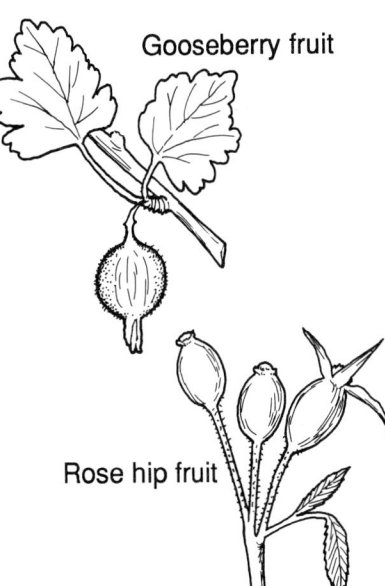

Gooseberry fruit

Rose hip fruit

46 THE WORLD OF PLANTS

Details of Some Fruits

Burdock
Using a hand lens it can be seen that the fruits of this plant are covered in hooks which work like Velcro. They allow the fruit to be firmly attached to the coat of an animal, but readily detached again when the animal brushes against a wall or bushes, for instance.

Tomato
The tomato is a very juicy and attractive fruit. Humans are very fond of eating them and animals eat related wild species. The seeds are very resistant to the digestive juices of the human gut. Look at your local sewage works and you may see young tomato seedlings growing!

Dandelion
Detailed study of the dandelion fruit shows that it is extremely well suited to dispersal and survival. It will not be dislodged from the parent plant unless the wind strength and humidity are just right – a casual puff of wind is not enough.

The parachute at one end causes the fruit to fall seed-bearing end first, ensuring that the seed ends up in the soil. The seed is equipped with tiny barbs which catch in the soil and anchor the seed firmly and securely.

Activities

○ 1 Copy and fill in this table with some plant examples.

Wind Dispersal	Internal Animal Dispersal	External Animal Dispersal

○ 2 Explain why plants need to disperse their seed.
◐ 3 Why is it important that a dandelion fruit cannot be dislodged by a casual puff of wind?
◐ 4 Why are burdock hooks like Velcro and not like superglue?
◐ 5 Explain why tomato seedlings sometimes grow at sewage works.
● 6 Examine the diagram opposite, which shows the number of sycamore seeds found at distances around the parent tree.
  (a) Where are most seeds found?
  (b) Suggest the direction of the prevailing wind.
  (c) Suggest how this data might have been collected.

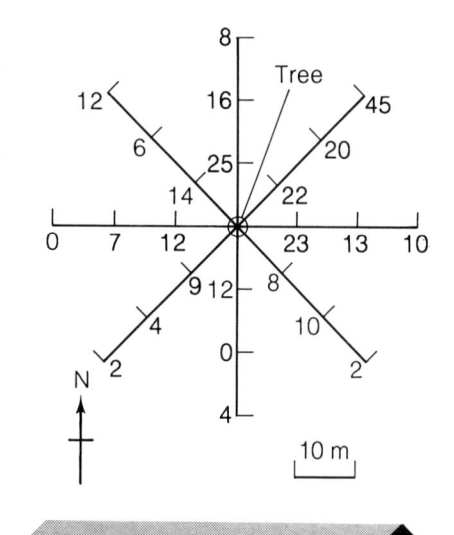

7 Asexual Reproduction

Key Ideas

Many plants reproduce by methods which do not involve sexual organs. These methods are collectively called *asexual reproduction*. They involve only one parent plant, and the offspring and parent have identical characteristics. There are many different methods of asexual reproduction.

Advantages of asexual reproduction are that mature plants are produced very fast and so plants can colonise new ground rapidly.

Runners

Runners are side-branches which grow from buds low down on the stems of the parent plant. The runner itself also has buds. The bud on the end of the runner is in contact with the ground and produces roots which work their way down into the soil. The bud also produces a green shoot which grows up into the air. In this way a new young plant is formed. Its connection with the parent plant ceases when the runner eventually rots and decomposes.

In time the new plant itself produces runners. Thus there is rapid colonisation of the ground surrounding the original plant.

Bulbs

You may have noticed that some plants, like daffodils, appear suddenly in early spring. They die back a few months later and before long all the plants have disappeared.

This type of plant actually spends most of its life below ground as a **bulb**. Bulbs are underground buds surrounded by fleshy leaves containing stored food and water. The stem at the base of the bulb is flattened and bears the buds and leaves, which are very tightly squashed together.

A bulb will lie dormant in the ground from early summer all through the autumn and winter until the spring. In early spring it grows rapidly using the starch stored after the previous year's growth. The early growth is followed by flowering and food is produced in the leaves and flower stems by photosynthesis. The flowers and leaves then die back and the food is transported to the leaf bases to form next year's bulb or bulbs.

New bulbs are produced from side buds of the original bulb in the same way. After a growing season, the bulbs can be dug up and the daughter bulbs split off and planted separately.

Side-branch (runner) grows out from the base of the main stem

Runner   Bud

New plants develop from the buds of the runner

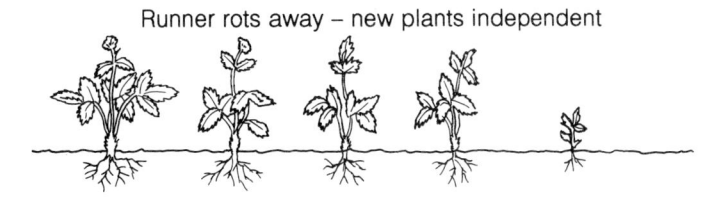

Runner rots away – new plants independent

Runners are produced in strawberry plants

48 THE WORLD OF PLANTS

Bulbs are produced in the daffodil

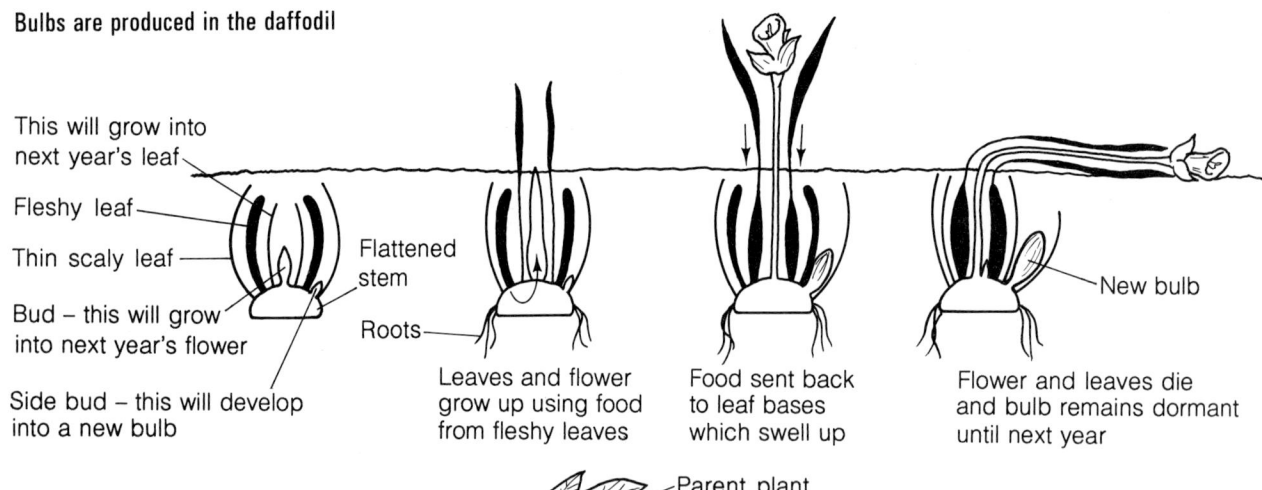

Labels on diagram: This will grow into next year's leaf; Fleshy leaf; Thin scaly leaf; Bud – this will grow into next year's flower; Side bud – this will develop into a new bulb; Flattened stem; Roots; New bulb.

Leaves and flower grow up using food from fleshy leaves

Food sent back to leaf bases which swell up

Flower and leaves die and bulb remains dormant until next year

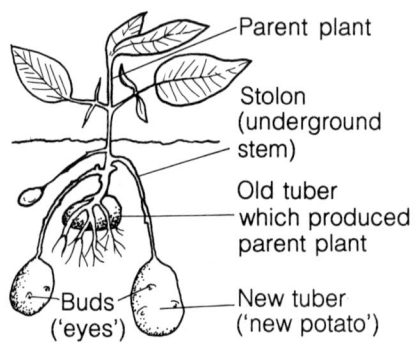

Labels on potato diagram: Parent plant; Stolon (underground stem); Old tuber which produced parent plant; Buds ('eyes'); New tuber ('new potato')

Stem tubers are produced in the potato

Stem Tubers

If a potato is examined closely, little buds called "eyes" can be seen. At the start of the growing season these eyes can produce shoots. Energy for the growth of these shoots comes from starch stored in the potato tissue. The shoot emerges from the ground and starts to grow green leaves. It can then produce its own food by photosynthesis.

At the end of the growing season a lot of food is transported to the ends of underground stems called **stolons**. The ends of these stolons swell and new **tubers** are formed. These tubers are the so-called "new potatoes". Each new potato can be dug up separately and planted out to produce a new generation of potato plants.

Activities

1. List three methods of asexual reproduction in plants.

2. Look at this graph of the runner lengths of a single strawberry plant produced in one summer.
   (a) What is the range of different runner lengths?
   (b) What is the commonest length of runner?
   (c) How many runners were 25 cm long?
   (d) What is the total number of runners the plant produced?

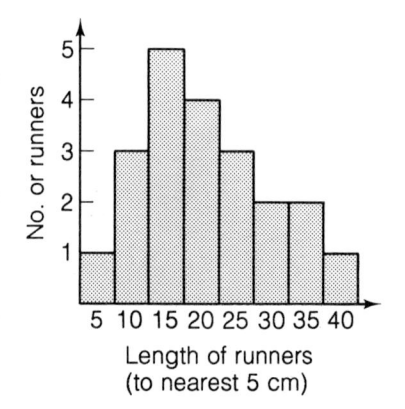

3. Where is the food supply for new growth in daffodil bulbs stored?

4. Where does the food supply for the formation of a new daffodil bulb come from?

5. A potato farmer decides to improve his yield of potatoes by applying fertiliser to one of his two fields. The fertiliser costs £15.00 per sack and his field needs 25 sacks to cover it properly.
   The yields of potatoes from his two fields that year are shown in the drawing. The farmer gets 10p per kilogram for his potato crop.
   (a) Was the fertiliser treatment a financial success for the farmer?
   (b) To make a fair comparison of the two fields, how should the farmer treat the two fields during the growing season?

Without fertiliser	With fertiliser
12 000 kg yield	15 000 kg yield

8 Artificial Propagation

Key Ideas

In garden centres and nurseries, plants are reproduced by *artificial propagation*. This uses the natural ability of many plant species to reproduce asexually. Artificial propagation ensures fast reproduction on a commercial scale of good quality, identical plant stock.

Cuttings

Young fast-growing shoots are cut from a parent plant with a sharp knife. These **cuttings** can be placed in water and allowed to root before planting out into soil, or they can be dipped in **hormone rooting powder** and then planted straight into moist sand.

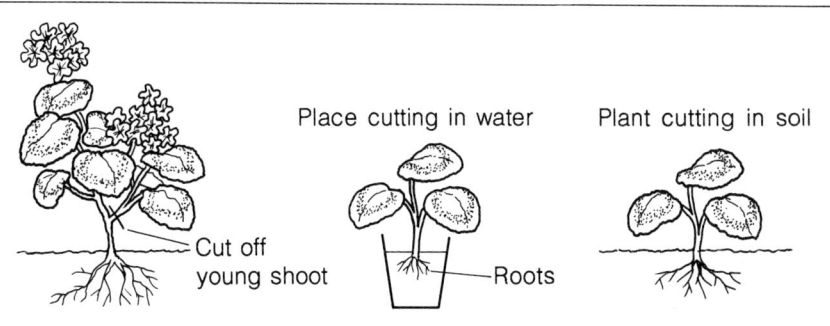

Cuttings are a good way of propagating geraniums

Grafting

This method is used by growers to produce many plants of the same variety in a short time. A grower chooses a plant of the variety required. A small piece of the chosen plant is fixed on to the root system of a well-established plant, often of a different variety. Many pieces can be taken from the same plant and "grafted" on to root systems in this way.

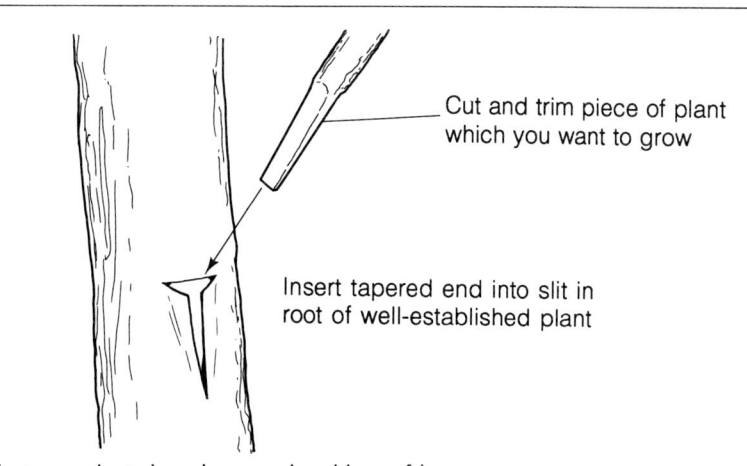

Most rose plants have been produced by grafting

Layering

This method is like the natural method of propagation with runners. A low side-branch, known as a **layer**, of the parent plant is pulled down on to the ground and is usually pegged into the soil. The grower hopes that the layer will produce roots and shoots and become an independent plant.

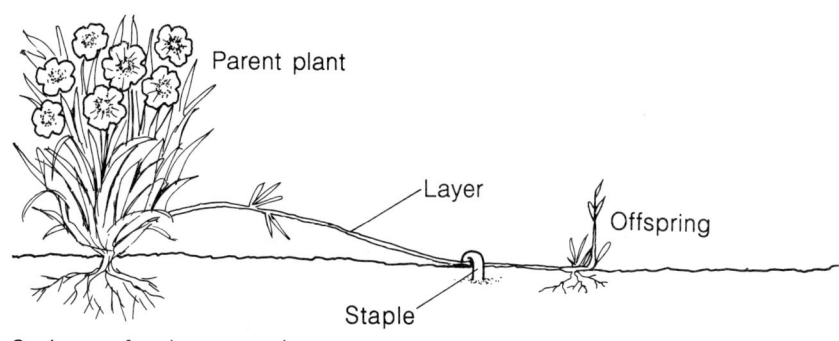

Gardeners often layer carnations

50 THE WORLD OF PLANTS

Clones

All forms of asexual reproduction, including artificial propagation, give rise to offspring that are identical to one another and to the parent plant. By "identical" we mean that they have exactly the same characteristics, such as leaf shape and flower colour. Collections of offspring produced from asexual reproduction are called **clones**.

It should be remembered that many plants can reproduce by natural and artificial propagation, and by sexual reproduction from seeds they produce.

What form of reproduction has produced this field of buttercups?

Reproduction Methods Compared

	Advantages to Humans	Advantages to Plant	Disadvantages
A S E X U A L	1. Good characteristics preserved. 2. Early and rapid growth.	1. Good characteristics preserved. 2. Clustered population cuts down **competition** from other species. 3. Able to colonise area around parent plant rapidly.	1. Lack of variety limits the ability of the species to respond to environmental change, e.g. drought, which may wipe out the population. 2. Lack of dispersal reduces scope for **colonisation** of different areas. 3. Clustered population produces competition within the species.
S E X U A L	1. Seeds exploited for food. 2. New **varieties** can be produced by **selective breeding**.	1. Variety within the species allows at least some of the plants to respond to environmental change. 2. Dispersal increases scope for **colonisation** of different areas and prevents competition between offspring.	1. Depends on meeting of the gametes. 2. Growth is often slow and young plants very fragile.

Activities

1. Name four plants which are propagated artificially.
2. Describe how you would take a cutting of the geranium shown below.

3. What is meant by the term "clone"?
4. (a) What are the advantages to a garden centre in propagating their plants artificially?
   (b) What are the advantages to a garden centre in propagating their plants sexually from seed?
5. The map below shows the distribution of some plants in a woodland. Explain how the method of reproduction in the daffodil accounts for its distribution in clumps with space between.

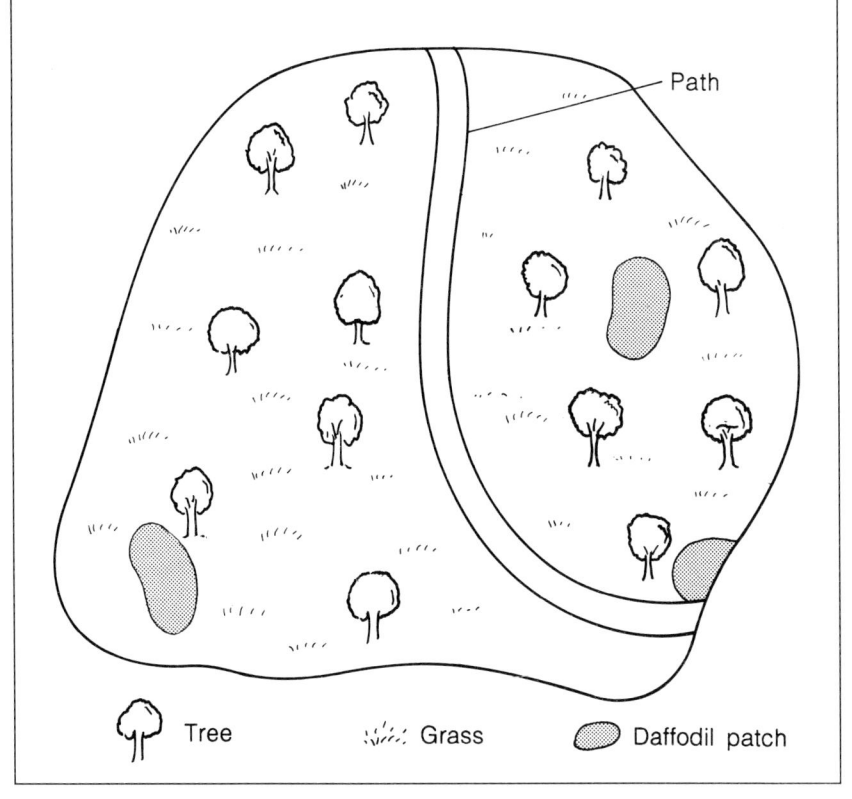

9 Photosynthesis

Key Ideas

Green plants are the producers in *food webs*. They make their own food in the form of *sugars*. To make food, the green parts of the plant must convert *light energy* into *chemical energy* which is stored in *starch*. The raw materials for *photosynthesis* are carbon dioxide and water.

When a green plant makes food it releases *oxygen* gas as a by-product. Most other living things obtain their food by eating green plants or other animals which have eaten green plants.

Sources of Food

Food contains chemical energy. We eat many different kinds of food, but if we trace foods back to their source we find that they all come from green plants. For instance, milk comes from cows, which eat grass, which is a green plant. Eggs come from chickens, which eat grain, which is the seed of a green plant.

Green plants make food and are called **producers**. Animals eat plants or other animals, and are called **consumers**. The relationships between producers and consumers allow us to construct a **food chain** or **food web**, e.g:

grass → caterpillar → shrew → owl

Green plants are the *source* of food for nearly all living things. They make their own food by a process called **photosynthesis**. "Photo" means "light". "Synthesis" means "making by putting together".

The food which a plant makes is **glucose**. It is made in the green parts of a plant, particularly the leaves. Glucose can be used by the plant or stored as **starch**.

Making Glucose

Glucose is a simple sugar. It is also a **carbohydrate**, which is a chemical containing **carbon**, **hydrogen** and **oxygen**. Green plants need three things to make glucose in photosynthesis:

1. a supply of energy,
2. a way of trapping the energy,
3. the raw materials, carbon dioxide and water, which contain carbon, hydrogen and oxygen.

1 Energy Supply

Although it is difficult to show that a green plant makes glucose, experiments can be carried out to prove that starch is made and stored in the plant.

It can be shown that a plant kept in the dark cannot make starch, and that the same plant kept in the light is able to make starch.

Light, usually in the form of sunlight, is the source of energy for photosynthesis.

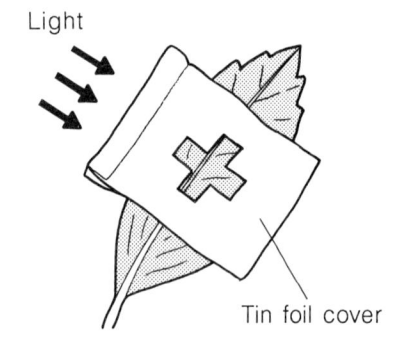

Light

Tin foil cover

Test leaf with iodine

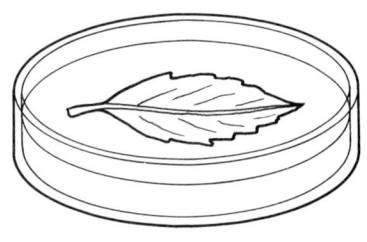

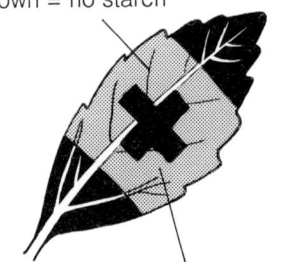

Brown = no starch

Black = starch present

2 The Energy Catcher

Some plants have leaves that are not green all over. The leaves may have white or other coloured patches. These are called **variegated** leaves.

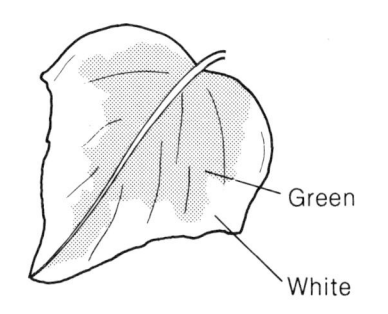

Variegated geraniums have white areas around the edges of their leaves

If one of these plants is kept in the light and then tested, starch is found only in the green areas of the leaves, *not* in the white patches.

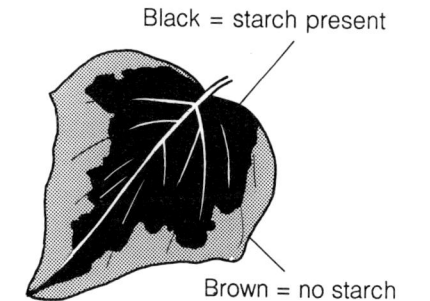

Black = starch present
Brown = no starch

The green colour is due to a chemical pigment called **chlorophyll** which the plant needs in order to make glucose and hence starch. The chlorophyll is able to trap the light energy and convert it into chemical energy. This chemical energy is used to make the glucose which can be converted into starch as a store of chemical energy.

3 Raw Materials

The plant needs raw materials which are chemically combined to make glucose.

The carbon and oxygen are obtained from carbon dioxide gas (CO_2) in the air. If the plant is kept without CO_2 and then tested, no starch is found in its leaves. Therefore CO_2 is needed for photosynthesis.

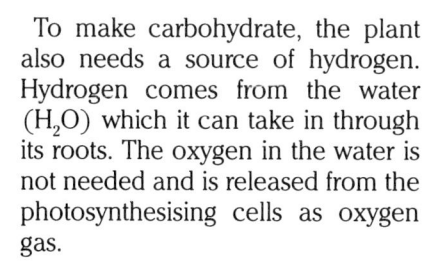

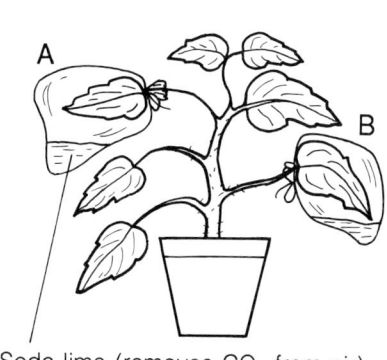

Soda lime (removes CO_2 from air)

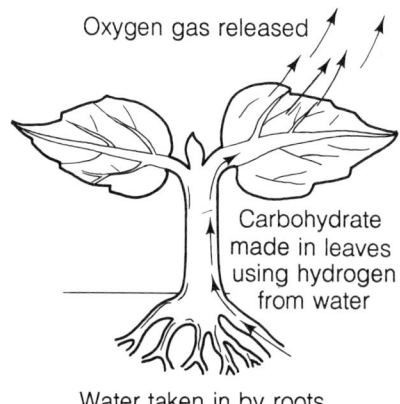

Test with iodine

Brown = no starch   Black = starch present

To make carbohydrate, the plant also needs a source of hydrogen. Hydrogen comes from the water (H_2O) which it can take in through its roots. The oxygen in the water is not needed and is released from the photosynthesising cells as oxygen gas.

Oxygen gas released

Carbohydrate made in leaves using hydrogen from water

Water taken in by roots

The process of photosynthesis can be summarised by the following equation:

$$\textbf{Carbon dioxide} + \textbf{water} \xrightarrow[\text{chlorophyll}]{\text{light energy}} \textbf{Glucose (starch)} + \textbf{oxygen}$$
$$\text{(chemical energy)}$$

Raw materials   Conditions   Products

54 THE WORLD OF PLANTS

Limiting Factors

Photosynthesis can only happen if the necessary raw materials and conditions are available. It needs **CO₂** and **H₂O**, and **light energy** which is trapped by **chlorophyll**. It will only work within a small temperature range – temperatures which are too low or too high will cause it to slow down or stop.

In order to see how these conditions affect photosynthesis, we need to be able to measure the rate at which photosynthesis is taking place. Fortunately this can be done easily by observing plants which grow in water, such as pondweed.

Oxygen is produced by photosynthesis in green plants. By measuring the amount of oxygen released from the plant over a certain time we can estimate the rate of photosynthesis. Using pondweed, the oxygen can be seen as bubbles of gas coming from the plant, which can be collected.

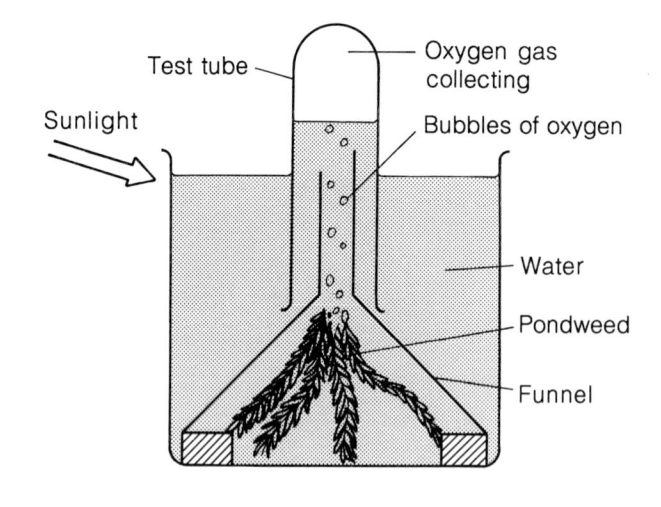

We can measure the rate of photosynthesis in pondweed by counting the number of bubbles of oxygen produced over a certain period of time

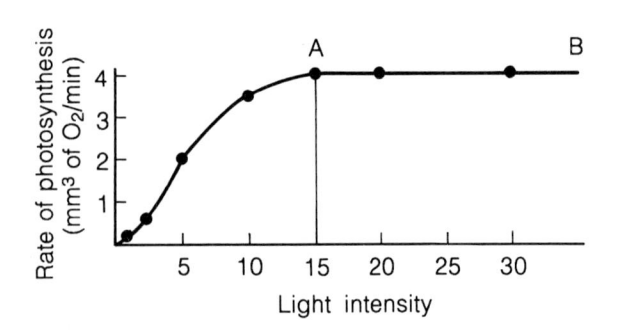

At point **A**, the rate of photosynthesis has reached a maximum. As the light intensity increases between **A** and **B**, the plant does not photosynthesise faster. This is because the reaction rate is being limited, either by the amount of CO_2 available, or by the temperature. In other words, the amount of CO_2 or the temperature is the **limiting factor**.

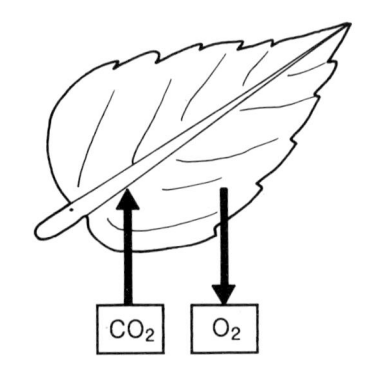

Photosynthesis

The glucose that is not needed as a source of energy for the plant can be used in other ways.

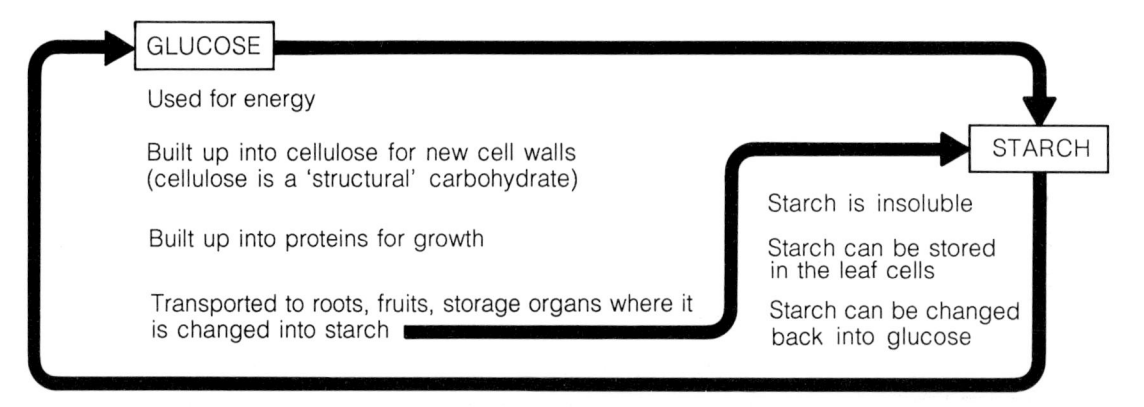

GLUCOSE

- Used for energy
- Built up into cellulose for new cell walls (cellulose is a 'structural' carbohydrate)
- Built up into proteins for growth
- Transported to roots, fruits, storage organs where it is changed into starch

STARCH

- Starch is insoluble
- Starch can be stored in the leaf cells
- Starch can be changed back into glucose

THE WORLD OF PLANTS 55

The Carbon Cycle

Both plants and animals produce carbon dioxide from the breakdown of food made originally in photosynthesis. Therefore the carbon dioxide from the air used by green plants eventually finds its way back into the air, possibly to be used again. This recycling of carbon in carbon dioxide is part of what is called the **Carbon Cycle**.

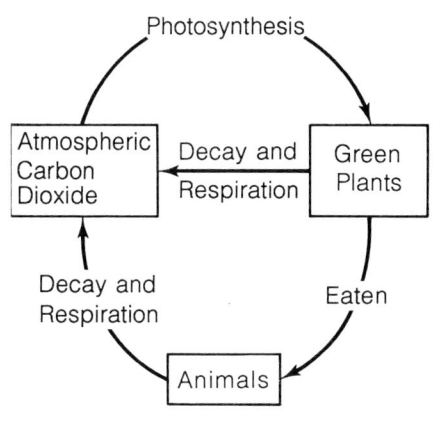

Part of the Carbon Cycle showing the cycling of carbon as carbon dioxide between plants, animals and the atmosphere

Respiration

Living cells are like chemical factories which need energy to maintain production. This energy can be obtained from the glucose made in photosynthesis.

Plants and animals need to release the energy in food to do work, such as in growing, moving, etc. Energy is released from food by a process called **respiration**. This needs oxygen to bring about the release of energy. Carbon dioxide is produced as a waste gas.

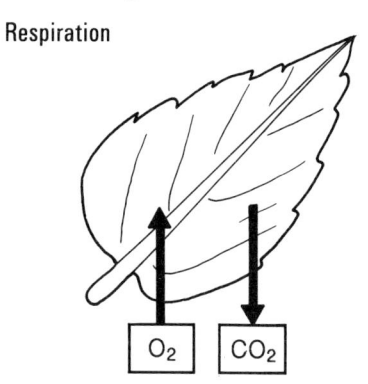

Respiration

Activities

○ 1 Copy and complete the following table to trace the source of each of the foods listed.

Food	Source
milk	
lamb	
chips	
steak	

○ 2 In the following food web, what would happen if all the green plants died?

Green Plants → Beetle → Fox
Green Plants → Rat → Stoat
Green Plants → Rabbit

○ 3 Which form of energy is available to plants in large amounts, and which form of energy do plants convert it into?

◐ 4 Describe how you might try to prove that a green plant cannot photosynthesise in the dark.

◐ 5 Make your own notes on how carbon dioxide is
(a) removed from, and
(b) added to the atmosphere.

● 6 The following data shows the effect which changing carbon dioxide concentration has on the rate of photosynthesis in pondweed. The rate is measured by counting the number of bubbles of oxygen gas produced.

CO_2 concentration (% dissolved in water)	0.1	0.2	0.3	0.4	0.5	1.0	1.5	1.8	2.0	4.0	5.0
mm^3 of O_2 gas/min (at constant light and temperature)	1.5	2.0	2.0	2.0	2.0	3.0	3.5	4.0	4.5	4.5	4.5

(a) Draw a line graph to show the relationship between CO_2 concentration and rate of photosynthesis.
(b) At what point does increasing the concentration of CO_2 no longer increase the rate of photosynthesis? Explain the reason for this effect.

● 7 (a) Using the data provided below, produce a line graph to show the relationship between temperature and rate of photosynthesis.

Temperature (°C)	5	10	15	17.5	20	21	22.5	25	30	40	50
mm^3 of O_2 gas/min (at constant light and CO_2 levels)	2	2.5	3.5	4	4.5	4.5	4	4	3	0	0

(b) What is the effect of temperature on the rate of photosynthesis?

10 Plant Leaves

Key Ideas

Plant leaves are specialised organs adapted for photosynthesise. To photosynthesise, they must trap light as an energy source. They also need to take in carbon dioxide from the air. This carbon dioxide is able to enter the leaf through tiny holes called *stomata*, found in the epidermis. Excess water vapour is also lost through the stomata.

A green plant needs to take in carbon dioxide and water to make glucose in photosynthesis. It also needs to be able to trap light energy. A plant leaf is specially adapted to take in carbon dioxide from the atmosphere, and to ensure that light is able to reach all points where photosynthesis is taking place.

Leaf Structure

In order to trap as much light energy as possible, the leaves of a plant are usually broad and flat to give a large surface area. The leaves are also very thin, so that at least some of the light hitting the top surface of a leaf gets through to reach the cells in the middle.

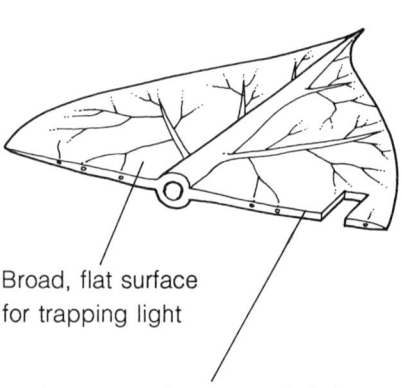

Broad, flat surface for trapping light

Leaf is thin so that as much light as possible reaches middle of leaf

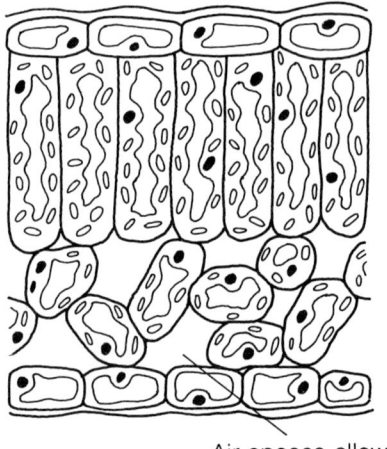

Air spaces allow gas exchange between cells

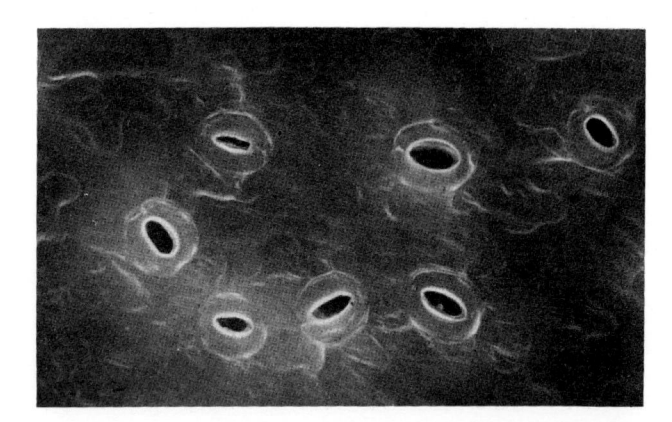

Closed stoma

Open stoma

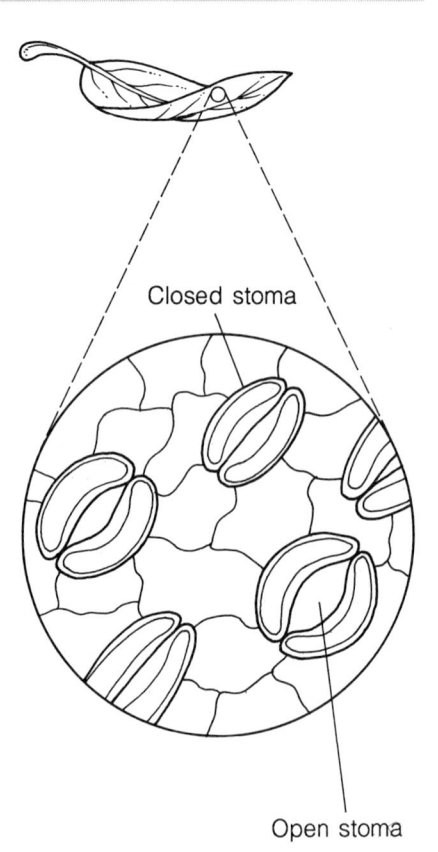

Gases need to be exchanged between leaf cells, and for this the leaf has many large air spaces between its cells. The leaf cells which photosynthesise need carbon dioxide which must enter the leaf during daylight. The gas passes through tiny holes in the undersurface of the leaf. These holes are called **stomata** (singular – **stoma**), and they can open and close.

Once the carbon dioxide has entered the leaf it can move through the air spaces to the cells where it is needed for photosynthesis.

Water, also needed for photosynthesis, is carried from the roots of the plant to the leaves. In the leaves it passes out of the veins and into the air spaces in the middle of the leaf. It can then be absorbed by the cells that need it.

Water not used by the plant is lost as water vapour from the leaf. It passes out of the leaf and into the atmosphere through the open stomata.

Stomata × 350

THE WORLD OF PLANTS

A plant leaf is made up of a series of layers.

Epidermis (upper) – single-cell layer which allows light to pass through and forms a protective covering. It does not usually have many stomata – often none. It has no chloroplasts

Cuticle – a waxy, non-cellular covering on the surfaces of leaves which prevents excess water loss. It is thicker on the upper surface

Palisade mesophyll – these cells are long and narrow and at right angles to the leaf's surface. Light can pass down through them easily. Each cell holds many chloroplasts, containing chlorophyll. This is the main site of photosynthesis in the leaf

Vein – composed of tubular cells which form the transport system of a plant, carrying water from the roots and food from the leaves

Spongy mesophyll – these cells have irregular shapes and are joined loosely with lots of air spaces between them to allow gas exchange between cells. They contain some chloroplasts

Epidermis (lower) – similar to upper epidermis, but usually with many stomata

Stoma – gases can pass in and out of leaf through this tiny hole (or pore). Water is lost through it by evaporation

Guard cells – pairs of cells which surround each stoma (one each side) and control the size of the opening

As water vapour is lost from the leaves of a plant it must be replaced. Water is taken in by the roots and transported up to the leaves. If a plant is losing too much water, the stomata may close to reduce the amount of evaporation.

The size of a stoma is controlled by the cells on each side of the pore. These cells are called the **guard cells**. They are the only cells on the lower epidermis of the leaf which have chloroplasts.

The loss of water from a leaf is called **transpiration**. We can measure the rate of transpiration by measuring the amount of water which the plant is taking in. This can be done using a potometer. (See the drawing in the Activities, page 58).

58 THE WORLD OF PLANTS

Activities

○ 1 For what purpose are there tiny holes (stomata) on the surface of a leaf?

○ 2 Draw a table listing the main parts of a leaf. Describe the function of each.

◐ 3 The underside of most plant leaves has more stomata than the upper surface. What do you think is the reason for this? (Hint: sunlight, heat, evaporation.)

◐ 4 Water plants have their stomata on the upper surface of their leaves. Explain why.

● 5 The equipment shown in the diagram is called a *potometer*. It can be used to measure the rate of transpiration of a plant. A series of experiments was carried out using a potometer. It was possible to vary the *temperature*, the *humidity* (amount of water vapour in the air) and the *wind speed*. In each experiment, two of these factors were kept constant and the third was varied. The results were written down as a list, shown below.

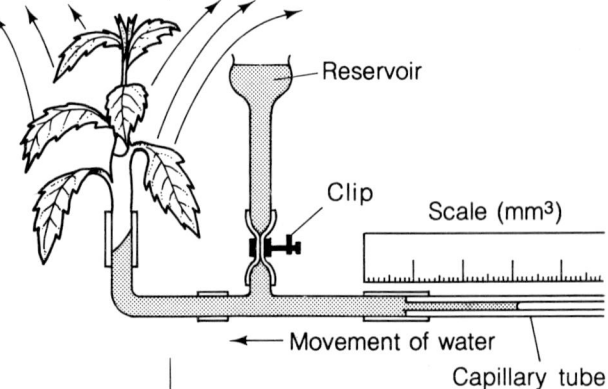

Temperature	high	med	med	med	low	med	med
Humidity	high	high	high	high	high	med	low
Wind speed	low	high	low	med	low	low	low
Rate (mm³/min)	3.3	5.1	1.1	4.3	0.5	6.4	2.5

(a) Draw up three tables of results to show how the rate of transpiration varied with (i) temperature, (ii) humidity and (iii) wind speed.
   The rate of transpiration is shown as mm³ water/minute.

(b) Describe the conditions which would produce the greatest water loss per minute in a plant.

● 6 A more detailed investigation was carried out into the effects of humidity on water loss. The results are given in the table below. Temperature and wind speed were kept constant.

Humidity (%)	0	10	20	30	40	50	60	70	80	90	100
Rate (mm³/min)	6.4	5.2	4.3	3.5	3.0	2.5	2.1	1.8	1.5	1.3	1.1

Draw a line graph to show the effect of increasing humidity on the rate of water loss from plant leaves by evaporation.

11 Plant Transport

Key Ideas

Plants need water for photosynthesis, which takes place mainly in the leaf cells. The water comes from the soil, and is transported to the leaves through *xylem vessels*.

Most food is made in the leaves, and parts of the plant without chlorophyll cannot make their own food. Food must therefore be transported to them from the leaves. This food is transported through *phloem tubes*.

Transport Systems

All green plants need water, mineral salts and carbon dioxide.

The water and carbon dioxide are needed to make glucose and other sugars. These sugars are made mainly in the plant's leaves. Therefore water, which is taken into the plant through the roots, must be transported to the leaves. Minerals, such as nitrates, which are needed to make proteins, are dissolved and transported in the water.

Water enters the plant from the soil through the root hairs. These are tiny outgrowths from cells on the outer surface of the root near its tip.

A mustard seedling, showing the root hairs clearly

From these cells the water has to cross the root, through many cells, to special tubes in the centre of the root, called **xylem vessels**.

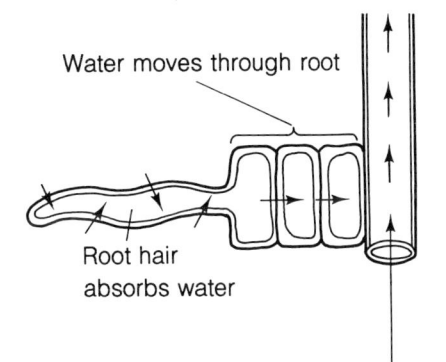

Once the water is in the xylem vessels it travels upwards from the roots to the stem and into the leaves.

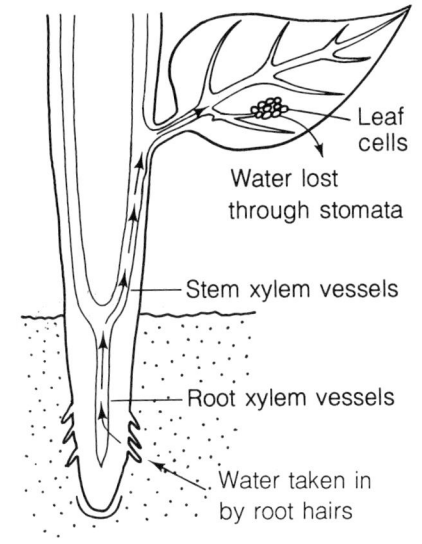

The **veins** that you can see in a plant leaf are the transport vessels – xylem and phloem.

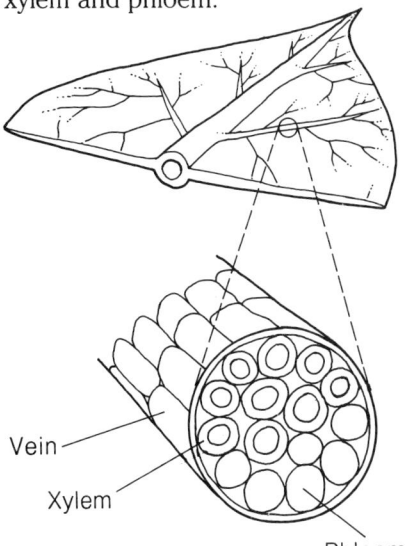

When the water reaches a leaf, it moves out of the xylem and enters the leaf cells, or it evaporates into air spaces between the cells.

In the leaf cells, some of the water will be used to make sugars. Many other cells in the plant, especially cells in the roots, cannot make their own sugars. All cells need sugars as a source of the plant's chemical energy, so it is necessary to transport sugars, dissolved in water, to these cells.

Sugars can pass, in solution, from the leaf cells into phloem tubes in the veins of the leaf. These phloem tubes carry the sugars to all other parts of the plant.

THE WORLD OF PLANTS

Structure of Xylem and Phloem

Xylem vessels are made up of dead cells which are long and narrow. These cells have lost their cytoplasm and nucleus and are joined end to end, making long tubes. Water can travel up the tubes easily because the end walls of the cells are broken down. The side walls of the xylem cells are strengthened by spiral or ring-shaped bands of **lignin**.

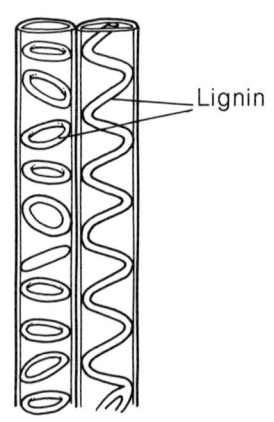

Phloem tubes are made up of cells which have no nucleus but some cytoplasm. The phloem cells each have a cell alongside, called a **companion cell**, which does have a nucleus. The phloem cells have holes in their end walls. Joined end to end, a row of cells forms a **sieve tube**.

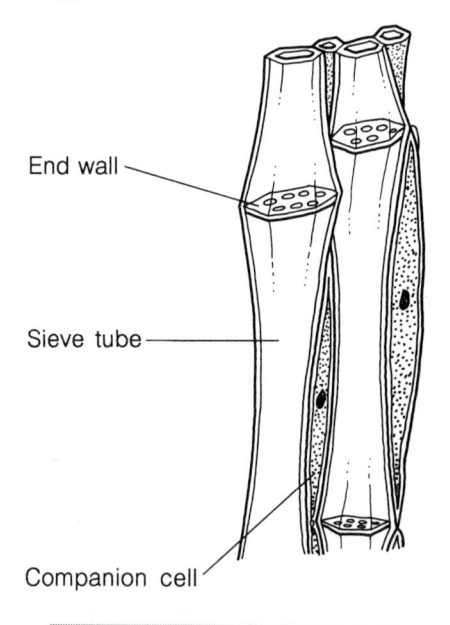

The xylem and phloem tubes are usually found next to each other. These clusters of tubes are often known as **vascular bundles**. The vascular bundles are found in the centre of the roots of a plant. They form a strong central core, and give the root strength and rigidity to push down through the soil.

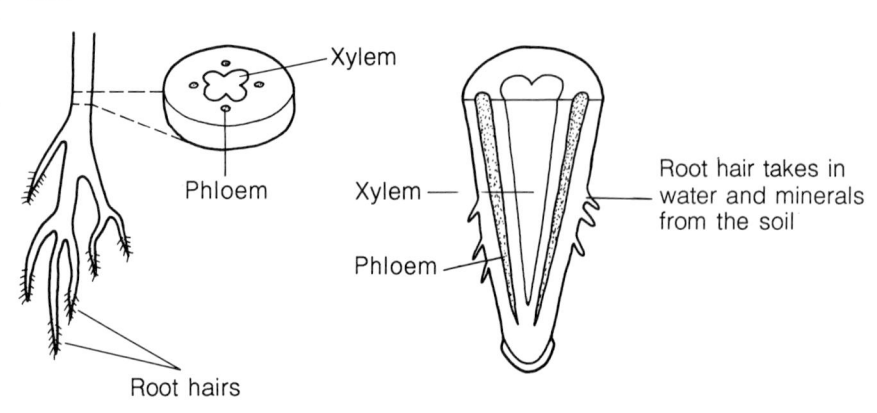

The transport system in a root. The phloem and xylem are grouped together in the middle of the root

In stems, the vascular bundles are found near the outside. The xylem vessels, with their woody skeleton of lignin, help to support the stem. They are arranged like a cylinder in the stem, and stop it from bending. Trees, being tall, need a lot of support. Their trunks are mainly xylem.

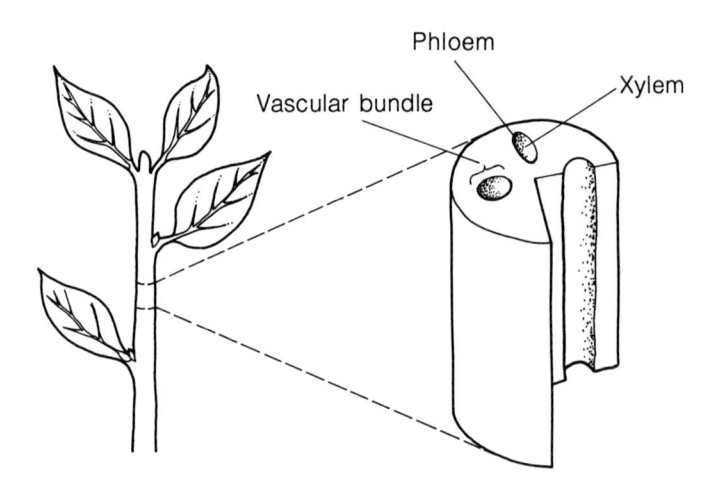

The transport system in a stem. The phloem and xylem are in a ring near the outside of the stem

Activities

1. Which part of a plant root takes in water and minerals from the soil? Where on the root is it found?

2. Describe, in your own words, how water reaches a leaf cell.

3. Explain the differences between the vascular bundles in a root and those in a stem, particularly their effect on support in a plant.

1 Food

Key Ideas

Animals need a food supply, to provide *energy* and raw materials for growth and repair. The major types of food are *carbohydrates, fats* and *proteins*. These food types are made from smaller, simpler substances containing three chemical *elements: carbon, hydrogen* and *oxygen*. Proteins also contain nitrogen and sometimes sulphur.

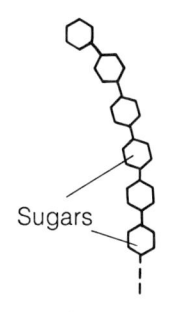

Food Types

As well as the three main food types – **carbohydrates**, **fats** and **proteins** – an animal's diet must also include **vitamins, minerals, water,** and also **fibre** which is sometimes called roughage.

Sugars

Starch

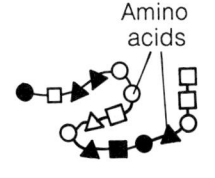

Amino acids

Protein

Food types	Their use to an animal
carbohydrates	as main energy source
fats	for storage of food, and for insulation
proteins	for growth and repair
vitamins	to help protect the body against disease
minerals	to maintain good health
water	to carry substances around the body; in all tissues
fibre	to give bulk to food, to help keep it moving through the gut

Structure of Food Types

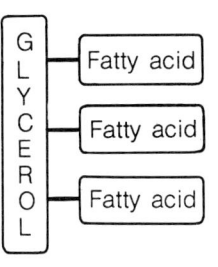

GLYCEROL — Fatty acid
— Fatty acid
— Fatty acid

Fat

There are two main groups of carbohydrates, called sugars and starches. The large starch molecules are made up of many sugar units joined together.

Fats, sometimes called **lipids**, are large molecules made up of smaller units called fatty acids and glycerol.

Proteins are large molecules built up from smaller amino acids. Most of our food is made up of the larger molecules of protein, carbohydrate and fat. The molecules of these substances are not small enough to pass into the blood to be taken to the cells of our bodies where they are needed. Therefore, when we eat food, we must break up these large molecules into their smaller parts. The sugars, fatty acids, glycerol and amino acids are able to enter the blood supply, because they are smaller.

For these foods to carry out their functions described in the table they must get into the cells of our body.

Animal Survival

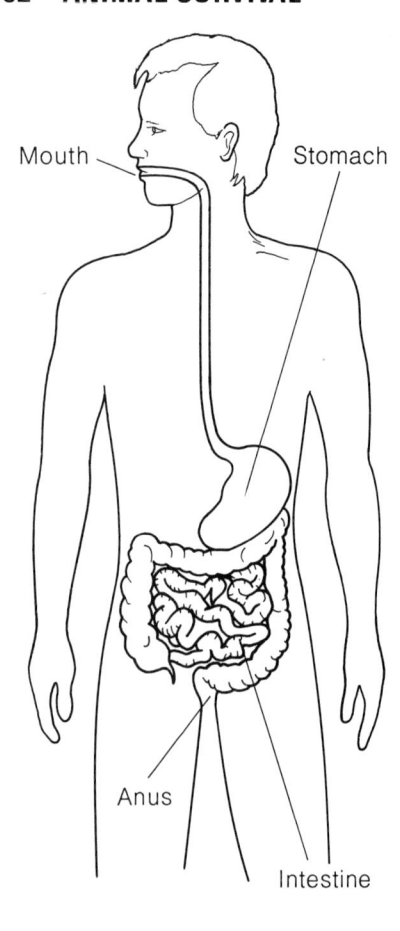

62 ANIMAL SURVIVAL

Digestive System

The digestive system is like a tube which begins at the **mouth** and ends at the **anus**.

Food enters at the mouth, is chewed and swallowed, then passes to the stomach. From the stomach it moves into the small intestine. The small intestine has a rich blood supply. Food substances have to enter the blood to be taken to the cells in the body where they are needed.

To understand how this happens, look at the diagram of a simple model of the intestine and read the experimental details.

The water in the dish represents the blood in vessels surrounding the intestine. At the start of the experiment the water does not contain *either* starch *or* glucose.

After 30 minutes the water is found to contain glucose but *not* starch. Glucose can pass through the Visking tubing but starch cannot. Starch is a large molecule. Glucose is a small molecule. Only small molecules can pass through the Visking tubing and through the intestine wall into the bloodstream.

Model of the Intestine

The experiment uses two carbohydrates, starch and glucose.

The Visking tubing is like the intestine. The carbohydrate food mixture is put into the Visking tubing and left for 30 minutes.

The water in the dish is tested at the start and at the end of the 30 minutes.

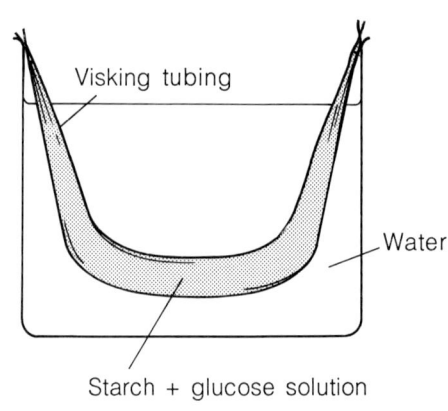

Digestion involves the breakdown of the large, insoluble molecules in our food – carbohydrates, fats and proteins. They are broken down into small, molecules – glucose, fatty acids and glycerol, and amino acids. The small molecules can then pass from the small intestine into the blood, like the glucose passing through the Visking tubing.

Activities

1. Why is a baby likely to need more protein than a healthy human adult?
2. What three chemical elements are found in carbohydrates, fats and proteins?
3. How are proteins chemically different from carbohydrates?
4. Why is roughage an important part of the human diet?
5. The diagram above shows the apparatus used in an experimental model of the small intestine.
   (a) Make your own drawing of the model and label it to show which parts represent: 1. the wall of the intestine, 2. the food, 3. the blood.
   (b) Name the substance which is able to pass through the Visking tubing into the water in the test tube.
6. Why is *undigested* food NOT able to pass through the wall of the intestine?

2 Feeding

Key Ideas

Food must be divided into small pieces before it can be swallowed. This mechanical breakdown is done by *teeth*.

There are three main types of teeth: *incisors, canines* and *molars*. Animals with differing diets have different shapes and numbers of each type of tooth.

Animals which eat plants and other animals (meat) are called *omnivores*.

Animals which eat other animals only are called *carnivores*.

Animals which eat mainly vegetation are called *herbivores*.

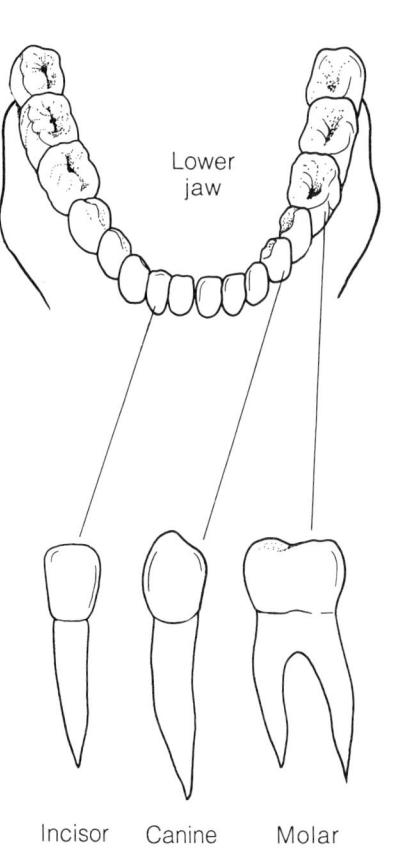

Teeth

Teeth grow from sockets in the **jawbone**. There are three main types of teeth, called incisors, canines and molars. The molars are sometimes divided into two groups called premolars and molars. The incisors are found at the front of the mouth. The rest are found at the sides. Incisors are used for biting. Canines are used by meat eaters for killing and tearing. Molars are used for grinding and chewing.

Omnivore Teeth

Omnivores eat plants and animals. They have chisel shaped incisors used for biting. The canine teeth are more pointed in shape. Their molar teeth are used for chewing and grinding.

Most humans are examples of omnivores.

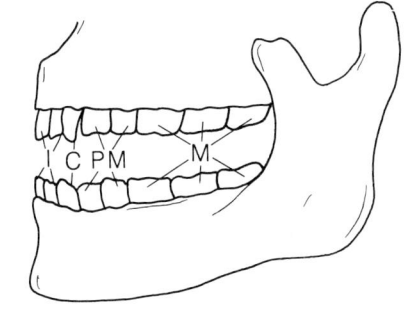

I   Incisors
C   Canines
PM Premolars
M   Molars

Human jaw

Herbivore Teeth

Herbivores eat plants. Herbivores have small canine teeth. Some herbivores, like sheep, have a horny pad replacing their upper canines and incisors. Their molars are ridged for chewing hard fibrous material. Most herbivores' teeth keep growing throughout life. This is because their molars are continually being worn down.

An example of a herbivore is a sheep.

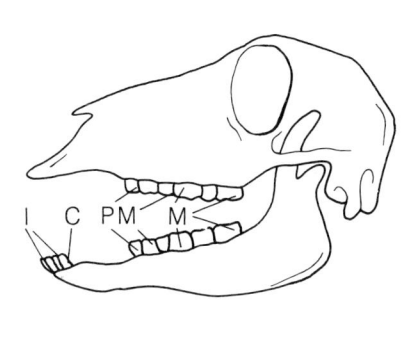

Skull of sheep

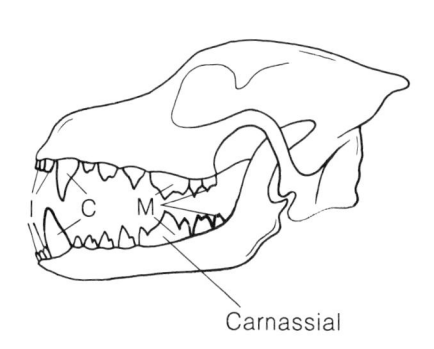

Carnivore Teeth

Carnivores eat meat (other animals). Their incisors are used for biting and bone scraping. Their canine teeth are long and pointed and are used for killing their prey and tearing meat off bones. They have special molar teeth called **carnassial** teeth which are used for slicing.

A dog is an example of a carnivore.

Skull of dog

64 ANIMAL SURVIVAL

Activities

○ 1 Draw a table to show the three main types of teeth and their uses.

○ 2 There are three main types of feeding with teeth. Animals may be omnivores, carnivores or herbivores. For each type, describe the type of diet and how the shape, number and arrangement of teeth in the jaw is different.

● 3 Tooth decay – A case study

When we eat food, **plaque** may form on the surface of our teeth. Plaque is a layer of bacteria feeding on the food. Action by the bacteria leaves an acid on the teeth which wears away the tooth enamel. This damage to our teeth is called **decay**. Tooth decay may be prevented by:

(a) the right diet – fewer sugary foods and more vitamin C and calcium in our diet.
(b) brushing our teeth regularly to remove the layer of plaque.
(c) **fluoride** in our drinking water or in toothpaste or in a mouthwash, to strengthen the enamel.
(d) regular checkups at the dentist, to spot decay before it becomes serious.

Fluoride is found naturally in the drinking water of some parts of Britain. The amount can vary. The table below shows the number of decayed teeth per child (average age 12 years) and the amount of fluoride in their drinking water. Fluoride is measured in parts per million: ppm.

No. of decayed teeth per child	8.0	8.0	6.5	4.0	3.5	3.0	2.8	2.6	2.5	2.5
Fluoride (ppm)	0.0	0.1	0.25	0.5	0.8	1.0	1.3	1.5	2.0	2.5

Q1 Draw a histogram to show the results given in the table.
Q2 What is the least amount of fluoride you think should be added to drinking water that will still have the best effect? Give a reason for your answer.

ANIMAL SURVIVAL 65

3 Digestion

Key Ideas

The food which we eat must be broken down into small, soluble molecules before it can get into the bloodstream. Once in the blood, the small molecules can be carried to the cells where they are needed.

As food passes through the *digestive system* it is mixed with digestive juices which contain chemicals called *enzymes*. These help to break down large molecules such as starch, protein and fats.

Food is moved through the digestive system by a muscular process called *peristalsis*.

The Mammalian Digestive System

Once food has been eaten it must be broken down – by **digestion**. Then it is moved into the bloodstream by **absorption**. These processes occur in the digestive system, also called the alimentary canal.

Digestion starts in the mouth. As food is chewed and broken up into pieces small enough to swallow, it is mixed with the liquid **saliva**, which contains an enzyme called salivary amylase. This begins the digestion of any starch in the food.

The saliva also contains a slimy substance called **mucin** which softens the food and makes it easier to swallow.

The **tongue** helps to mix the saliva and food together, and also forms it into lumps for swallowing.

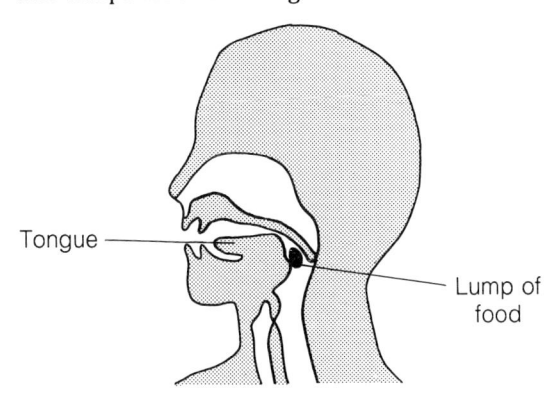

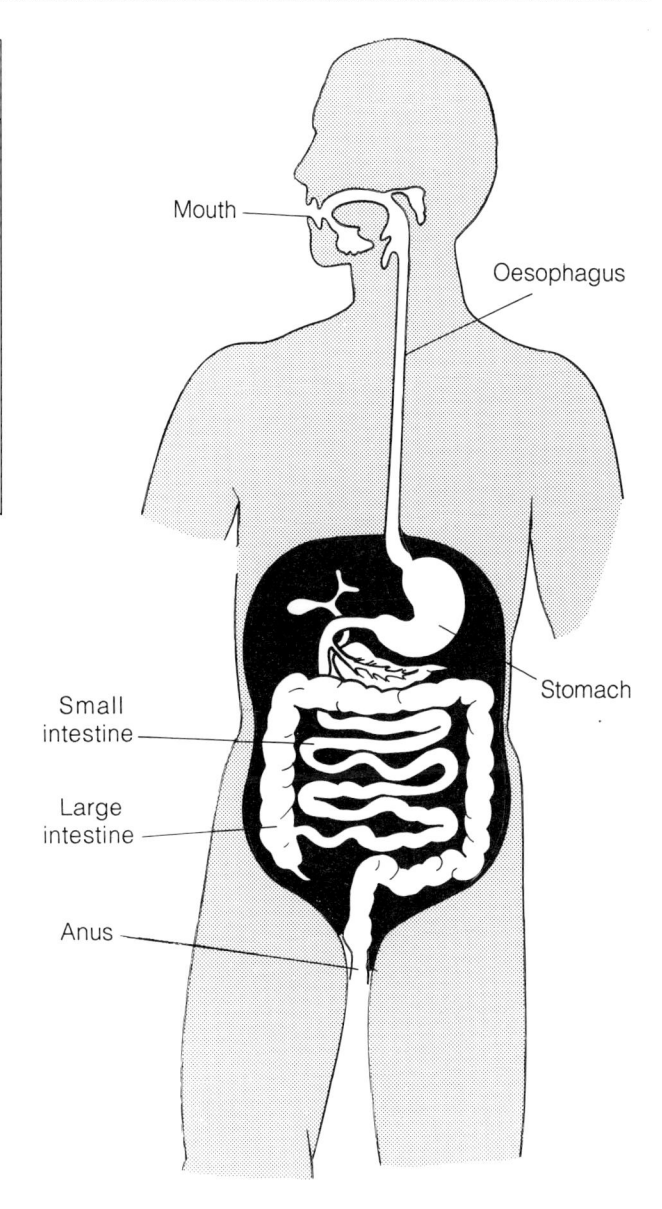

The digestive system

Food Intake, Digestion and Absorption

Small pieces of food are pushed to the back of the mouth by the tongue, and are then swallowed. They pass down a tube called the **oesophagus** to the **stomach**.

The food does not simply fall down the oesophagus, but is pushed down by muscles surrounding the tube. They contract just behind the food as it passes down, like squeezing toothpaste out of a tube. Try swallowing when you are upside down! This is possible and the food or drink will be pushed towards the stomach. This process is called **peristalsis**.

As you will know from experience, sometimes food goes "down the wrong way". Instead of passing down the oesophagus, the food passes into the **windpipe**, causing you to choke. Normally this does not happen because during swallowing a small flap of tissue, called the **epiglottis**, covers the entrance to the windpipe. This prevents food from going into the lungs.

From the oesophagus, the food enters the stomach. The stomach is a muscular bag which can stretch when filling up with food.

The food is churned up by the muscular walls of the stomach. It is also mixed with **gastric juices** which help in the digestion of some of the food. Food can stay in the stomach for 2 or 3 hours, until it is squirted out through the **pyloric sphincter**, which opens at regular intervals.

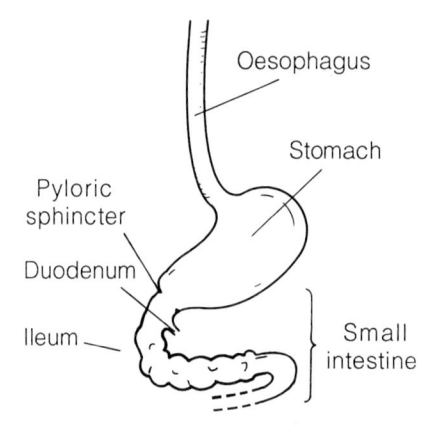

From the stomach, the food passes into the first section of the **small intestine** called the **duodenum**, which is a short tube. Once again, peristalsis is the process that moves the food through the tube.

In the duodenum more digestive juices, from the gall bladder and pancreas, are mixed with the food. It passes from the duodenum into the main section of the small intestine called the **ileum**.

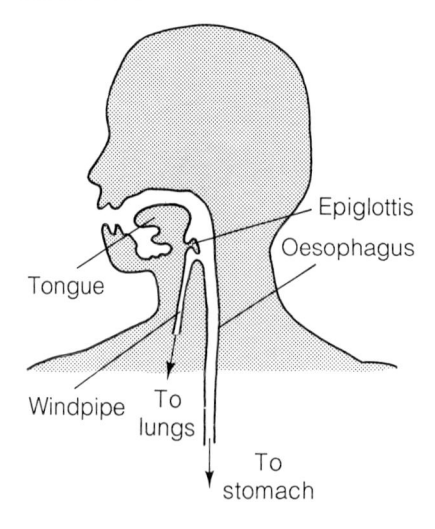

The ileum is a very long tube, up to six metres or more. The wall of the ileum has many folds and the inner lining is covered with tiny finger-like projections called **villi**.

Each villus has blood capillaries running through it. It is here that the small molecules produced by digestion are absorbed.

At the end of the small intestine the undigested materials from the food, together with water, pass into the **large intestine**. This is made up of four sections, the **colon, rectum, caecum** and **appendix**. The caecum and appendix have no function in humans.

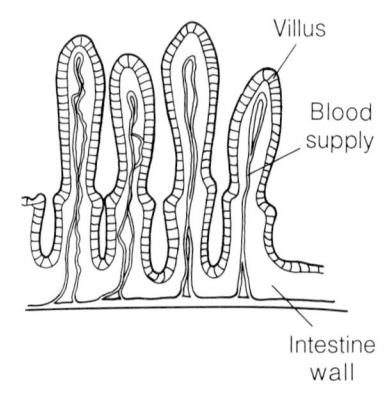

The material which enters the colon is made up mainly of fibre, dead bacteria and dead cells, mixed with water. Most of the water is absorbed by the lining of the colon. The dry remains called **faeces** are stored in the rectum and eventually forced out through the **anus** by muscular contractions similar to peristalsis.

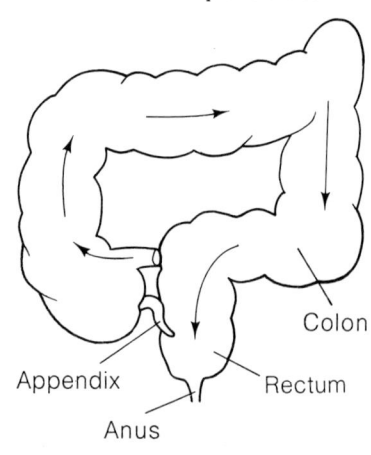

Peristalsis

The oesophagus has two layers of muscle fibres surrounding it. There are circular muscles around the lining of the oesophagus, and longitudinal muscles running down its length outside the layer of circular muscles.

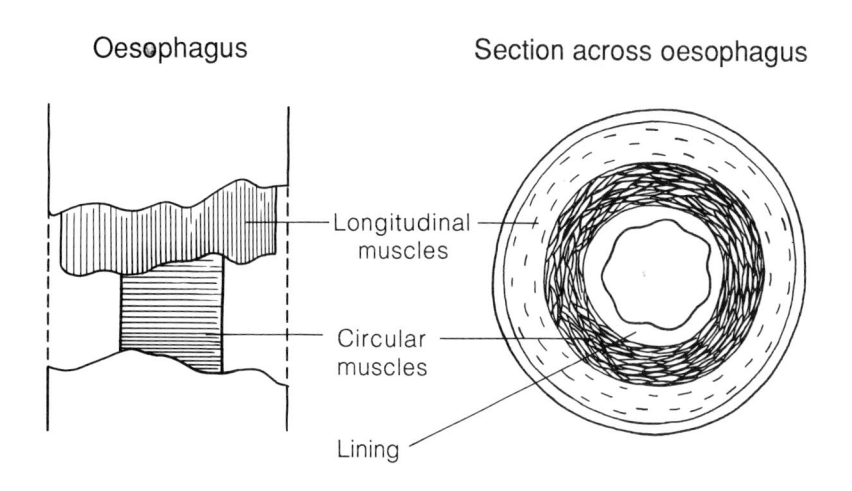

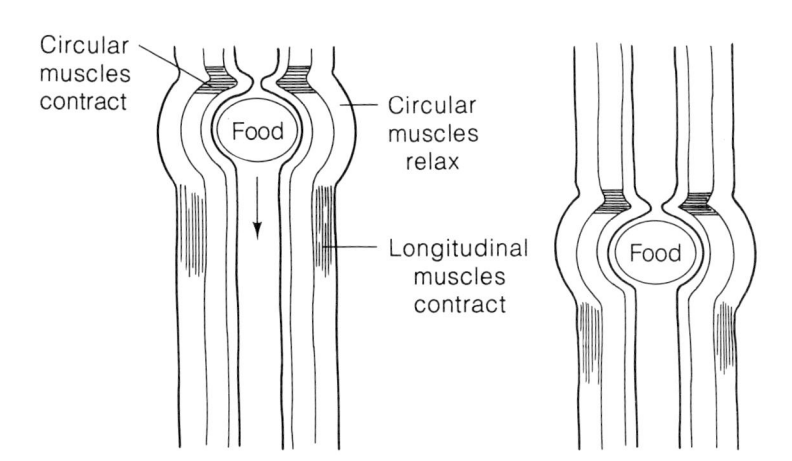

As food is swallowed the circular muscles above the food contract, pushing the food towards the stomach. Meanwhile, below the food the longitudinal muscles contract and the circular muscles relax, allowing the food to pass further down the oesophagus. "Waves" of muscular contractions like this force food right through the whole length of the digestive system.

Activities

- 1 Describe what happens to food in your mouth.
- 2 Describe how it is possible for food to get to your stomach even if you are upside down.
- 3 Describe *how* food is *moved* through the digestive system.
- 4 What chemicals are required for the breakdown of food?
- 5 Copy and complete the following table to summarise the passage of food through the digestive system.

Part of system	What happens here
mouth	

4 Digestive Enzymes

Key Ideas

Large food molecules are broken down into smaller ones by chemicals called *enzymes*.

There are three main types of digestive enzymes. *Amylases* break down carbohydrates into sugars. *Proteases* break down proteins into amino acids. *Lipases* break down fats into fatty acids and glycerol. These enzymes are found in digestive juices produced by glands in the body.

Enzyme Action

Enzymes are very **specific** in their action on the different foods.

Amylases will only break down carbohydrates into sugars. Proteases will only break down proteins, first into peptides, then into amino acids. Lipases will only break down fats into fatty acids and glycerol.

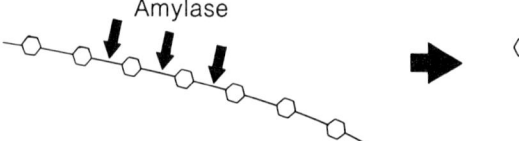

Starch: a carbohydrate

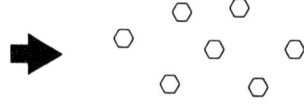

Sugars

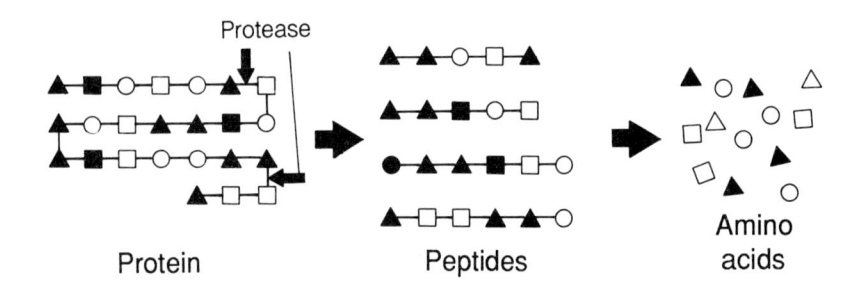

Protein → Peptides → Amino acids

Pepsin is a "protease" enzyme, which means it "breaks down protein". In addition to lipase (shown in the table), the pancreas produces a protease enzyme and an amylase enzyme.

Fat → Glycerol + Fa + Fa + Fa

There are many different types of enzyme involved in digestion. We shall concentrate on three: one amylase, one protease and one lipase. The table below shows one of each of these three types of enzyme, the digestive juices in which they are found, and what each does.

Name of enzyme	Digestive juice	Food acted on	Product
salivary amylase	saliva	starch	maltose sugar
pepsin	gastric juice	protein	peptides
lipase	pancreatic juice	fats	fatty acids and glycerol

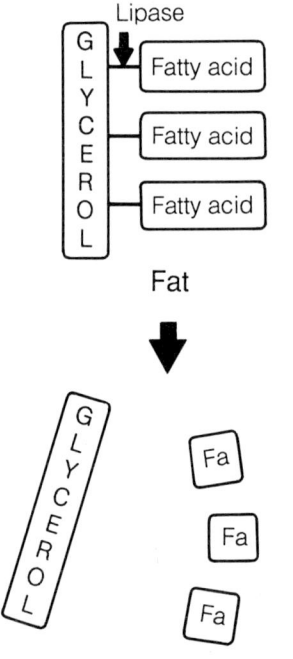

ANIMAL SURVIVAL 69

Each of these enzymes is produced from different glands, in or leading into, the digestive system. The diagram shows the position of these glands in the digestive system.

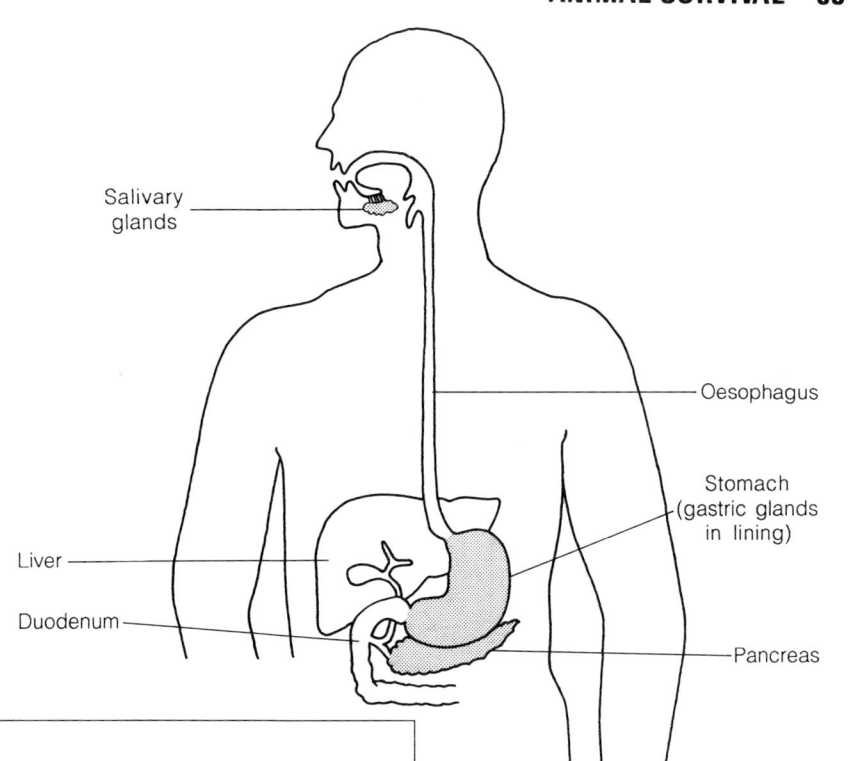

Labels on diagram: Salivary glands, Oesophagus, Liver, Duodenum, Stomach (gastric glands in lining), Pancreas

Activities

○ 1 Rearrange the word lists below to match the correct enzymes with the foods which they break down and their products.

amylase	protein	fatty acids and glycerol
protease	fats	sugars
lipase	starch	amino acids

◑ 2 Copy and complete the table below, showing which enzymes are found in which digestive juices.

Digestive juice	Amylase	Protease	Lipase
saliva			
gastric			
pancreatic			

● 3 Copy and complete the table below which outlines the digestion of a roast beef sandwich.

Food	Part of digestive system where most digestion occurs	Enzyme involved	Final product of digestion
bread		amylase	
butter	duodenum		
beef			amino acids

5 Absorption

Key Ideas

For food or water to be of any use to us it must reach the parts of the body where it is needed. Simple substances from food leave the digestive system and enter the blood by *absorption*. Glucose, amino acids, fatty acids and glycerol are absorbed in the ileum. Water is absorbed in the colon.

The intestine is long, and villi provide a *large, inner surface area*. The thin walls of the villi and their rich blood supply help to increase the efficiency of absorption.

The Small Intestine

It is in the small intestine that the molecules from food are *absorbed* into the body. The smaller molecules of glucose, amino acids, fatty acids and glycerol pass out from the small intestine and are transported to cells in the body where they will be used or stored. The model gut in Chapter 1 showed that only small molecules could pass out from the intestine.

Enormous numbers of molecules have to be absorbed as food is carried along the length of the small intestine. To absorb as much as possible, the small intestine needs to be a long tube – about 6 metres – and needs to have a *large surface area*.

To understand this, try to picture a wide corridor, 25 metres long, packed with hundreds of people running down it. The smaller people are trying to escape from the corridor before they are swept towards its end.

There are small escape doors along the corridor. Increasing the number of doors would allow more people to escape. However there is a limit to the number of doors which can be fitted into flat walls.

Having a corridor with "wavy" walls increases the area of the walls, allowing for more doors. The corridor is still 25 metres long, but more small people will be able to escape. It will also tend to slow down their movement, making it easier to escape.

ANIMAL SURVIVAL

The inner lining of the small intestine is "wavy", like the second corridor. Its surface is covered with many tiny finger-like projections called villi, each about 0.5 mm high.

The surface of each villus is very thin, making it easier for small molecules to pass through. The villi also have a rich blood supply. The blood carries the digested food substances to where they are needed.

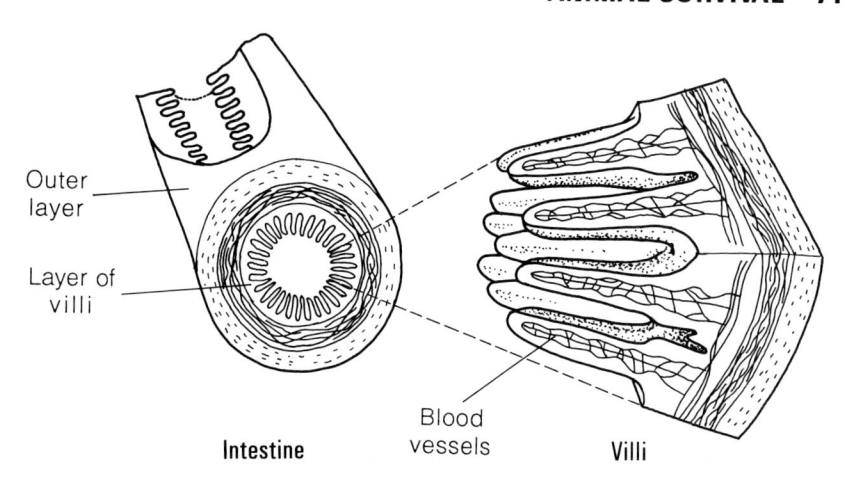

Glucose and amino acids are carried away from the small intestine by the blood. They are transported to the liver by the **hepatic portal vein**. In the liver, excess glucose is converted to insoluble **glycogen** which is stored until it is needed.

Amino acids are used to make new proteins for growth and repair in the body. In the liver, amino acids which are not needed are changed into glycogen (stored) and **urea**, by a process called **deamination**. The urea is later excreted by the kidneys.

Vitamins and minerals are absorbed into the blood in the small intestine.

Fatty acids and glycerol are absorbed into vessels called **lacteals** in the villi. The lacteals form part of the **lymphatic system**. From the lymphatic system, fatty acids and glycerol are passed to the blood system. They may be converted back into fat to be stored under the skin, or they may be broken down and used as a source of energy within cells.

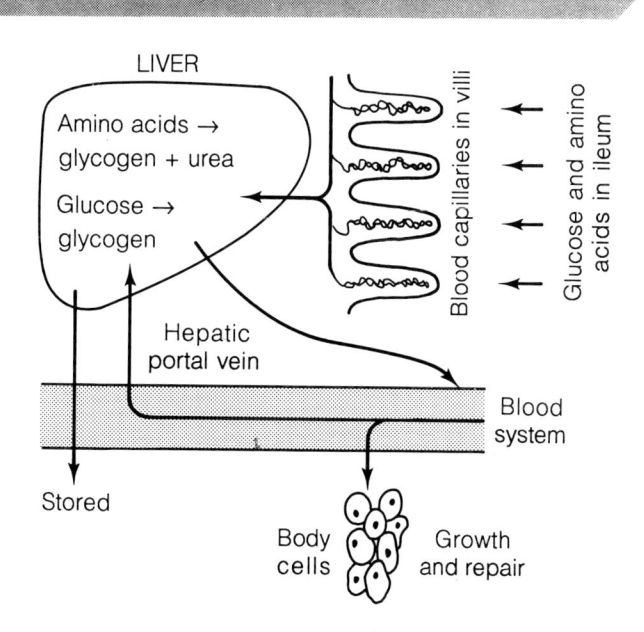

Activities

1. Describe what is meant by absorption.
2. What has to happen to food before it can be absorbed?
3. Describe *three* features of the small intestine which make it well designed to carry out absorption.
- 4. State the difference between the absorption of glucose and fatty acids.
- 5. Copy and complete the following table to show the different fates of each of the four products of digestion.

Product	Absorbed into	Use in body

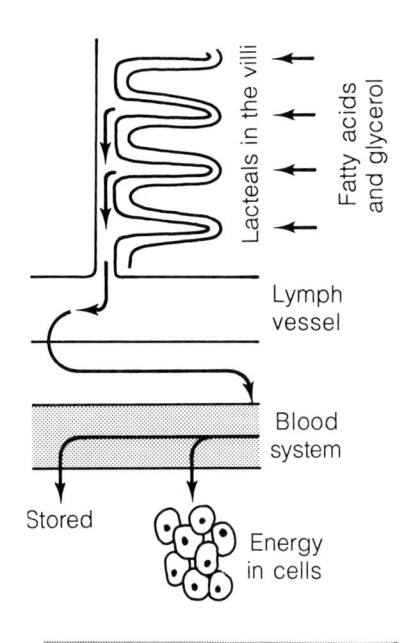

6 Sexual Reproduction

Key Ideas

Most animals produce young by *sexual reproduction*. This requires a *male sex cell (sperm)* to join with a *female sex cell (egg)*. The joining process is called *fertilisation*.

Sperms are attracted to eggs by chemicals and swim towards them. When a sperm meets an egg, the *nuclei* of the two cells join to form a *zygote*. In fish this happens outside the body. In mammals it happens inside the female's body.

Fertilisation

An animal does not live forever. New animals must be produced to take the place of those which die. In animals this usually involves sexual reproduction. Specialised sex cells called **gametes** are produced:
1. Male gametes called **sperms** which are small and able to move.
2. Female gametes called **eggs** which are large and do not normally move by themselves.

Fertilisation occurs when male and female gametes meet and their *nuclei join* together to form a single *fertilised egg cell* called a **zygote**.

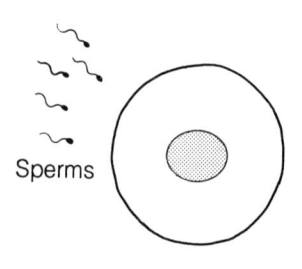

Sperms

Human egg (× 500)

Nuclei join together

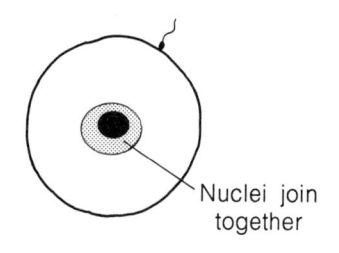

Zygote

Fertilisation must always take place in watery conditions to prevent the gametes from drying out and so that the sperm can swim to the egg. In mammals, this happens inside the female's body, and fertilisation is said to be *internal*.

If the watery liquid is outside the bodies of the parents, then fertilisation is said to be *external*. External fertilisation occurs in many organisms. We shall look at one example, the trout.

Trout

A female brown trout prepares a simple nest in the bed of a river by making a trench in the gravel with her tail. She then lays about 3000 eggs in the trench and waits for the male to swim over the eggs and release millions of sperms onto the eggs. Attracted by chemicals from the eggs, the sperms swim towards them.

Many of the eggs are fertilised. The female trout then sweeps gravel roughly over the eggs to cover them until they hatch.

Trout egg   Human egg

Relative size

Internal Fertilisation

Internal fertilisation occurs in insects, reptiles, birds and mammals. This is necessary to prevent the eggs and sperms from being exposed to the dryness of the land. Also, animals which live on the land must produce a liquid to carry the sperms to the eggs.

The sperms of these animals are released with fluid, in which they can swim to the eggs. The sperms are chemically attracted to the eggs and swim towards them. When one sperm meets an egg, its nucleus enters the egg and joins with the nucleus of the female egg cell.

ANIMAL SURVIVAL

Internal fertilisation has some other advantages over external fertilisation:

1. Eggs and sperms are not washed away by water currents before fertilisation occurs.

2. Because sperms are placed inside the female's body, their chance of meeting eggs is increased.

3. While they are inside the female's body, the fertilised eggs are protected as they develop.

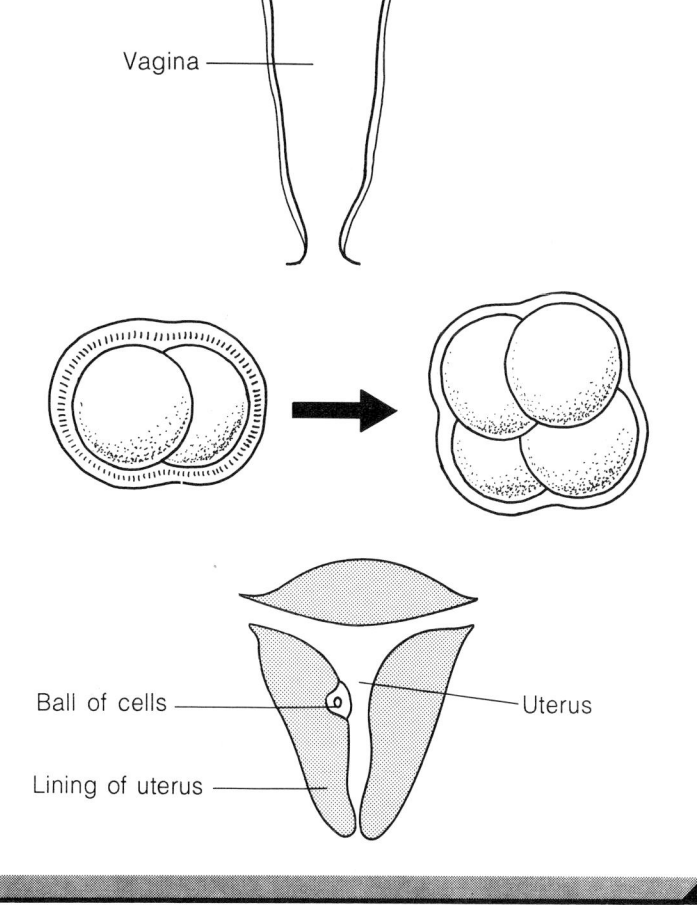

Egg (just released from ovary), Oviduct, Ovary, Uterus, Sperm moving through uterus and oviducts, Vagina, Ball of cells, Lining of uterus, Uterus

Activities

1. State the difference between external and internal fertilisation.
2. Describe the features which are common to both types of fertilisation.
3. Describe the advantages of internal fertilisation when compared with external fertilisation.

7 Reproductive Organs

> ### Key Ideas
>
> Eggs are made in the *ovaries* of female animals. Sperms are made in the *testes* of male animals.
>
> A female mammal releases eggs from the ovaries. The eggs pass along the *oviducts* to the *uterus*. In a male mammal, sperms pass from the testes through a *sperm duct* to the *penis*.

Human Reproductive Organs

As human children grow up, they each an age when chemical and physical changes take place in their bodies. This period of change is called **puberty**.

The time when puberty starts varies from person to person, but it is usually between the ages of 10 and 18. The chemicals produced in the body which bring about the changes are called **hormones**.

Females

When a girl is born she has thousands of undeveloped eggs in each ovary. As she approaches puberty the breasts start to develop, and the hips widen. Some of the eggs in the ovaries start to develop and eventually, at puberty, the first egg is released from an ovary. This process is called **ovulation**.

Ovulation is repeated about every 4 weeks, unless an egg is fertilised. After the egg is released it passes along the oviduct towards the **uterus**.

The egg takes about two to three days to move along the oviduct. During that time, the lining of the uterus becomes thicker. It also develops a greater blood supply, ready to accept a fertilised egg.

If the egg is not fertilised, the uterus lining and some blood are lost through the vagina. This "**period**" or **menstruation** usually lasts a few days.

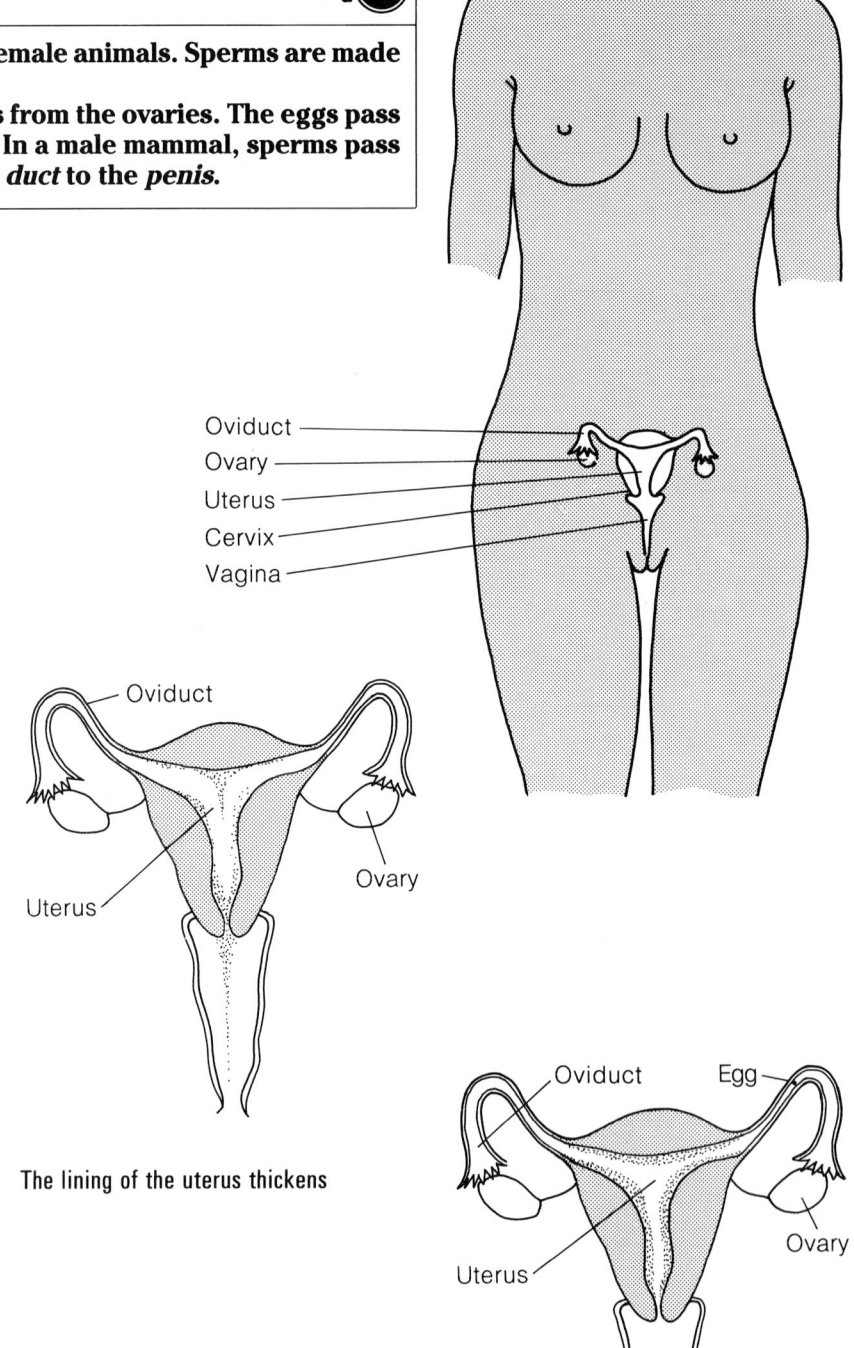

The lining of the uterus thickens

The lining is shed

ANIMAL SURVIVAL 75

Males

As boys grow older their bodies change. Boys are born with a **penis** and two **testes**. The testes are oval shaped and hang under the penis in a bag called the **scrotum**.

When a boy reaches the age of puberty his testes start to produce sperms. Also at this time, hair begins to grow on his body, and his vocal chords get longer, making him speak with a deeper voice.

As well as carrying urine out of the body, the penis is now able to carry sperms out of the body. Sperms travel from the testes through the sperm ducts to the penis. In the ducts the sperms mix with liquid called **semen**. Semen can be ejected from the penis if the penis becomes erect in sexual arousal.

An extra flow of blood from the body into the penis causes it to expand and become stiff. If, at this time, the penis is placed inside the female vagina, then the sperms may be able to swim through the uterus and into the oviducts to fertilise an egg.

Fertilisation in Humans

Fertilisation takes place in the oviducts. Sperms deposited in the vagina swim through the uterus and up into the oviducts where they meet an egg (or eggs).

After one sperm has fertilised one egg, the fertilised egg, which is called a zygote, passes down the oviduct towards the uterus. At this stage the zygote starts to divide into identical cells. One cell becomes two, then two become four, and so on.

This small group of dividing cells becomes a ball. It reaches the uterus and buries itself into the thickened lining.

Early Development in Trout

After the eggs are fertilised, they take in water and swell up. They then divide by mitosis. As in mammals, one cell becomes two, then two become four, and so on.

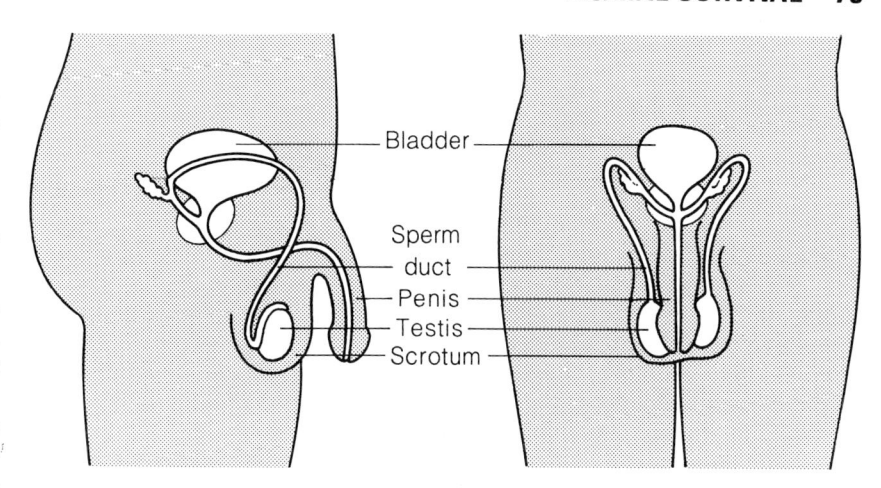

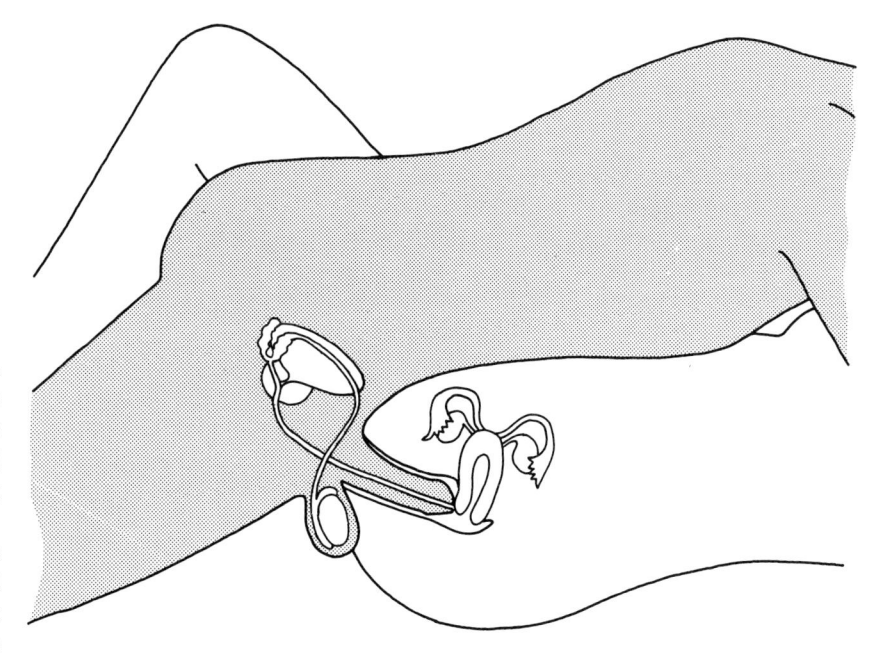

Labels: Bladder, Sperm duct, Penis, Testis, Scrotum

Activities

○ 1 State two physical changes which happen to girls at puberty.
○ 2 State two physical changes which happen to boys at puberty.
○ 3 Where are sperms made in humans?
　　Where are eggs made in humans?
○ 4 Describe the sequence of events which results in a sperm fertilising an egg.
● 5 Describe what happens to a human zygote after fertilisation.

8 Development

Key Ideas 🔑

Animals whose eggs are fertilised externally, like trout, lay their eggs in water. The fertilised eggs have little protection and the developing young get their food from the egg *yolk*.

In mammals the egg is fertilised in the oviduct and starts to develop as it passes to the uterus. It then becomes attached to the lining of the uterus where the *embryo's* blood supply can gain food from the mother's blood. It is protected by the *amniotic sac* containing fluid and by the mother's body surrounding it.

Young mammals continue to be protected by their parents after *birth*.

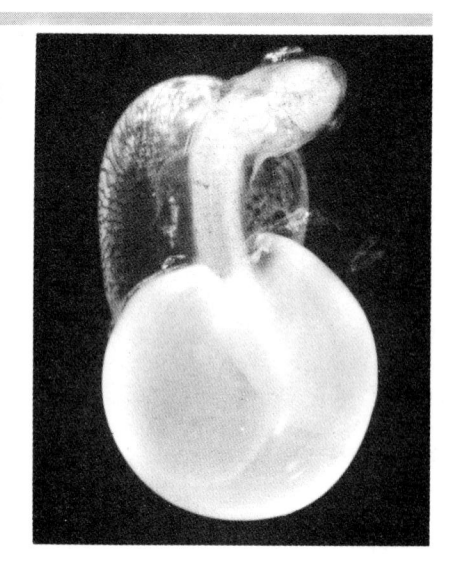

Developing Eggs of Fish

Female brown trout lay their eggs in late autumn. Male trout release their sperms at the same time. The female covers the fertilised eggs with gravel.

A fish egg is protected to some extent by a flexible surrounding membrane. The trout embryo obtains food for its growth and development from yolk within the egg.

In the spring the eggs hatch out as baby trout called **alevins**. They feed at first from an orange coloured yolk sac. Blood vessels run over the surface of the yolk, absorbing food from it. When the yolk is fully absorbed the trout begins to feed on moving food, such as insect larvae.

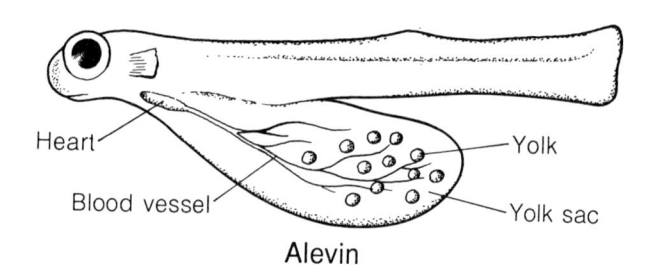

Alevin

Developing Eggs in Mammals

Fertilisation occurs in the oviduct. The egg divides by mitosis to form a ball of cells. After travelling down the oviduct the ball of cells buries itself in the thick lining of the uterus.

The lining of the uterus has a rich blood supply which prepares it to accept the ball of cells. Further development can now take place. The cells of the uterus lining start to grow around the ball of cells, which is now called an **embryo**.

Human embryo 6 weeks old

ANIMAL SURVIVAL 77

Connections form between the embryo and the uterus to provide the embryo with **food** and **oxygen** from the mother's blood supply. These connections gradually develop to form the **placenta**. As the embryo grows it is protected by the mother's uterus and by being inside a fluid filled bag called the **amniotic sac**.

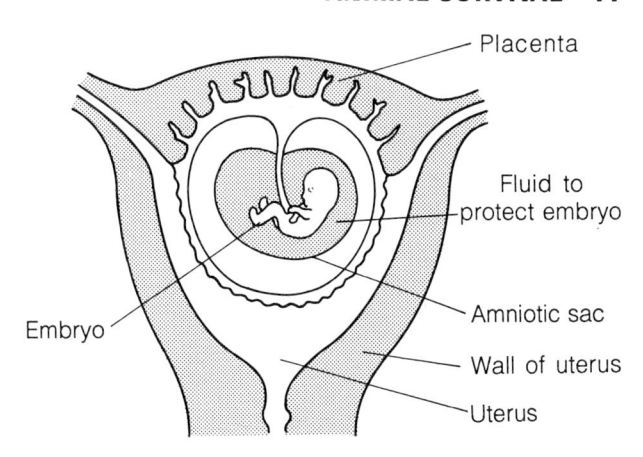

The Placenta

The placenta is where blood vessels from the mother are close to blood vessels from the embryo. The embryo receives food and oxygen from the mother's blood while the mother's blood can accept, and carry away, carbon dioxide and other waste products from the embryo's blood.

After the second month of the pregnancy, the embryo will have grown to about the size of a peanut and is now called a **foetus**.

When the foetus has developed sufficiently to survive outside the mother, it is ready to be born as a baby. This happens about 40 weeks after fertilisation.

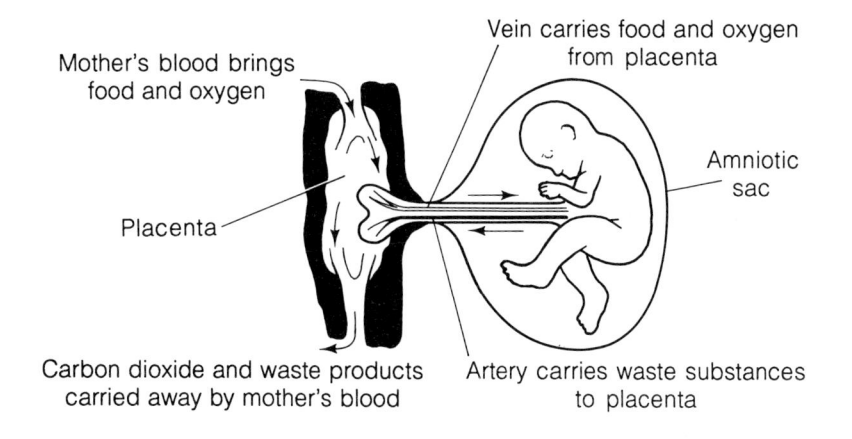

Activities

○ 1 Describe and compare the protection given to the eggs of a trout and a human.

○ 2 Describe and compare how baby trout and human embryos get their food.

◐ 3 Name three substances which can pass through the placenta.

9 Development and Care

Key Ideas

Some animals are able to survive on their own immediately after birth. Trout do not get help from their parents in the first weeks of life. They are less likely to survive than the young of mammals, such as humans, which are protected and fed by their parents for some time after they are born.

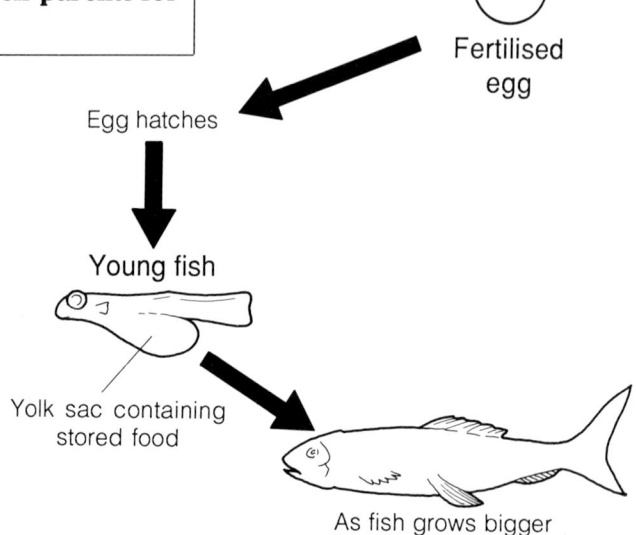

Trout

The young fish hatches out of its egg and is able to survive without help from its parents. The parents are likely to be many miles away when it hatches. At first the young fish feeds from a yolk sac attached to its underside. As it grows and the yolk is used up, the young trout also feeds on small animals in the water.

Survival of an animal species depends on enough young living to an age when they are able to reproduce.

A female trout has to lay thousands of eggs because:
1. some eggs will not be fertilised,
2. some eggs will be eaten,
3. some young fish will be eaten before they become adults and reproduce.

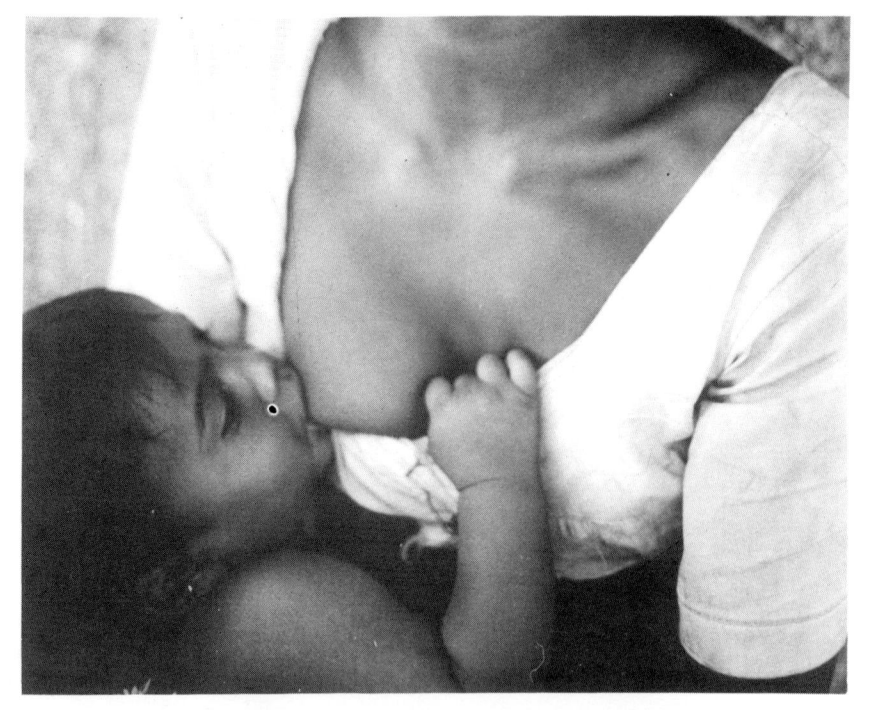

Fertilised egg

Egg hatches

Young fish

Yolk sac containing stored food

As fish grows bigger it feeds on small animals in the water

Humans

When a human baby is born, it is totally dependent on its parents for food and protection. If it were to be abandoned for more than a short while it would die.

Soon after birth a human baby is usually fed with milk from the mother's breasts. Milk not only provides it with food, but substances in the mother's milk help to protect the baby from infection.

Human parents continue to look after their young for many years after birth. They feed and protect them and also teach them the skills needed for survival to adulthood.

Hygiene and medical care have improved so much in the last hundred years that many more humans survive than are necessary to replace the people who die. The consequence is that the world human population is growing at a tremendous rate.

Successful development

There is usually a relationship between the number of eggs produced by an animal and the method of fertilisation. This is coupled with the amount of parental care given to the young.

Animals which fertilise their eggs outside the body produce more eggs than those in which fertilisation is internal.

Animals which have little parental care also produce more eggs than animals which care for their young.

This is summarised in the diagram.

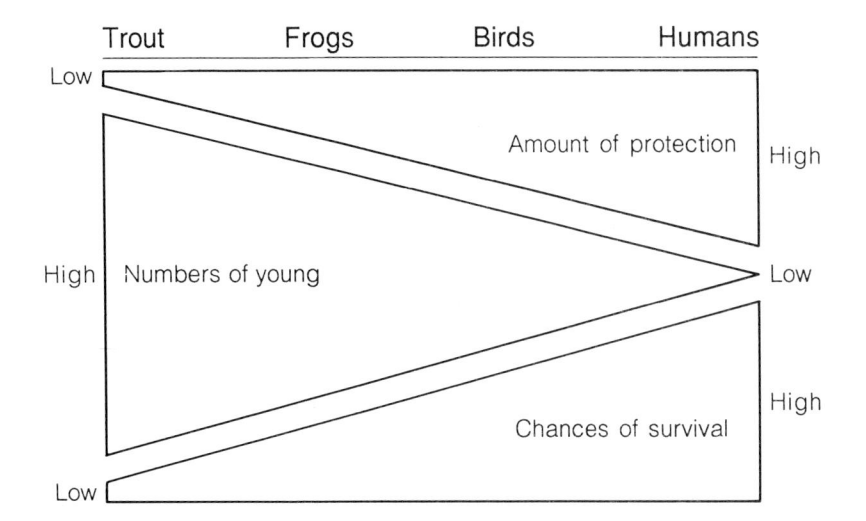

Activities

1. State three reasons why a trout must lay thousands of eggs.
2. State the needs of a human baby when it is born. Describe how these needs are met.
3. This chapter contains descriptions of three factors which contribute to the successful development of young animals. Describe each one and explain how each increases the chances of survival.

10 Water Balance

Key Ideas

All living things contain a high percentage of water. Most foods come from living things which contain a large amount of water. Animals must be able to maintain the correct amount of water in their bodies by balancing water lost with water gained. Water is taken in by *eating* and *drinking*. Water can be lost in *urine* and *faeces* and by *sweating* and *breathing out*. In mammals the *kidneys* are the main organs for controlling the amount of water in the body.

The Importance of Water

Water is essential in living things for the following purposes:
1. **Synthesis** – water is used as a raw material for many chemical reactions, such as photosynthesis in green plants.
2. **Reproduction** – sperms need a liquid in which to swim towards eggs.
3. **Transport** – water can carry materials around the body. Blood is mainly water.
4. **Cooling** – sweat cools an animal: heat energy is needed to evaporate water from the surface of an animal.
5. **Dissolving** – water is a good solvent. Chemicals can move about in solution and take part in the many chemical reactions necessary for life.
6. **Lubrication** – mixing food with saliva (mainly water) makes it easier to swallow.
7. **Support** – water gives support to the bodies of some animals, such as earthworms.

Some animals do not need to drink liquids at all. Gerbils, often kept as pets, normally live in dry climates and get all the water they need from their food. The food itself contains water and additional water is gained from respiration. This is balanced by the water lost in urine and faeces.

Gerbil feeding in the wild

How Animals Gain Water

The human body gains water in three main ways:
1. We **eat** foods containing water.
2. We **drink** liquids.
3. Respiration – the chemical breakdown of food to release energy – produces water as a waste product.

How do Animals Lose Water?

1. In liquid waste: **urine**.
2. In solid waste: **faeces**.
3. Cooling down: **sweat**.
4. Breathing out.

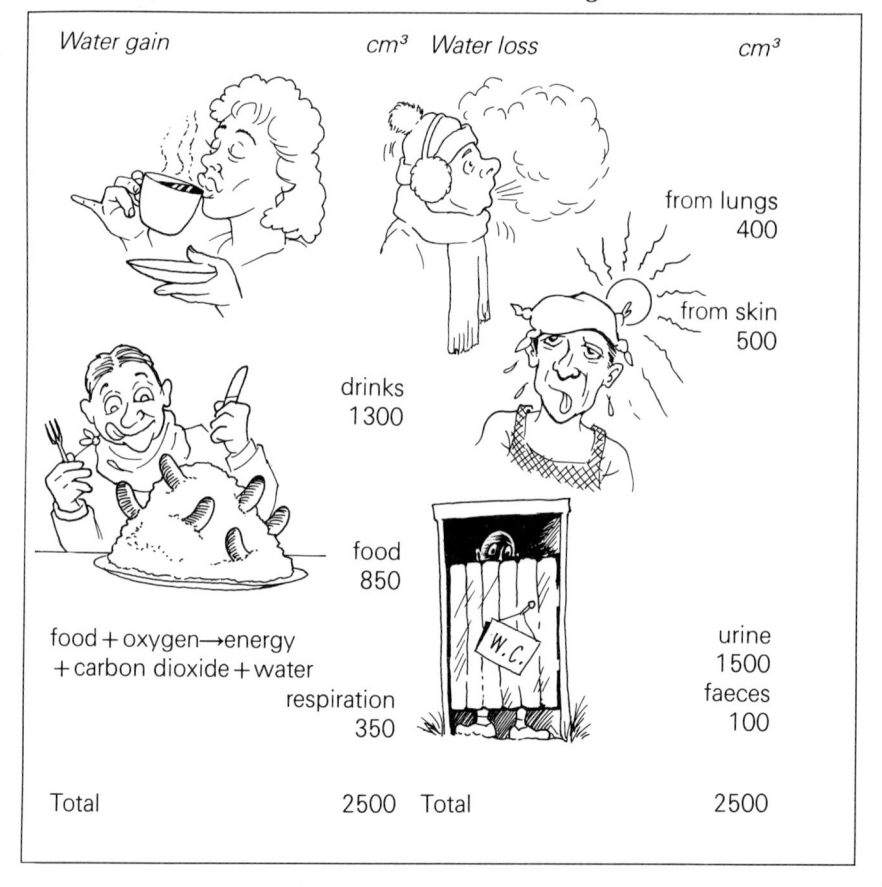

Water gain	cm^3	Water loss	cm^3
		from lungs	400
		from skin	500
drinks	1300		
food	850		
food + oxygen → energy + carbon dioxide + water respiration	350	urine	1500
		faeces	100
Total	2500	Total	2500

Controlling Water Content

Our blood must contain the right concentration of water: not too much, not too little. The normal concentration of water in our blood is about 98%. Our kidneys get rid of excess water, salts and urea.

If there is too high a concentration of water in the blood, then the kidneys produce a large volume of very dilute urine. If the water concentration in the blood is too low, then the kidneys excrete less water. The urine is more concentrated and more water is kept in the body.

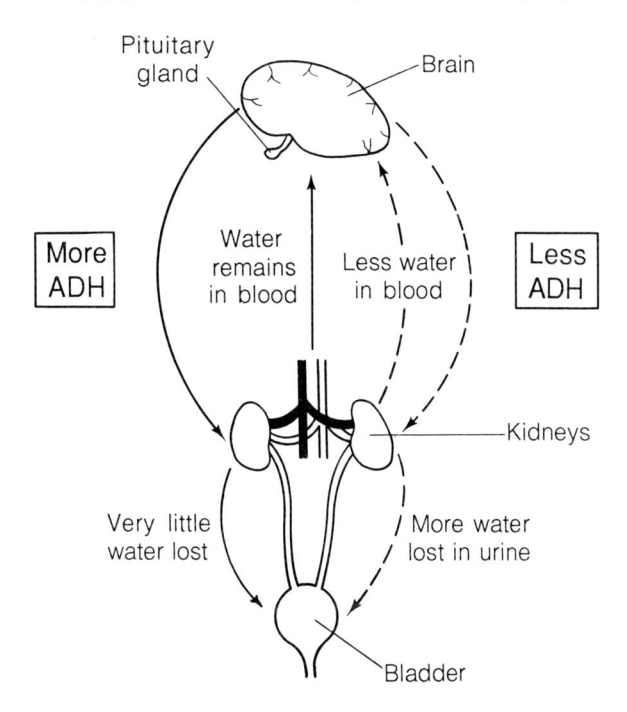

The brain detects the concentration of water in the blood. If water in the blood is at a low level, the pituitary gland produces a chemical called **anti-diuretic hormone** (ADH). This hormone is released into the bloodstream and is carried to the kidneys. It causes the kidneys to reabsorb water into the blood system and so lose much less water in the urine. Therefore very little water is lost from the blood and its water concentration stays nearly the same.

If more water is taken in, then the water concentration in the blood will increase. When this is detected the pituitary gland produces less ADH. This is an example of **feedback control**.

Activities

1. Draw a table listing and describing the important properties of water.
2. Draw a histogram using the table of data on page 80 to show the comparison of water gain with water loss.
3. Describe the sequence of events occurring in the body if the concentration of water in the blood rises.

11 Waste Removal

Key Ideas

Undigested food does not leave the digestive system until it reaches the anus. It leaves the body as faeces, containing some water.

One of the main waste products carried in the blood is *urea*, which is removed from the blood by the kidneys. Blood is carried to the kidneys through the *renal artery*.

From the kidneys, urine containing dissolved urea is transported through the *ureter* to the *bladder*, to be stored and later excreted.

Kidney Function

The kidneys have two main functions:
1. maintaining the water and salt balance in the body;
2. removing the poisonous waste urea from the body.

There are two kidneys in a mammal. They receive blood from the renal artery. This blood is **filtered** in the kidneys which remove unwanted substances. The blood then leaves the kidneys through the **renal vein**.

Glucose, salts, amino acids, urea and water are filtered from the blood in the kidneys. The glucose, amino acids and some salts and water are then **reabsorbed** back into the blood. Only excess water, some salts and the waste urea form the urine, which passes from the kidneys through the ureter, to be stored in the bladder.

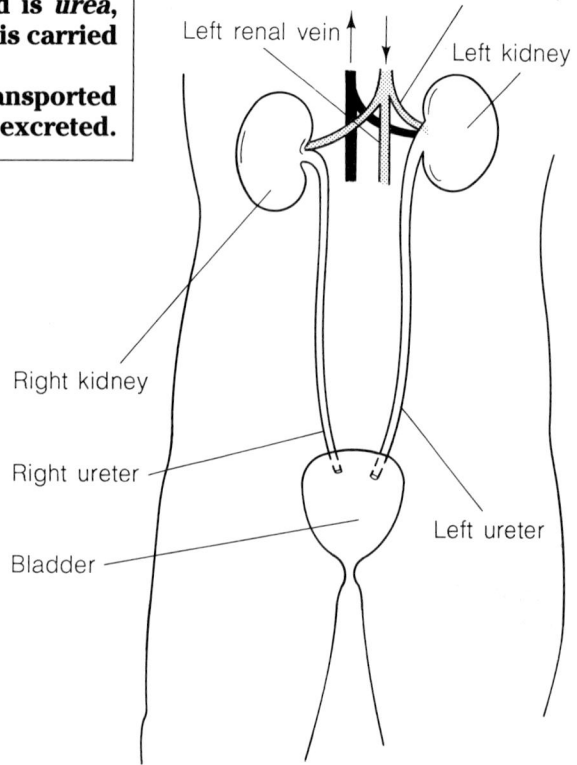

Filtration in the Kidney

The kidney contains about a million **kidney tubules** called **nephrons**. Each of these tubules starts at a bowl-shaped **Bowman's capsule**. In the bowl of each capsule there is a bundle of blood capillaries which are subdivisions of the renal artery. This bundle of blood vessels is called a **glomerulus**.

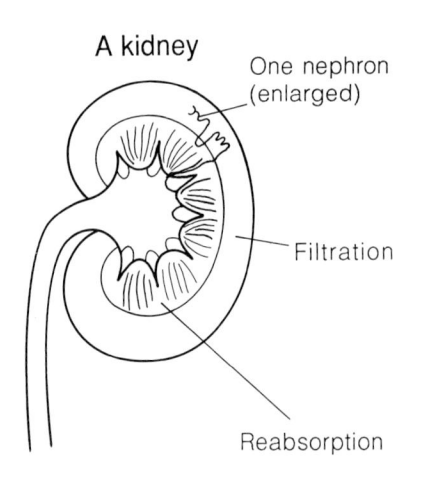

A nephron

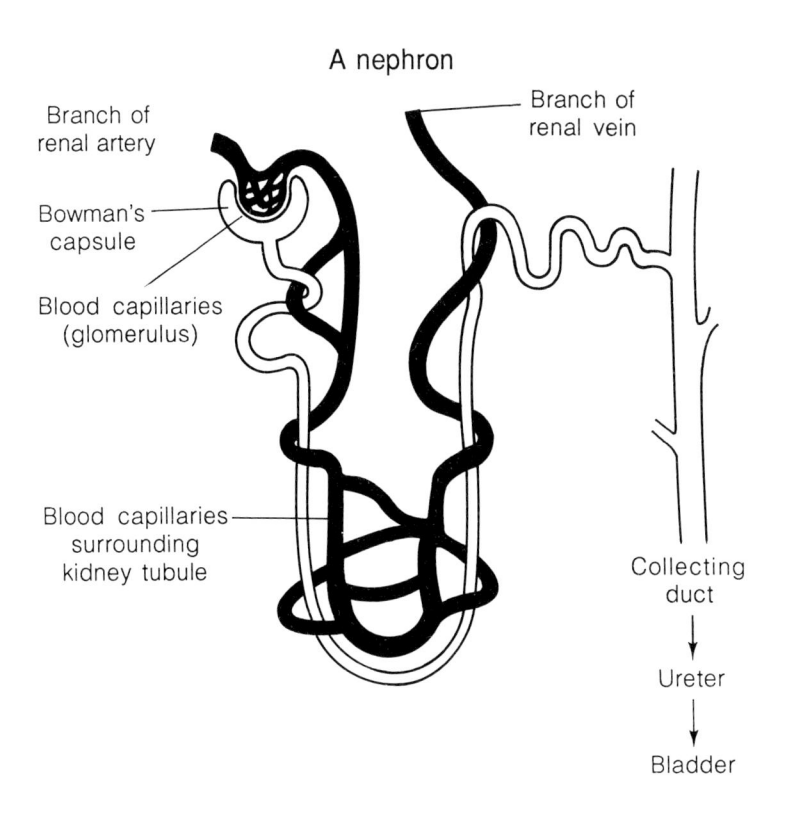

- Branch of renal artery
- Branch of renal vein
- Bowman's capsule
- Blood capillaries (glomerulus)
- Blood capillaries surrounding kidney tubule
- Collecting duct → Ureter → Bladder

Most of the liquid part of the blood – mainly water with some chemicals dissolved in it – passes out of the capillaries and into the Bowman's capsule. This filtrate contains glucose, salts, amino acids and urea. Larger parts of the blood such as cells and proteins are too big to pass out of the capillaries.

Reabsorption

The filtrate passes down the kidney tubule, which is surrounded by blood capillaries – continuations of the blood vessels found in the Bowman's capsule. Most of the useful substances are reabsorbed back into the blood. The rest is passed out of the kidney as urine.

Activities

○ 1 Which blood vessels carry blood to and from the kidneys?
○ 2 List the substances which are filtered from the blood by the kidneys.
○ 3 Which of these substances are reabsorbed back into the blood?
● 4 Describe where filtration occurs in the kidney.

12 Kidneys – Real or Artificial

Key Ideas

A person whose kidneys are damaged cannot produce urine to get rid of the poisonous waste urea. The person can be kept alive by being linked to an *artificial kidney machine* or by having a kidney *transplant*. The human body can function normally with only one working kidney.

Kidney Damage

If one of your kidneys stops working you can still survive. Sometimes, however, both kidneys can be damaged. This could happen in an accident or because of an infection, or through abusing your body with excess alcohol, or other drugs and chemicals. Total kidney failure can be treated in two ways.

1. You can be linked to an artificial kidney machine. This machine takes over the role of the kidneys. You need to be attached to it for about six to eight hours, at least twice a week.

A needle is inserted into a vein, usually in your arm, which carries blood out of your body through a tube to the machine. The blood flows over a thin membrane, rather like the Visking tubing described in Chapter 1. The soluble substances in the blood, including the waste urea, pass through the membrane. Liquid flowing over the other side of the membrane carries the waste away. This filters the blood in a similar way to a real kidney. The filtered blood is then returned to your body through a tube attached to another needle entering the vein further up your arm.

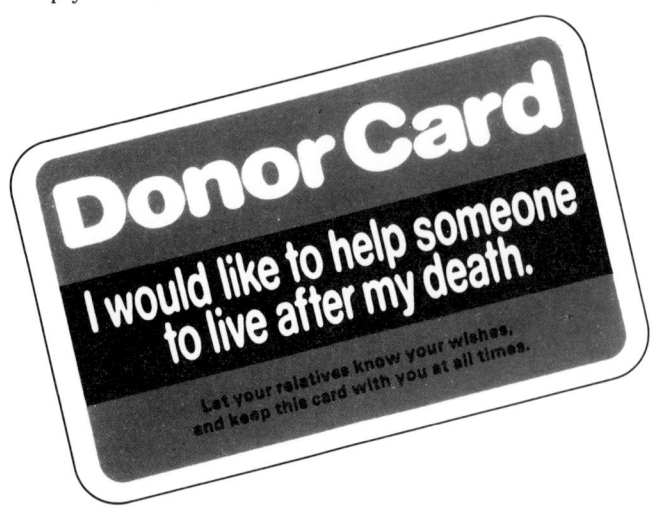

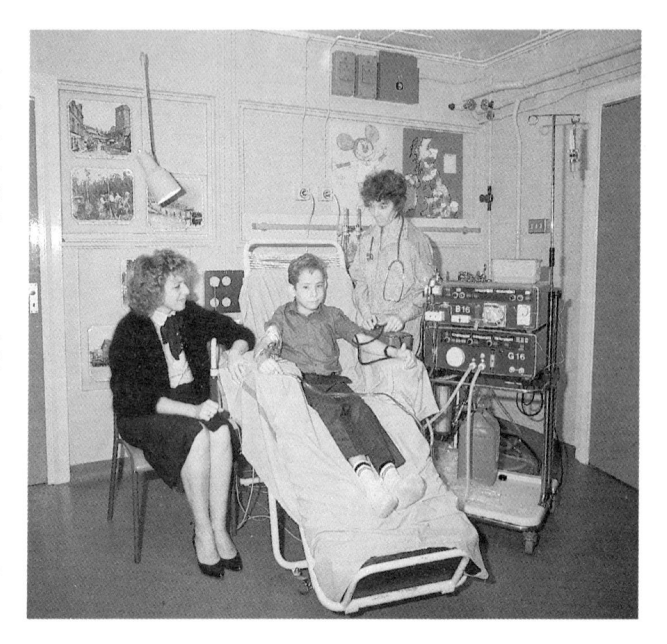

2. Kidney machines are very expensive and inconvenient to use. There are not enough kidney machines available in this country to treat all the patients suffering from kidney failure.

The alternative is a kidney transplant operation. It is possible to transplant a kidney from a living donor, usually a close relative. Kidneys can also be transplanted from dead donors, where death has not involved damage to the kidneys.

The problem with transplants is that the new kidney has to match the body of the patient. The donor kidney must be from a person with the same blood and tissue type as the patient's. If it is not, it will be attacked by the patient's body defences and rejected as "foreign".

Another difficulty is that permission must be obtained to remove a kidney from a dead person to use for a transplant. You may be able to help someone to live by carrying a donor card, or by allowing your name to be included in a computer data base of donors.

Effects of Kidney Damage

If the kidneys are damaged then they may cease to filter the blood. This causes a variety of symptoms. Firstly, the level of urea in the blood will increase. Normally urea makes up about 0.03% of the liquid part of the blood. If this rises to more than 0.2% it would cause death.

Also, the amount of salts in the blood would increase, which could cause cell damage. If reabsorption of water from the filtrate back into the blood stops, then the kidneys produce vast quantities of very dilute urine.

To get an idea of the rate of filtration, with no reabsorption at all, the kidneys take less than 5 minutes to remove a volume of water from the blood equal to the total volume of water in your body.

Urine		Glomerular filtrate	
Substance	Concentration	Substance	Concentration
water	96.0%	water	98–99%
urea	2.0%	urea	0.03%
total salts	1.8%	total salts	1·0%
glucose	none	glucose	0.1%
other substances containing nitrogen	0.2%	other substances containing nitrogen	a trace

Activities

1. Describe the problems which you think would occur if you had to use a kidney machine.
2. State the difficulties involved in providing kidneys for transplants.
3. Describe how a transplant might improve the life of a patient who had been using a kidney machine.
4. Draw a histogram to compare the proportions of **dissolved** substances in urine and the liquid filtered from the blood in the glomerulus. Do not include amounts of water in your histogram.

86 ANIMAL SURVIVAL

13 Responding to the Environment

Key Ideas

Living things can detect changes in environmental factors. These changes, called *stimuli*, are usually detected by sense organs. When a stimulus is detected by an organism, it may respond to the change in some way. Responses to stimuli make up the *behaviour* of the organism. Most behaviours increase the survival chances of the organism.

Detecting Environmental Factors

An organism must be able to detect changes in its surroundings so that it can react to improve its conditions or to protect itself from harm.

Humans have many sense organs to detect stimuli. Our abilities to detect different stimuli are called our **senses**. If we include the different types of stimuli which our skin can detect, and our sense of balance, we have more than the traditional five senses.

Sense	Stimulus	Sense organ
sight	light	ears
hearing	sound	ears
smell	chemicals (usually gases)	nose
taste	chemicals (solids/liquids)	tongue and throat
balance	movement/position	part of inner ear
touch	contact	skin
temperature	heat/cold	skin
pain	damage	skin
pressure	force	skin

Detecting Change

Responding to Change

ANIMAL SURVIVAL 87

Responses to Stimuli

The underlying reason for virtually all responses to stimuli is survival. The following examples explain the significance of some specific responses to stimuli.

Woodlice

Woodlice dry up and die if they are out in the open for too long. They respond to dryness and light by moving quickly. If, by chance, they move to darker or damper surroundings, their response is to slow down. Therefore they tend to remain for longer in damp and dark surroundings, and are less likely to dry out and die.

Humans

Human sperms are attracted to eggs by chemicals released from the eggs. This response increases the chances of sperm reaching the eggs and of fertilisation taking place. This increases the chances of survival of the species.

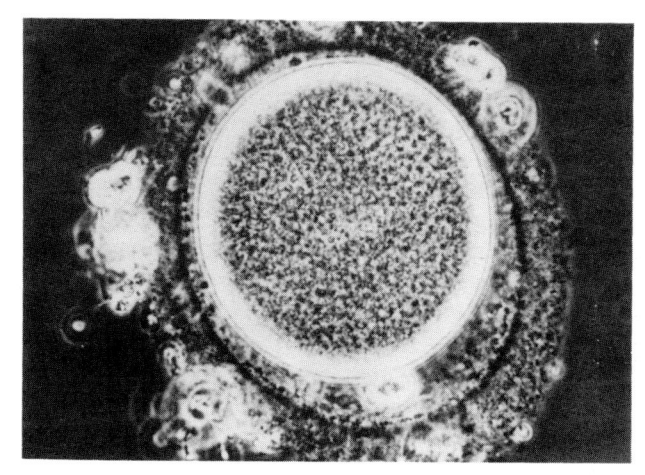

Activities

1. How are changes in your environment detected?
2. Describe three examples of responses to stimuli.
3. Explain the advantages of the responses which you described in your answer to question 2.
4. For a named organism, explain the significance of a response it makes to a stimulus.

14 Biorhythms

Key Ideas

Certain factors in the environment regularly change. Day and night, the tides and the seasons are examples. Changes of this type may produce specific responses in some organisms. For example, changing day length causes some plants to flower. This kind of stimulus is called a *trigger stimulus*.

There are changes in our environment due to changes in time. In the daytime the sun shines. At night-time, without the help of artificial light it is difficult to see our surroundings. These changes are due to the Earth turning. The length of daytime varies throughout the year as the Earth moves around the Sun.

Even without clocks or calendars, we, and many other living things can respond to the passing of time. Experiments have shown that some living things seem to have a kind of "internal biological clock". Humans kept in constant darkness go through waking and sleeping periods. They will wake from a long sleep period approximately every 24 hours.

Tidal Cycles

For the cycles of marine creatures, the trigger stimulus seems to be changes in the tides. Some crabs come out of their burrows twice a day to feed, always at low tide, which happens every $12\frac{1}{2}$ hours in Great Britain.

Daily Cycles

Aspects of behaviour are often repeated at the same time in each 24-hour cycle. Some animals are active during the day – called **diurnal**. Others are active at night – **nocturnal** – as anyone having a hamster in their bedroom at night will know!

The trigger stimulus is either dawn or dusk.

Annual Cycles

Other time cycles are seasonal.

In the springtime, increasing day length causes many birds in regions near the equator to fly north and prepare to breed. The trigger stimulus for this migration is when a particular day length is reached.

Rhythmical Behaviour

A great many animals can tell the compass direction from the Sun. Since the Sun's position changes during the day, it follows that these animals must have some kind of internal clock that takes into account the Sun's movement during the day.

The leaves and flowers of many plants show regular movements in a 24-hour cycle, even if the plants are kept under constant lighting conditions. Many insects emerge from pupae at a particular time of day, regardless of conditions. Certain crabs become darker in the morning and lighter in the afternoon.

ANIMAL SURVIVAL

Experiments indicate that all these 24-hour cycles can operate independently of external conditions. If the plant or animal is placed in a closed dark box, its behaviour will still show this cycle, even though it cannot detect what time of day it is from the Sun.

The cycles that occur over monthly or yearly periods can also be independent of environmental conditions. However, they can get out of step with the "real world". For example, a plant kept in constant light exhibits its circadian rhythms, but on return to normal conditions, its biological clock will be "reset" by dawn/dusk trigger stimuli. This shows that the clock is "internal" but is adjustable by external stimuli.

It is not only whole organisms that have biological clocks, but also internal organs and cells. Release of hormones and enzymes tends to vary during the day, and a sudden change in the day/night rhythm can disturb things. An example of this in humans is jet-lag. A jet plane leaving Glasgow airport at dawn and flying west for 10 hours will arrive in America 5 hours after sunrise. The passengers will experience a day length which is 5 hours longer than their internal clock is used to. It takes time to readjust to the change.

Benefits to Organisms

Nearly all rhythmical behaviours are adaptations which are likely to improve the survival chances of the species concerned.

Birds which do not migrate to warmer climates for the winter may die from extreme cold or starve from lack of food.

Male and female animals need to produce sperms and eggs at the same time if reproduction is to be successful. Plants of the same species must flower at the same time of year for cross pollination to occur.

Activities

1. State what is meant by a "trigger stimulus".
2. Describe three examples of rhythmical behaviour. For each example identify the trigger stimulus.
3. Describe what is meant by a "biological clock".
4. Describe the type of advantage gained from most rhythmical behaviours.
5. Explain why all the midge larvae in a pond tend to change into flying adults at nearly the same time on the same day. What is the advantage for the midges?

Investigating Cells

1 Microscopes and Cells

Key Ideas

Since the 17th century scientists have used *microscopes* to study living things. With them, they discovered that all living things are made up of tiny units called *cells*. If cells are *stained* using coloured dyes, details of their structure can be seen more clearly.

Cells from different organisms appear similar in some ways. So do cells from different parts of the same organism, but there are important differences. The differences usually depend on the job that the cell has to do.

Plant cells differ in many ways from animal cells.

Microscopes

In order to see tiny details of the parts of plants and animals, you need to use a **microscope**. The type of microscope which you will use in your biology class will probably be similar to the one shown in the drawing.

A microscope has an **eyepiece lens** and an **objective lens**. You look through the eyepiece lens, while the objective lens is the one just above the **specimen** which you want to see magnified. Many microscopes have a choice of two or three objective lenses. The different objective lenses give different **magnifications**. Magnifications of 100 times or more are needed to study the details of parts of the body of an animal or plant.

The specimen is usually mounted on a **glass slide** and placed on the **stage** of the microscope. Light from a lamp or a window is reflected from a **mirror** and up through a hole in the stage. This reflected light then passes through the specimen and up through the lenses into your eye. The microscope is focused by turning the **focus knob** which usually works by changing the distance between the objective lens and the specimen.

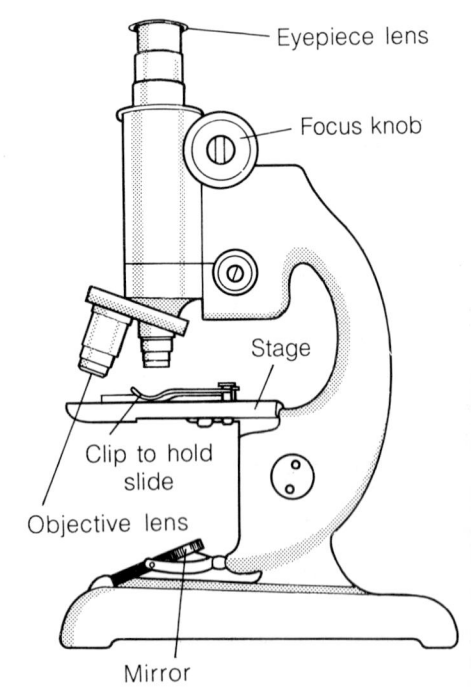

A basic light microscope

Magnification

The lenses of a microscope are usually each stamped with a number. This number is the magnification of the lens. To find the total magnification of a microscope, the number on the eyepiece must be multiplied by the number on the objective lens being used. If an eyepiece was marked ×10 and the objective was marked ×20, then the **total magnification** would be:

$$10 \times 20 = 200 \text{ times } (\times 200)$$

Looking at Cells

In 1665 Robert Hooke used a simple microscope to look at a thin piece of cork from the bark of a tree. He saw that cork was made up of tiny units which he called **cells**. This word has stuck and biologists use the word nowadays to mean the basic blocks that make up all living things.

So as to be seen clearly down the microscope, specimens of animal and plant material must be carefully prepared. Most biological specimens are prepared as **wet mounts**.

> I Took a good clear piece of Cork, and with a Pen-knife ſharpen'd as keen as a Razor, I cut a piece of it off, and thereby left the ſurface of it exceeding ſmooth, then examining it very diligently with a *Microſcope*, me thought I could perceive it to appear a little porous; I could exceeding plainly perceive it to be all perforated and porous, much like a Honey-comb, but that the pores of it were not regular ... theſe pores, or cells, were not very deep, but confiſted of a great many little Boxes.

Hooke's cork cells and an extract from his notes

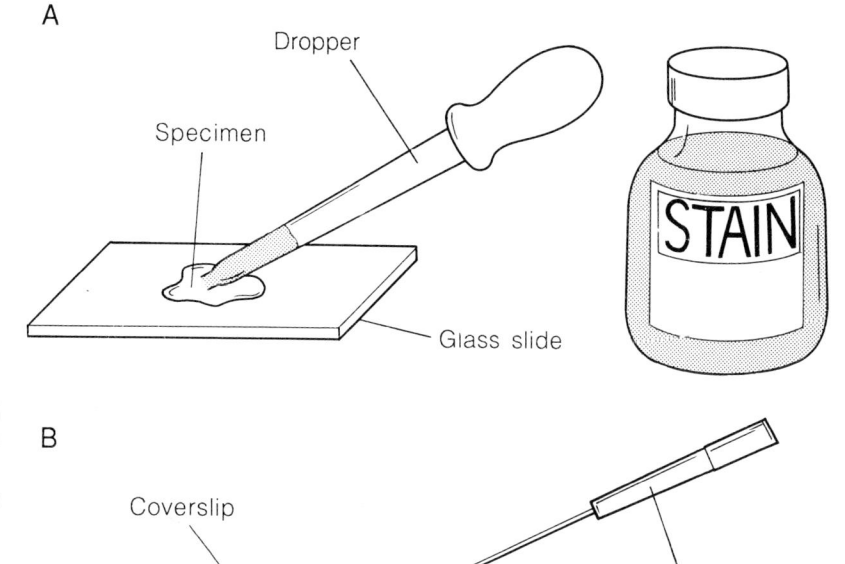

1. The material should be very thin. Some types of material can be smeared onto the glass slide.

2. Most cell material is transparent and is stained with one or more coloured dyes. This makes different parts of the material stand out and easier to see.

3. The material should be covered with a **coverslip** to stop it drying out. The coverslip should be lowered with a mounted needle. This helps prevent air bubbles being trapped in the preparation.

A

B

Preparation of a wet mount

92 INVESTIGATING CELLS

Animal Cells

The photograph is of some cells from the lining of the human mouth. Below the photograph is a drawing of the cells. There is a boundary to each cell called the **cell membrane**. The main body of the cell is a watery jelly called **cytoplasm** which has a dark stained body called the **nucleus** in it. These basic features are found in most animal cells.

Cells from different parts of an animal do differ in some ways – they may be different sizes and shapes depending on the job they have to do.

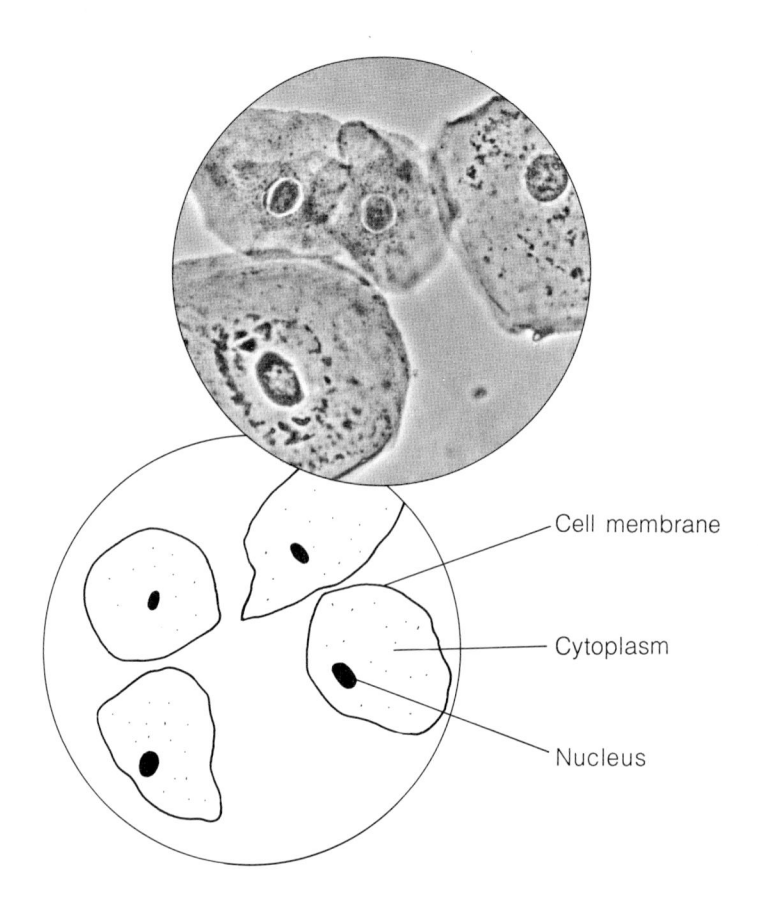

Human cheek lining cells, × 600

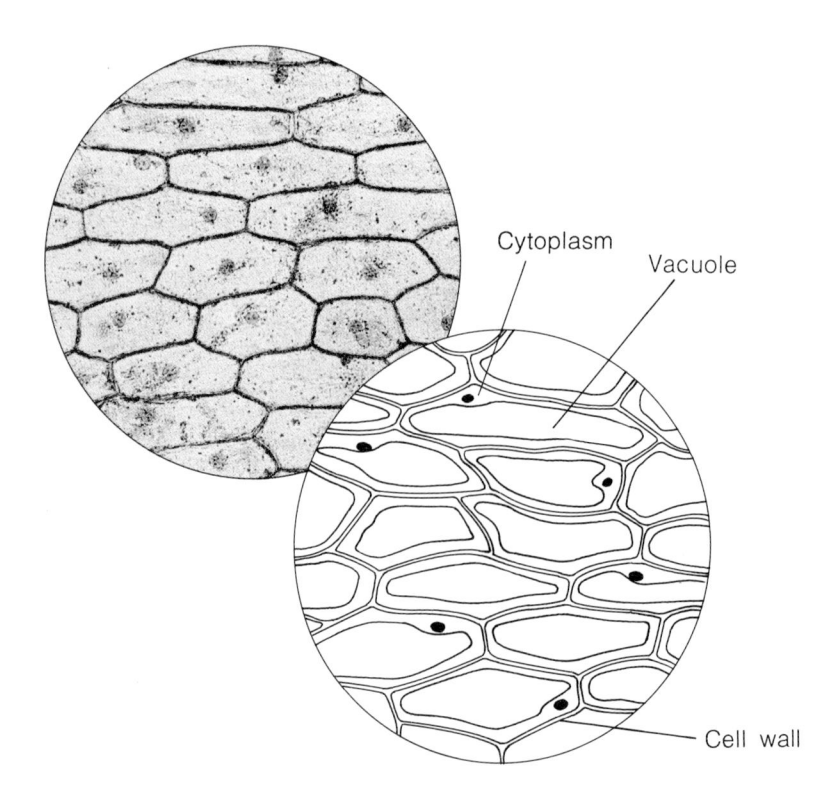

Plant Cells

The photograph shows a piece of thin tissue from the skin of an onion. A labelled drawing is shown with the photograph.

Compare these cells with the animal cells above. There are some similarities and some differences. Apart from the membrane, cytoplasm and nucleus, there is a thicker outer boundary called the **cell wall**. The cytoplasm is pushed to the outer part of the cell by a bag called the **vacuole** which is filled with **sap**. Cells from the green parts of plants have bright green beads called **chloroplasts** in their cytoplasm.

Onion leaf skin cells, × 100

INVESTIGATING CELLS 93

Differences Explained

What are the different parts of cells for? All cells need the basic three structures:

The Nucleus

The nucleus controls and coordinates the cell activities. It is vitally important in cell division. It carries inherited information.

HUMAN CHEEK CELLS

The Cytoplasm

In the cytoplasm, all the special chemical activities of the cell happen. Energy is released from food, wastes are destroyed, useful substances are made from raw materials.

The Cell Wall

Plants do not have a skeleton in the way that most animals do. The cell walls of a plant act like cell skeletons, giving the plant support and preventing it from being floppy.

The Cell Membrane

The membrane is the effective boundary of the cell. It can control which substances are allowed into the cell. It controls which substances are allowed out of the cell. Membranes like this are called **selectively permeable membranes**. The cell must gain water, food and oxygen. It must lose wastes.

GREEN LEAF CELLS

The Vacuole

If plants are short of water they tend to wilt. When watered, the vacuoles swell with sap, and push against the cell wall thus helping the plant to regain its shape.

In addition to these basics, plant cells need some other structures:

The Chloroplast

Plants do not eat. They get food by making it themselves during **photosynthesis**. Photosynthesis takes place in the chloroplasts.

94 INVESTIGATING CELLS

Activities

1. What name is given to the basic units from which living things are made?
2. Explain why cells to be viewed down the microscope are stained with coloured dyes.
3. Make up a table like the one below showing the jobs of the different cell parts.

Name of Cell Structure	Function

4. List the similarities and differences between plant and animal cells.
5. This drawing shows the field of view of a microscope at ×100. A piece of onion skin is also shown with one cell labelled **A**. A ruler with a scale in millimetres is also shown in view. There are 1000 micrometres in every millimetre.

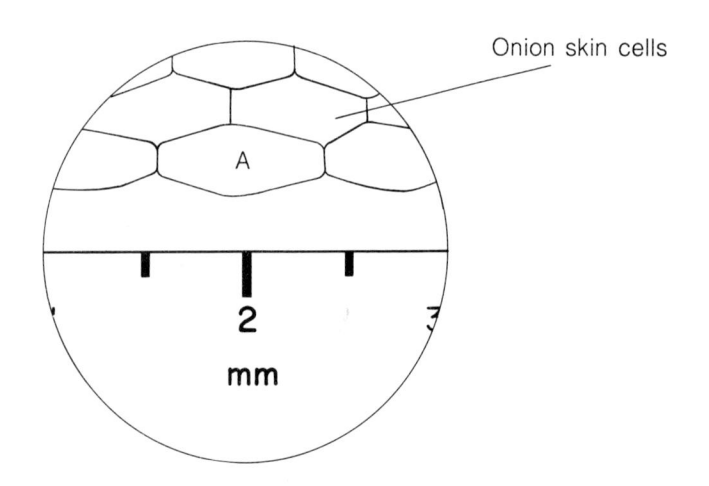

(a) How wide is the field of view in millimetres?
(b) How wide would the field of view be if the magnification were changed to ×200?
(c) How many cells 50 micrometres wide could be placed across the field of view as shown?
(d) How wide is cell **A** in micrometres?
(e) How many onion cells are fully visible in the field?

2 Cell Division

> ## Key Ideas
>
> The number of cells in the bodies of living things needs to increase at certain times of their lives. The cell number increases during enlargement of their bodies in growth and when their bodies need to be repaired after injury. This is achieved when existing cells divide in two by a process called *mitosis*. The nucleus of the cell controls this process. During mitosis, a number of objects called *chromosomes* become visible within the nucleus, and their movement marks different stages in the process.

Chromosomes and Genes

When cells treated with a stain such as **acetic orcein** are viewed by microscope, threads of material known as chromosomes are seen inside the nuclei. In an ordinary cell these chromosomes are difficult to see because their threads are so fine – see **A**.

If a cell which is dividing is examined the chromosomes are more easily visible. This is because they become shorter and thicker at this time – see **B**. Each chromosome consists of a chain of units called genes. Each gene controls an aspect of the organism's characteristics. In humans for example, genes control characteristics such as eye colour and blood group. You can read more about this on page 160 of Inheritance.

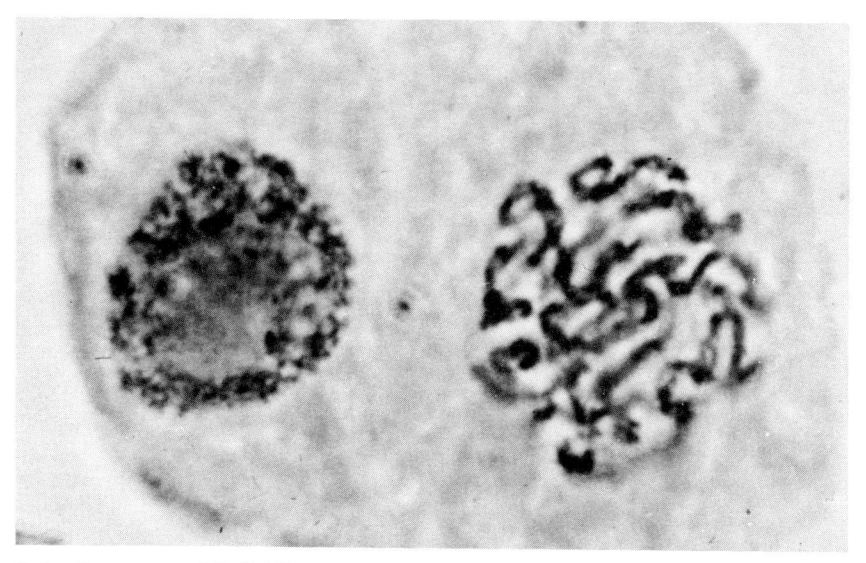

Cells: **A** at rest, and **B** dividing

Chromosome Number

Every living organism has a specific number of chromosomes in the nuclei of its cells. This number is the same for all members of a species. There are two similar chromosome sets in each nucleus. Each set was inherited from one parent at fertilisation.

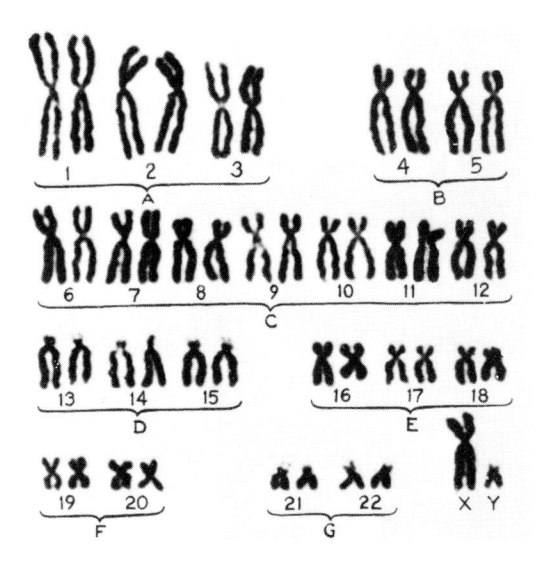

Human chromosome set

96 INVESTIGATING CELLS

The table below shows the numbers of chromosomes in different organisms.

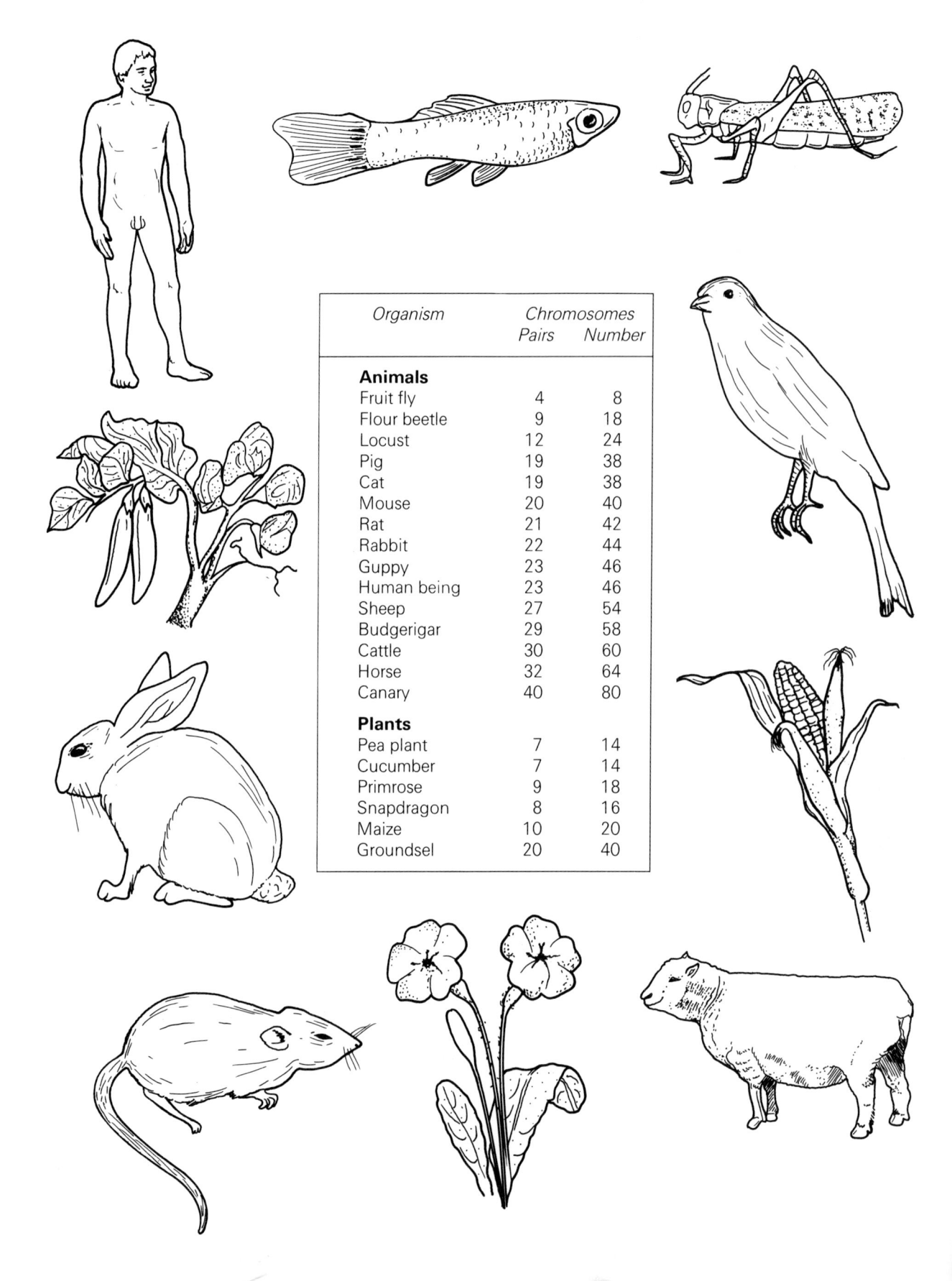

Organism	Chromosomes Pairs	Number
Animals		
Fruit fly	4	8
Flour beetle	9	18
Locust	12	24
Pig	19	38
Cat	19	38
Mouse	20	40
Rat	21	42
Rabbit	22	44
Guppy	23	46
Human being	23	46
Sheep	27	54
Budgerigar	29	58
Cattle	30	60
Horse	32	64
Canary	40	80
Plants		
Pea plant	7	14
Cucumber	7	14
Primrose	9	18
Snapdragon	8	16
Maize	10	20
Groundsel	20	40

Cell Division

The number of chromosomes must be kept the same in all the cells of an organism. When a human cell with 46 chromosomes divides, it must produce two daughter cells each with 46 chromosomes. This means that the cell has to double its chromosomes just before division.

The phase of the cell's life during which the chromosomes double is called **interphase**. At the end of interphase the number of chromosomes will have doubled. The doubling process produces identical copies of the chromosomes called **chromatids**. This means that the daughter cells will be identical to the parent cell.

During the next phase of the division, the chromosomes become visible as double strands. This phase is called **prophase**. By the end of prophase a fibrous structure called the **spindle** appears in the central area of the dividing cell. The spindle is produced by structures called centrioles. The chromosomes are attached to the spindle by their centromeres.

At **metaphase** the double chromosomes move to the equator of the spindle. They line up, and at **anaphase**, the two chromatids of each double chromosome are pulled apart. The chromatids are moved to either end of the spindle. When they reach the end, new nuclei are formed from the chromatids during **telophase**. Shortly afterwards, the cytoplasm splits and the formation of two identical daughter cells is complete.

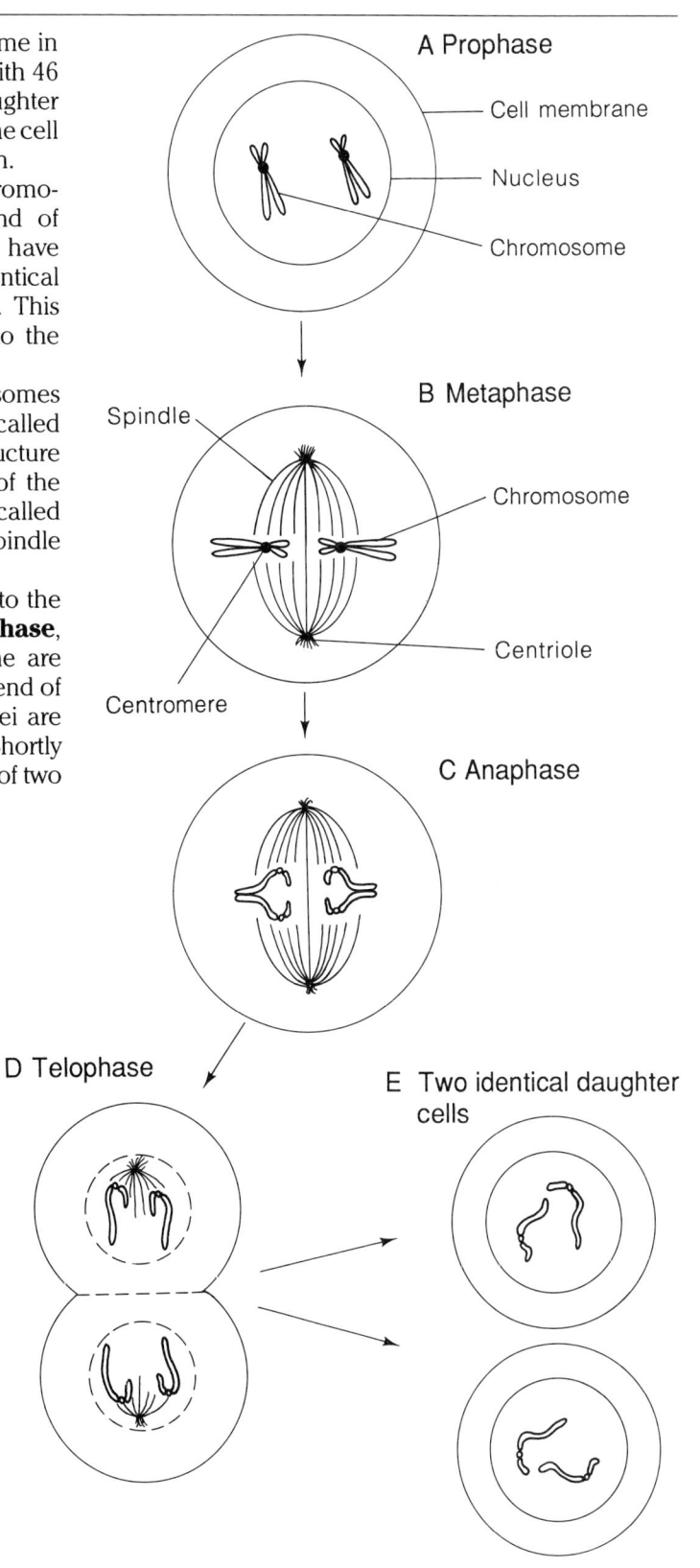

Stages of mitosis — only one pair of chromosomes shown

98 INVESTIGATING CELLS

Chromosome Problems

Occasionally mistakes occur during cell division and a daughter cell contains the wrong number of chromosomes. In a fertilised human egg cell an extra chromosome, number 21, very occasionally appears. This causes the baby to have Down's syndrome, named after Langdon Down who first discovered it in 1866. People with Down's syndrome often have round faces and narrow eyes. They may be short in stature and mentally retarded. This example shows how important it is for cells to have exactly the correct number of chromosomes. You can read more about this on page 172 in Inheritance.

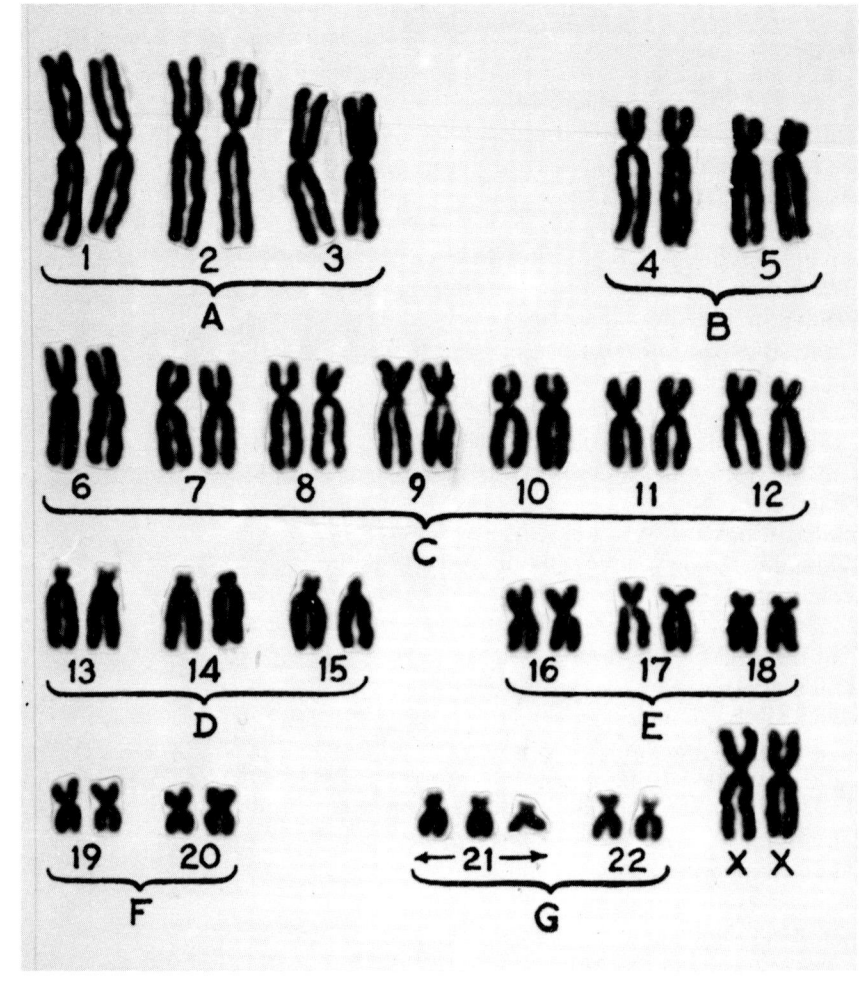

Chromosomes of a human female with Down's syndrome. Notice the extra chromosome number 21

Activities

1. A single cell divides by mitosis for 5 generations. How many cells will result?

2. Which part of a cell controls the process of mitosis?

3. Why must the chromosomes of a cell double just before cell division?

4. Place these statements into the correct order of their occurrence in cell division.
   the chromosomes move to centre of spindle
   chromatids are pulled apart
   ✓the chromosomes become visible
   the spindle forms
   daughter cells form

5. What causes Down's syndrome?

6. Why should the chromosome number be the same in all cells of an organism?

3 Cells and Diffusion

What is Diffusion?

All substances are made up of tiny particles. Substances can be **solids**, **liquids** or **gases**. In solids the particles are close together and are not free to move about. In liquids and gases the particles are free to move about.

Particles in liquids and gases tend to move from where they are tightly packed or concentrated to areas where they are less tightly packed. The movement of gases and liquids from areas of high concentration to areas of low concentration is called **diffusion**.

If a lump of sugar is dropped into a cup of tea, all of the tea will eventually become sweet. This is because the sugar particles have moved from the concentrated lump to all parts of the tea. This diffusion causes all parts of the tea to be sweet.

If gas is leaking from a gas tap in your laboratory, even people far away from the tap will eventually smell the gas. This is because the gas particles will diffuse through the air from where they are concentrated to all corners of the room.

Key Ideas

Cells need to take in substances such as food and oxygen in order to continue living. They must also lose substances such as wastes which are harmful in large quantities. The *cell membrane* controls this gain and loss of substances.

One of the ways in which the living cell gains and loses substances is by the process of *diffusion* through the cell membrane. In diffusion substances move from areas where they are highly *concentrated* to areas where they are less concentrated.

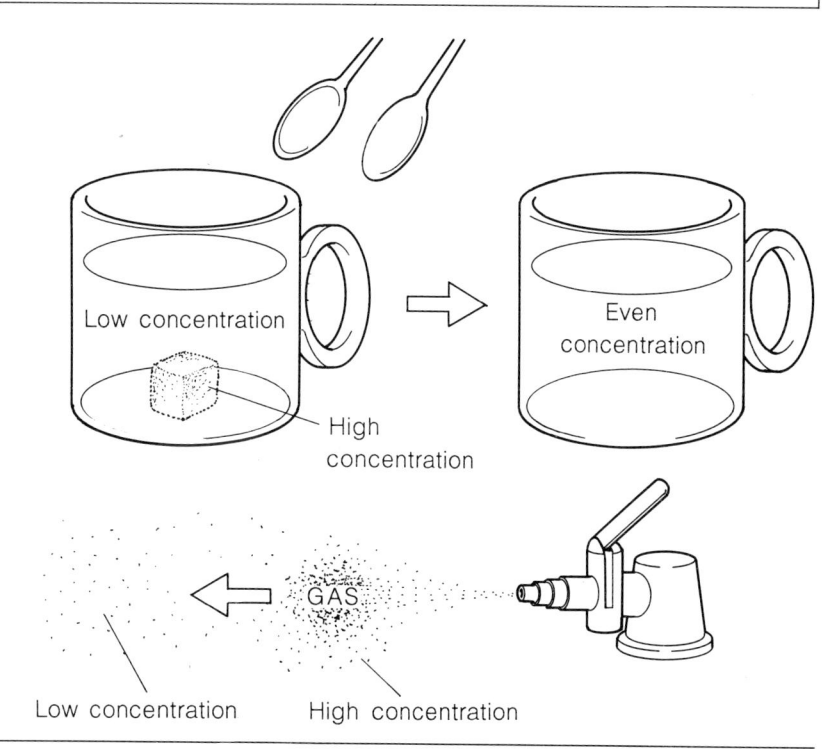

The Cell Membrane

Diffusion is very important to the life of cells as it allows them to gain and lose substances. They gain substances such as dissolved foods and oxygen, and lose others like wastes and carbon dioxide. In order to enter or leave the cell, any diffusing substance must pass through the cell membrane.

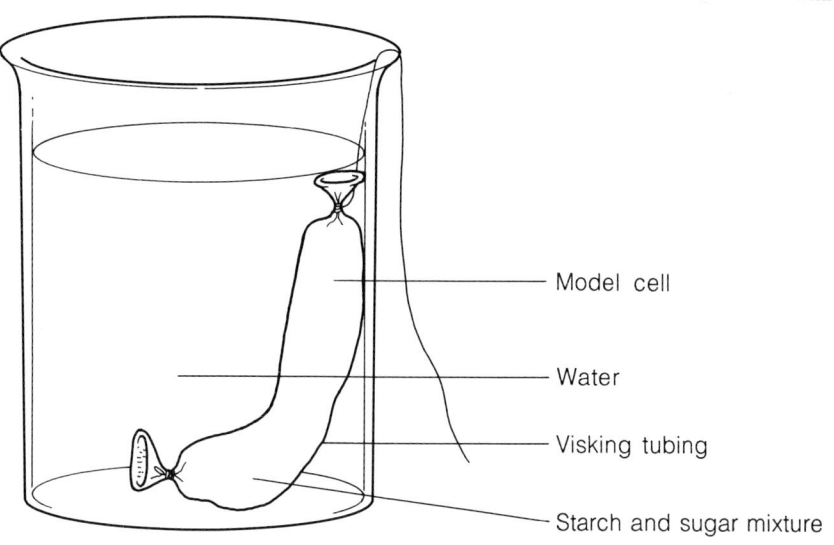

Visking tubing experiment

100 INVESTIGATING CELLS

Look at the experiment shown on page 99. A model cell has been made out of Visking tubing. The tubing acts just like the cell membrane. The "*cytoplasm*" of the model cell is a mixture of large starch particles and small sugar particles in water.

After 10 hours the water surrounding the model cell is tested for the presence of sugar and starch. Only sugar is found. It is thought that the cell membrane has tiny pores in it. These pores let sugar diffuse through the membrane but are too small to let large starch molecules through. The membrane can therefore control the movement of substances by diffusion depending on their size.

Think of a net bag full of fruit. Large fruits such as apples and oranges cannot fall out of the bag. Small fruits like cherries and single grapes can get through the net and fall to the ground. The bag acts like a cell membrane, letting some things through but stopping others.

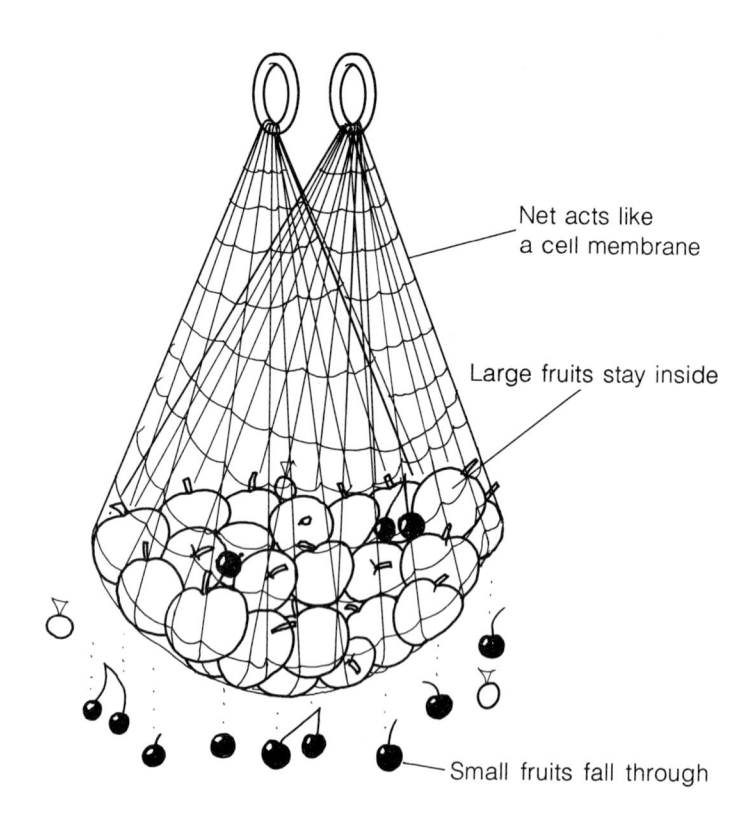

Net bag idea of the cell membrane

Diffusion and Cells

The single-celled **Amoeba** lives in the mud on the bottom of ponds. It gains its oxygen from the water by diffusion of gas particles through its membrane. Carbon dioxide is lost from its body in the same way.

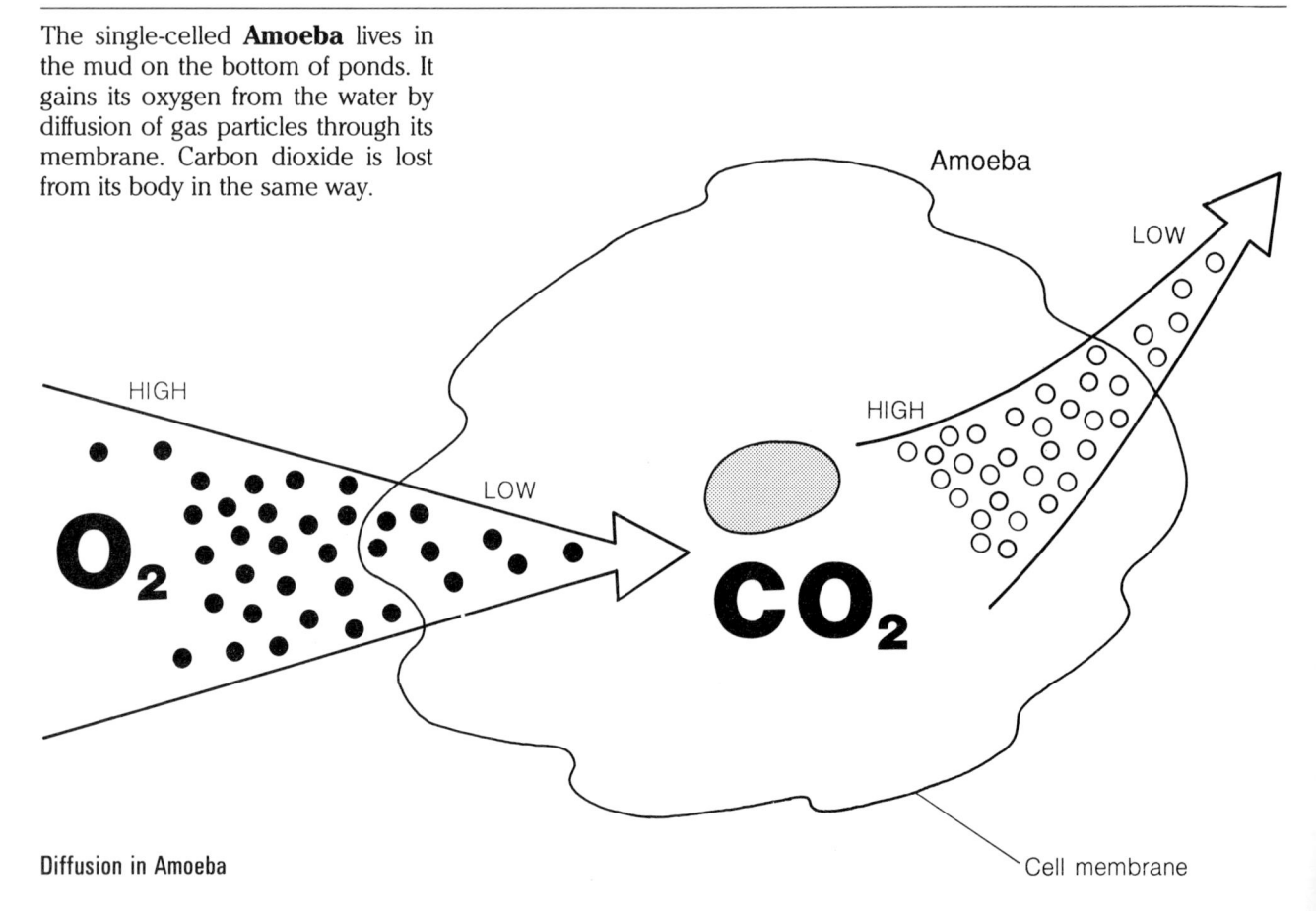

Diffusion in Amoeba

Diffusion and Organisms

In larger organisms such as humans, diffusion is also very important. Imagine a cell somewhere in the body. It has to be supplied with a range of substances to keep it alive. Wastes and carbon dioxide have to be removed. Diffusion takes place between the cell and the blood supply.

How does the bloodstream pick up the useful substances in the first place, and how does it get rid of the wastes it collects from the cells? Diffusion is the answer again.

Let's take oxygen and carbon dioxide as examples. When blood passes into the lungs, oxygen which has come into the lung air spaces during breathing in, diffuses into the blood. At the same time, carbon dioxide diffuses from the blood into the air spaces and is removed from the body during breathing out.

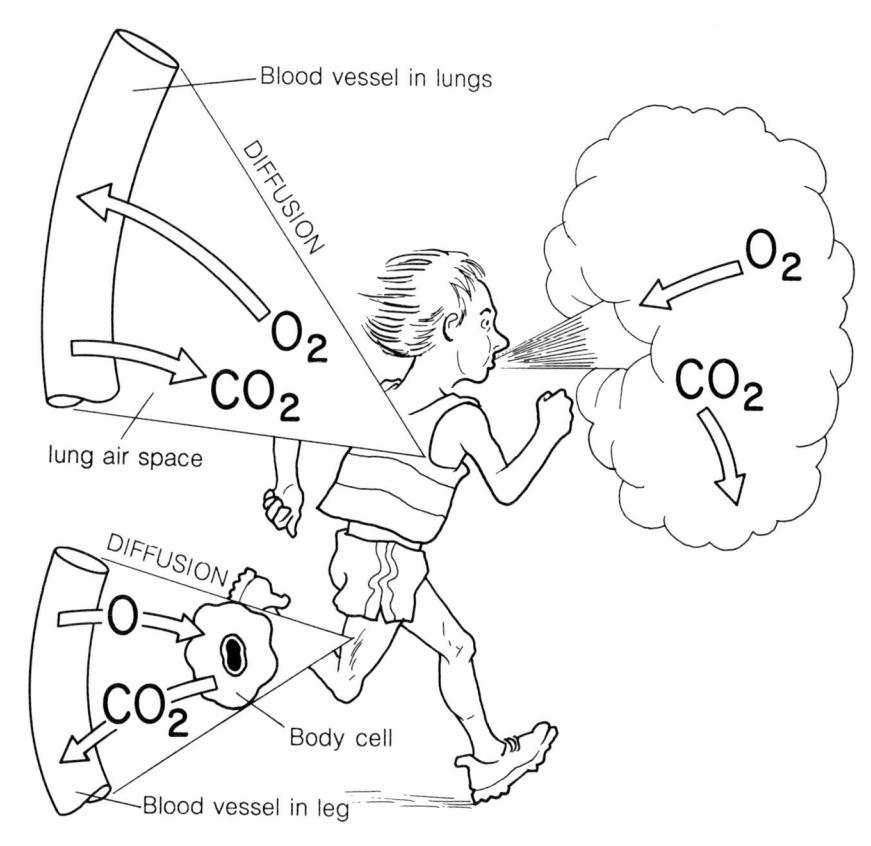

Diffusion in a whole organism

Activities

1. Write a sentence or two saying what is meant by the term "diffusion". You must use every word in the word bank given:

   movement   low concentration   high concentration   substances

2. Why is diffusion so important to an organism like Amoeba?

3. Make up a table to show some of the substances which move in and out of cells by diffusion. Set the table out as shown:

Diffuse In	Diffuse Out

4. Which cell structure controls diffusion of substances?

5. Study the diagram opposite. What would happen to the contents of the tube after 24 hours?

● 6. Study the diagram of the athlete above.
   Write a short account of the importance of diffusion to the whole organism. Base your account on the picture of the athlete.

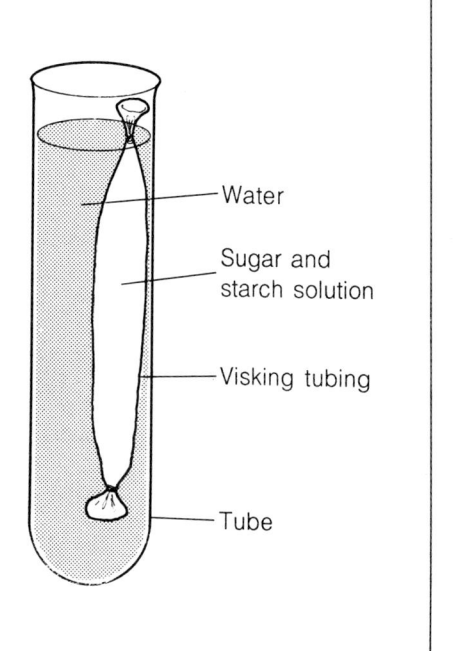

4 Cells and Water

Key Ideas

Water is one of the important substances needed by living cells. It can enter or leave the cells through the cell membrane. The diffusion of water through the membrane is called *osmosis*. In osmosis, as in diffusion, the water moves from an area of high water *concentration* to an area of lower water concentration. This means that sometimes water will enter a cell and at others it will leave the cell.

Osmosis in Animal Cells

The red blood cells of mammals float in a liquid called **plasma**. The cells and the plasma together make up what is called whole blood. Normally, the level of water and dissolved substances in the plasma is the same as that in the red blood cell cytoplasm. This ensures that no movement of water by osmosis will occur through the membranes.

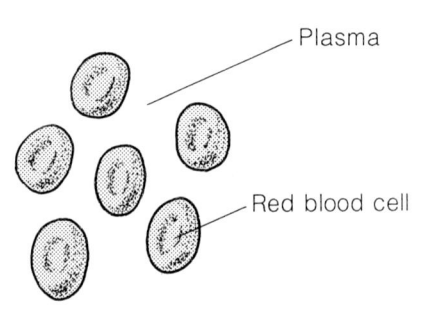

Whole human blood

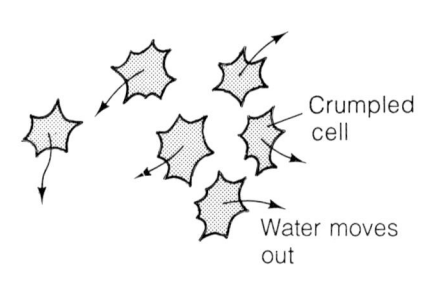

Low water concentration in plasma

If the water concentration of the plasma becomes low compared with the cell cytoplasm, then water will move out of the cells into the plasma by osmosis. The cells could crumple if they lost too much water in this way. Crumpled cells will not function properly and the organism will be damaged. You can read more about blood on page 131 of The Body in Action.

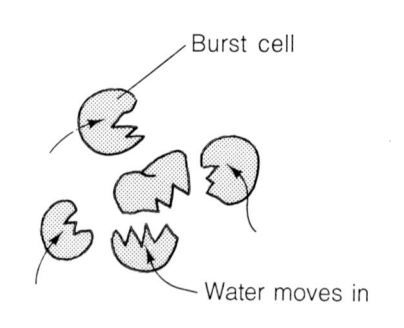

High water concentration in plasma

If the water concentration of the plasma becomes high, then water will move into the cells by osmosis. If too much water moves into the cells they will swell and could burst. Burst cells cannot function and the organism will be damaged.

Normally the kidneys of the mammal will react to any changes in the water level of the plasma. The kidneys keep the water level constant and the blood cells are protected from damage. You can read more about this on page 81 of Animal Survival.

Osmosis in Plant Cells

The effect of osmosis on plant cells is different from the effect on animal cells, because of the presence of the stiff cellulose wall around the cells.

In an experiment a cylinder of potato tissue was placed in a beaker of pure water. Another was placed in a similar beaker of strong sugar solution. The next day both cylinders were examined. The cylinder which had been in pure water had swollen and felt hard because it had taken in water by osmosis. The other cylinder seemed to have shrunk and felt soft, also because of osmosis. This time the potato cylinder had lost water.

Some cells from each cylinder are shown below. Cells which are full of water are **turgid**. Cells which have lost a lot of water have shrunken vacuoles and are **plasmolysed**.

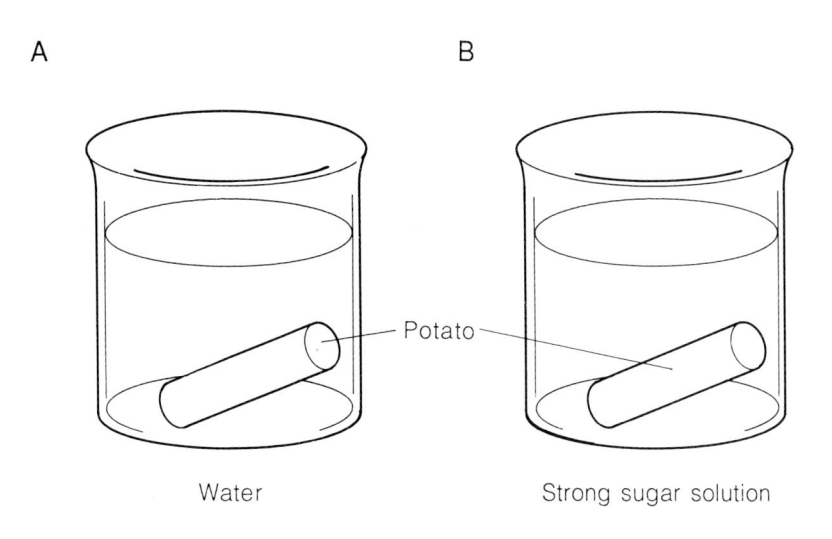

A — Water
B — Strong sugar solution

Potato experiment

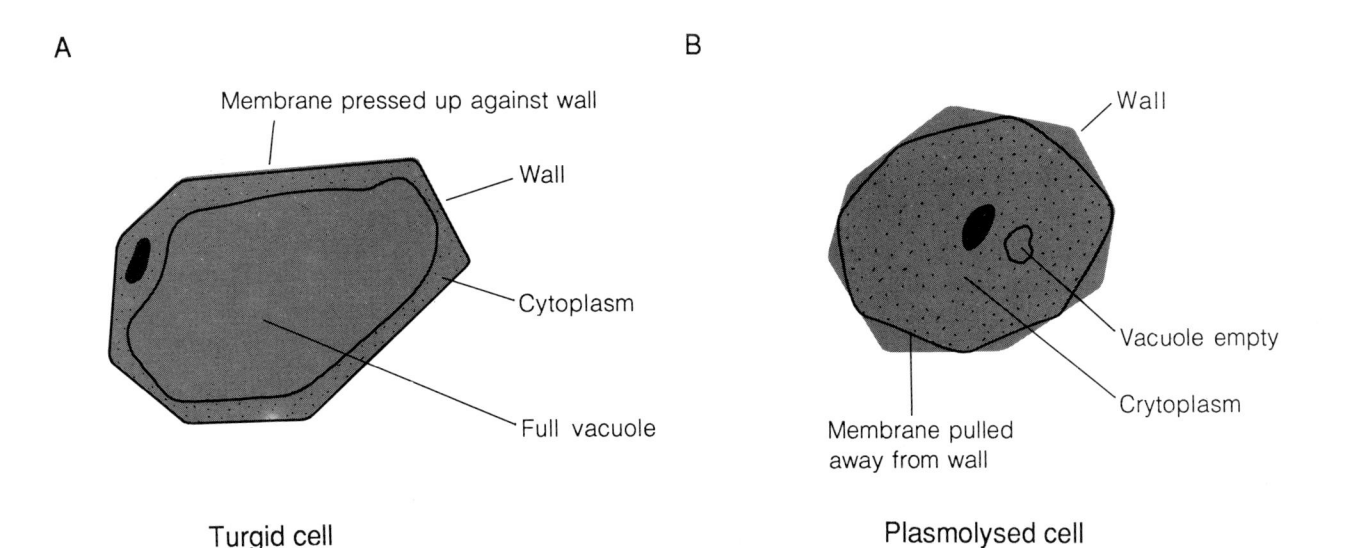

A — Turgid cell
- Membrane pressed up against wall
- Wall
- Cytoplasm
- Full vacuole

B — Plasmolysed cell
- Wall
- Vacuole empty
- Crytoplasm
- Membrane pulled away from wall

Cells from the potato experiment

INVESTIGATING CELLS

Concentration Gradients

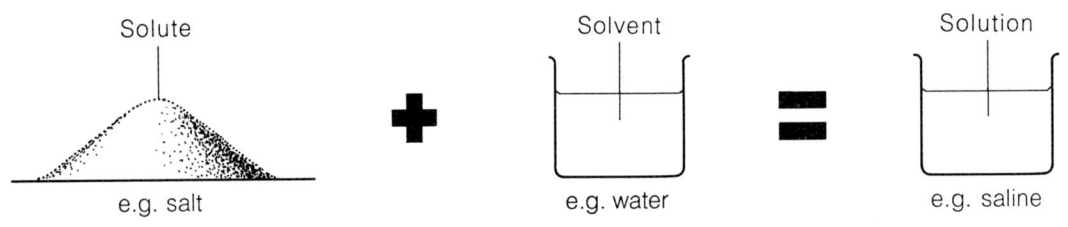

A SOLUTION = A SOLVENT + A SOLUTE

What do we really mean when we talk about concentration? We mean the particular amount of solute (sugar or salt) dissolved in a particular amount of solvent (usually water). If 10 grams of a solute like sugar were to dissolve in 1 litre of water, the resulting solution would have a concentration of:

10 grams per litre

Think of two solutions of differing concentration separated from each other by a **selectively permeable** membrane. There is a concentration gradient between the two solutions and osmosis can occur. Water moves along the concentration gradient from high water concentration to low water concentration, as shown in the diagram.

Concentration gradient

Activities

○ 1 What is meant by the term "osmosis"? Use the following list of words to explain your answer:

water   diffusion   cell membrane
high water concentration   low water concentration

○ 2 Describe a situation which could lead to the plasma of a human's blood becoming too watery.

○ 3 Describe a situation which could lead to the plasma of a human's blood becoming too salty.

○ 4 Study the following pairs of plant cells. In each case explain whether the water will move from **X** to **Y** or from **Y** to **X**.

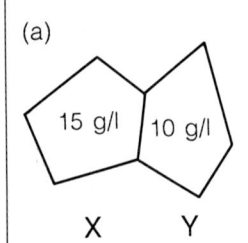

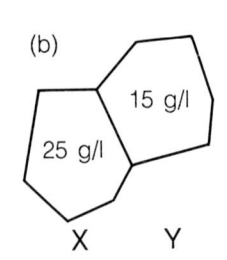

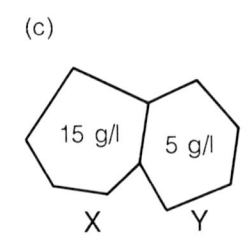

(a) X: 15 g/l   Y: 10 g/l
(b) X: 25 g/l   Y: 15 g/l
(c) X: 15 g/l   Y: 5 g/l

● 5 In an experiment some pieces of dandelion stalk were placed in pure water. The pieces have an **impermeable** coat on the outside. After the experiment the pieces were observed to have curled as shown below. Try to explain the results of this experiment in terms of osmosis.

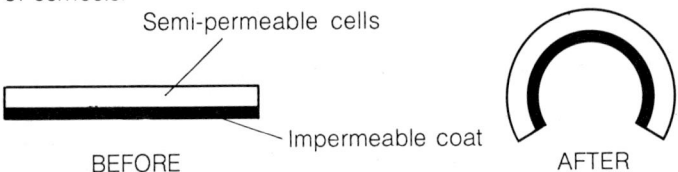

BEFORE — Semi-permeable cells / Impermeable coat
AFTER

● 6 What might happen if the stalk pieces were placed in strong sugar solution?

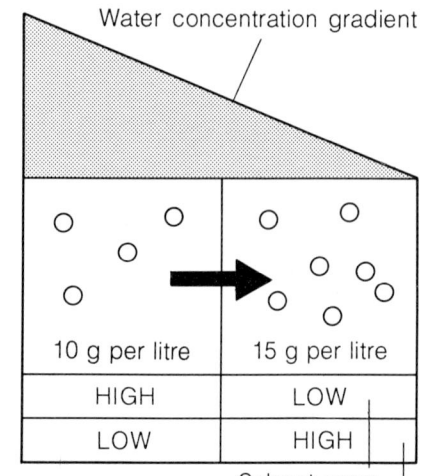

5 Chemical Reactions in Cells

Key Ideas

Many chemical reactions are needed for the life of a cell. Some of these reactions involve the breaking down of substances. Food is broken down to release energy and poisonous wastes are broken down to make them harmless. Breakdown reactions are called *degradations*.

Other reactions involve the building up of new substances needed by the cell. Build-up reactions are called *synthesis* reactions.

Most cell reactions would normally happen very slowly, but cells have very special substances called *enzymes* which make these reactions go fast enough to keep the cell alive.

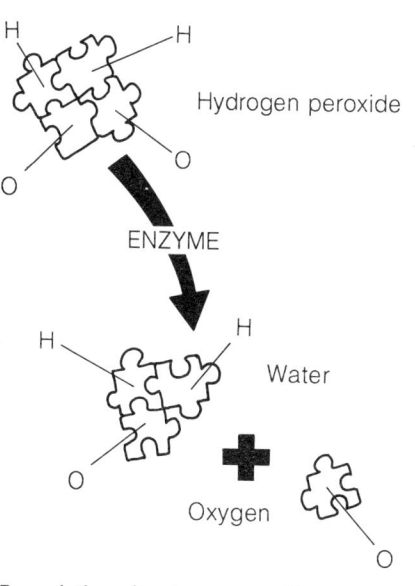

Degradation of hydrogen peroxide

What are Enzymes?

Substances which speed up chemical reactions are called **catalysts**. Catalysts are often used in the chemical industry. The photograph shows a **catalytic cracker** in which catalysts are used to produce petrol from oil.

Living cells have their own natural catalysts. These are called enzymes. You may have seen **biological washing powders** in the supermarket. These powders contain enzymes which are used to break down natural stains such as blood, egg and grass.

An Enzyme Which Degrades

Catalase is a degrading enzyme found in almost all living cells. This enzyme breaks down a cell waste called **hydrogen peroxide** into the harmless substances oxygen and water, as the diagram shows. The hydrogen peroxide is known as the **substrate** and the water and oxygen are known as the **products**. The enzyme is not destroyed by the reaction and can be used again and again.

A piece of living tissue such as liver may be sliced to break open some of its cells. The slice is dropped into a beaker of hydrogen peroxide. Catalase from the liver cells starts to break down the hydrogen peroxide and lots of bubbles of oxygen are seen in the beaker, as shown in the photographs.

Catalytic cracker

The effect of liver on hydrogen peroxide

Enzymes Which Synthesise

Green plants make glucose during the process of photosynthesis. The glucose dissolves very easily in water, and for this reason the plants cannot store their extra glucose. Instead, they build up the glucose into starch, an insoluble substance which is easy to store.

The glucose is synthesised into starch by an enzyme called potato **phosphorylase**. In the underground tubers of potato plants, this enzyme builds small glucose molecules made by the potato leaves into larger starch molecules. The diagram of potato cells shows stored starch grains.

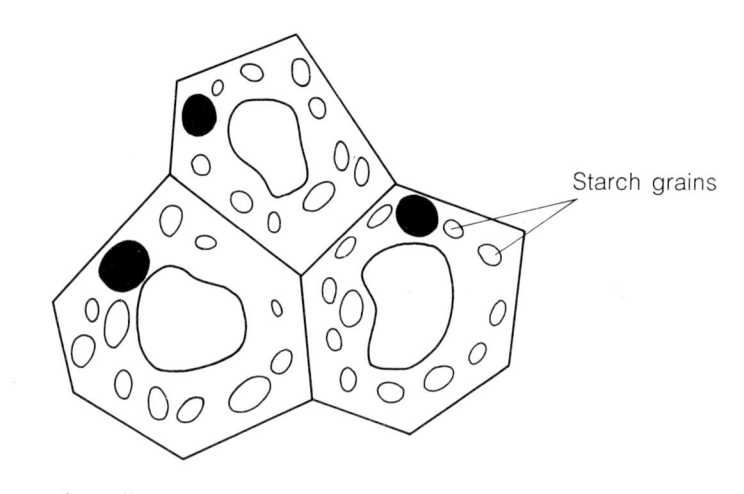

Potato tuber cells

Obtaining Potato Phosphorylase

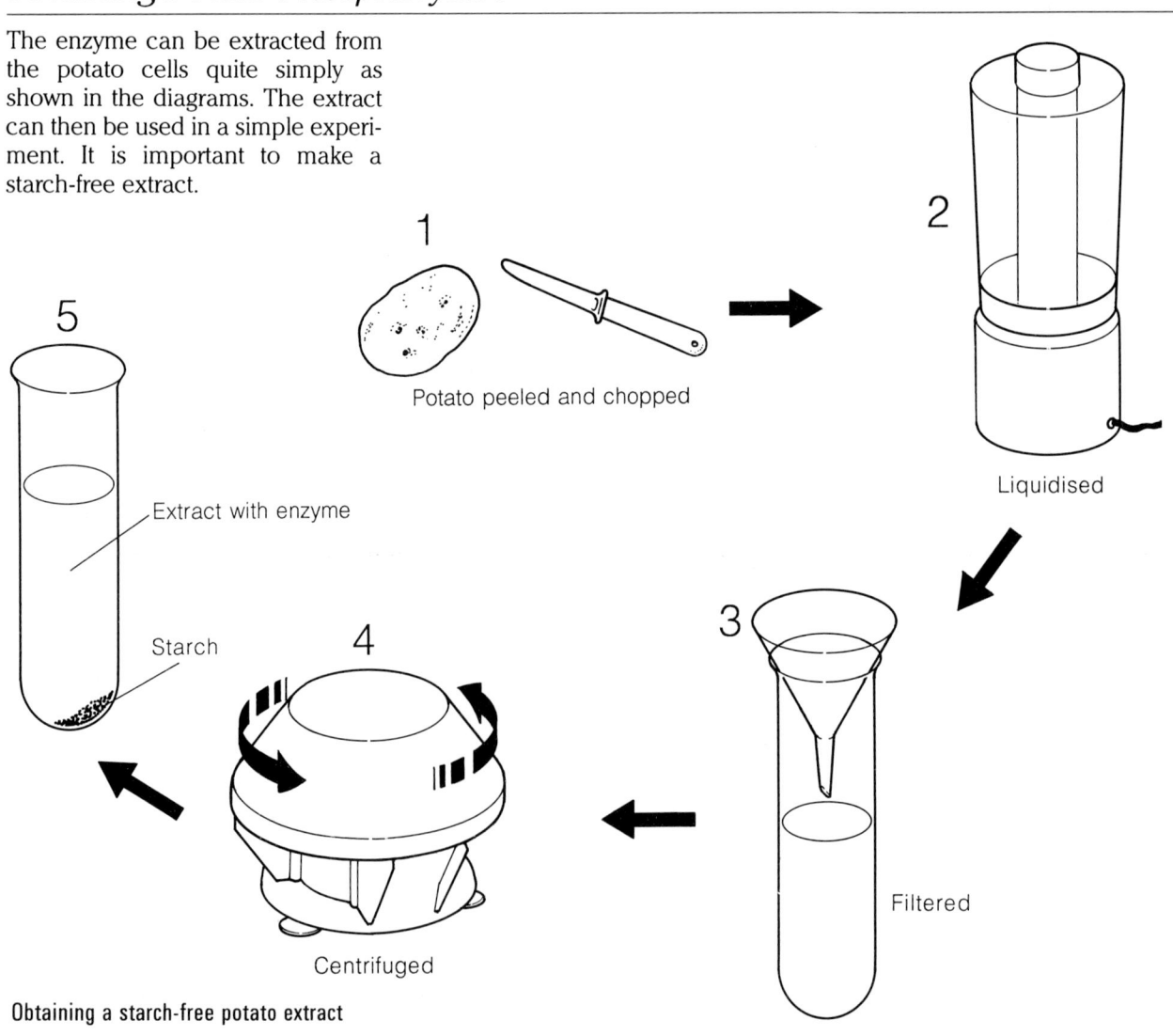

The enzyme can be extracted from the potato cells quite simply as shown in the diagrams. The extract can then be used in a simple experiment. It is important to make a starch-free extract.

1 Potato peeled and chopped

2 Liquidised

3 Filtered

4 Centrifuged

5 Extract with enzyme / Starch

Obtaining a starch-free potato extract

An Experiment with the Extract

The diagrams show a simple experiment which can be done with the potato extract.

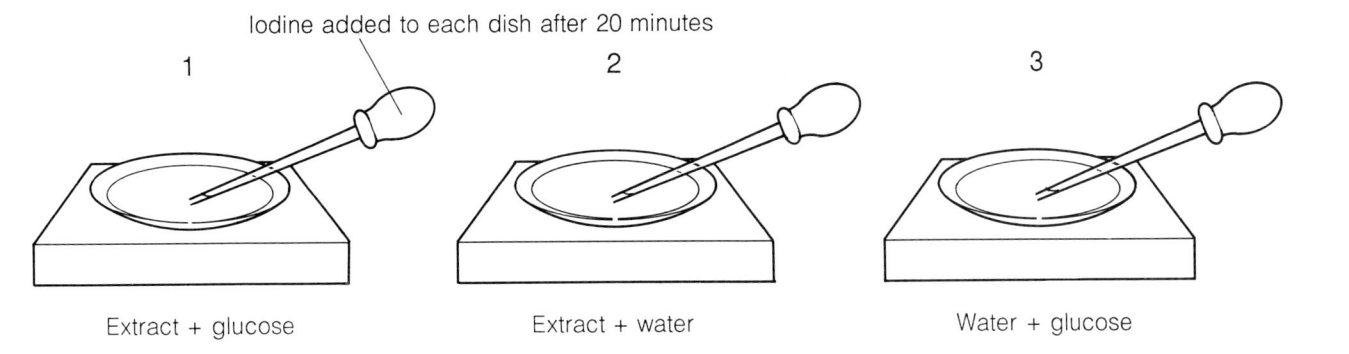

Iodine added to each dish after 20 minutes

1 — Extract + glucose
2 — Extract + water
3 — Water + glucose

Controls

After 30 minutes the contents of the dishes are tested to see if any starch has been made. To check for the presence of starch, **iodine solution** is added to the dishes. If starch has been made then the iodine solution will turn a blue-black colour.

Dishes 2 and 3 are controls. Dish 2 shows that the extract is starch free. Dish 3 shows that glucose will not change into starch by itself.

Dish no.	Iodine colour	Starch
1	Blue-black	Yes
2	Brown	No
3	Brown	No

A student's notebook

108 INVESTIGATING CELLS

Why are Enzymes Needed?

If enzymes were not present in cell cytoplasm, reactions such as the breakdown of hydrogen peroxide would be very slow. If the peroxide were not broken down fast enough it might accumulate and poison the cell. Just think what peroxide does to hair!

How Enzymes Work

It is helpful to try to imagine how an enzyme might actually carry out its job. Think of enzymes as having particular shapes – like keys. These shapes exactly fit the shape of the substrate just as a key exactly fits the shape of a lock.

The enzyme identifies its substrate by shape. The enzyme is said to be **specific** for its substrate. After the enzyme has fitted to its substrate, it changes the substrate into the products very quickly. Following the change the enzyme comes away from the products and is ready to start again. An enzyme can be used many times just as a key can open a lock many times.

Enzyme "key"

Substrate

The "key" fits the substrate exactly

"Key" unchanged

Product formed

Activities

1. What is meant by the term "catalyst"?
2. Name an enzyme which breaks down its substrate.
3. Name an enzyme which builds up its substrate.
4. A small piece of liver is added to a test tube of hydrogen peroxide to which a drop or two of washing-up liquid had been added. A lot of foam is produced in the test tube. When a glowing splint was put into the foam it was seen to relight.

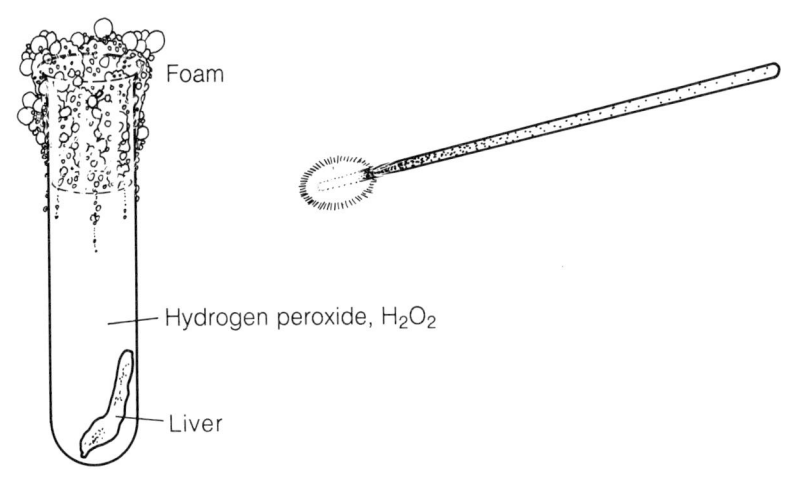

   (a) What has made the foam appear?
   (b) What gas is in the foam bubbles?
   (c) Why was the washing-up liquid used in the experiment?

5. Describe the lock and key idea of enzyme action in your own words.
6. Why do cells need enzymes?
7. What is meant by the word "specific" when applied to enzyme action?
8. The following experiment was set up to investigate catalase activity in different tissues.

   Catalase breaks down hydrogen peroxide into water and oxygen. Catalase activity can be measured by amount of oxygen produced.

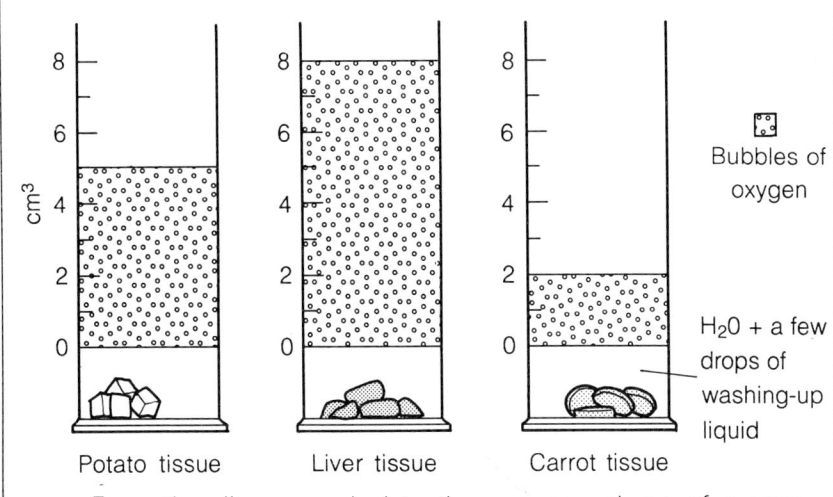

   From the diagram, calculate the average volume of oxygen produced by potato, liver and carrot.

6 More About Enzymes

> ### Key Ideas
>
> Enzymes are made of delicate chemicals called *proteins*. If the protein is damaged in any way, the enzyme will not work properly. This means that in the wrong *pH* or *temperature* conditions enzyme activity will be reduced.

Enzymes in Barley Grains

Barley grains store starch which they use for food during germination. To be of use the starch must be degraded to sugar. During germination the grain uses an enzyme called **diastase** to convert the starch to **malt sugar**. Malt sugar is usually known as **maltose**.

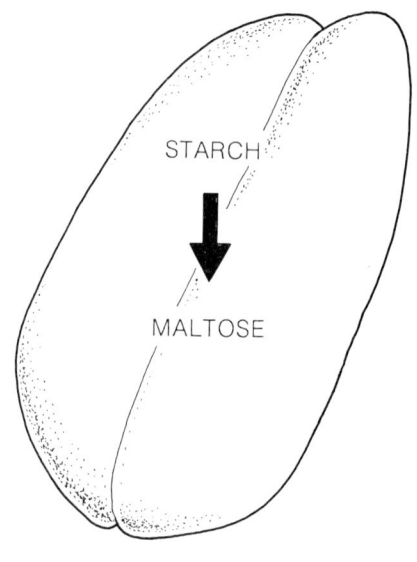

Diagram of a barley grain

Diastase and Temperature

The diastase is a protein which is very delicate and is affected by heat. The demonstration shown on page 111 is repeated at a range of temperatures including 10°C and 60°C. Each dish contains starch jelly with a well cut into the centre. The wells are filled with diastase.

The extent of the degraded starch in each dish is estimated by measuring the diameter of the clear area around the well. The results are plotted on the graph also shown on page 111. It can be seen that the enzyme does not work very well in the extreme conditions. At high temperatures the enzyme is permanently damaged or **denatured**.

Diastase at Work

A germinating barley grain can be cut in half with a sharp scalpel. The cut surface is pushed down into a starch jelly in a shallow petri dish and left for 24 hours. Diastase will leak out of the grain and into the starch jelly, breaking down some of the starch into maltose.

If the plate is flooded with iodine solution, the area around the grain does not turn blue-black because the starch would have been degraded by the enzyme.

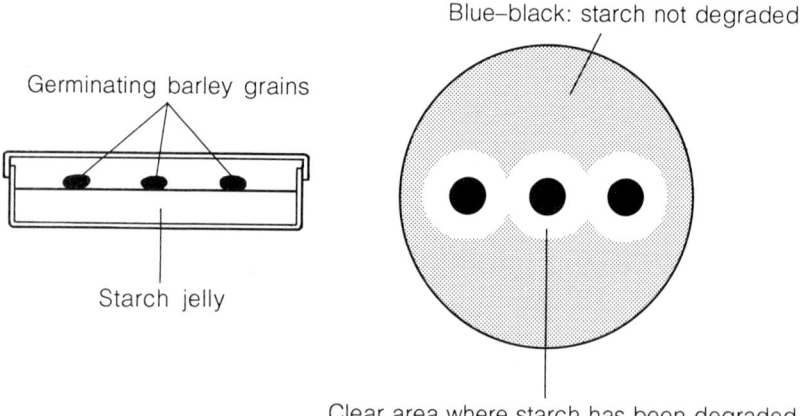

A barley grain experiment

INVESTIGATING CELLS 111

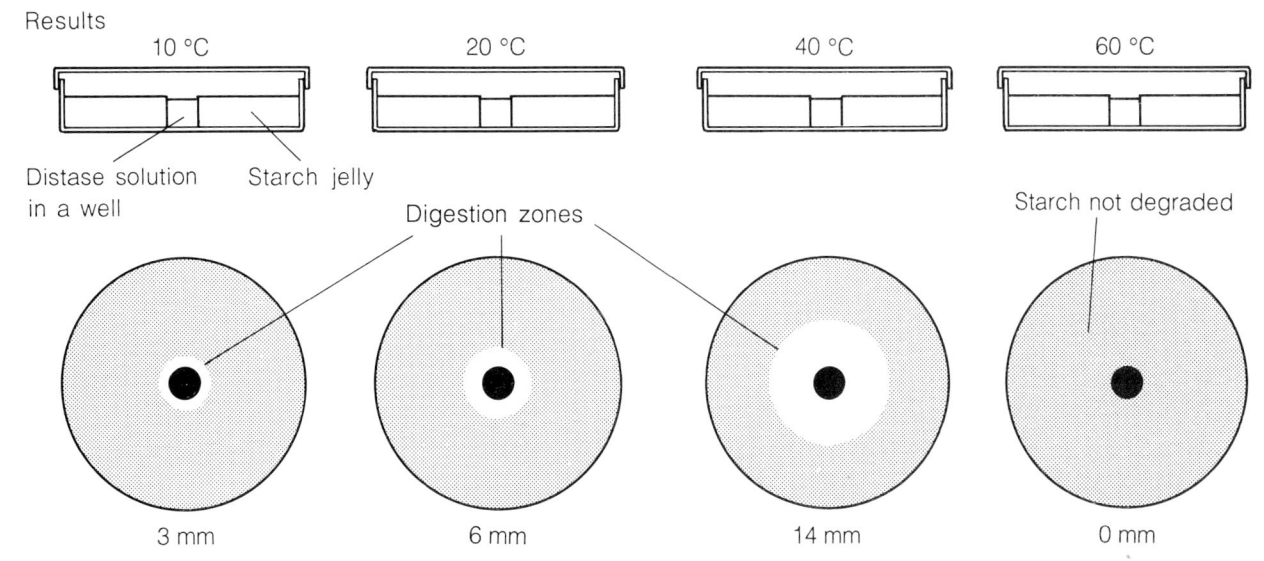

Results

10 °C   20 °C   40 °C   60 °C

Distase solution in a well — Starch jelly

Digestion zones

Starch not degraded

3 mm   6 mm   14 mm   0 mm

Diastase and temperature experiment

Diastase and pH

Acidity and alkalinity are measured on a special scale called the pH scale. The scale has 14 points with 1 the most acid and 14 the most alkaline. Point 7 is taken as neutral.

Some starch jelly plates are made at different pHs by adding special chemicals called **buffers** to them. Wells are cut in the jelly as before, and diastase solution is placed in each well. The plates are incubated at 40°C.

The amount of starch degradation is found to relate to the pH of the jelly. Diastase, like most enzymes, works best at about neutral pH.

Pepsin from mammal stomachs works best in acid conditions about pH 2.

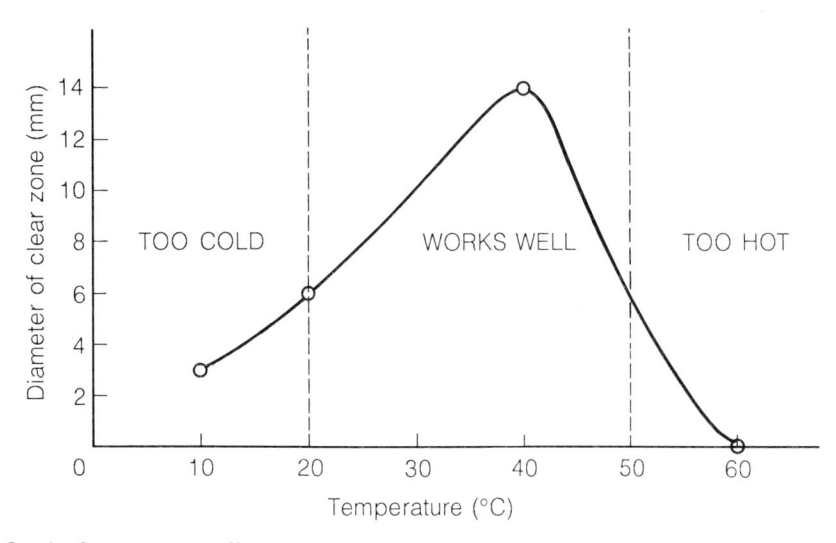

Graph of temperature effect

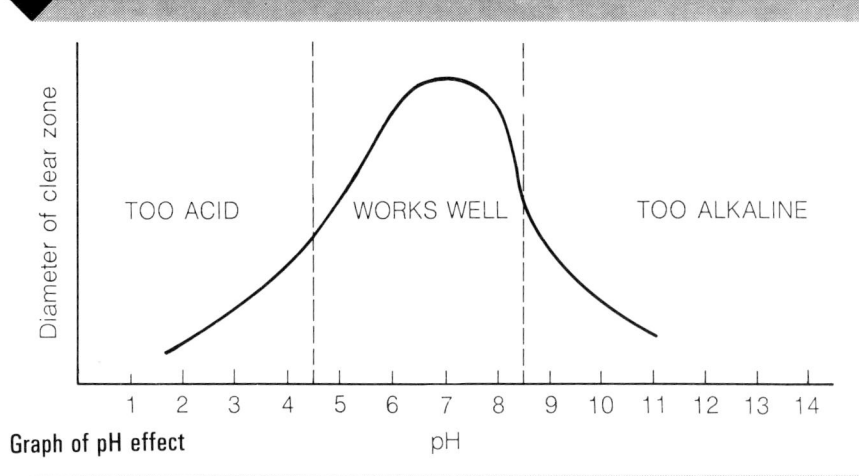

TOO COLD — WORKS WELL — TOO HOT

Graph of pH effect

TOO ACID — WORKS WELL — TOO ALKALINE

Enzyme Shape

Enzymes have a special shape. If the shape of the enzyme is altered by damage due to extremes of pH or temperature, then the enzyme will not be able to do its job, just as a key which has been bent or twisted will not be able to open a lock. The temperature or pH at which an enzyme works best is called its **optimum** temperature or pH.

112 INVESTIGATING CELLS

Activities

1. What are enzymes made of?
2. Name the starch-degrading enzyme from barley grain cells.
3. What is the product of the activity of this enzyme?
4. Study the diagram showing the diastase and temperature experiment on page 111. What would be a suitable temperature to germinate barley grains at? Why would this temperature be suitable?
5. What is measured on the pH scale?
6. At which pH do most enzymes work best?
7. Plot these figures for a starch jelly diastase experiment on a piece of graph paper.

Temperature	Diameter of Clear Zone (mm)
0	0
10	3
20	6
30	14
40	17
50	4
60	0

8. Pepsin is an enzyme produced by cells which line the stomach of mammals. This graph shows how its activity varies with pH.
   (a) What is the optimum pH for this enzyme?
   (b) Other cells in the stomach lining produce acid. Why is this useful for the action of pepsin?

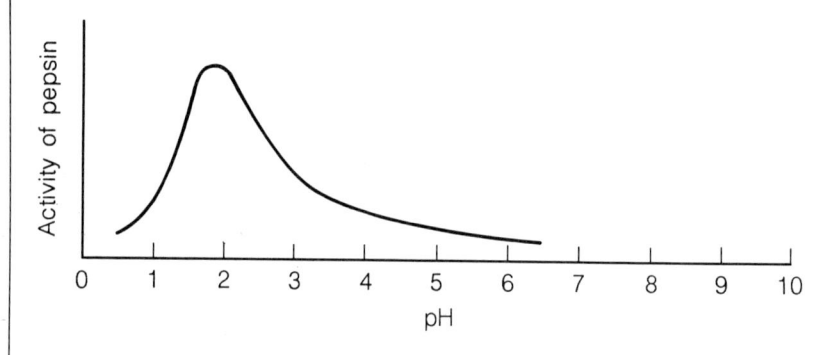

9. What is meant by the term "optimum"?

7 Cells and Energy

Key Ideas

All cells require energy to stay alive. This energy is obtained from food. Plant cells are able to make their own food using the energy from sunlight. Animal cells obtain foods in a ready-made form when the animal eats.

Energy is released from the food in a process called *respiration*. The chemical energy released during respiration can be converted into other forms of energy such as heat and movement.

Uses of Energy

All living cells need energy for growth, cell division and for carrying out chemical reactions.

Plants and Energy

Green plants are able to trap the energy they need from sunlight. They absorb the light and the energy is converted to chemical energy in the products of photosynthesis. The plant cells can release this energy as they need it during respiration.

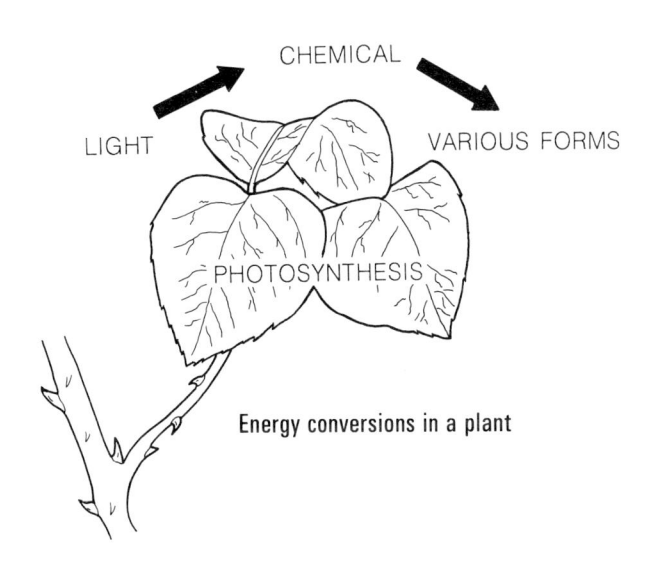

Energy conversions in a plant

Animals and Energy

Animals must eat ready-made food. They are able to release the chemical energy from their food during the process of respiration.

Think about the cells of the human body shown in the diagram. Each of these cells has a special job to do. Each cell will release chemical energy from food during respiration and convert it to the form of energy it needs.

Cells	Job	Energy released
Brain	Coordination	Electrical
Liver	Chemical reactions	Heat
Muscle	Motion	Movement

Energy conversions in a human

114 INVESTIGATING CELLS

Energy Foods

The hamburger shown in the drawing consists of different food types. Each type can supply a certain amount of energy per gram. Energy is measured in kilojoules (kJ). The bread is mainly **carbohydrate** which provides 17 kJ per gram. The butter is mainly **fat** which provides 39 kJ per gram. If the meat is lean it will be mainly **protein**. Protein provides about 17 kJ per gram.

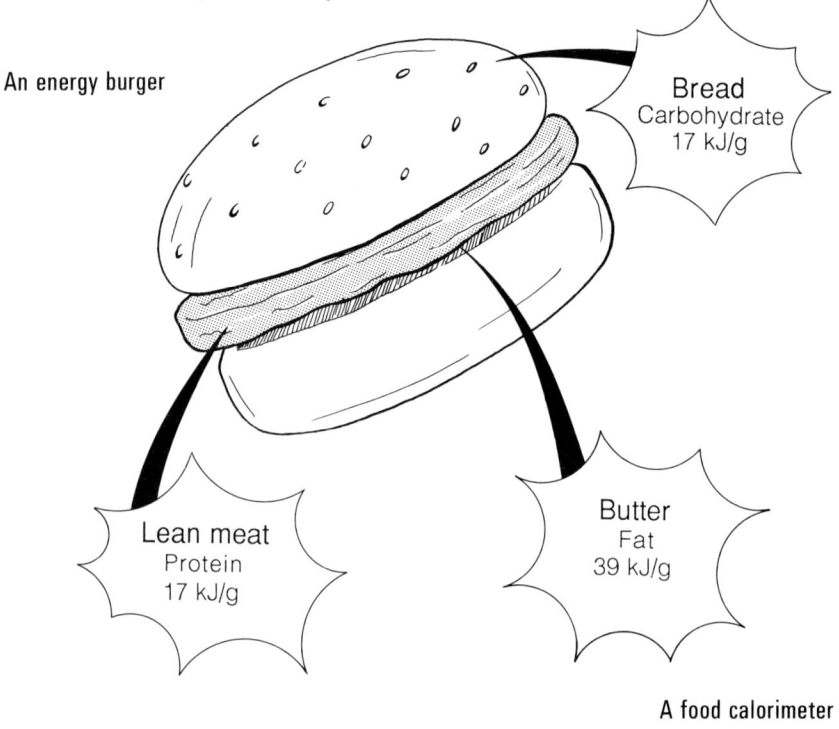

An energy burger

Bread
Carbohydrate
17 kJ/g

Lean meat
Protein
17 kJ/g

Butter
Fat
39 kJ/g

A food calorimeter

What's in a Kilojoule?

One kilojoule is enough energy to raise the temperature of 4.2 litres of water by 1 degree Celsius.

The energy of foods can be tested experimentally using equipment called a **calorimeter**. In the calorimeter, food is burned in pure oxygen and the heat energy given up is used to heat a known volume of water. The rise in temperature of the water is carefully measured.

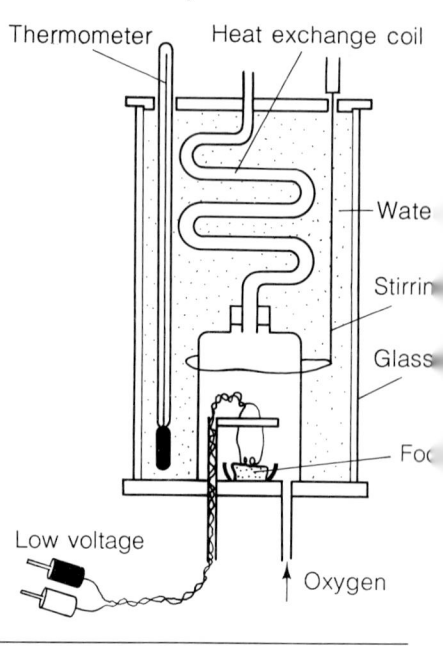

Thermometer   Heat exchange coil

Wate

Stirrin

Glass

Foc

Low voltage

Oxygen

The Energy Values of Human Foods

Most everyday foods are mixtures of carbohydrate, protein and fat. Oils are liquid fats. This table lists some everyday foods and their approximate energy values per gram.

Food From Plants	Energy Value (kJ per g)
bread	10.6
plain cake	18.0
breakfast flakes	15.3
rice	15.1
spaghetti	15.3
potato	3.2
baked beans	3.9
onion	1.0
carrot	0.8
cabbage	0.8
peas	2.0
tomato	0.6
lettuce	0.5
apple	1.9
banana	3.2
orange	1.5
pear	1.7
strawberries	1.1
peach	1.6
peanuts	24.6
olive oil	39.0

Food From Animals	Energy Value (kJ per g)
beef	10.2
chicken	7.8
liver	8.4
pork	21.0
bacon	20.0
sausage	15.3
white fish	4.0
sardines	6.7
butter	31.3
cheese	17.3
milk	2.7
eggs	6.6

Activities

1. Give three uses of energy in living cells.
2. Write down the energy change which takes place in plant cells during photosynthesis.
3. Write down the energy change which takes place in the muscle cells of an athlete during a race.
4. Which class of foodstuff contains the most energy per gram?
5. A one gram sample of food is burned in a food calorimeter. The calorimeter contains 500 cm³ of water. The temperature of the water is raised from 15°C to 21°C.
   Calculate the energy value of the food in kilojoules.
6. Work out the total energy value of the following snack using the information in the chapter.

   Chicken sandwich with salad – 50 g chicken
   – 100 g bread
   – 10 g butter
   – 20 g tomato
   – 20 g lettuce
   Glass of milk – 100 g milk
   Piece of cake – 30 g plain cake
   Apple – 100 g apple

7. A student tries to work out the energy value of a peanut by doing an experiment as shown in this drawing. Criticise the experimental method used.

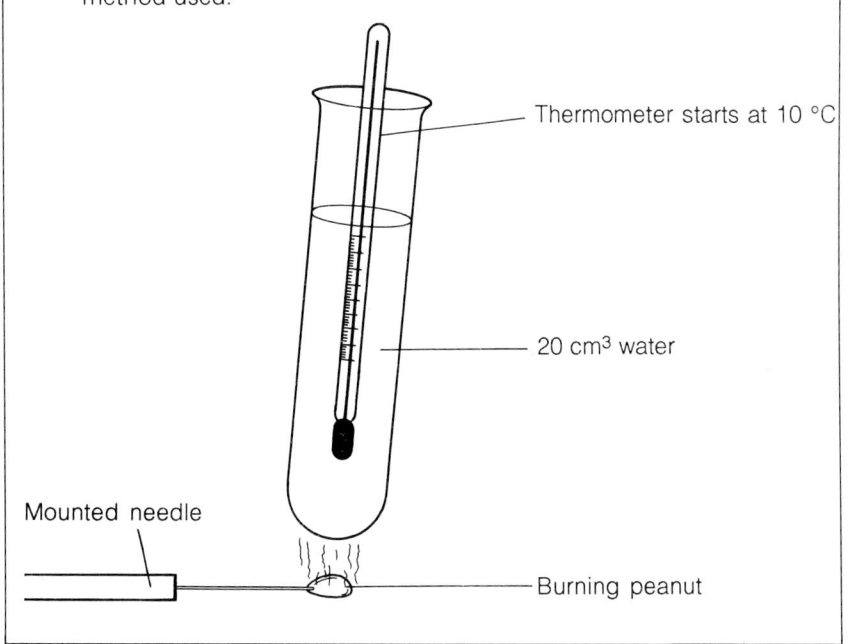

   Thermometer starts at 10 °C
   20 cm³ water
   Mounted needle
   Burning peanut

8 Aerobic Respiration in Cells

Key Ideas

During the process of *aerobic respiration* of foods, cells use oxygen from their environment. They produce the waste products carbon dioxide and water and release the energy from the food. Experiments can confirm that respiring tissues do indeed use up oxygen, release carbon dioxide and release energy.

The Word Equation for Aerobic Respiration

If all the requirements and the products of aerobic respiration are combined together they form a **word equation**. The word equation is shown below:

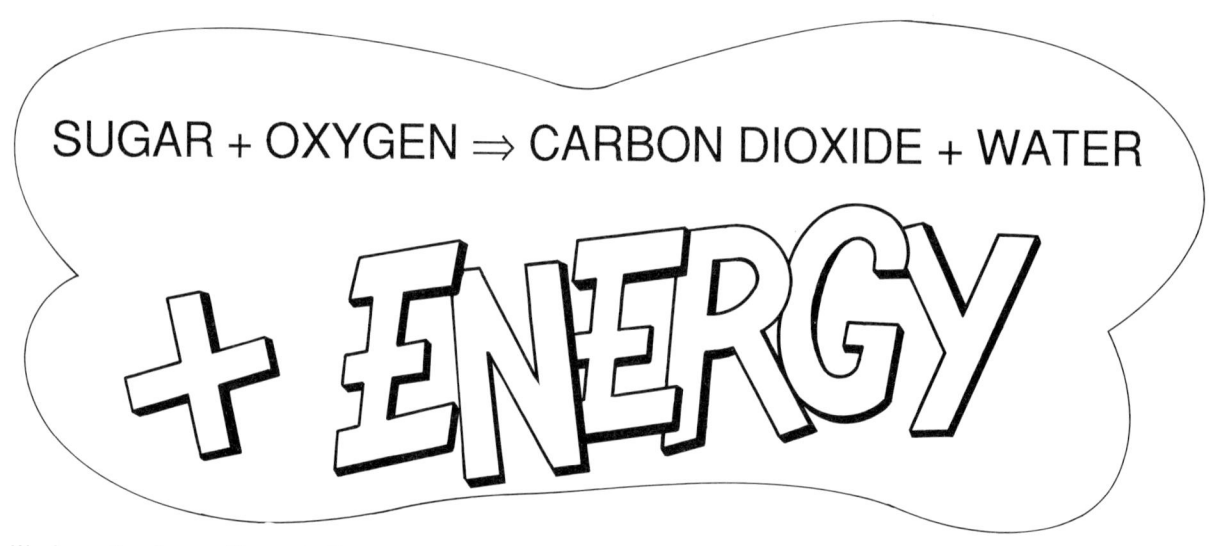

SUGAR + OXYGEN ⇒ CARBON DIOXIDE + WATER + ENERGY

Word equation for aerobic respiration

The Use of Oxygen

A **respirometer** can be used to show that living organisms remove oxygen from the air during respiration. A simple respirometer is shown in the diagram. If this respirometer is left for 24 hours the level of the coloured liquid in the fine tube rises from point **X** to point **Y** on the scale. The *soda lime* is a mixture of chemicals which absorb any carbon dioxide produced by the small animals. The control for this experiment can be set up using the same respirometer apparatus but not including the small animals.

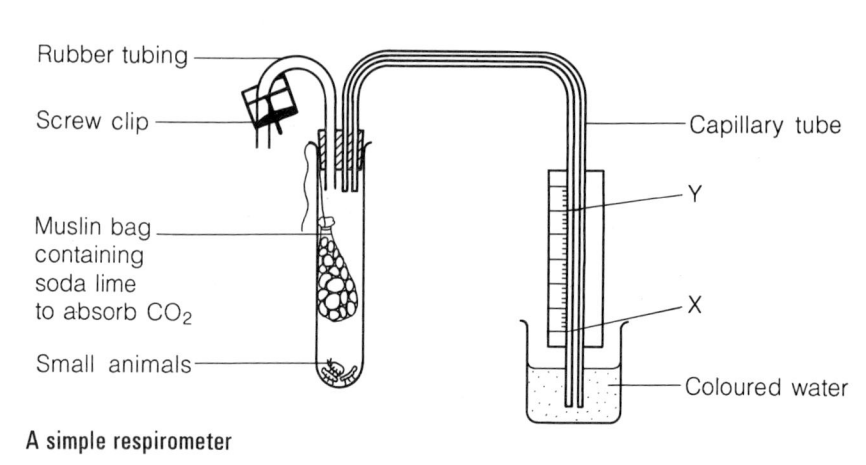

A simple respirometer

INVESTIGATING CELLS

The Production of Carbon Dioxide

An experiment such as that shown in the diagram above will show that respiring cells produce carbon dioxide. The **bicarbonate indicator** used in the experiment is a test for the amount of carbon dioxide present.

Amount of CO_2	Indicator Colour
none	purple
little	rosy red
a lot	yellow

If the experiment is left set up for 24 hours the indicator in the experimental tube will turn yellow.

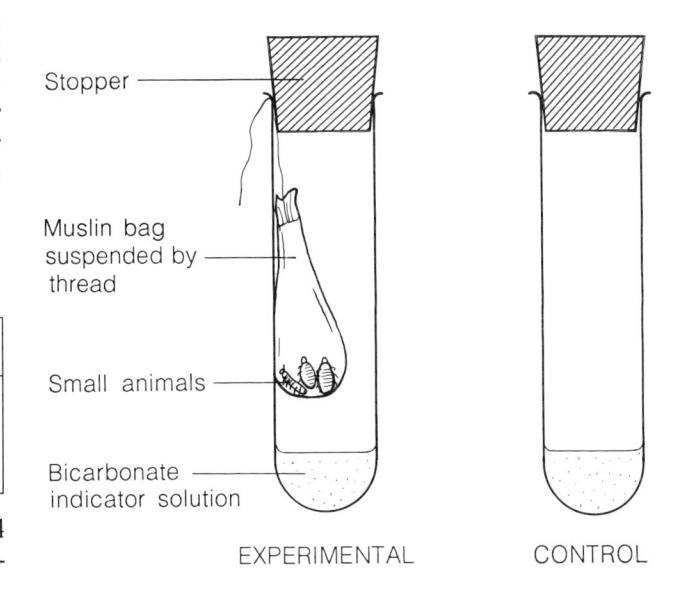

Labels: Stopper; Muslin bag suspended by thread; Small animals; Bicarbonate indicator solution

EXPERIMENTAL   CONTROL

A bicarbonate indicator experiment with control

The Release of Energy

The release of heat energy by respiring pea seeds can be shown by the experiment in the diagram. After 24 hours the temperature on the thermometer had gone up by 5 degrees Celsius.

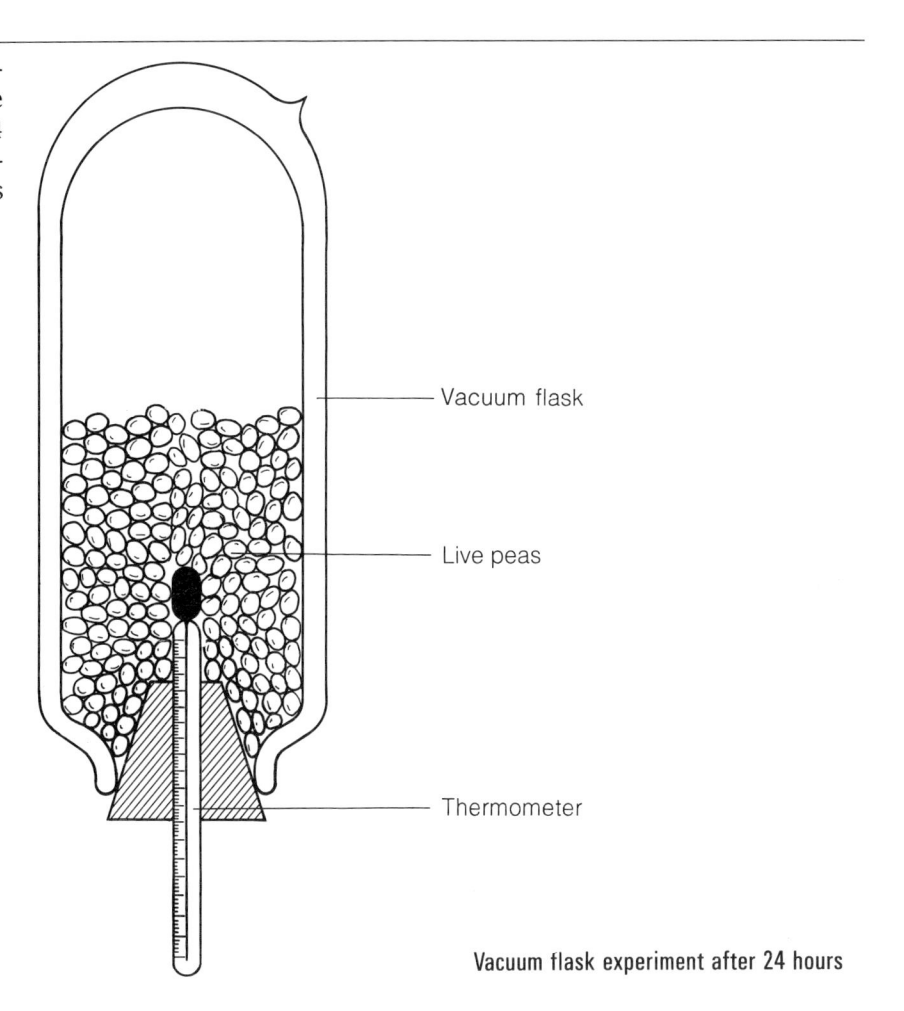

Labels: Vacuum flask; Live peas; Thermometer

Vacuum flask experiment after 24 hours

118 INVESTIGATING CELLS

Energy and Metabolism

As we have already seen, many chemical reactions take place inside the cells of living organisms. If this chemistry stops for any reason the organisms will die. All of the reactions together are known as **metabolism**.

Some of the chemical reactions build up new compounds. An example is the synthesis of starch by the enzyme phosphorylase in potato cells. Synthesis reactions require energy to make them happen.

Some other reactions involve the breakdown of compounds. An example of a breakdown reaction is respiration, sugar being broken down into carbon dioxide and water. These degradation reactions release energy. The energy-release reactions are vitally important because they supply the energy for the synthesis reactions in cells.

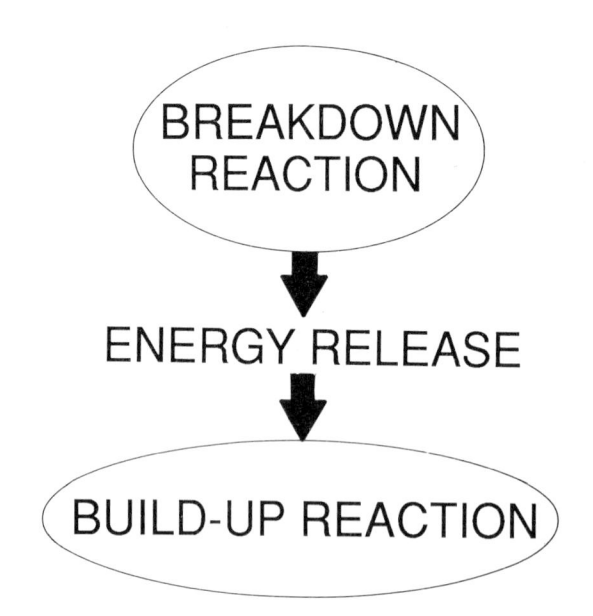

BREAKDOWN REACTION
↓
ENERGY RELEASE
↓
BUILD-UP REACTION

Metabolism diagram

Activities

○ 1 Write the word equation for respiration.

○ 2 Predict what would happen to the drop of coloured liquid in the respirometer shown here. Why would this happen?

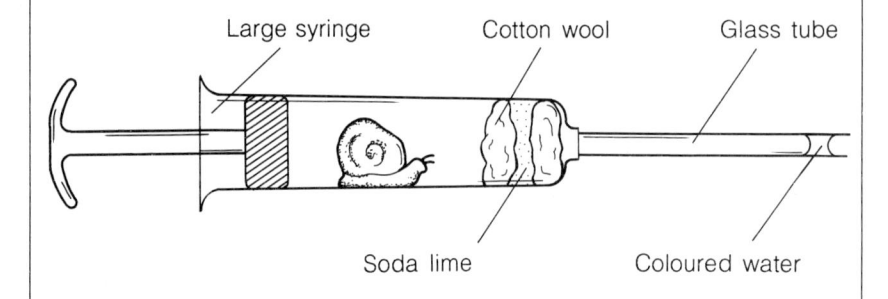

Large syringe — Cotton wool — Glass tube
Soda lime — Coloured water

○ 3 Try to explain why a control is needed in the experiment using a respirometer on page 116.

○ 4 Study the control in the bicarbonate indicator experiment on page 117. Try to explain why the control is needed.

○ 5 Study the vacuum flask experiment shown on page 117.
 (a) Why is a vacuum flask used instead of a glass flask?
 (b) Why is the vacuum flask held upside down?

● 6 What is meant by the word "metabolism"?

● 7 Explain the importance of degradation reactions such as respiration for the metabolism of cells.

1 Food and Energy

Key Ideas

The food we eat provides us with our *energy*. This energy allows us to do many things including moving about. Different types of food provide different amounts of energy. *Fats* provide twice as much energy per gram as *carbohydrate*.

Energy taken into the body must balance the energy used in activity. If the input is bigger than the output, *obesity* can result. If the input is too small to meet the minimum requirements, then *starvation* results. The amount of energy required by an individual depends on many factors such as age, sex, body size, and activity.

Human Energy Requirements

Each person needs a different daily energy intake. This is measured in **kilojoules**. The minimum intake is found to be about 9500 kJ per day. The figure for a particular individual depends on factors such as age, sex and level of activity. The diagram shows how the energy requirements of humans vary.

person	age	kJ per day
baby	0–1	4 200
child	2–6	6 800
boy	7–11	9 650
	12–15	12 000
girl	7–11	9 200
	12–15	9 600
male	adult at rest	7 300
	light work	11 550
	heavy work	14 700
female	adult at rest	6 300
	light work	9 450
	heavy work	12 600
	breast feeding	11 300
senior citizen	65 +	9 000

Human energy requirements

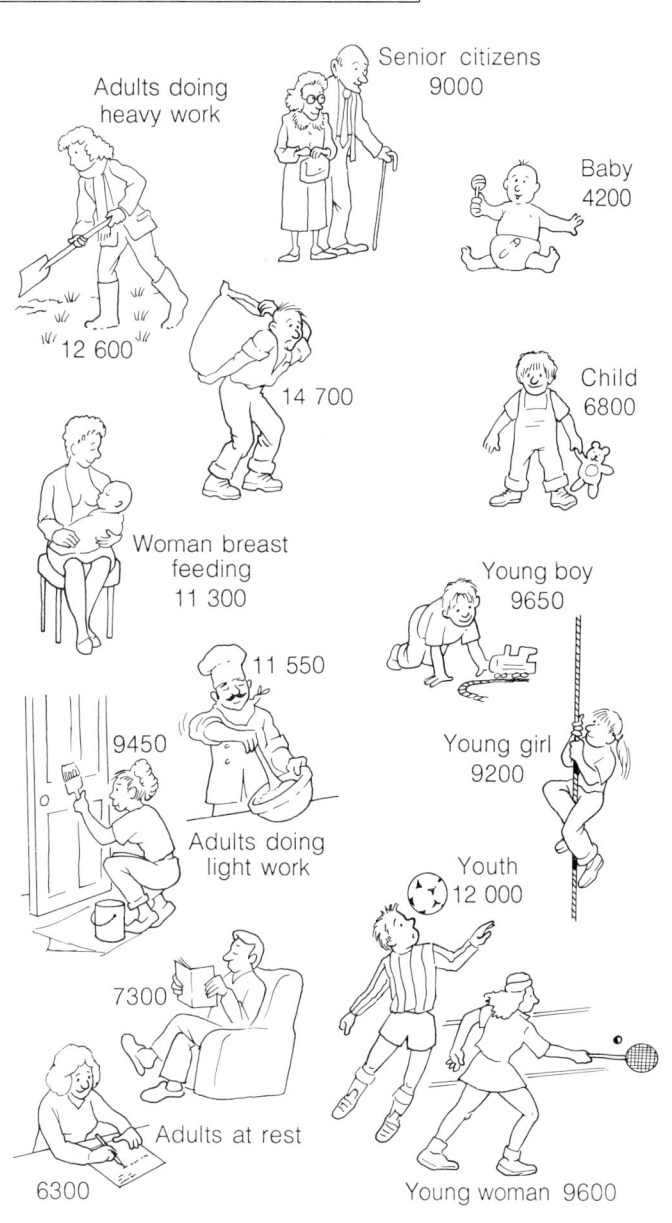

Energy through life

- Adults doing heavy work 12 600
- Senior citizens 9000
- Baby 4200
- 14 700
- Child 6800
- Woman breast feeding 11 300
- 11 550
- Young boy 9650
- 9450
- Young girl 9200
- Adults doing light work
- Youth 12 000
- 7300
- Adults at rest 6300
- Young woman 9600

The Body in Action

120 THE BODY IN ACTION

Eating Too Much

What happens if someone eats more food than they need? The extra food will be turned into fat and stored below the skin. The person will be overweight and look fat. This is called obesity.

Obese people can reduce their weight by dieting or by exercising and using more energy. To reduce weight it is usually best to combine these two methods.

An overweight person has more chance of having a **stroke** or a heart attack because the heart has too much strain put on it.

A day in the life

Eating Too Little

If a person eats too little they will begin to lose weight. At first they will use up fat. If they continue eating too little their muscle tissue will be used up as an energy source. Eventually a person could die. This would take an adult about 9 weeks without any food at all. The wasting away of the body through starvation is called **marasmus**.

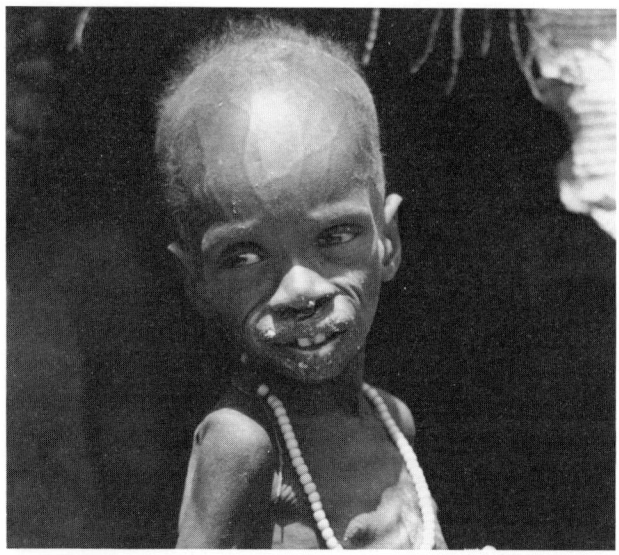

The effects of marasmus in children

Activities

1. Which type of food provides the most energy per gram?
2. List the factors which affect the energy requirements of a human.
3. Draw a bar chart of the energy requirement figures given in the table on the previous page.
4. What is meant by
    (a) obesity
    (b) marasmus?

2 Breathing

Key Ideas

The release of energy from food usually needs oxygen from the air. Carbon dioxide gas is produced as a waste product of the release of the energy and must be removed from the body. Mammals exchange these two gases during breathing. They have special organs called lungs in the chest which are designed to allow these gases to be exchanged between the air and the bloodstream.

The Gases of the Air

The table shows the percentage of different gases in the air and in breathed out air. It shows that oxygen gas is removed from the air and carbon dioxide is added to the air during breathing.

The oxygen is used in a chemical reaction called **respiration**. Respiration takes place in all living cells. It is controlled by enzymes and results in the release of energy from food. Waste products of respiration are carbon dioxide and water.

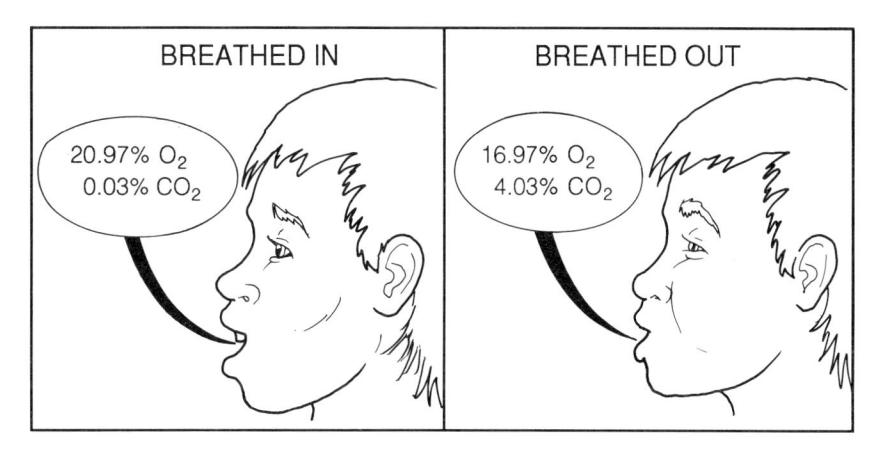

BREATHED IN: 20.97% O_2, 0.03% CO_2

BREATHED OUT: 16.97% O_2, 4.03% CO_2

Sample	% O_2	% CO_2	% N_2 and others
air	20.97	0.03	79.00
exhaled breath	16.97	4.03	79.00

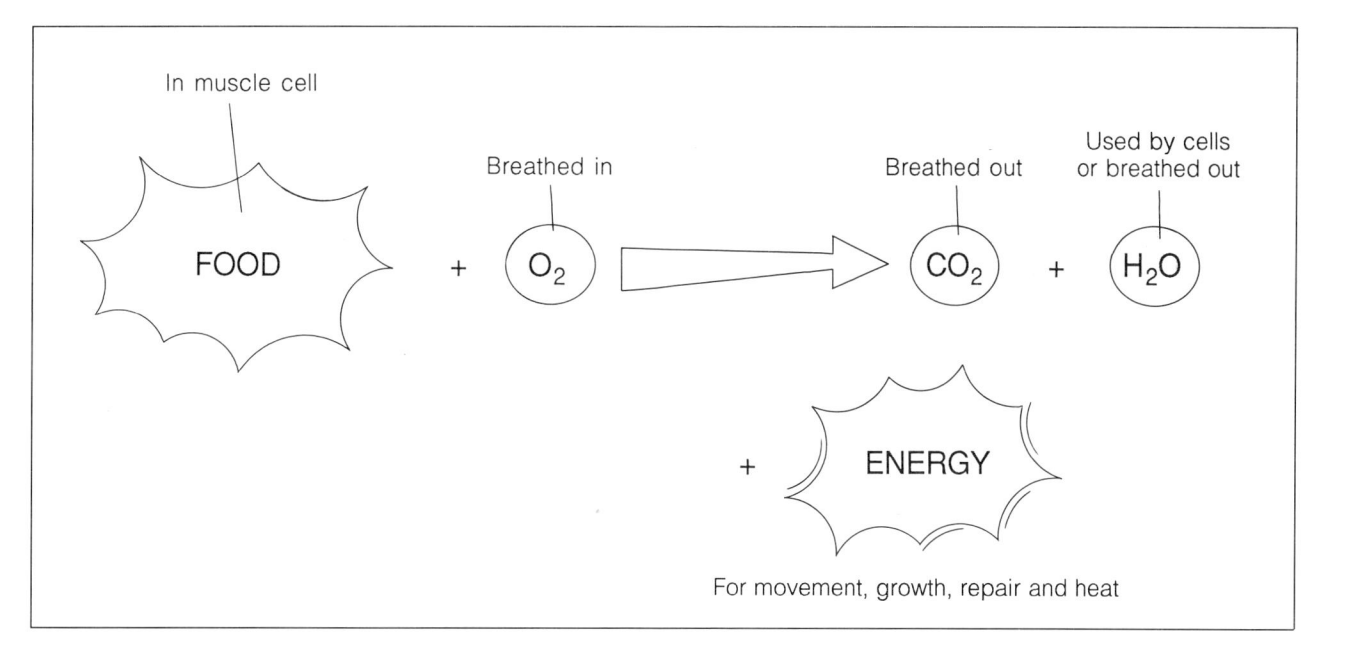

In muscle cell

FOOD + O_2 (Breathed in) → CO_2 (Breathed out) + H_2O (Used by cells or breathed out) + ENERGY

For movement, growth, repair and heat

122 THE BODY IN ACTION

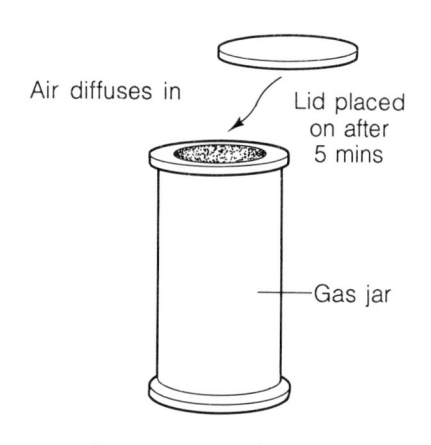

Collecting atmospheric air

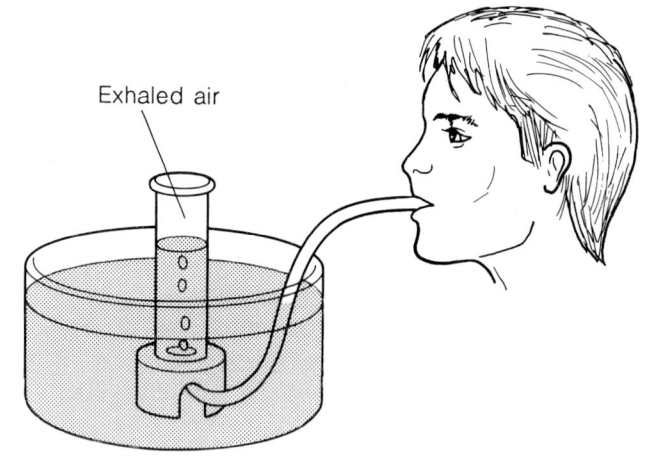

Collecting exhaled air

Oxygen

It is easy to collect samples of atmospheric air and breathed air, as shown in the diagrams.

Oxygen is needed to allow burning. When the oxygen runs out burning stops. By estimating how long a candle burns in each of the gas jars, a rough idea of the amount of oxygen present can be obtained. A candle will burn for a few seconds in a jar of atmospheric air. In a jar of breathed air the candle will go out almost at once.

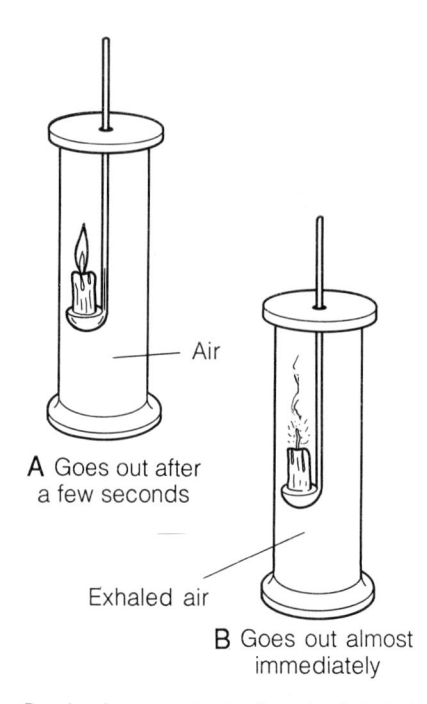

A Goes out after a few seconds

B Goes out almost immediately

Burning in atmospheric air and exhaled air

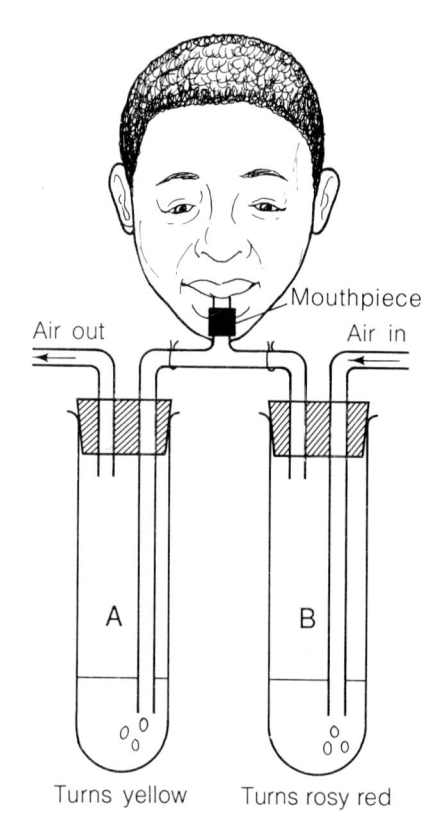

Carbon dioxide

The apparatus in the diagram can be used to show the carbon dioxide differences in breathed and unbreathed air.

Bicarbonate Indicator

Indicator colour	Carbon dioxide
purple/dark red	zero
rosy red	a little
yellow	a lot

Turns yellow   Turns rosy red

Activities

1. Draw a pie chart to show the composition of exhaled air (use the data in the table on page 121).
2. Write the word equation for respiration.
3. Give two ways in which the energy released during respiration is used by the body.
4. Sketch the apparatus for burning a candle in atmospheric and exhaled air. Explain why the candle goes out almost right away in jar **B** and stays alight for a few seconds in jar **A**.
5. Describe the effect of carbon dioxide on bicarbonate indicator.

3 The Lungs

Key Ideas

Lungs are special organs in mammals used for gas exchange. Air is taken into the lungs through a series of branching tubes. The widest of these tubes are held open by rings of *cartilage*. The thinnest branching tubes end in structures called *air sacs*. Here gases are exchanged between the blood and the air.

The Passage of Air

During breathing, air is drawn into the nostrils to the **nasal cavity**. From there it passes into the **pharynx** and on to the windpipe or **trachea**. The air then enters each lung through branches of the windpipe called **bronchi** (singular **bronchus**). Each bronchus splits into numerous bronchioles. The smallest bronchioles end in swellings called **air sacs**. An air sac is made up from several **alveoli** (singular **alveolus**). The huge numbers of alveoli in each lung provide a very large surface area for gas exchange.

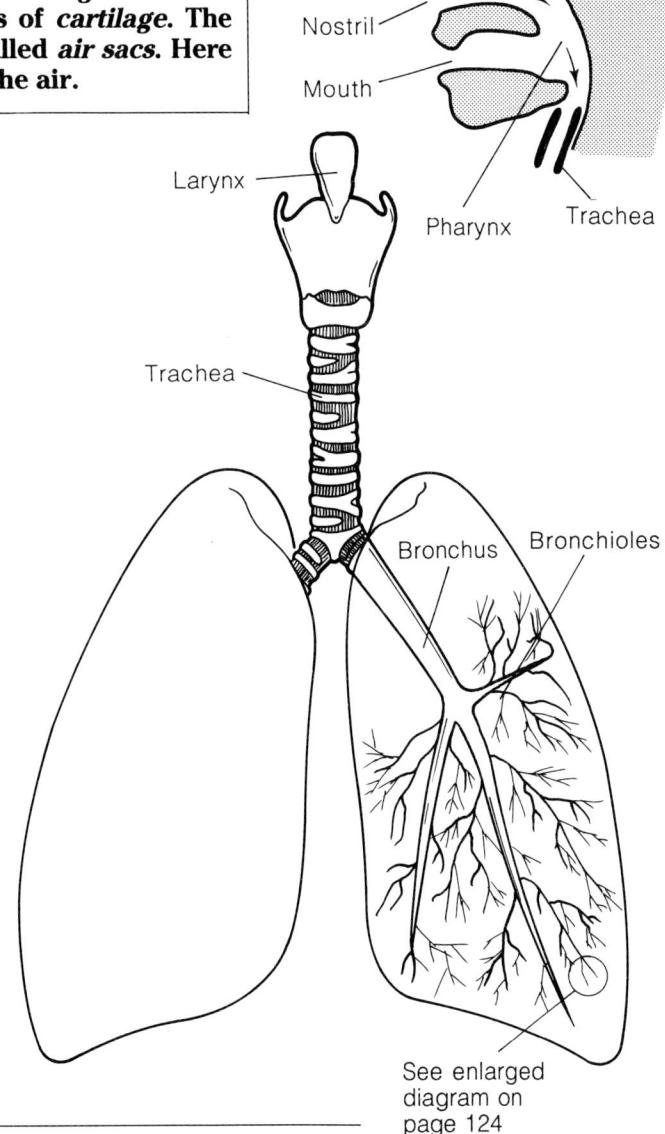

The Need for Cartilage

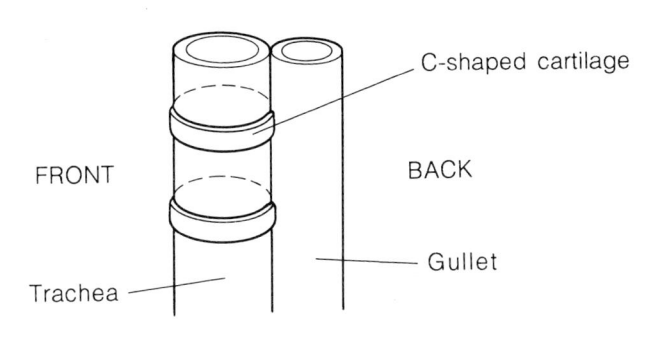

The tube you can feel at the front of your neck is the trachea. Your gullet lies behind this. You can feel rings of a substance called cartilage. These rings support the windpipe and bronchi and hold them open. The rings in the trachea are not quite complete but are C-shaped. The open parts of the C allow the gullet to enlarge so that food can pass down it during swallowing.

124   THE BODY IN ACTION

The Air Sacs

The drawing on the right circles one air sac. The sac can be seen to be made up of many alveoli.

A branch of a bronchiole

- Bronchiole
- Alveolus
- One air sac

The Alveoli

The alveoli are the gas exchange surfaces. There are about 300 million alveoli in one person's lungs. It is reckoned that if they were spread out flat, their surface would be as big as a tennis court.

- Blood in
- Air passage
- Blood out
- Alveolus
- Fine blood vessels

A group of alveoli

What a surface!

The Exchange of Gases

Each alveolus is richly supplied with blood through tiny blood vessels called lung capillaries. Blood coming to an alveolus from the general blood circulation is rich in carbon dioxide. Most of this gas will diffuse into the alveolar air. At the same time oxygen from the air will diffuse into the bloodstream. The red blood cells carry the oxygen in the bloodstream. The plasma carries most of the carbon dioxide. The diagram on the right shows what happens at an alveolus.

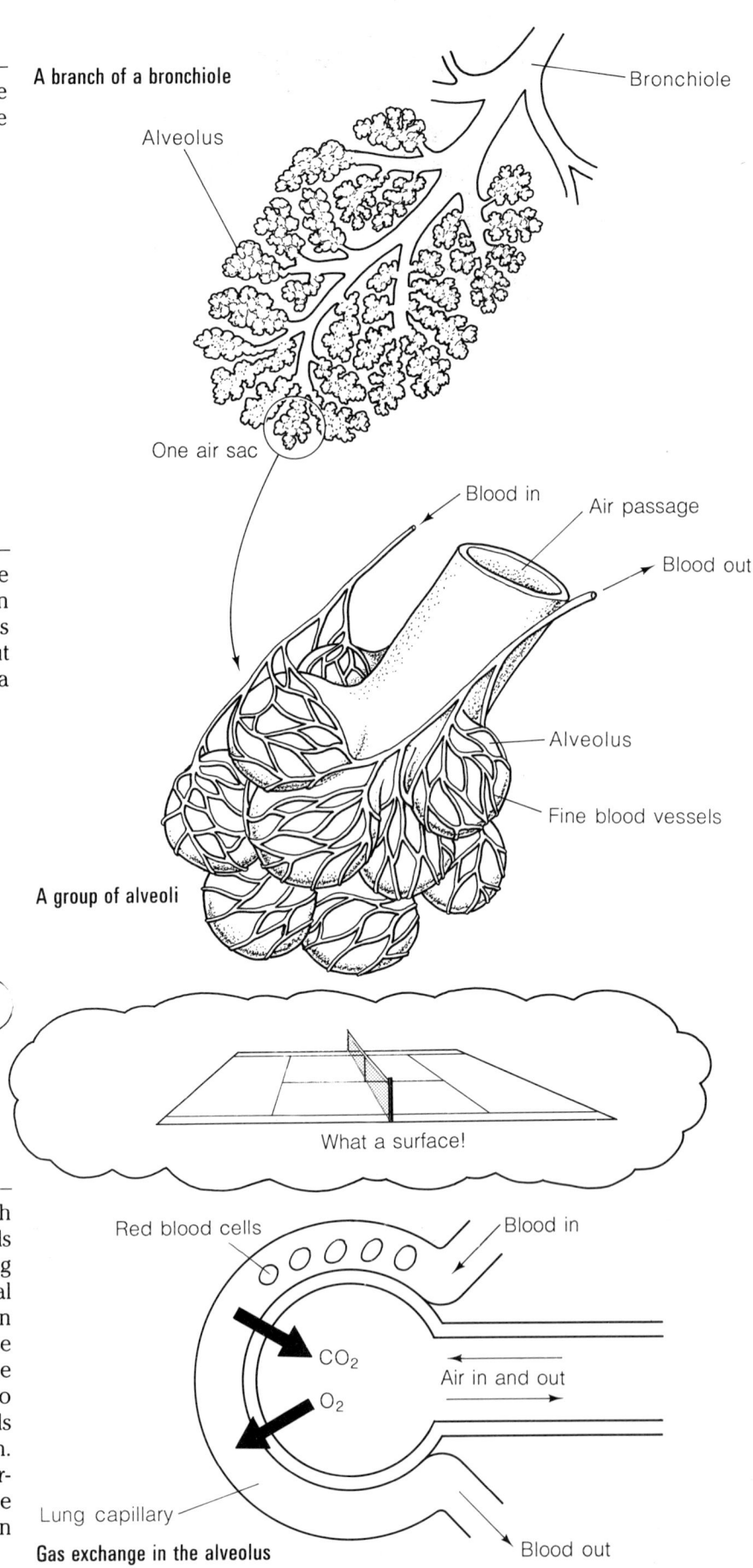

- Red blood cells
- Blood in
- CO_2
- O_2
- Air in and out
- Lung capillary
- Blood out

Gas exchange in the alveolus

MORE ABOUT GAS EXCHANGE

1. Cleaning Mechanism of the Lung

Atmospheric air drawn into the lungs is likely to be polluted. It contains particles of dust and germs such as bacteria and viruses. These impurities are dangerous and must not be allowed to reach the delicate gas exchange surfaces of the alveoli.

Adaptations are features of an organism which make it well suited to its environmental conditions. The trachea has adaptations to prevent impurities from reaching the alveoli. The inner lining or **epithelium** of the trachea has two types of cell which are important in keeping the lungs clean. **Goblet cells** secrete **mucus** which forms a continuous layer on the epithelium. Any dust or germs which are breathed in will be trapped on this layer.

Ciliated cells then beat in waves to drive the dirtied mucus upwards towards the **larynx**. It is then driven into the gullet where it can be swallowed, passed to the stomach and made harmless. When you have a cold, mucus is produced in large quantities and this material may be coughed up into the mouth.

2. Gas Exchange Adaptations

The gas exchange surface of the alveoli of mammal lungs has various adaptations which make it highly efficient at doing its job.

1. The total surface area of the alveoli is massive, which allows a large volume of air to make contact with their surfaces during each breath.

2. The surface is very thin, only one cell thick, thus allowing more speedy diffusion of gases.

3. Gases can only diffuse into living cells if the gases are in solution, so the surface is kept moist.

4. There is a rich blood supply on the surface of each alveolus. This allows lots of oxygen to enter the bloodstream for transport to the cells where it is used in respiration. It also allows for rapid diffusion of carbon dioxide from the bloodstream into air to be exhaled.

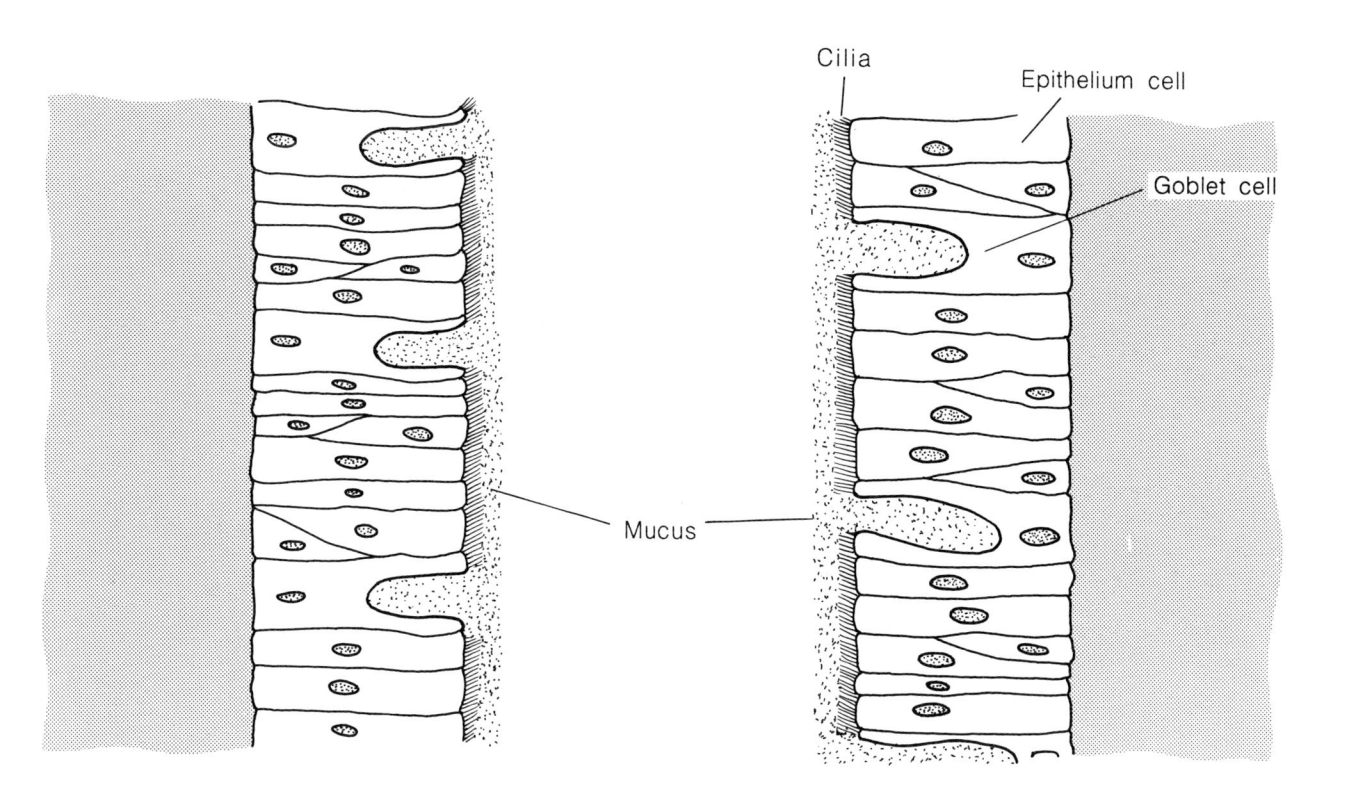

Cells of inner surface of trachea

126 THE BODY IN ACTION

3. Mechanism of Breathing

Inspiration

During inspiration air is drawn into the lungs. Some intercostal muscles relax and others contract to raise the rib cage. At the same time the diaphragm contracts and is thus lowered, flattening it out.

The combined muscular actions increase the volume of the cavity inside the chest. This increase in volume causes reduction of pressure and thus air is drawn into the lungs from the atmosphere where the pressure is higher.

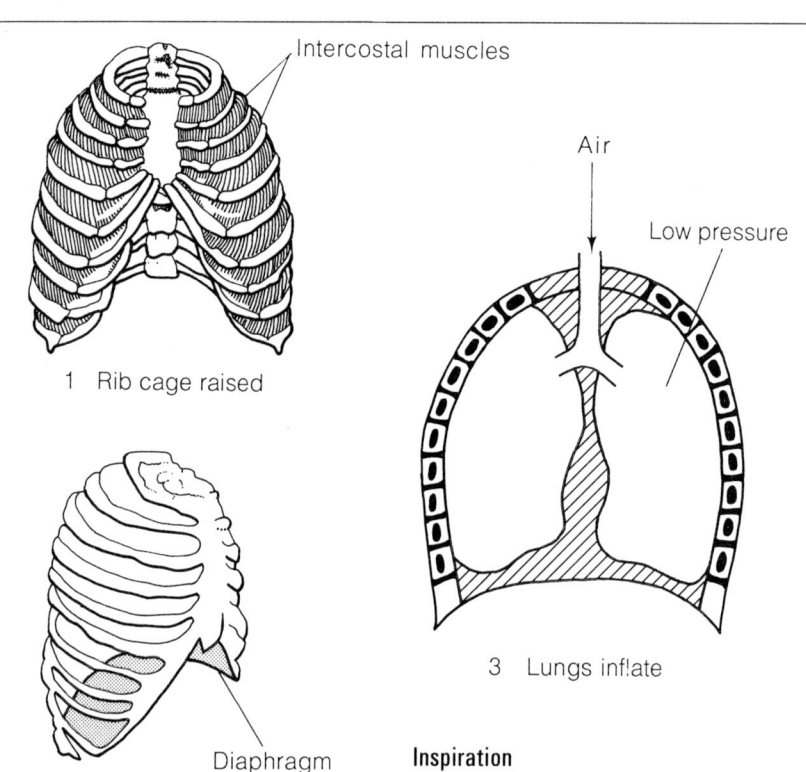

1 Rib cage raised — Intercostal muscles

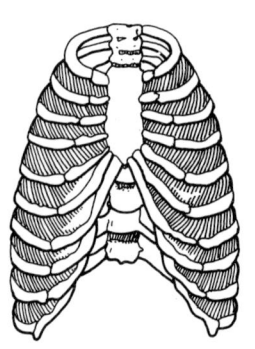

2 Diaphragm lowered

3 Lungs inflate — Air, Low pressure

Inspiration

Expiration

During expiration, air is forced out of the lungs. Some intercostal muscles contract and others relax, to lower the rib cage. At the same time the diaphragm relaxes and is drawn up into the chest cavity.

These changes result in the reduction of volume within the chest cavity. The volume reduction causes an increase in the pressure within the chest. This pressure squeezes the air out of the lungs.

1 Rib cage lowered

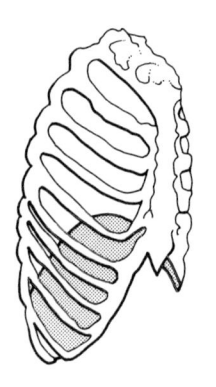

2 Diaphragm raised

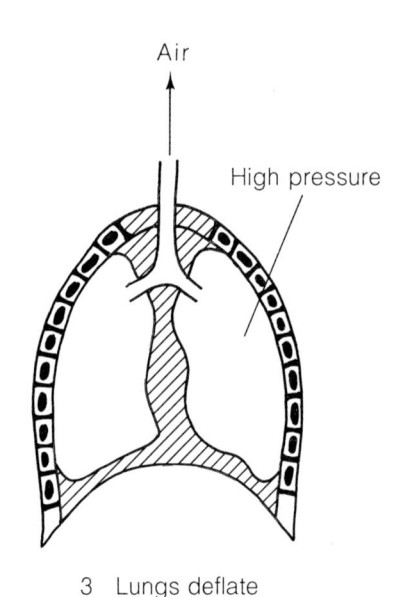

3 Lungs deflate — Air, High pressure

Expiration

A Model of Breathing

The mechanism of breathing is a little easier to understand if we consider two models of what happens. The plastic drink bottle represents the chest. The glass tubes represent the windpipe and bronchi, and the lungs are represented by the balloons. The diaphragm is the rubber sheet stretched across the bottom of the bottle.

When the rubber sheet is pushed up, the volume of the air inside the bottle is decreased. This raises the pressure and air is forced out of the balloons.

When the rubber sheet is flat, the volume of the air inside the bottle is increased. This decreases the pressure and air is drawn into the balloons.

In the rib action model, pieces of wood represent the bones in the chest. Elastic bands represent the intercostal muscles. The action of the elastic bands shows how the muscles move the bones.

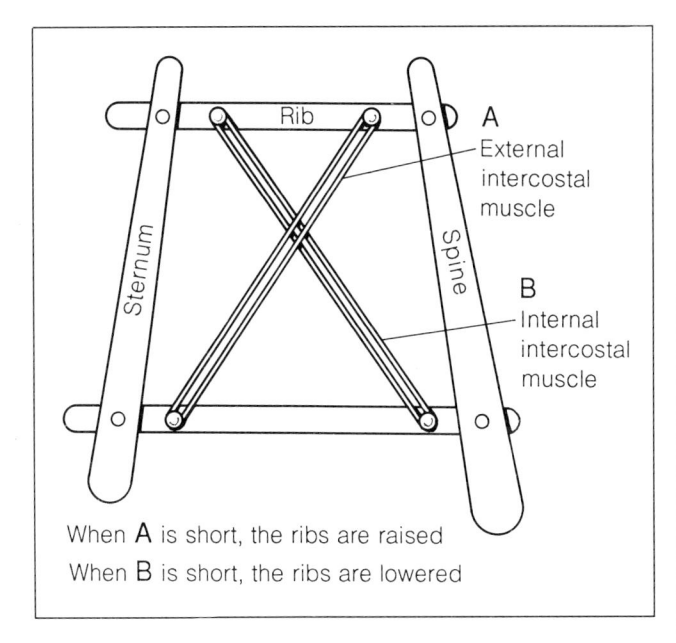

When **A** is short, the ribs are raised
When **B** is short, the ribs are lowered

Rib action model

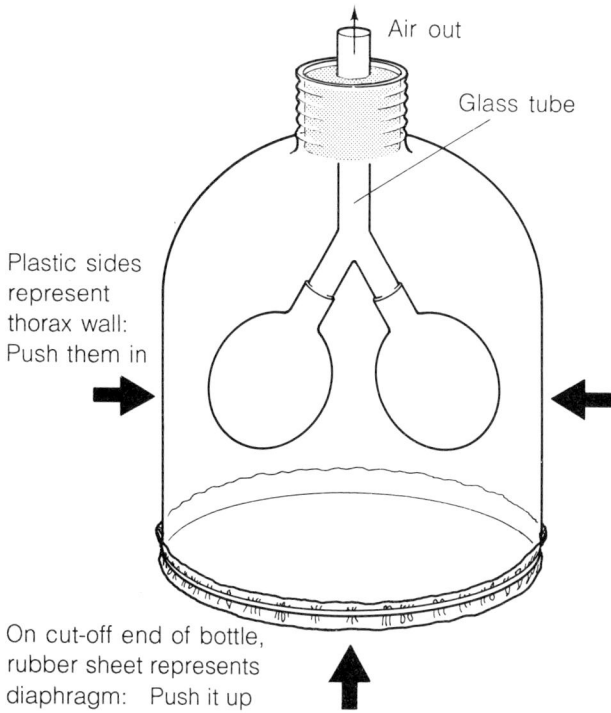

Plastic drinks bottle model of thorax

On cut-off end of bottle, rubber sheet represents diaphragm: Push it up

Plastic sides represent thorax wall: Push them in

A — External intercostal muscle
B — Internal intercostal muscle

Activities

1. Put the following words into order to show the route taken by breathed-in air.
   trachea alveolus bronchiole air sac bronchus
2. What is the job of the cartilage in the trachea?
3. Which gas is absorbed into the blood vessels on the surface of the alveolus?
4. Which gas is released by the blood vessels on the surface of the alveolus?
5. Write a criticism of each of the two breathing models. (Hint – why are they not lifelike?)
6. What are the jobs of
   (a) cilia
   (b) mucus
   in the trachea?
7. Copy and complete the following table on the lungs:

Feature	Reason
large surface area	
	quick diffusion
moist surface	
	gases diffuse into blood

4 The Heart and Circulation

Key Ideas

Foods and oxygen, and wastes including carbon dioxide are delivered to and from the body tissues by the bloodstream. The blood flows round in various types of tubes called blood vessels. The bloodstream is kept circulating by the beating of the *heart*. The heart is a strong muscular pump in the chest cavity between the lungs.

The arteries carry blood out of the heart to all the tissues of the body. In the capillaries the exchange of materials between blood and tissue cells takes place. The veins return the blood to the heart.

The Structure of the Heart

The heart is a hollow sac divided into four chambers. It is mostly made of **cardiac muscle**.

The upper two chambers of the heart are called **atria**, one on the left and one on the right. These atria have the thinnest walls.

The lower two chambers are called **ventricles**, one on the left and one on the right. They both have very thick muscular walls since they actively pump blood. The wall of the left ventricle is noticeably thicker than the wall of the right ventricle as the left ventricle has to pump the blood round the whole body, whereas the right pumps only to the lungs.

The heart beats at about 70 beats per minute throughout a person's life. It speeds up during exercise.

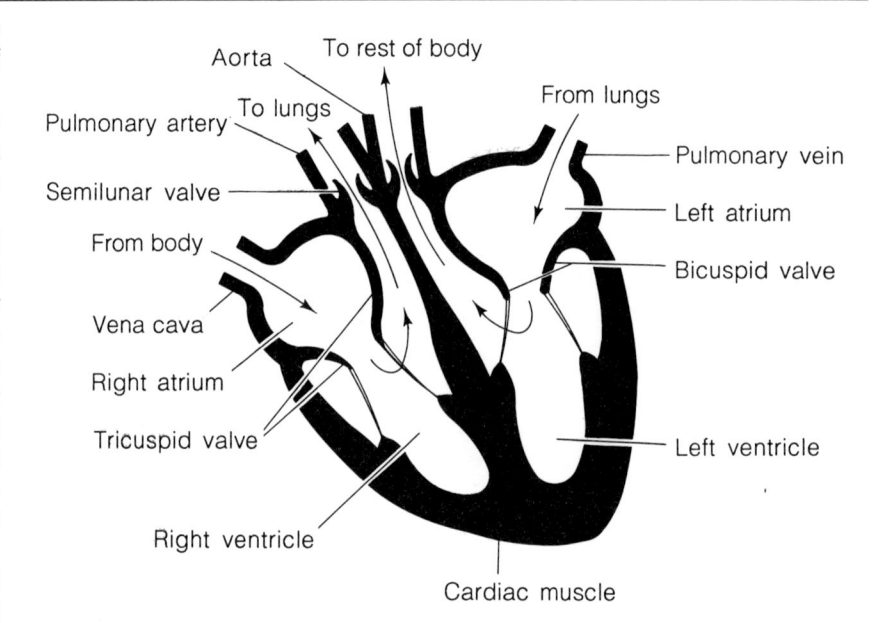

The heart, front view

One-Way System

Blood flows through the heart in a one-way system. The blood is not allowed to flow backwards. Valves in the heart prevent the blood flowing in the wrong direction. The main **bicuspid** and **tricuspid valves** close to prevent blood going into the atria when the ventricles contract. The **semilunar valves** shut to allow the ventricles to fill with blood from the body and lungs during relaxation of the cardiac muscle.

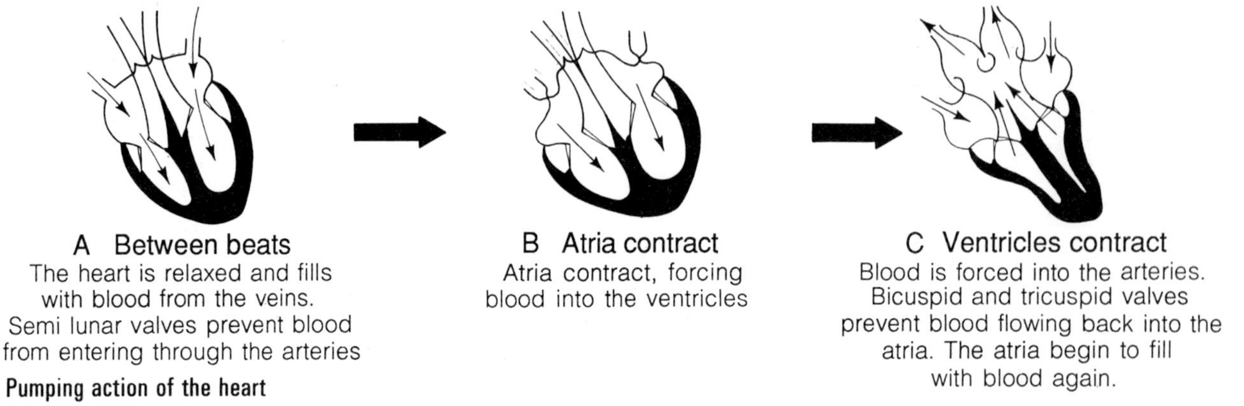

A Between beats
The heart is relaxed and fills with blood from the veins. Semi lunar valves prevent blood from entering through the arteries

B Atria contract
Atria contract, forcing blood into the ventricles

C Ventricles contract
Blood is forced into the arteries. Bicuspid and tricuspid valves prevent blood flowing back into the atria. The atria begin to fill with blood again.

Pumping action of the heart

THE BODY IN ACTION 129

Coronary Arteries

Blood is pumped to all parts of the body by the action of the heart. If you think about it, this means that the heart itself will need a blood supply.

Branches of the main artery leaving the heart visit the heart walls as shown in the diagram. These vessels are called **coronary arteries** and they supply the heart muscle with food and oxygen.

People with diets high in animal fats tend to have fat deposited in their blood vessels. If the coronary arteries become clogged up with these fatty deposits, the blood supply to the heart muscle is cut off. This can lead to a coronary heart attack and part of the heart muscle dies.

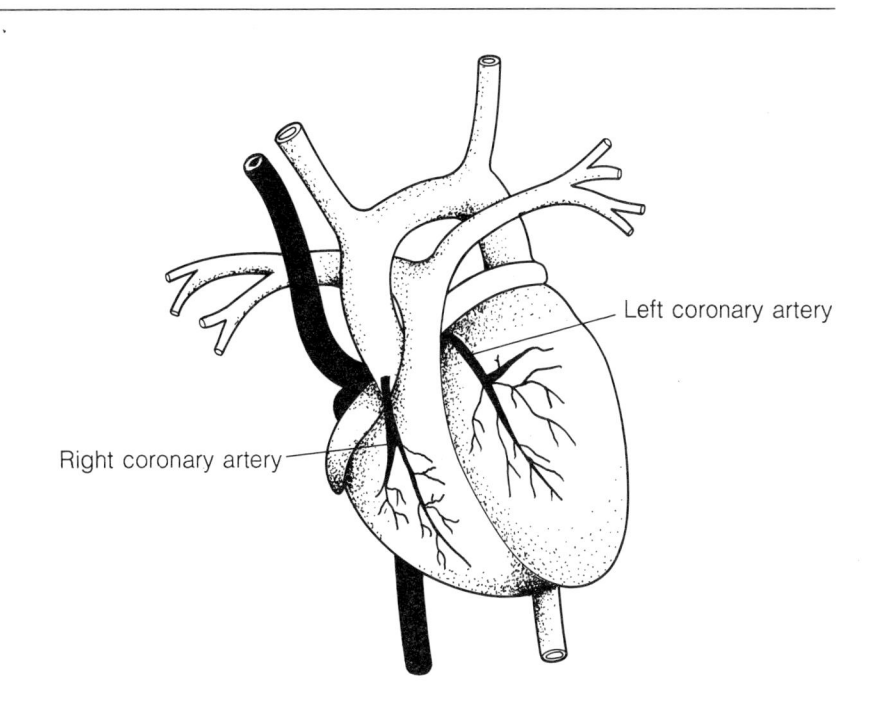

Blood Vessels and Circulation

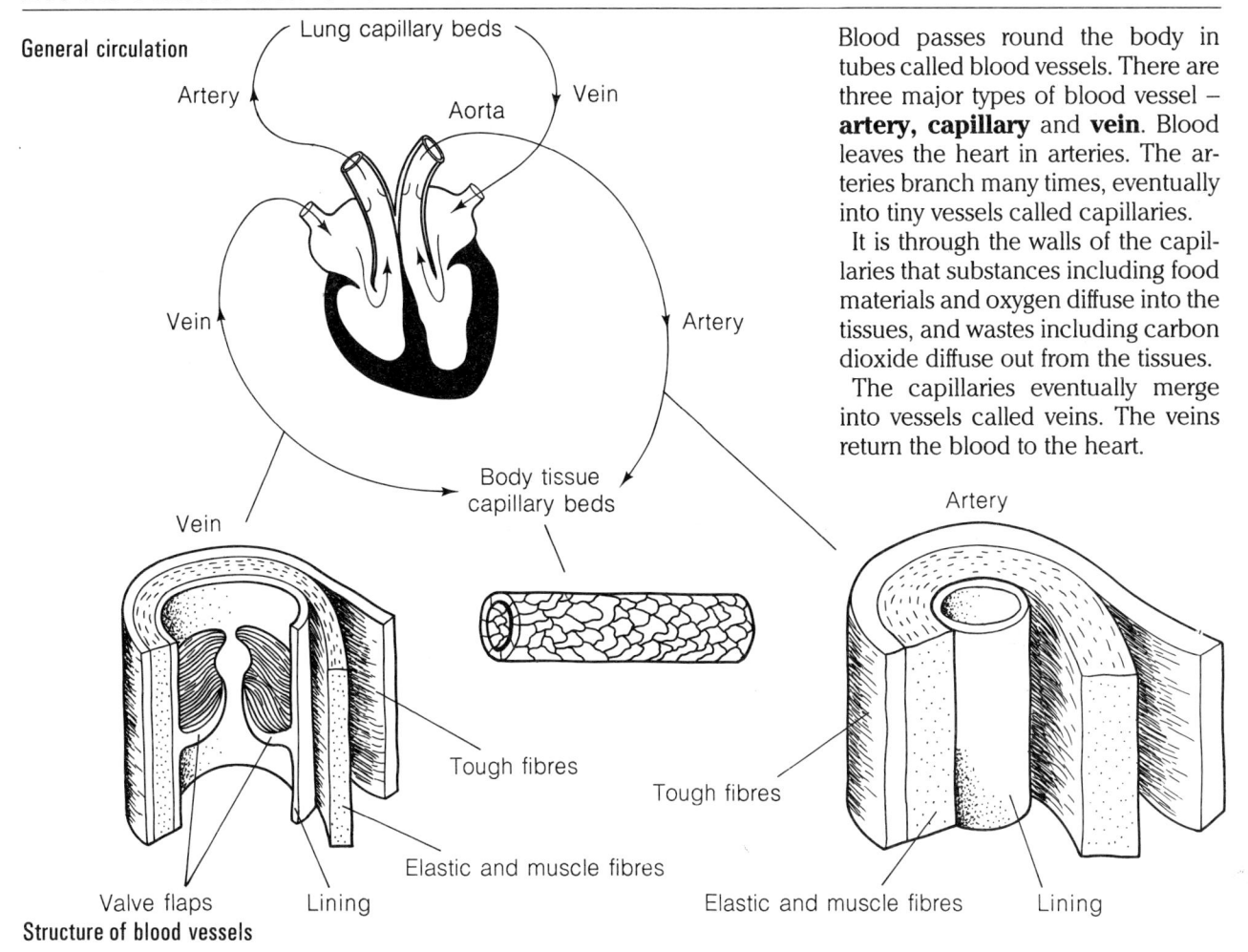

Blood passes round the body in tubes called blood vessels. There are three major types of blood vessel – **artery, capillary** and **vein**. Blood leaves the heart in arteries. The arteries branch many times, eventually into tiny vessels called capillaries.

It is through the walls of the capillaries that substances including food materials and oxygen diffuse into the tissues, and wastes including carbon dioxide diffuse out from the tissues.

The capillaries eventually merge into vessels called veins. The veins return the blood to the heart.

Structure of blood vessels

Capillary Beds

The capillary beds are highly branched to give a large surface for exchange of materials. The walls of the capillary vessels are no more than one cell thick to allow for the rapid movement of substances.

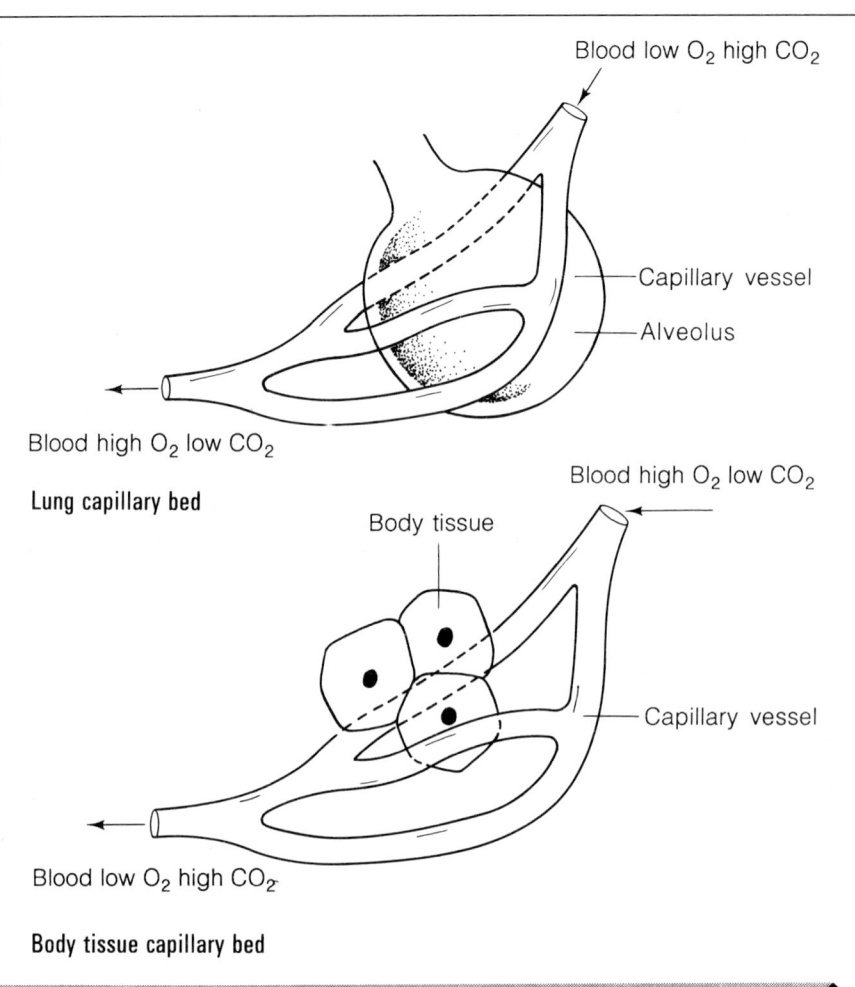

Blood low O_2 high CO_2
Capillary vessel
Alveolus
Blood high O_2 low CO_2

Lung capillary bed

Blood high O_2 low CO_2
Body tissue
Capillary vessel
Blood low O_2 high CO_2

Body tissue capillary bed

Activities

1. Name the four heart chambers.
2. Which chamber has the thickest wall, and why?
3. Place these in order to give the direction of blood flow:
   right auricle   right ventricle   left auricle   left ventricle
   vena cava   pulmonary vein   pulmonary artery   aorta
   body tissue   lung tissue
4. What is the general function of heart valves?
5. Describe the function of the coronary arteries.
6. Suggest which foods to avoid to help keep the coronary arteries healthy.
7. Make up a table to show the differences between arteries and veins.
8. Describe the features of a capillary bed which make it efficient for gas exchange.

5 The Structure of Blood

Key Ideas

The blood is a liquid called plasma with millions of cells floating in it. There are *red cells* and the much less numerous *white cells*. Each part of the blood has a special job to do.

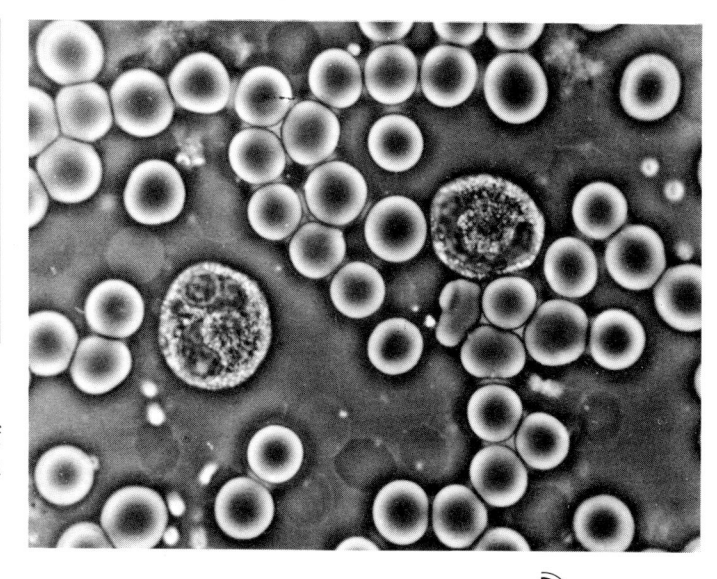

The photograph shows a drop of human blood viewed under a high power microscope.

Red Blood Cells

The red cells are much more common than white cells. There are about 5 million per cubic millimetre of blood.

The red cells are disc-shaped and have a dimple in each side. They have no nucleus when fully grown and their cytoplasm is coloured red by a substance called **haemoglobin**. They are less than 10 micrometers in diameter and their function is to carry oxygen and help in the transport of carbon dioxide.

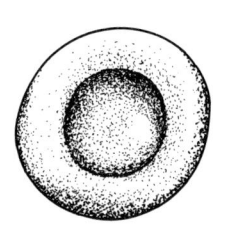

Red blood cell

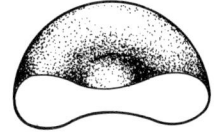

Cut in half to show biconcave shape

The shape of a red blood cell

White Blood Cells

There are only about 7000 white blood cells per cubic millimetre of blood. They have a very distinct nucleus which can be bean-shaped or like a short string of beans. The cells with the bean-shaped nuclei are called **lymphocytes** and they produce proteins called **antibodies** which help fight disease. The other white cells are called **phagocytes** and they also help to fight disease by engulfing bacteria.

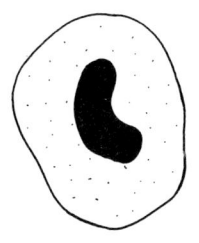

Phagocyte   Lymphocyte

Plasma

Plasma is a pale yellow liquid in which the cells float. The plasma carries many substances in solution like foods and wastes. It also carries a number of special substances like proteins and hormones.

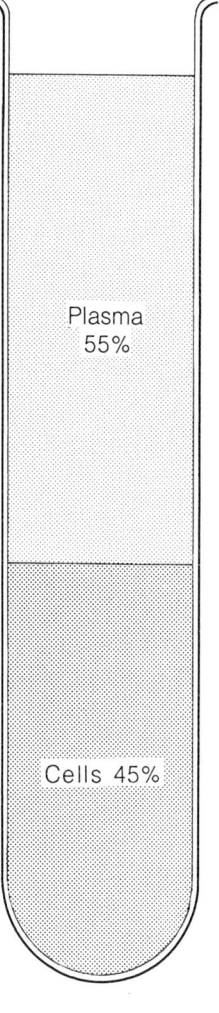

Plasma 55%

Cells 45%

The relative amounts of plasma and cells in blood

Haemoglobin

Haemoglobin is a protein found in the cytoplasm of red blood cells. The protein molecules contain iron. Haemoglobin gives the red cells their purple-red colour.

Haemoglobin can combine with oxygen to form oxyhaemoglobin which is bright red. This combination is reversible. At the lung tissues the reaction is:

$$Hb + O_2 \longrightarrow HbO_2$$

Haemoglobin (purple)   Oxygen   Oxyhaemoglobin (bright red)

At the body tissues the reaction is:

$$HbO_2 \longrightarrow Hb + O_2$$

Activities

1. Make up a table of the jobs of blood cells and plasma.
2. Draw diagrams of:
   (a) a red blood cell
   (b) a phagocyte
   (c) a lymphocyte
- 3 Explain the function of haemoglobin in the transport of oxygen.

6 Support and Movement – The Skeleton

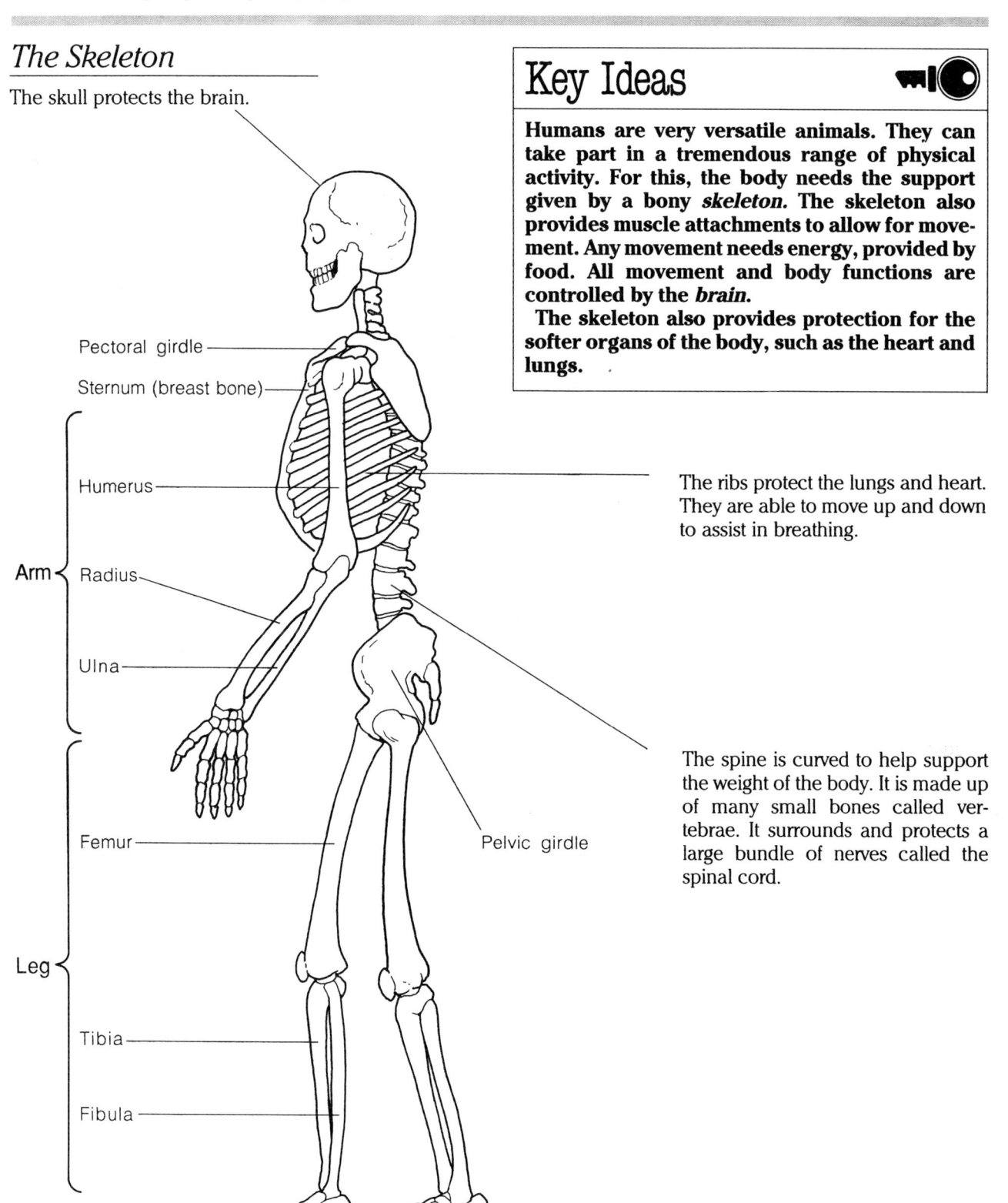

The Skeleton

The skull protects the brain.

Pectoral girdle
Sternum (breast bone)

Arm
- Humerus
- Radius
- Ulna

Leg
- Femur
- Tibia
- Fibula

Pelvic girdle

Key Ideas

Humans are very versatile animals. They can take part in a tremendous range of physical activity. For this, the body needs the support given by a bony *skeleton*. The skeleton also provides muscle attachments to allow for movement. Any movement needs energy, provided by food. All movement and body functions are controlled by the *brain*.

The skeleton also provides protection for the softer organs of the body, such as the heart and lungs.

The ribs protect the lungs and heart. They are able to move up and down to assist in breathing.

The spine is curved to help support the weight of the body. It is made up of many small bones called vertebrae. It surrounds and protects a large bundle of nerves called the spinal cord.

134 THE BODY IN ACTION

Muscles from the arms and legs are joined to the pectoral and pelvic girdles.

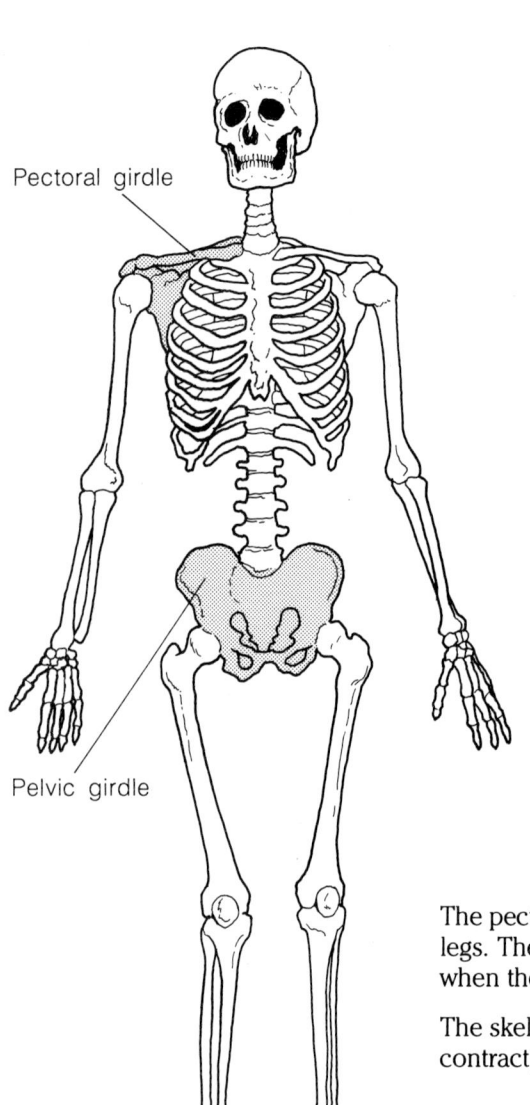

Pectoral girdle

Pelvic girdle

The pectoral and pelvic girdles are like hangers which support the arms and legs. They provide the arms and legs with something solid to push against when they move.

The skeleton provides a framework for muscles to attach to. When muscles contract, they pull on bones of the skeleton which causes movement.

Activities

1. The skeleton has three main functions. Draw a table to show these functions and, for each one, give examples of parts of the skeleton which are involved.
2. Give three examples of parts of the body protected by the skeleton. In each case, state which bones give the protection.
3. Explain why the skeleton is needed for an animal to move.

7 Bones and Joints

Key Ideas

Your skeleton is a framework of bones. Bones are made up of soft flexible fibres, hard minerals and living cells.

Where bones of the skeleton meet, their ends are covered in a layer of *cartilage* which helps to reduce friction between the two bones which make up a *joint*. The joints of the skeleton are held together by *ligaments*. Some joints are rigid, while others allow for movement. *Hinge* joints and *ball and socket* joints are examples of two moveable joints.

Bones

If you were able to see a long bone from your leg, it would look something like this, if it were split down the middle.

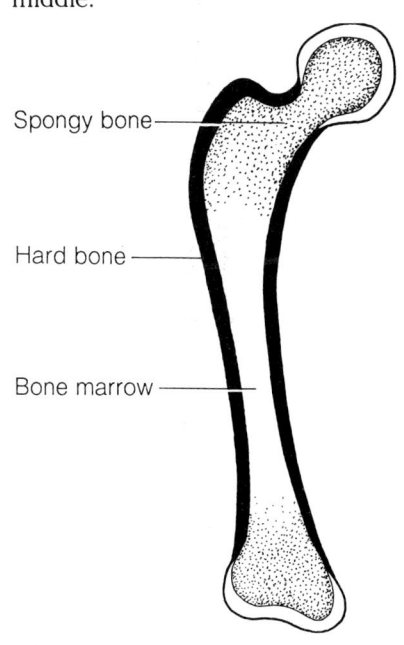

Spongy bone

Hard bone

Bone marrow

The bone is made up of three regions.

1 The outside is made of hard dense bone. Calcium and other minerals give the bone great strength.
2 Inside the outer layer is a region of spongy bone. This is made up of many flexible fibres.
3 A hollow space in the bone is filled with bone marrow in which new red blood cells are made. A hollow bone is lighter than a solid one without losing much strength.

Joints

The body has three main types of joints:
1 Joints which do not move. These exist where bones have grown together, such as in the skull.
2 Joints which are able to move slightly, such as those between the vertebrae of the spine.
3 Joints which are able to move freely, such as the joints in the arms and legs.

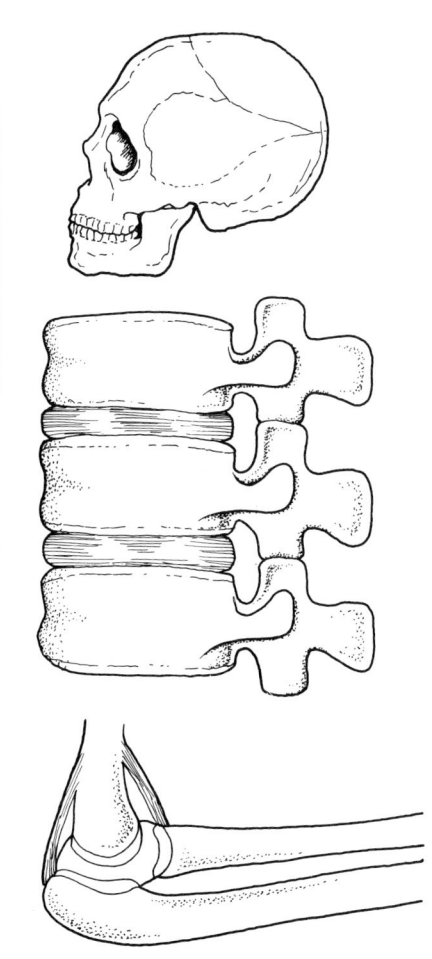

Movement

The range of movement which is possible in the human skeleton depends on the types of joints where bones meet.

Your elbow joint is a **hinge** joint which, like a door hinge, only allows movement in one direction.

Your leg is attached to the hip by a **ball and socket** joint, which allows movement in more than one direction. Some adjustable car rear-view mirrors have this type of joint.

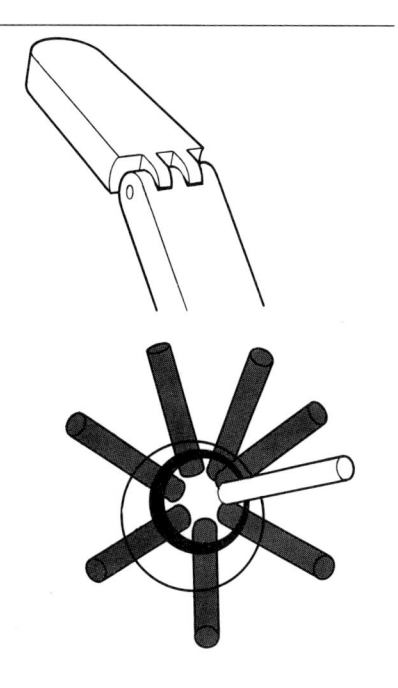

136 THE BODY IN ACTION

Structure of Joints

Bones are held together at joints by **ligaments**. The ends of the bones where they meet in a joint are covered with a layer of **cartilage**. This is softer than bone and provides a smooth, slippery surface which cuts down the friction and "wear and tear" of the bone ends when they rub against one another.

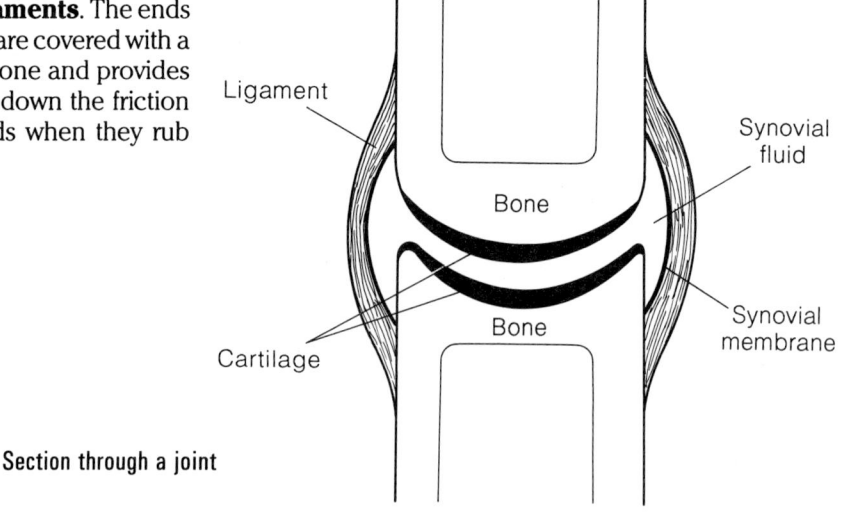

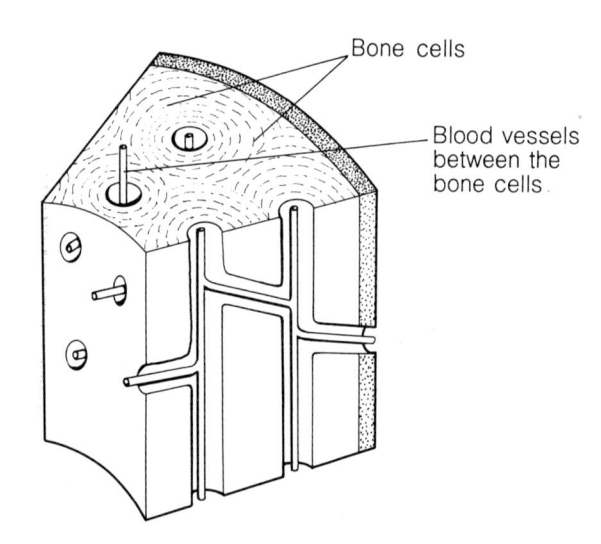

Section through a joint

A section of a bone

Synovial Joints

Joints are weak points in the skeleton and need to be well protected. The ligaments which hold the bones of a joint together are very strong, but are also flexible enough to allow the joint to move freely. They prevent a joint from becoming dislocated. The cartilage on the end of the bones, as well as reducing friction between the bones, also acts as a shock absorber, being softer than bone. Surrounding the joint, inside the ligaments, is the synovial membrane. This produces a liquid, called synovial fluid which acts like oil. It lubricates the joint, further reducing friction. It also helps to cushion movement in the joint.

Living Bone

Although the bones of a skeleton appear dead, the bone in a living animal is living tissue. It has a blood supply and nerves. It has bone cells which make new bone and also repair damaged bone.

Activities

1. Find the following joints in your body or on a model skeleton and find out how they move:
   shoulder, hip, toes, fingers, knee, elbow.
   Make a table to show whether each is a hinge or a ball and socket joint.

2. State two parts of a moveable joint which help to reduce friction. For each part, describe how it reduces friction.

3. Make a labelled diagram of a synovial joint.

8 Muscles and Movement

Key Ideas 🔑

Muscles are needed to move your body or parts of it. Muscles which move the skeleton are attached to the bones by *tendons*. When a muscle gets shorter by *contracting*, it pulls a tendon which in turn pulls a bone. Muscles can only actively contract. If a muscle is not contracting it is *relaxed*, and can be pulled longer by another muscle contracting. This is why muscles always work in pairs: one contracts as the other relaxes.

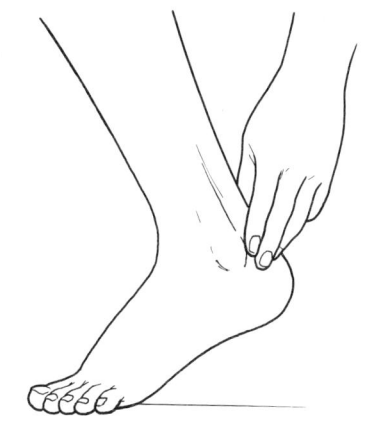

Muscle Attachment

Muscles cause bones to move. Muscles are attached to bones by tendons.

If you touch the back of your heel as in the diagram, you should be able to feel a hard ridge which is your Achilles tendon. This tendon attaches your calf muscle to your heel bone.

Keep touching this tendon and bend your toes up. You should feel the Achilles tendon pulling on your relaxed calf muscle to stretch it.

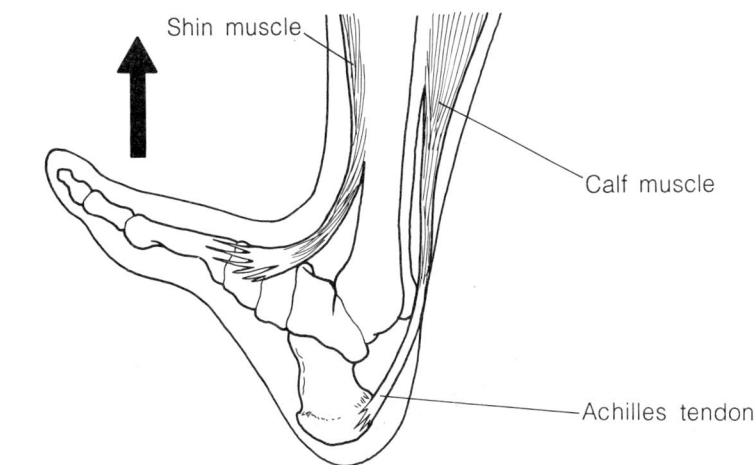

Muscle Contraction

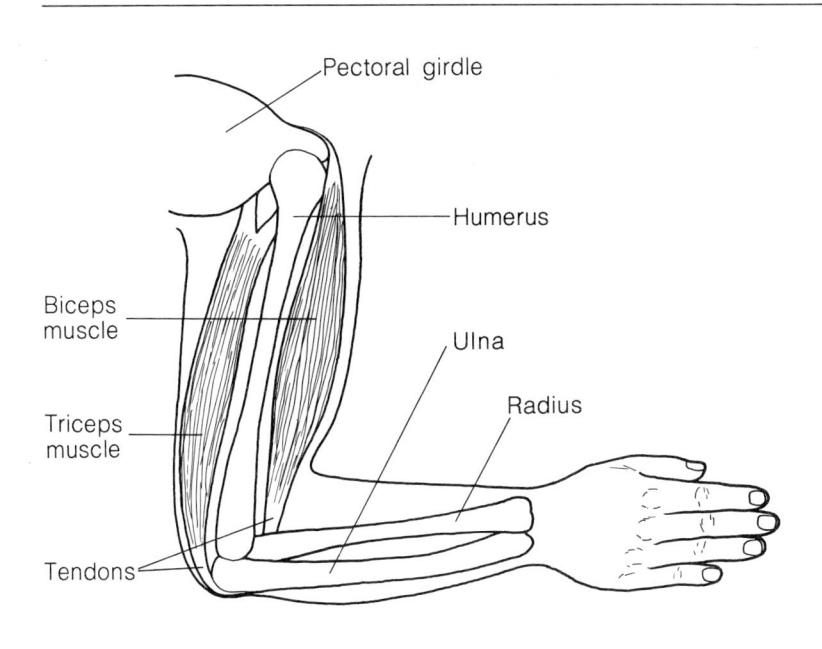

The muscles, which are attached to bones and can cause them to move, are made up of hundreds of bundles of muscle fibres. These muscle fibres can contract if they receive a signal from the nervous system.

Muscles can only actively contract. They cannot make themselves longer, although, if they are relaxed, they can be pulled longer.

For movement to occur at a joint, one end of the muscle causing the movement must be attached to a fixed part of the skeleton, such as the pectoral girdle. The other end is attached, by a tendon across a moveable joint, to the bone which is to be moved. When the muscle is signalled to contract, it gets shorter, and pulls on the tendon, which in turn pulls the bone.

Muscles of the upper arm

138 THE BODY IN ACTION

Antagonistic Muscles

If a limb bends at a joint by muscle contraction (see **A**) then it can only straighten if another muscle contracts (see **B**).

Muscles therefore usually work in pairs with each muscle pulling across a joint in different directions. These muscle pairs are termed **antagonistic**.

A To bend at elbow:
- Biceps contracts
- Triceps relaxes

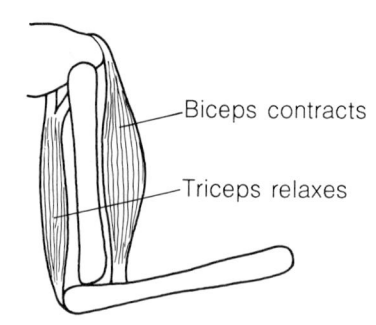

B To straighten at elbow:
- Biceps relaxes
- Triceps contracts

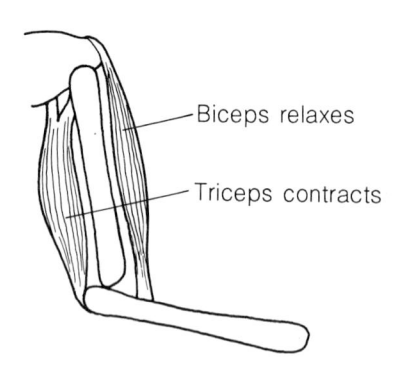

Injuries

Most muscles and joints are almost continually under stress. Sometimes that stress will be greatly increased due to very strenuous activity. This may occur at work but will often occur when people are involved in sporting activity.

There are many types of injury which can occur. Here are a few examples.

1. *Sprains* – if a joint, such as the ankle, is suddenly twisted, the ligament at the side of the joint can be torn.
2. *Dislocations* – If a joint is forced beyond the limit of its normal movement, the bone end can be pulled out of the joint, for example at the ball and socket joint of the shoulder.
3. *Muscle damage* – If a muscle is forced to do too much work, for instance in the case of a person bending the back to lift a heavy weight, then the muscle can be overstretched, causing a strain. Sometimes a muscle (such as the large hamstring muscle at the back of the thigh) can be pulled so badly that muscle fibres are broken, causing the muscle to tear.

The humerus bone no longer fits into the socket of the scapula and is displaced to one side
- Humerus
- Shoulder blade

- Achilles tendon
- Snap

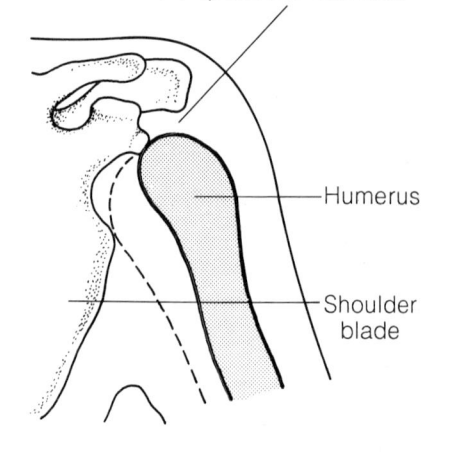

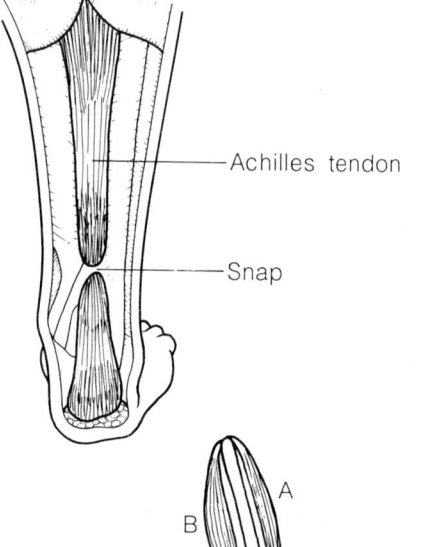

Tendons are inelastic: they cannot stretch very much. If this were not the case, then when a muscle contracted it would simply stretch the tendon and not pull on the bone. In cases of severe stress the tendon attaching a muscle to a bone may be pulled so sharply that the tendon snaps. This will prevent further movement of the joint.

Activities

○ 1 What will happen to bone **X** if muscle **A** contracts?
○ 2 What will happen to bone **X** if muscle **B** contracts?
○ 3 Describe what is meant by "antagonistic muscles".
● 4 Describe the difference between a tendon and a muscle.
● 5 A tennis player snaps an Achilles tendon. What effect will this have on her movement?

9 Levels of Performance

Time no. of beats over 30 s

Use fingers as shown

Take pulse at base of thumb

Measuring pulse rate

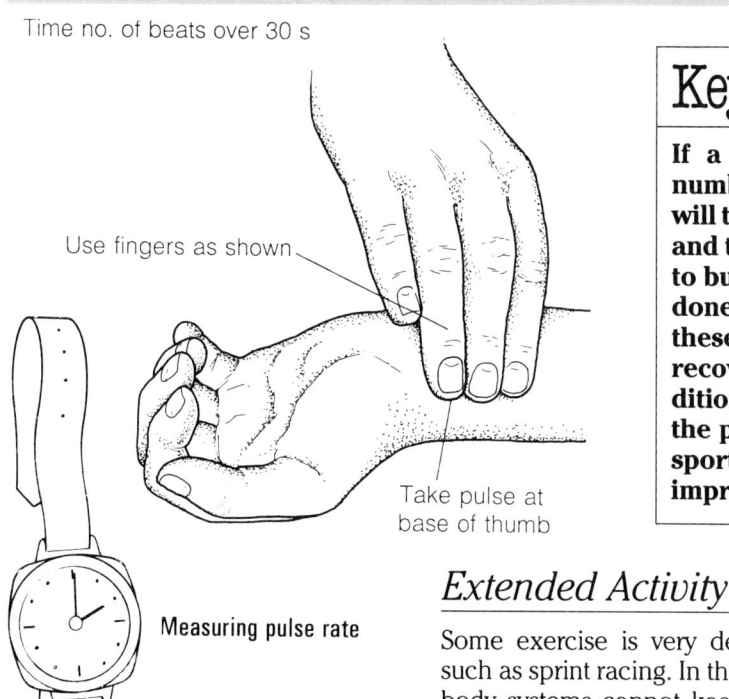

Key Ideas

If a person trains for a particular sport, a number of changes in his or her performance will take place. Exercise increases the pulse rate and the breathing rate. It also causes *lactic acid* to build up in the muscles. A fit person who has done the right training will show less increase in these levels than an unfit person. Fit people also recover much more quickly after exercise. Additionally, if the training programme involves the practice of skills involved with a particular sport then factors like reaction time will be improved.

What Happens During Exercise

During physical activity, increased demand is made on the muscles. Working muscles require extra food and oxygen to keep going. Waste materials like carbon dioxide must be removed.

In order to meet these demands, various changes take place within the body. The breathing rate goes up so that more oxygen and carbon dioxide are exchanged with the air. The heart rate goes up in order to send more blood containing food and oxygen to the muscles and to remove carbon dioxide more quickly. The table shows the effects of some of the changes which occur.

Extended Activity

Some exercise is very demanding, such as sprint racing. In this case the body systems cannot keep up with the demand from the muscles. The muscles start to respire anaerobically. This type of respiration does not require oxygen but does result in the build-up of a poisonous waste called lactic acid. The build-up of this and other waste substances can cause pain in the muscles. Eventually the muscles become fatigued and will stop contracting. In a trained person the build-up is less and hence the effects are reduced.

Muscle fatigue can be demonstrated simply. The diagram below shows the procedure. The weight is lowered and raised as shown for 3 minutes. The number of times the weight can be lifted is recorded. The results of such an experiment are shown below. As the number of three-minute trials increases, the weight-lifting ability decreases. This is due to a lack of oxygen and a build up of lactic acid.

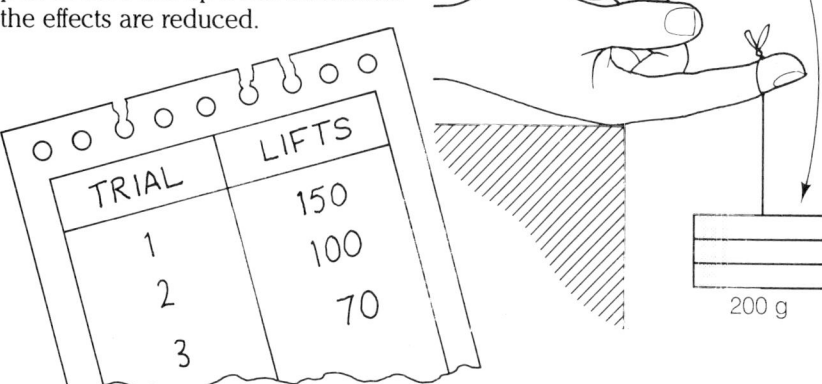

TRIAL	LIFTS
1	150
2	100
3	70

200 g

	At rest (per minute)	During activity (per minute)
Breathing	8 litres	25 litres
Pulse rate	75 beats	200 beats
Oxygen used	250 cm^3	5 litres

Recovery Time

Recovery time is the period taken to return to normal pulse rate, breathing and lactic acid levels after exercise. This period is shorter for a person who is fit.

140 THE BODY IN ACTION

Reaction Time

The time taken for a person to react to a stimulus is called the reaction time. This time can be shortened with practice in a given test situation. The diagram shows a very simple reaction time test. The subject leans on the edge of a bench as shown. The experimenter drops a ruler from the position shown. The subject attempts to catch the ruler as it falls through his or her open hand. The distance the ruler falls before being caught is a crude measure of that person's reaction time.

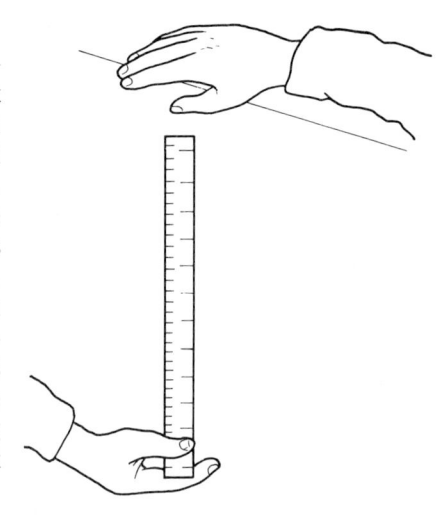

Training

The effects of training are very obvious in the early stages of a training programme. There is increased amount of regular stress being placed on the body during the training activity, and it results in improvement of the parts of the body being trained.

The most obvious improvements occur in the lung efficiency and the efficiency of blood circulation. The body also recovers more quickly after the exercise period, as is shown in the method of fitness measurement known as the Harvard Step Test.

The Harvard Step Test

This is a test designed to measure physical fitness. It is based on the principle that a short recovery time is an indication of physical fitness.

1 Step up onto a 40 cm high box and down again every two seconds for four minutes.

2 Sit down for one minute.

3 Record the pulse rate over 30 seconds after the minute.

4 Record the pulse rate in the same way after a further 30 seconds' rest.

5 Take a final pulse rate in the same way after a further 30 seconds.

6 Calculate the step test score in the following way:

$$\text{Score} = \frac{120 \times 100}{2 \times \text{total of 3 pulse rates}}$$

7 Compare the results to this table:

Score	Performance
over 90	outstanding
80–89	excellent
70–79	good
60–69	fair
50–59	poor
below 50	very poor

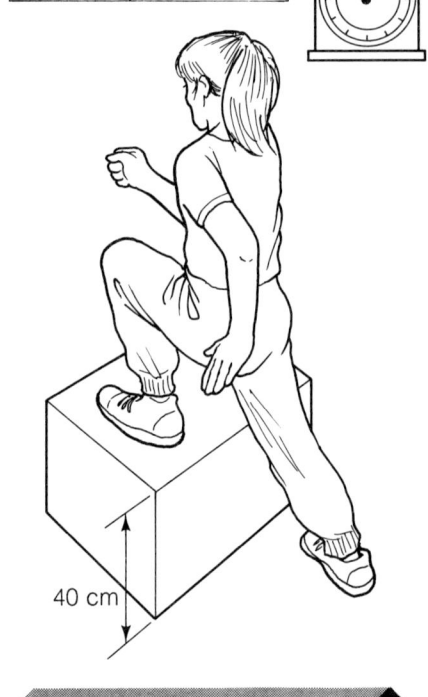

Activities

○ 1 Explain why the pulse rate rises during exercise.

○ 2 What causes muscles to fatigue during exercise?

○ 3 What is meant by the term "recovery time"?

○ 4 Describe the effects of training on a person's body performance.

○ 5 A student takes the dropping ruler reaction test. The results of 10 trials are recorded in the graph shown.
  (a) What happens to the student's level of performance after 5 trials?
  (b) What is the difference in reaction time between trial 1 and trial 10?

● 6 These results for the Harvard step test were obtained from an 18-year-old university student. Calculate his fitness level using the table above.

   pulse 1: 50   pulse 2: 39   pulse 3: 32

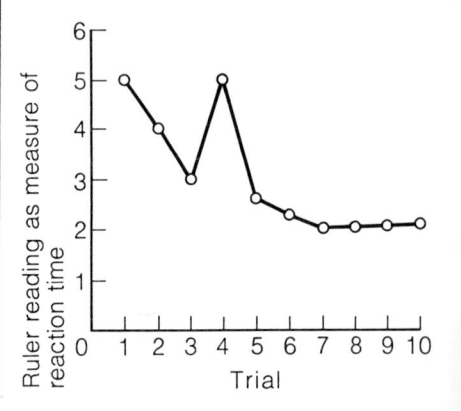

10 Senses and Reactions

Key Ideas

We are continually responding to changes in our environment. In order to do this we must receive information from our surroundings through our senses. Much of our waking lives is spent in physical activity, such as walking, playing and running. Any reaction to change, or physical activity of any type, requires control by our *central nervous system* and response by our muscles. This type of control is called *coordination*.

The Senses

Our sense organs receive information from the environment and pass it on to our central nervous system. This is made up of the brain and the spinal cord which is the bundle of nerve fibres running down a channel in our vertebrae.

Our sense organs are made up of cells called **receptors**. Information which they detect is called a **stimulus**. On receiving a stimulus, the receptor cells convert it into electrical signals which pass along nerve fibres to the central nervous system. If a response to the stimulus is needed, then another electrical signal is sent from the central nervous system to produce an effect. This signal may go to one or more muscles, or to glands in the body which can release hormones to affect other parts of the body. These muscles and glands are called **effector** organs because they effect (bring about) a response to a stimulus.

Human beings have six main senses: **sight, hearing, touch, taste, smell** and **balance**.

Our sense of touch is able to detect **contact, pain, pressure** and **temperature**.

These senses, the sense organs involved and the types of stimulus they can detect, are summarised in the table.

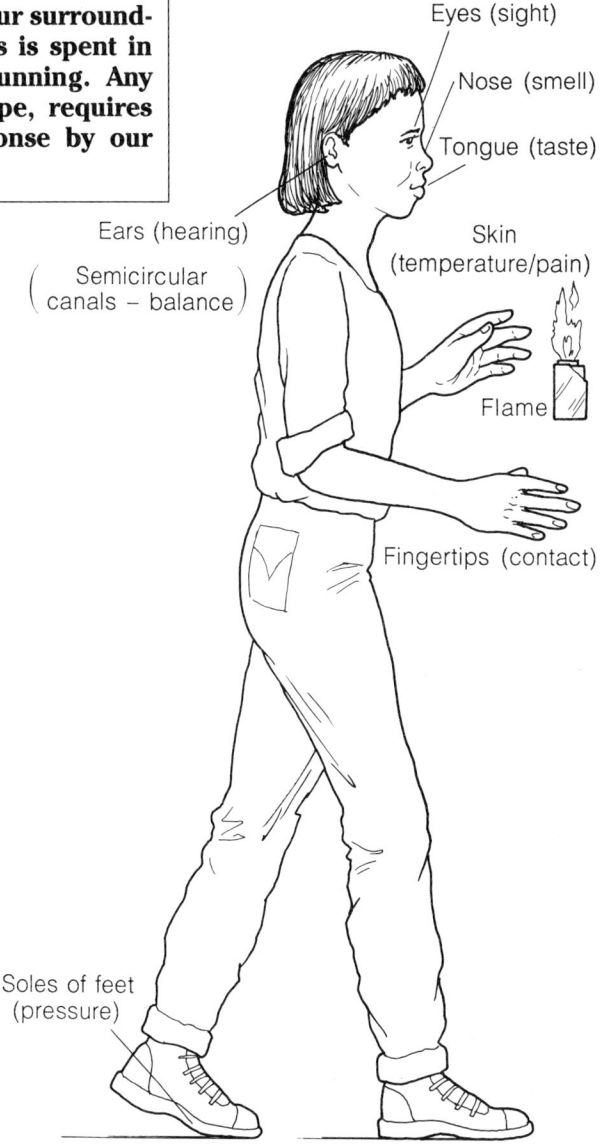

Sense	Stimulus	Sense organ/s
sight	light	eyes
hearing	sound	ears
smell	chemicals (usually gases)	nose
taste	chemicals (solids/liquids)	tongue and throat
balance	movement/position	part of inner ear
touch	contact	skin
temperature	heat/cold	skin
pain	damage	skin
pressure	force	skin

Activities

1. For each of the following situations give the main stimulus and main response:
   (a) touching a hot iron
   (b) reading a book
   (c) drinking sour milk
   (d) the school bell ringing

11 The Eye and Sight

Key Ideas

Most of the information we receive from our surroundings is detected by our sense of sight – through our eyes. The main parts of the eye are: the *cornea*, protecting the front of the eye; the *iris*, allowing light into the eye; the *lens*, focussing light on the *retina*, which passes signals to the brain through the *optic nerve*. Two eyes on the front of our head allow us to judge distance more accurately than one eye.

Structure of the Eye

The cornea is a transparent disc on the front of the eye. It protects the front of the eyeball, while allowing light to enter the eye.

The iris is the coloured part of the eye, which has a hole in the middle called the **pupil**. The iris can control the amount of light entering the eye by altering the size of the pupil.

The retina is the inner layer at the back of the eye. It is made up of light-sensitive cells. There are two types of cells in the human eye: one type detects colour, while the other type is sensitive to shades of grey.

Light entering the eye through the pupil then passes through the lens. The lens is elastic and transparent. It can change shape. It is able to bend rays of light to focus on the retina. This produces a clear image.

Electrical signals pass from the retina along the optic nerve to the brain. At the point where the optic nerve leaves the eye there are no light-detecting cells. Because no light signals can be detected, this is called the **blind spot**.

THE BODY IN ACTION

Humans have two eyes on the front of the head. Obviously if one eye is damaged, then you have a spare. However, this is not the only reason for having a pair of eyes. Each eye looks at the world from a slightly different angle.

Close your right eye and hold your right forefinger out in front of your face. As in diagram **A**, position your left forefinger about 10 centimetres behind the right so that the left finger is completely hidden. Open your right eye and close your left eye. Your left finger should sudden appear as in diagram **B**.

With both eyes open, your eyes are seeing two slightly different pictures which are combined into one by your brain. This allows you to judge distances more accurately. A one-eyed tennis player has never won Wimbledon!

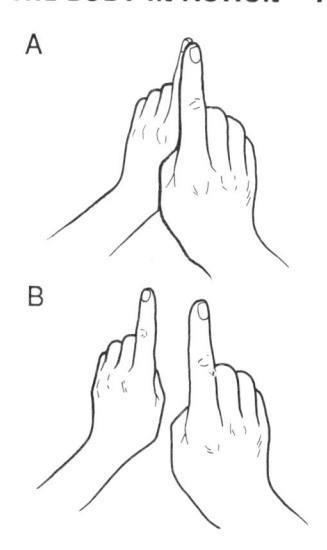

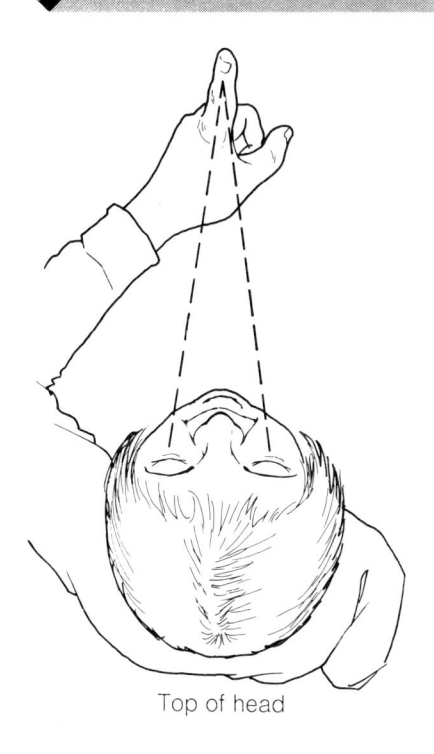

A

B

How does having two eyes allow us to judge distance? Two eyes positioned on the front of the head gives us **binocular vision**. This means that when you look at your finger held in front of your face your brain is receiving two pictures of it. Your brain is able to combine these two pictures so that you see only one finger. For this to happen, each eye must be looking directly at the finger. Therefore if your finger is close to your face each eye must turn inwards slightly. Nerve signals from the muscles which turn the eyes inwards send signals to the brain telling it how far round the eyes have moved. This allows the brain to judge how far away your finger is. This is fairly accurate for objects close to your eyes, where the movement inwards of the eyes is able to be detected. Beyond 10 to 15 metres this becomes less accurate.

Top of head

Activities

1. Draw a table to show the main parts of the eye and their functions. List the cornea, iris, pupil, lens, retina and optic nerve.
2. Describe why having two eyes is better than one.
3. Lay a pencil on the desk in front of you with its point towards you. Close one eye. Hold another pencil above your head. Bring it down to touch its point against the point of the pencil on the desk. Do this 10 times. Count how many times you are successful. Repeat the same test with both eyes open. Again count your successes. Describe your test and explain your results in terms of binocular vision.

12 Hearing and Balance

Key Ideas

Humans have two ears, one on each side of the head. This allows us to judge more accurately the direction from which a sound is coming.

Sound vibrations enter the *outer ear* and are passed through the *ear drum* to the *middle ear bones*. From there they are passed into the *cochlea* where they are converted into electrical signals which pass along the *auditory nerve* to the brain.

Next to the cochlea are found the *semi-circular canals*, which are not involved in our sense of hearing. They allow us to sense our position and keep our balance.

Parts of the Ear

The outer ear is filled with air and collects sounds.

The cochlea is a fluid-filled, coiled tube. Sound vibrations pass through the fluid in the cochlea and cause tiny hairs along its length to move. These hairs are attached to nerve cells.

The semi-circular canals are filled with fluid. Movements of the head are detected by movement of this fluid.

The ear drum is a thin membrane separating the outer ear from the middle ear. It vibrates when sounds reach it. These vibrations are passed to the middle ear bones.

The middle ear is a small cavity filled with air, found in the skull. There are three bones in the middle ear: the hammer, anvil and stirrup. These bones are attached to each other and connect the eardrum with the oval window at the other side of the middle ear.

Signals produced by the nerve cells in the cochlea are passed to the brain along the auditory nerve.

As with your eyes, you have two ears. This helps you to detect the direction from which sounds come. Your ears are positioned at the side of your head. Therefore a sound from your right will reach your right ear first. The same sound takes slightly longer to reach your left ear. The brain can detect this small time gap. With experience it is able to judge the direction of the sound, unless the sound is coming from directly in front, above or behind your head.

Semi-circular Canals

Above the cochlea, in the inner ear, there are three semi-circular canals, see **A**. These are tubes filled with liquid. The liquid is able to move in each tube. At the end of each tube there is a flap of tissue, able to move in two directions. If the fluid in the tube pushes against this flap, the flap will move, see **B**. The base of the flap is connected to nerve cells which can detect its movement and send a message to the brain. Therefore if your head or body moves, your brain will know your position.

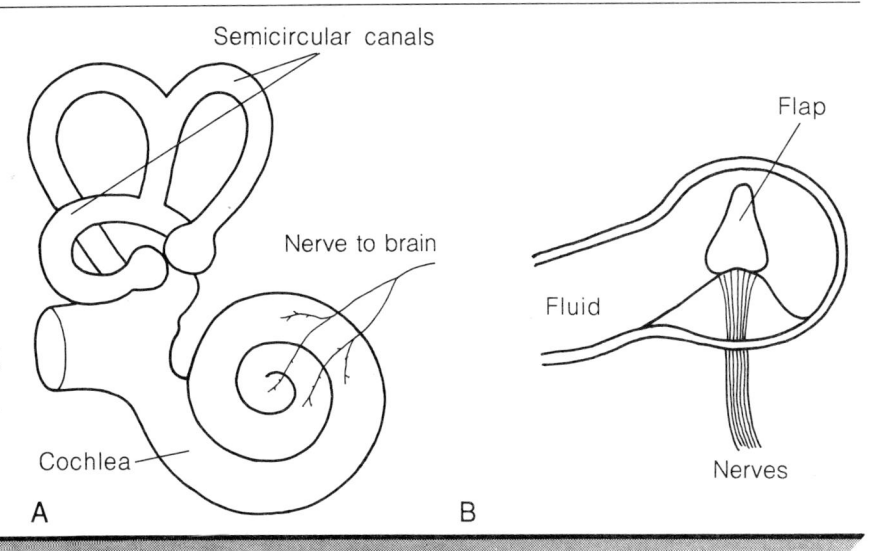

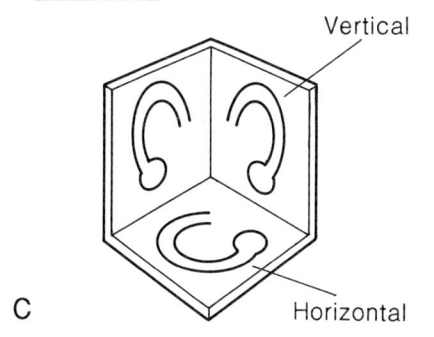

There are three semi-circular canals. Two are positioned vertically and one horizontally, see **C**. The two vertical canals are in planes at right angles to each other. If your head moves in one direction, the fluid moves slowly in the canal corresponding to that plane of movement. This pushes against the flap at the end of the canal. Most movements which you make are not precisely in the same plane as any one canal. The brain will usually have to interpret signals coming from two or three of the canals. It is able to combine the information to detect the direction of movement or the position of the body, see **D**.

Position of the cells stimulated by the movement

Position of the cells stimulated by the movement

Position of the cells stimulated by the movement

Activities

○ 1 Draw a table listing the different parts of the ear and the function of each.

○ 2 Explain why your brain would find it difficult to detect the direction of a sound from directly above your head.

◐ 3 What might you be able to do to help your brain to trace the direction of a sound from above your head?

● 4 Describe a type of movement which might stimulate all of your semi-circular canals.

13 The Nervous System

The Nervous System

Every part of the body is connected to the **spinal cord** and **brain** by a network of nerves.

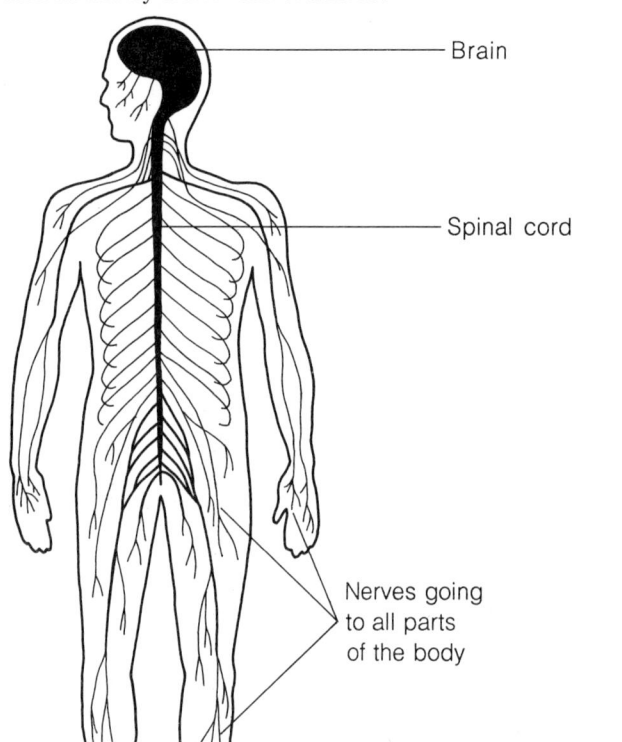

- Brain
- Spinal cord
- Nerves going to all parts of the body

Key Ideas

The human nervous system is made up of *nerves* and the *central nervous system*, which is the *brain* and the *spinal cord*. The brain is made up of three parts, the *cerebrum*, the *cerebellum* and the *medulla*.

Some nerves carry messages from the sense organs to the central nervous system, while other nerves carry signals from the central nervous system to the muscles. The central nervous system interprets messages from the senses and coordinates any responses which the body needs to make to stimuli.

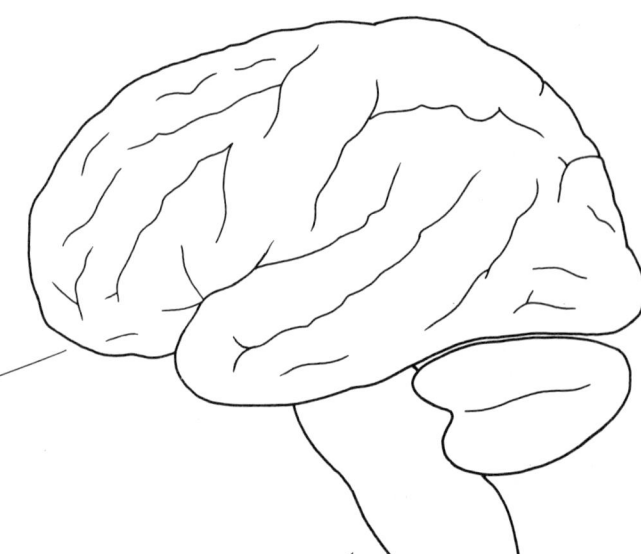

The Brain

The **cerebrum** is the largest part of the brain. The cerebrum interprets messages from the sense organs and can send out signals to parts of the body telling them what to do.

The cerebrum is the centre of thinking, memory and reasoning. If you are playing tennis and want to make a serve, the cerebrum will send signals to the muscles in the arms and legs to make them move together in the correct order to allow the racket to hit the ball correctly.

The **medulla** is the part of the brain which controls many automatic actions, such as breathing, heartbeat, coughing and swallowing.

If you are playing a difficult game, you do not want to have to think about every breath you take!

The **cerebellum** is found at the back of the head. It controls balance and coordinates all the actions of the muscles involved in moving the parts of your body. If a tennis player wants to run across court, the cerebellum will make sure that the muscles in the arms and legs move together in the correct order, so that the player runs without falling over.

This allows you to concentrate your conscious thinking (which goes on in the cerebrum) on what shot to hit when you reach the ball.

Nerves

Nerves carry information from the sensory organs, such as the eye or ear, to the spinal cord and brain. Electrical and chemical changes take place in a nerve. These changes cause a message or **nerve impulse** to travel along the nerve. A nerve is made up of a bundle of thin nerve fibres.

Nerves also carry information from the brain and spinal cord to **effector organs**. These can be muscles being made to contract, or glands which may release chemicals, called hormones, into the blood. Nerve impulses can only travel in *one* direction along a nerve.

Sensory Nerves

These are nerve cells which carry messages to the central nervous system.

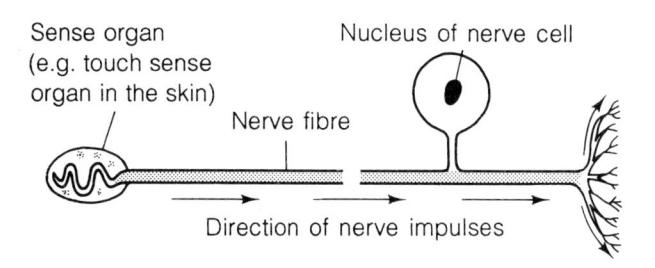

This information is called a **stimulus**.

Motor Nerves

These are nerve cells which carry signals from the central nervous system to effector organs.

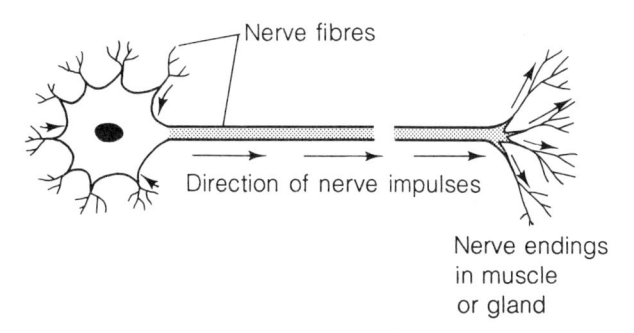

This information is called a **response**.

The brain is continually receiving vast amounts of information from the different sense organs. It is important that all the different parts of the body work together. The control of this is carried out by the central nervous system. This is called **coordination**.

As information comes into the central nervous system, the brain puts the information together. It may also compare it with previous information, stored in your **memory**. In this way your brain can use your past experiences and compare these with the current information. This comparison is called **association**. Then a decision may be made in the brain to respond to the stimulus. In this case, nerve impulses will be sent out along motor nerves to effector organs.

Most types of responses to stimuli are **voluntary actions**, which require some thought, such as answering a teacher's question!

148 THE BODY IN ACTION

Reflex Actions

A reaction to a stimulus involves messages travelling to the brain, which works out the best response to the stimulus. The brain then sends signals to the muscles or glands to produce a response. The fastest time that this can happen in humans is normally about 0.15 seconds.

Sometimes a faster response may be required, particularly to reduce possible damage to the body. A common example of this is touching a very hot object with your hand. In the time taken for a normal voluntary response, your skin could become badly burned.

Therefore, in this type of situation, a message is carried along a sensory nerve to the spinal cord. From there a signal is carried quickly and automatically to a motor nerve which leaves the spinal cord and goes to a muscle. This signal causes the muscle to contract and remove your hand from the hot object before you are consciously aware of what is happening.

This type of response is called a reflex action. The response time to a stimulus in this case will be about three times shorter than for a normal action.

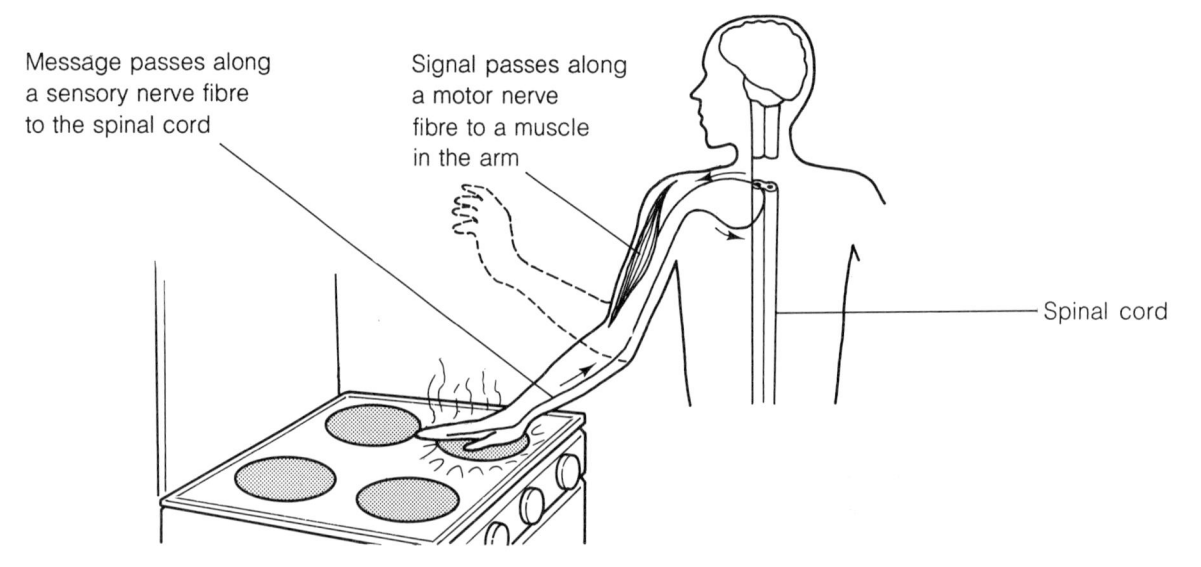

Route taken by a nerve impulse in a reflex action – called a reflex arc.

Another advantage of reflex actions, apart from speed of response, is that you do not have to consciously think about a response. The response happens automatically. Such actions include coughing, sneezing and blinking.

Activities

1. Copy and complete the following table to describe the function of each of the main parts of the brain.

Part	Function
cerebrum	
cerebellum	
medulla	

2. State the difference between motor nerves and sensory nerves.
3. Describe what might happen in the nervous system if you wanted to pick up a pencil which had fallen to the floor.
4. Describe, in your own words, how coordination occurs.
5. Explain, in terms of your nervous system, what would happen if you tried to pick up a tripod stand which you did not know was very hot.
6. Describe, in your own words, the advantages of a reflex action.

1 Variation

Key Ideas 🗝

Each different type of living thing in the world is described as a *species*. Organisms which can breed and produce offspring which are fertile are members of *one* species.

Differences between organisms are called *variations*. Variations exist between different species. Variations also occur within species.

Variations which have many "in-between" forms are called *continuous* variations.

Variations which show extremes and have no "in betweens" are called *discontinuous* variations.

Interbreeding

If a male organism mates with a female organism, young are produced. If these young are also able to reproduce then the original parents must belong to the same species.

Variation within Species

All dogs belong to the same species, although you might not think so when comparing a Great Dane and a Chihuahua.

As can be seen in the photographs of dogs shown on this page, different members of one species can look quite different from each other. Dogs have been cross-bred by humans for different purposes, such as hunting or racing. They can show extreme differences.

Donkeys and horses are two separate species.

You may know that a donkey and a horse can mate and produce young. The young are called mules. A male and female mule can mate, but will not produce offspring.

Horse and mule (right)

Different breeds of dog

Two different breeds of dog and their mongrel offspring

Inheritance

150 INHERITANCE

Being Human

All human beings belong to the same species. No two people are identical, although they all share many similar features.

People look different because of individual variations. Some of this variation is acquired during a person's lifetime. It is not passed on to the next generation. Examples of this include: scars, hairstyles and muscle development.

Many of the features showing variation may be passed on from generation to generation. These are inherited variations, and include: eye colour, fingerprints and ear lobes.

The branch of biology which studies inherited variations is called **genetics**.

- Dark wavy hair
- Brown eyes
- Straight nose
- Projecting chin
- Lobed ears

- Blonde straight hair
- Blue eyes
- Upturned nose
- Receding chin
- Unlobed ears

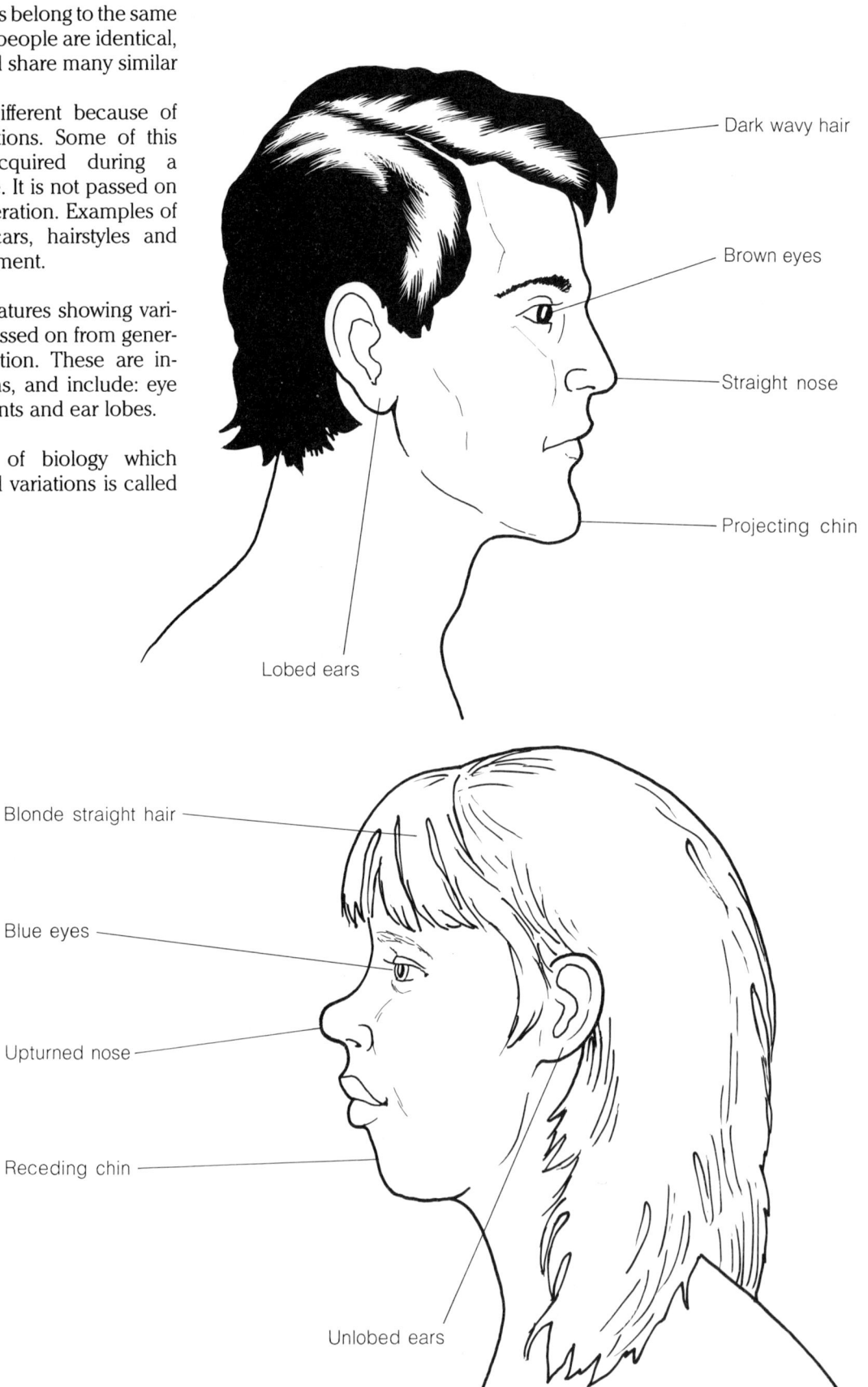

INHERITANCE 151

Describing Variation

Below are two histograms of features that can be measured which vary between people – adult height and tongue rolling.

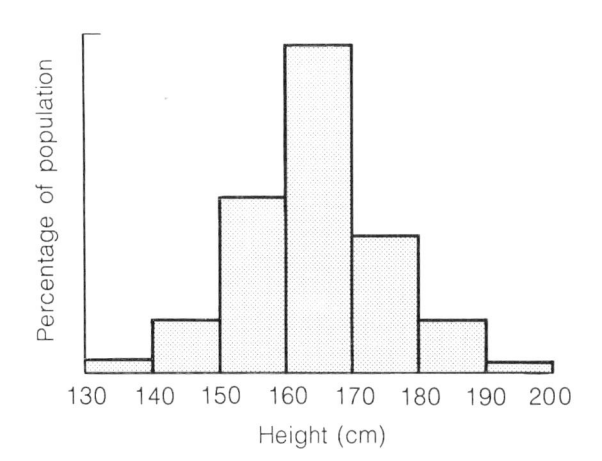

Adult height

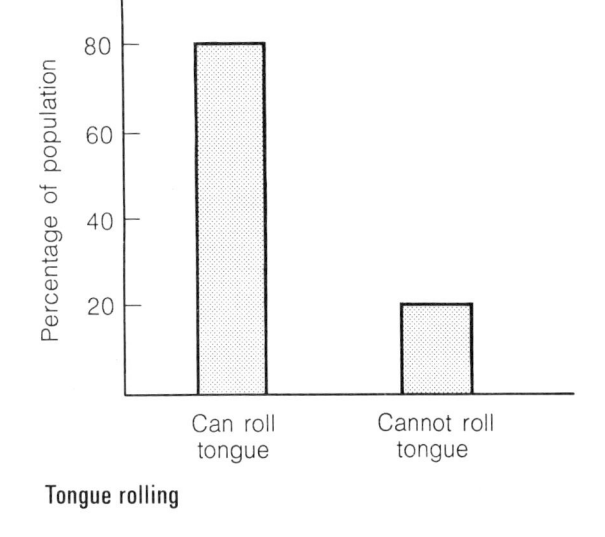

Tongue rolling

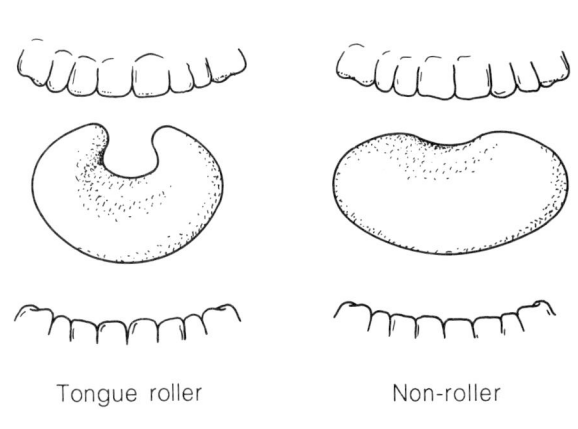

Tongue roller   **Non-roller**

Tongue rolling ability

The variation in height has many "in between" forms and people can be any height from one extreme to the other.
 This type of variation is called **continuous variation**.

The variation in tongue rolling ability has no "in between" forms. People can either roll their tongues or they cannot.
 This type of variation with clear-cut differences between individuals is called **discontinuous variation**.

A continuous variation is one which shows gradual changes between individuals throughout a population.
 A discontinuous variation is one which can be seen in two or more quite clearly defined groups in a population.
 Some of the activities for this chapter ask you to identify characteristics as being examples of either continuous or discontinuous variation.

152 INHERITANCE

Activities

○ 1 Write out a list of the characteristics which might allow someone to identify you, for example if you were lost. State whether each is a continuous or discontinuous variation. Underline those you have acquired during your lifetime.

○ 2 When a new baby is born, friends and relatives tend to say things like "she's got her mother's eyes" or "he's got his father's nose". Think about a friend or relation whom you know well and whose parents you also know well. Try to identify which characteristics he/she has inherited from the mother or father.

● 3 Five hundred wheat seeds were sown and after 21 days a random sample of the seedlings was removed. The seedling lengths were measured in centimetres. The results are shown below:
15, 19, 14, 20, 17, 12, 21, 17, 24, 16, 23, 16, 23, 19, 12, 20, 17, 19, 23, 19, 19, 19, 19, 20, 25, 18, 20, 21, 22, 16, 20, 18, 20, 18, 18, 20, 19, 20, 18, 21, 25, 19, 20, 15.
Group the results into 3 cm lengths and draw a histogram to show the variation in seedling length.

(a) From the results above, calculate the average length of the wheat seedlings.

(b) What type of variation is shown in wheat seedling length?

(c) Describe the shape of the histogram.

● 4 Humans do not all have the same blood group. Blood groups can be identified as being either A, B, AB or O. In a sample population the following frequencies of blood groups were identified:
48% of the population were Group O.
34% of the population were Group A.
13% of the population were Group B.
5% of the population were Group AB.
Draw a bar graph to show the distribution of blood groups in the population.

● 5 What type of variation is shown by human blood groups?

● 6 Select some human characteristics and, by making comparisons and collecting data from your classmates, try to identify whether they show continuous or discontinuous variation.

2 A Visit to the Zoo

Key Ideas

Zoological gardens are places where a wide variety of wild animals are kept for study, breeding and exhibition to the public. For many animals special enclosures have to be provided. The animal enclosures are often grouped together to show similar types of animals near each other, such as all the monkeys in cages in one large "Monkey House". Animal enclosures are usually labelled with the name of the animal, its diet and where it comes from in the wild.

There are almost one million different species of animal in the world. These can be divided into two main groups: invertebrates, of which there are about 900 thousand species, and vertebrates.

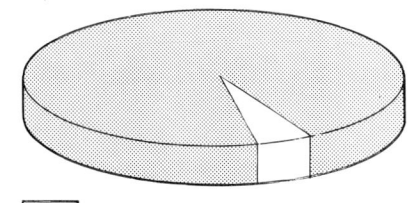

☐ Vertebrates
▓ Invertebrates

The vertebrates are divided into five main groups: fish, amphibians, reptiles, birds and mammals.

Zoological gardens usually concentrate on keeping animals from these five vertebrate groups. Most of the animals kept are mammals.

Within a zoo, animals of similar types are usually grouped together as shown in the sample zoo map.

154 INHERITANCE

The five main vertebrate groups can be identified by the features shown in the table.

Vertebrate group	Main features
Mammals	have hair or fur; young born alive; young suckle on mother's milk
Birds	have feathers, wings and lay eggs with hard shells
Reptiles	have dry scaly skin and lay eggs
Amphibians	young have gills, while adults have lungs and skin without scales
Fish	have fins and skin with scales

Genus and Species

The large groups of animals are split into smaller groups each called a genus. A genus contains several species.

In most zoos, an animal has a label giving its scientific name, with details of habitat, distribution, diet and breeding patterns. The label here might be found on a leopard's cage.

The scientific name for the leopard is *Panthera pardus*. *Panthera* is the genus to which the leopard belongs and *pardus* is the species name.

Variation between Species

Members of the genus *Panthera* are similar, but differences can be seen between each species. Members of this genus, such as lions, tigers, jaguars and snow leopards, have different fur colourings and patterns.

LEOPARD

Panthera pardus

Distribution	Africa, Asia.
Habitat	Varies from dense forest to open dry country, and up into mountains.
Habits	Solitary, except during mating season. Hunts by night and takes prey into tree. Spends day in cover of trees or rocks.
Food	Wide range of birds and mammals; particularly partial to monkeys and baboons.
Breeding	Gestation period 3 months. Litter of 2-3 cubs.

Activities

1. A lion's scientific name is *Panthera leo*. What is its genus name and what is its species name?
2. Name the five main vertebrate groups of animals and state one identifying characteristic for each.
3. Describe the main functions of zoological gardens.

3 A Visit to the Botanic Gardens

Key Ideas

Botanic gardens are places where collections of plants are kept. The idea behind them is to let the public see the variety of plant life on earth. They usually have greenhouses and hothouses so that exotic plants and tropical species can be grown. Often there are ponds to grow aquatic species. The plants are usually laid out in a systematic way and are labelled to show names and where in the world they come from.

Plant Variety

The variety of plants is enormous. There are more than half a million different **species** in the world. The species can be placed into groups for easy reference. Membership of groups often depends on the presence (or absence) of such features as flowers, spores or chlorophyll.

There are five main groups of plants, most of which can be found in a botanic garden. The groups are **algae, fungi, mosses, ferns,** and **seed-bearing plants**, which include coniferous trees, monocotyledonous species, like grasses and palm trees, and dicotyledonous species like deciduous trees, shrubs and herbs. The diagram shows examples of the different groups. You can read more about plant varieties on page 32 of World of Plants.

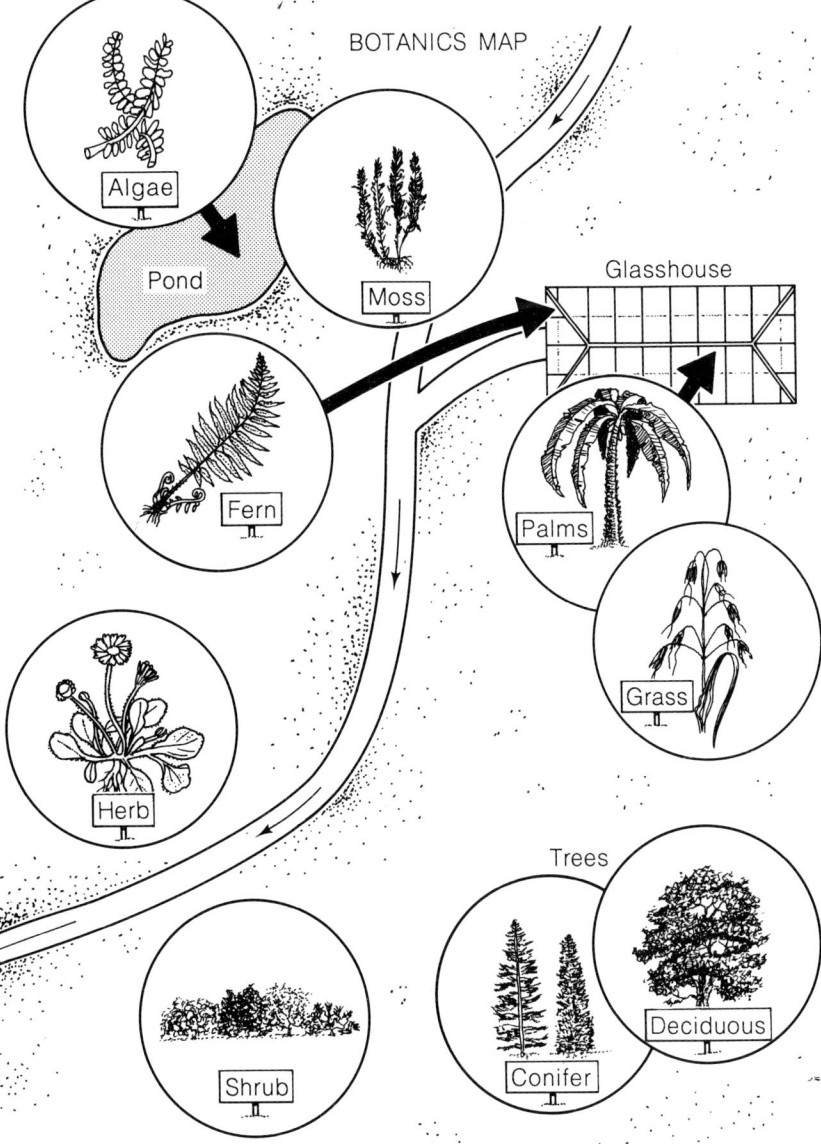

156 INHERITANCE

Plant group	Main features
Fungi	No chlorophyll; feed on dead or dying material
Algae	Usually aquatic; some species single-celled
Mosses	Produce spores; small leaves; no true roots
Ferns	Produce spores; leafy body; roots and stems
Seed-bearers:	
{Conifer Trees	Produce flowers and seeds; seeds contained in cones
Grasses	Produce flowers and seeds; leaves with parallel veins
Trees & Shrubs	Produce flowers and seeds; thick woody stems
Herbs}	Produce flowers and seeds; soft stems and leaves

Ilex aquifolium (Holly)

Distributed: in woodland throughout British Isles

Flowers: May – June

Fruits: ripen in Sept – March

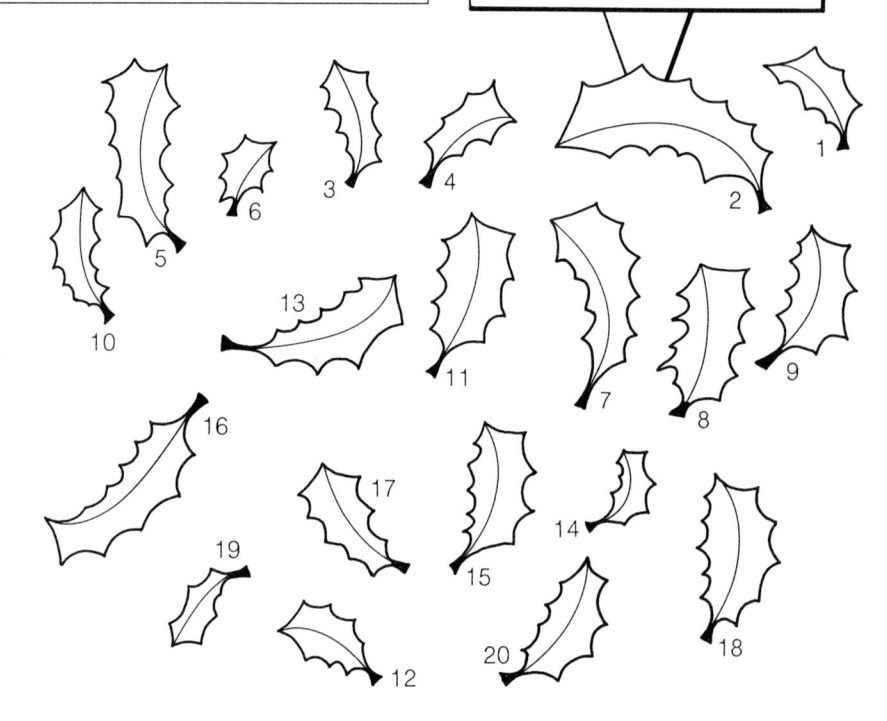

Genus and Species

The large groups of plants are split into smaller groups, each called a **genus**. A genus contains several species.

In most botanic gardens, each plant has a label giving its scientific name, details of habitat and distribution. The label shown might be found on a holly tree.

The scientific name for holly is *Ilex aquifolium*. *Ilex* is the genus to which the holly tree belongs and *aquifolium* is the name of the species. The label also gives details of distribution, habitat, and flowering and fruiting time.

Variation within a Species

Although members of a species are very alike, they are not identical. Differences can be seen. For example, if the point number on a collection of holly leaves is counted, a range of data is obtained. The drawing shows a collection of twenty holly leaves. Notice how the point number varies within the species.

Activities

○ 1 Copy and complete the following branched diagram which shows the different plant groups.

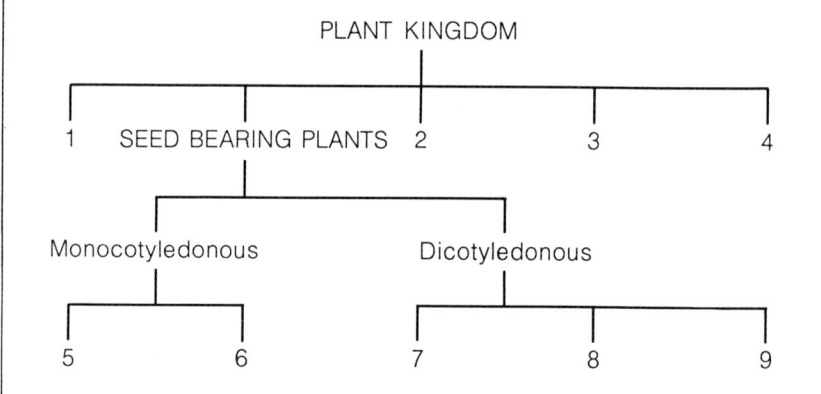

```
                    PLANT KINGDOM
         ┌──────────────┬──────────┬──────────┐
         1    SEED BEARING PLANTS  2    3    4
              ┌──────────┴──────────┐
         Monocotyledonous      Dicotyledonous
           ┌────┴────┐        ┌────┬────┐
           5         6        7    8    9
```

○ 2 Draw a bar chart to show the variation in point number of the twenty holly leaves shown in the drawing.

4 Inheritance of Characteristics

Key Ideas

Features which can be used to identify individuals are called *characteristics*. Acquired characteristics are those features, such as height or weight, which are affected by an individual's environment. *Inherited* characteristics are those, such as fingerprints, which are passed on from parents to offspring.

The characteristics of an organism – usually its physical appearance – are used to describe its *phenotype*.

So far we have looked at variation which is passed on from parents to offspring.

The first person to find out how inherited characteristics are passed on was an Austrian monk called Gregor Mendel. In 1865, he chose to begin some breeding experiments using garden pea plants. Mendel was successful, partly due to luck, but mainly due to particularly good experimental methods.

1. He looked at only one inherited characteristic at a time.

2. The characteristics he looked at had distinctly different forms with no "in betweens", i.e. they showed discontinuous variation.

The characteristics he studied included plant height (some pea plants are tall and some dwarf) and type of seed coat (some smooth and some wrinkled).

3. Pea plants grow quickly and can be either cross pollinated or self pollinated.

For cross pollination, pollen from one flower fertilises the egg cell in another flower of the same species. For self pollination the pollen from one flower pollinates the egg cells in the same flower head.

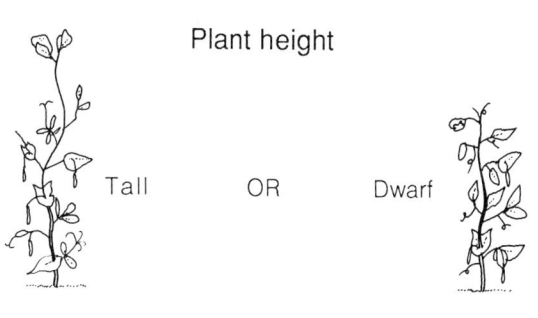

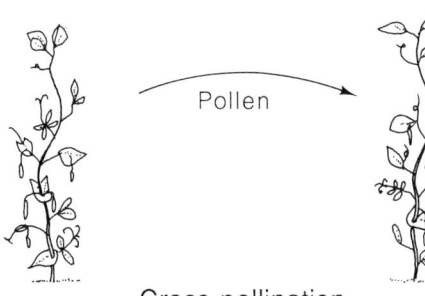

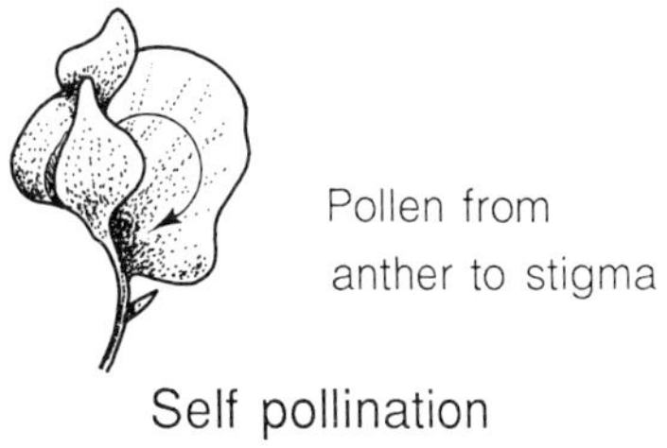

Plant height

Tall OR Dwarf

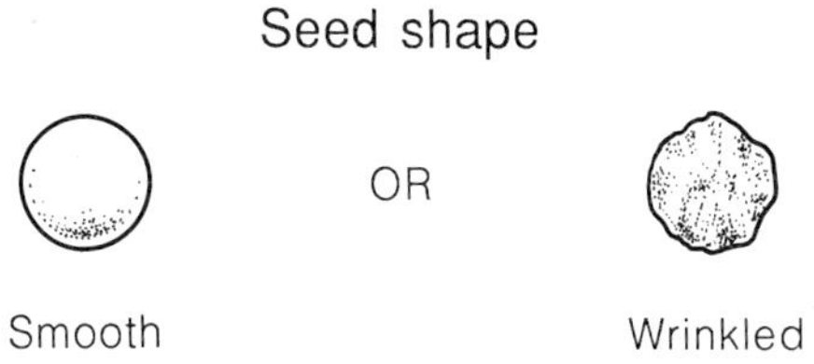

Seed shape

Smooth OR Wrinkled

Cross pollination

Self pollination

Pollen from anther to stigma

158 INHERITANCE

4. Mendel always began his experiments with **pure-bred** lines of plants. These plants, when self pollinated for many years, always show the same characteristics.

His method was to cross two different pure-bred plants. When two different organisms are bred together their young are called hybrids. He usually crossed plants which differed by only one characteristic. This type of cross is called a **monohybrid** cross.

In a cross such as the one shown on the right the parents are identified as generation P and the young are identified as the F_1 generation. Where crosses are made between individuals of the F_1 generation, the offspring are called the F_2 generation.

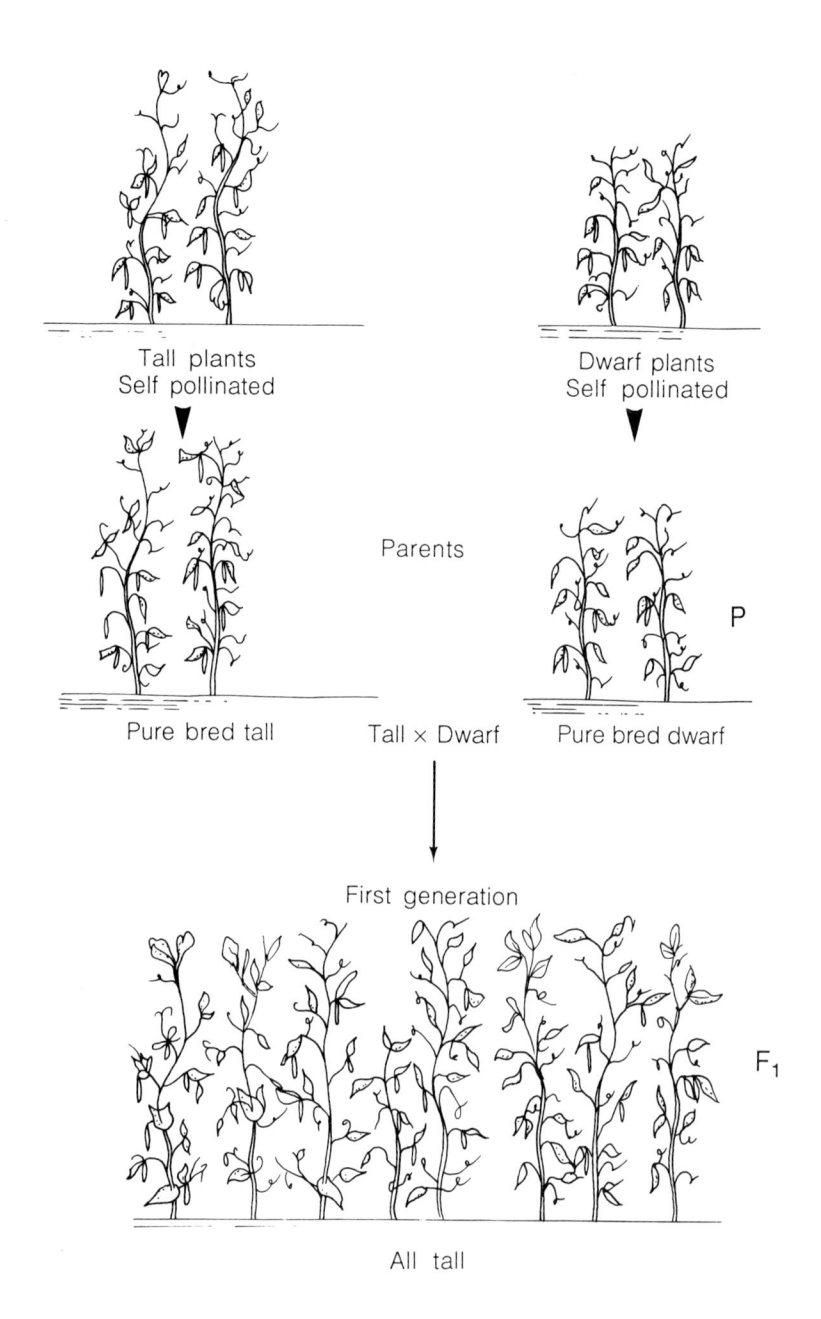

Tall plants
Self pollinated

Dwarf plants
Self pollinated

Parents

Pure bred tall   Tall × Dwarf   Pure bred dwarf   P

First generation

All tall F_1

As all the hybrid offspring were tall, Mendel called tallness a **dominant** characteristic and dwarfness was called a **recessive** characteristic. In these crosses the dominant characteristic masks the recessive characteristic. The physical appearance of an organism is called its **phenotype**. Tall plants show the dominant phenotype. Dwarf plants show the recessive phenotype.

For a cross between pure-breeding plants, the phenotypes of the F_1 offspring are always identical to each other.

When any two individuals are mated with each other, the young of the cross inherit some characteristics from one parent and some from the other. The phenotypes of the young will usually be a mixture of the phenotypes of both parents.

However in experimental crosses where one characteristic is being studied – monohybrid crosses – the phenotypes of all the offspring are usually identical for the characteristic studied. All the offspring show the dominant phenotype. This is because one parent is pure-breeding for the dominant phenotype and the other parent is pure-breeding for the recessive phenotype. When mating occurs, the dominant form of the characteristic masks the recessive form of the characteristic.

Activities

1. Describe the difference between acquired characteristics and inherited characteristics.
2. Describe the difference between cross pollination and self pollination in plants.
3. In breeding experiments with plants, why is it important to self pollinate plants for several generations before carrying out a monohybrid cross?
4. In pea plants, flower colour can be red or white. If a red-flowered parent is crossed with a white-flowered parent, all the F_1 generation are red-flowered.
   Which flower colour is the dominant form of the characteristic?
5. Describe what is meant by the term phenotype.

160 INHERITANCE

5 Gametes, Chromosomes and Genes

Key Ideas

The cells of living organisms have nuclei which contain information. This information is held on *chromosomes*.

Normal body cells have two matching sets of chromosomes. To reproduce sexually, sex cells called *gametes* must be produced. These specialised cells have a single set of chromosomes. For sexual reproduction, a male gamete must join with a female gamete. This is called *fertilisation* and produces a cell which combines the two sets of chromosomes of the gametes to give two matching sets again.

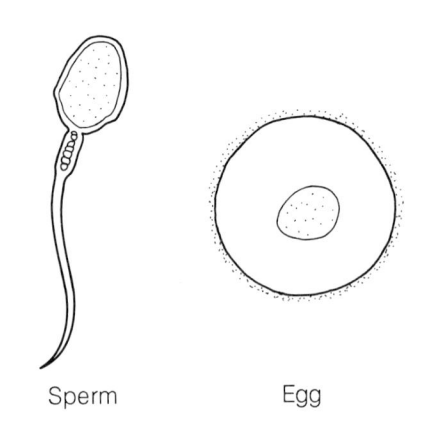

Sperm   Egg

The Genetic Material

The only way an individual can inherit characteristics is by information being passed on in the gametes of its parents.

This information is found in the nucleus of a cell, which contains fine thread-like strands called chromosomes. Each chromosome carries a number of sections of information, each called a gene. Some of your characteristics – such as whether you can roll your tongue or not – are controlled by a single gene.

A fruit fly called *Drosophila* has giant chromosomes in its salivary gland cells. Magnified under the microscope, these chromosomes show visible bands. The bands are thought to show the position of one or more genes.

In sexual reproduction, a single cell, the **zygote**, is formed when two parental gametes join together. This means that we can inherit genetic material from both parents. This genetic material is present for the whole of the organism's life in every cell nucleus.

It is passed on to future generations by the gametes.

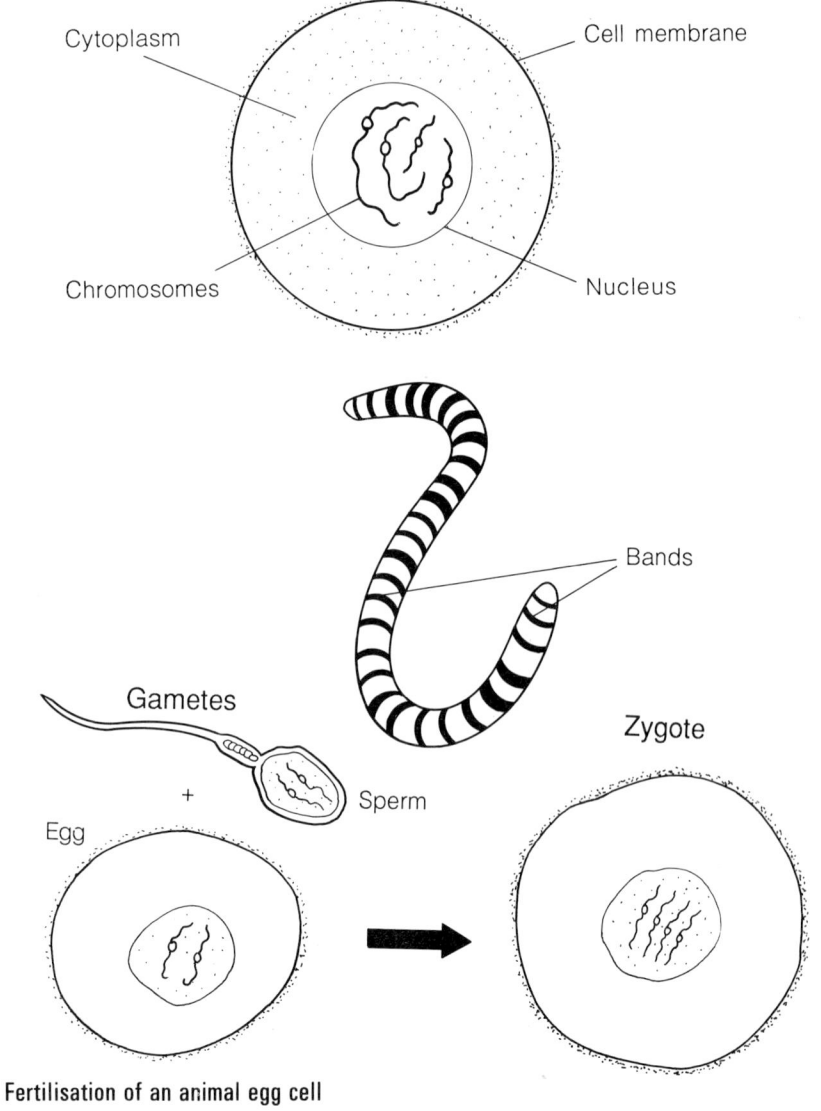

Cytoplasm — Cell membrane
Chromosomes — Nucleus

Bands

Gametes
Egg + Sperm → Zygote

Fertilisation of an animal egg cell

Producing Gametes

There are two types of sex cells. In mammals, male gametes are called sperms. Female gametes are called eggs. Most of the cells in the human body contain two matching sets of chromosomes. Some cells, the gametes, contain only one set of chromosomes. These special cells are made in a way that reduces two sets of chromosomes per cell to only one set.

Human cells have 46 chromosomes arranged in two sets of 23. In other words, each normal human cell has 23 pairs of chromosomes. Of each pair, one chromosome comes from each parent.

Human sex cells have only one set of 23 chromosomes.

The cell shown in the drawing is not a human cell. It has only one pair of chromosomes. If it is going to divide to produce sex cells it must go through three stages.

1. Its chromosomes double in number, making a second, identical set of chromosomes.

2. The cell divides once to produce two cells, each again having one pair of chromosomes.

3. The two cells then divide again, with one chromosome going into each cell produced.

One cell with a normal number of chromosomes has produced four new cells, each with half the normal number of chromosomes. Each of these new cells is a gamete.

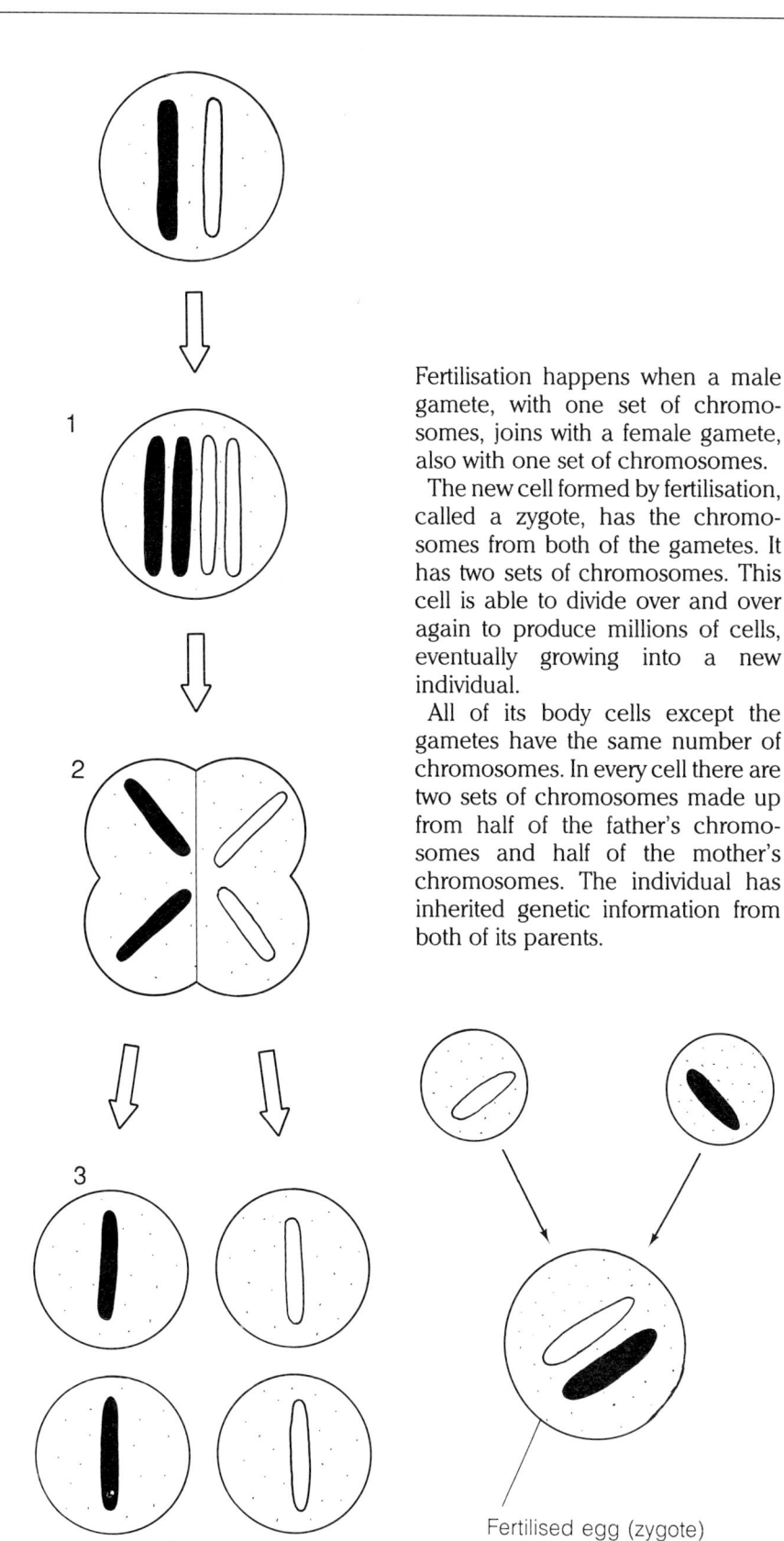

Fertilisation happens when a male gamete, with one set of chromosomes, joins with a female gamete, also with one set of chromosomes.

The new cell formed by fertilisation, called a zygote, has the chromosomes from both of the gametes. It has two sets of chromosomes. This cell is able to divide over and over again to produce millions of cells, eventually growing into a new individual.

All of its body cells except the gametes have the same number of chromosomes. In every cell there are two sets of chromosomes made up from half of the father's chromosomes and half of the mother's chromosomes. The individual has inherited genetic information from both of its parents.

Gametes

Fertilised egg (zygote) with two chromosomes

Activities

1. Where in a cell are the chromosomes found?
2. If an animal has 40 chromosomes in its body cells, how many chromosomes will there be in each of its gametes?
3. Describe what happens to the chromosomes in a cell when it forms gametes.
4. Explain why it is important for gametes to have half the number of chromosomes found in other body cells.

6 Monohybrid Crosses

> ## Key Ideas
>
> **Chromosomes are made up of many "bits" called *genes*. Each gene may contain information to control a particular characteristic. The number and type of genes on an organism's chromosomes make up its *genotype*. There may be different forms of one gene. Cells have pairs of chromosomes. When gametes are formed only one chromosome from each pair goes into each gamete.**

Mendel used pea plants in most of his experiments. One of the characteristics which he studied was plant height.
Mendel said that tallness and dwarfness must be controlled by "factors", which we now call genes. He then said that these factors work in pairs.

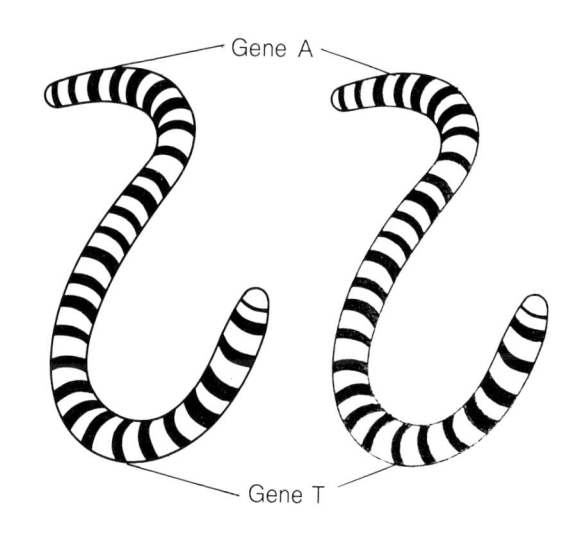

Each chromosome is made up of many hundreds of genes. Chromosomes exist in pairs and each chromosome in a pair carries genes for the same characteristics along its length. Therefore each individual has a pair of each of its genes.
The two genes in each pair can be of the same form or they can be different forms.

Since tallness is dominant over dwarfness, Mendel made the code for tallness **T** (capital letter). Since dwarfness is recessive to tallness, he made the code for dwarfness **t** (small letter).
Therefore pure-breeding tall plants would have two identical copies of the plant height gene for tallness, i.e.:

tall plants = **T T**

and pure-breeding dwarf plants would have two identical copies of the gene for dwarfness, i.e.:

dwarf plants = **tt**.

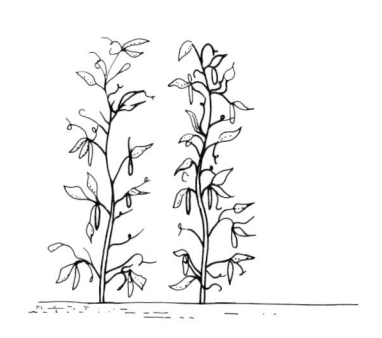

Pure breeding tall plant

Pure breeding dwarf plant

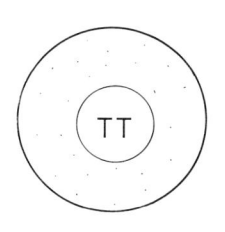

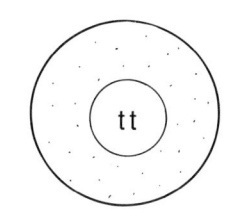

164 INHERITANCE

"Tall" and "dwarf" are different forms of the same gene. This gene carries information which controls plant height.

The forms of the pair of genes which an individual has is called its genotype. The forms may be the same or different.

The effect of these two forms of a gene on the characteristic of an individual is called its phenotype.

If an individual has one of each of the different forms of the gene for height, then its genotype will be **Tt**. Because the dominant form of the gene controls the characteristic, the phenotype of this individual plant will be tall. The effect of gene **T** dominates the effect of gene **t**.

A gamete has only a single set of chromosomes, therefore it has only one chromosome from each of the pairs that exist in other body cells.

A gamete from a tall plant **TT** will only have one tallness gene, **T**.

A gamete from a small plant **tt** will only have one dwarfness gene, **t**.

If the tall plant's gamete fertilises the small plant's gamete then the zygote formed will inherit one form of the gene from each parent.

It will have the genotype **Tt**.

It will look tall because gene **T** dominates the effect of gene **t**.

Characteristic – tall

Genotype — TT

Phenotype

Characteristic – tall

Phenotype

Genotype — Tt

Gametes

	t	t
T	Tt	Tt
T	Tt	Tt

Genotypes

Zygotes

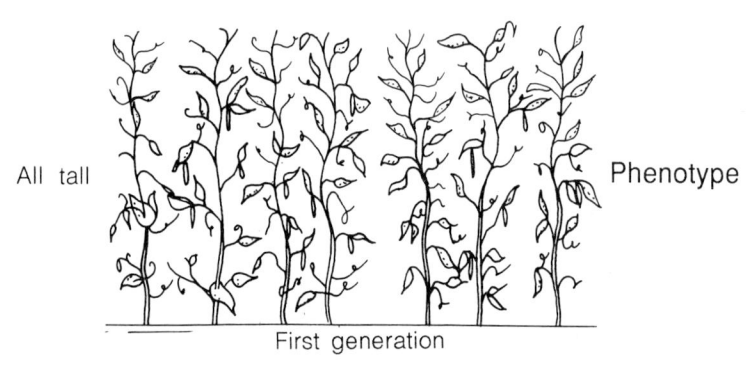

All tall — First generation

Phenotype

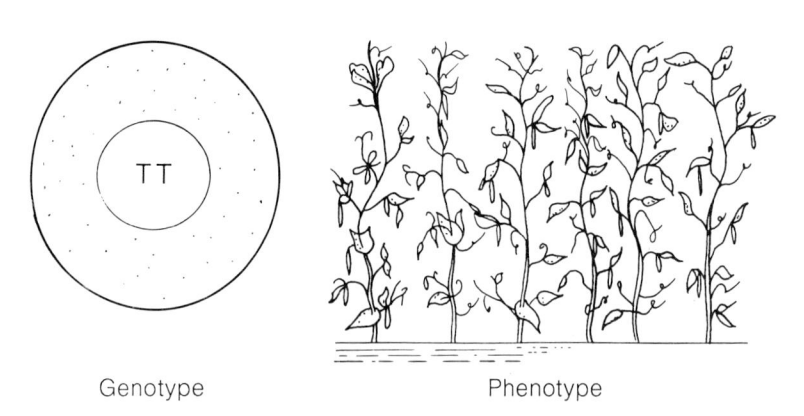

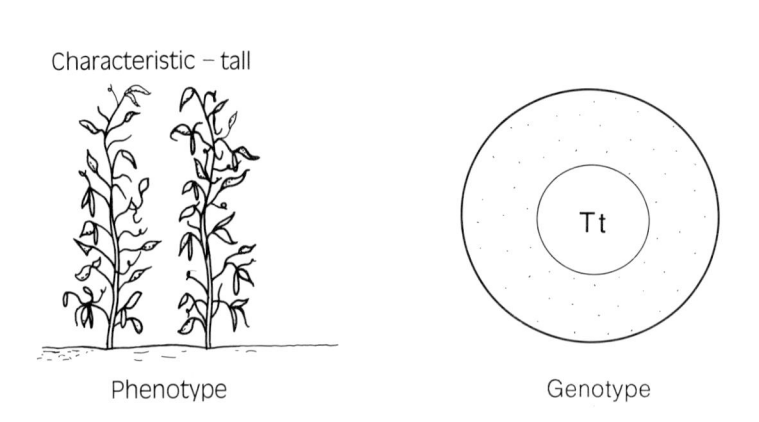

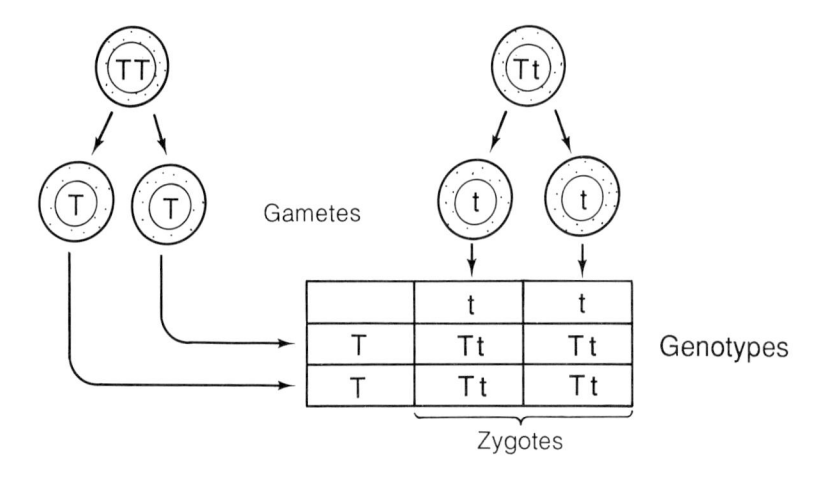

The site (position) on a pair of chromosomes where a particular factor is found is called the gene. This gene can control the phenotype of one characteristic. The different forms of the gene which can be found at that site on the chromosome are called the **alleles** of that gene. Therefore the alleles for tallness and dwarfness are alternative forms of the same gene.

If the two alleles for one gene are identical, **TT** or **tt**, then the individual is said to be **homozygous** for that gene. Individuals like this are called pure bred.

If the two alleles are different, **Tt**, then the individual is said to be **heterozygous** for that gene.

When two different types of pure bred parents are crossed with each other, the individuals of the next generation will be heterozygous. Individuals like this are called **hybrids**.

The hybrid offspring have one of each type of allele:

hybrid plants = **Tt**

The hybrids will always be tall because tallness **T** is always dominant over dwarfness **t**.

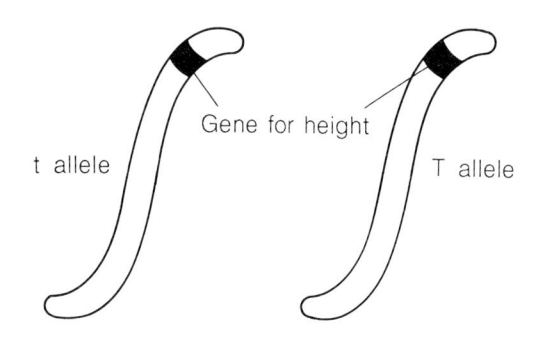

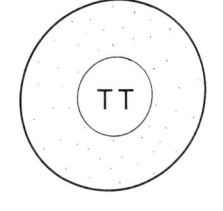

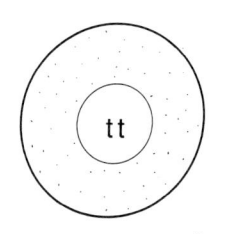

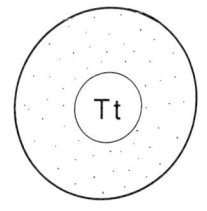

Crosses

A cross occurs when a male gamete fertilises a female gamete. Gametes only contain one allele of each gene.

For a pure-bred tall plant each gamete will have **T**.

For a pure-bred dwarf plant each gamete will have **t**.

Therefore the hybrid formed from a cross between a tall plant and a dwarf plant will have the alleles **Tt**. However, it will grow into a tall plant.

This does not mean that dwarfness has been lost forever.

If a male hybrid **Tt** produces sperm, they will be of different types, **T** or **t**.

Similarly, if a female hybrid **Tt** produces eggs, they will be of different types, **T** or **t**.

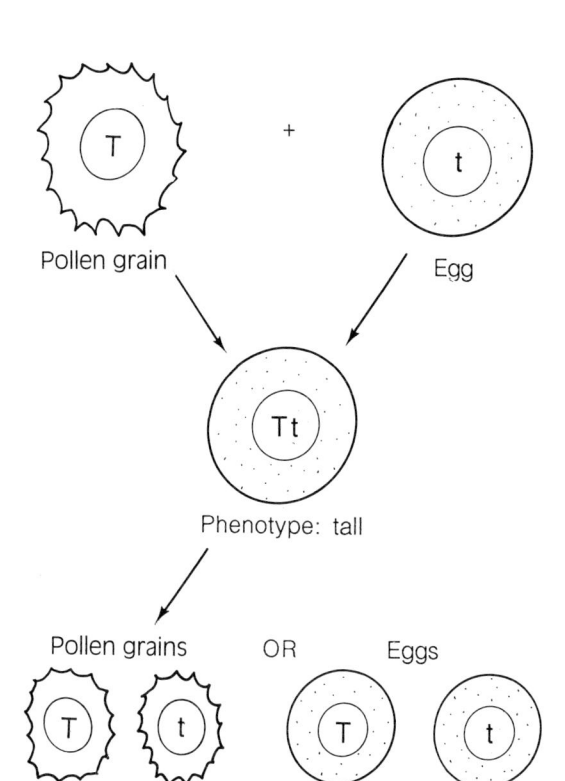

166 INHERITANCE

The diagrams below show how the gene which controls tongue rolling is inherited.

R is the allele for tongue rolling.
r is the allele for being unable to roll your tongue.

P₁ Parents

Normal body cell in father with a pair of alleles for tongue rolling

Normal body cell in mother with a pair of non tongue rolling alleles

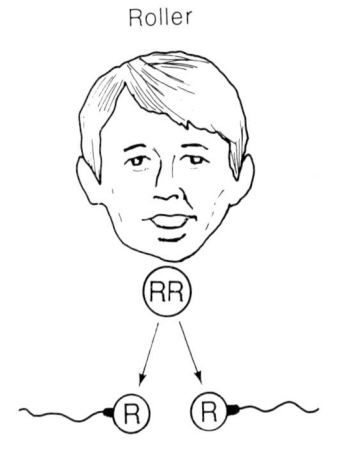

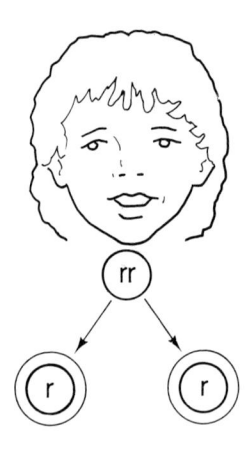

Roller

Gametes

Each sperm has an allele for tongue rolling

Each egg cell has an allele for non tongue rolling

At fertilisation

There are four possible combinations of sperms joining with eggs.

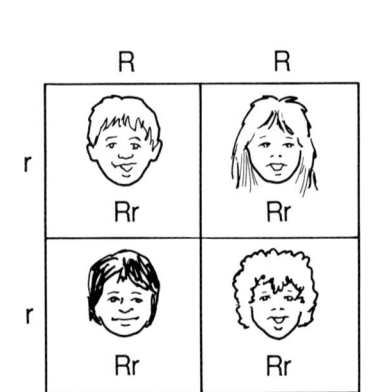

All the children inherited the alleles **Rr**. All the children can roll their tongues.

Fruit Fly Crosses

Fruit flies (*Drosophila melanogaster*) are often used for genetics experiments because they have a short life cycle and results for a cross can be obtained in two or three weeks. They are easy to keep, being small, and they produce large numbers of offspring. It is also fairly easy to tell the difference between males and females.

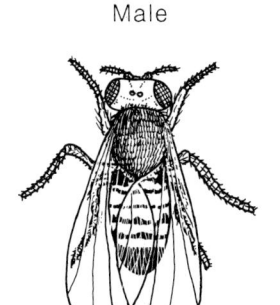

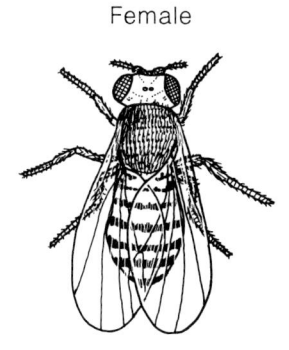

Male

Female

Some fruit flies have normal wings and some have vestigial wings, which are short and misshapen and do not allow flight. The wing phenotype is determined by one gene.

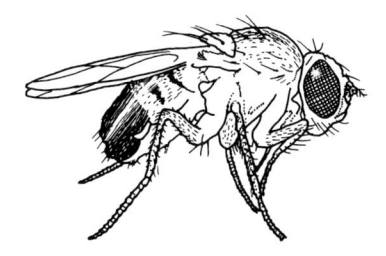

Female with curly wing mutant phenotype

Normal winged

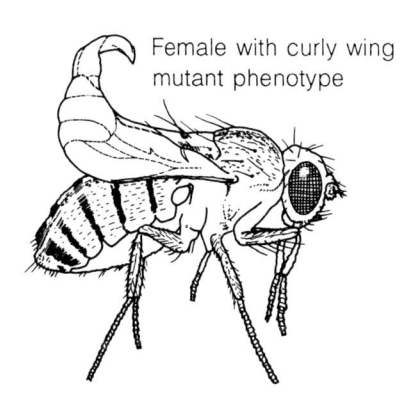

Vestigial winged female fruit flies were crossed with normal winged male fruit flies. Both varieties of fly came from the pure-breeding populations. The offspring of this cross all had normal wings. Using the symbols **N** for the dominant normal wing and **n** for the recessive vestigial wing, the following table shows the results of this cross.

P_1 Parents	Phenotype	Normal wing × vestigial wing
	Genotype	**NN** **nn**
	Gametes	**N** **n**
F_1	Phenotype	All normal wing
	Genotype	**Nn**

168 INHERITANCE

Crossing the F₁

The F₁ flies from the cross **NN** × **nn** were all found to be normal winged flies. This is the phenotype of these flies, that is, what they would look like. If we cross the F₁ flies with each other the cross would be as shown in the table.

F₁	Phenotype	Normal wing	×	normal wing
	Genotype	**Nn**		**Nn**
	Gametes	**N** or **n**		**N** or **n**
F₂	Phenotypes	Normal winged		Vestigial winged
No. of flies		150		50

The genotypes of the normal winged flies could be **NN** or **Nn**.
The genotype of the vestigial winged flies would be **nn**.
The ratio of normal winged flies to vestigial winged flies is 3:1.

Activities

1. If a pea plant has the genotype **Tt** (where **T** and **t** are the genes for plant height) what will be the plant's phenotype?

2. If a pea plant with genotype **TT** is crossed with a pea plant of genotype **tt**:
   (a) What are the phenotypes of the parents?
   (b) What would be the genotypes of the parents' gametes?
   (c) What would be the genotype of the F₁ offspring?
   (d) What would be the phenotype of the F₁ offspring?

3. Mendel cross pollinated pure-breeding plants which produced round seeds with pure-breeding plants which produced wrinkled seeds. All the offspring produced round seeds.
   (a) Which is the dominant allele?
   (b) Using the symbols **R** and **r** for the alleles, copy and complete the following table to show the genotypes of the parents and offspring in the spaces.

Parent genotypes:		×	
	round seeds		wrinkled seeds
Offspring genotype (F₁):			
		all round seeds	

   (c) The F₁ generation were self pollinated and the offspring examined for seed type. What phenotypes of seeds would you expect to be found and in what ratio?

7 Sex Determination in Humans

Key Ideas

Human sex cells carry a complete set of 23 *chromosomes*. In egg cells there is a total of 22 chromosomes controlling almost all of the characteristics of the offspring. The remaining chromosome is called the *X chromosome* and is concerned with the sex of the offspring. In sperm cells there is a total of 22 chromosomes concerned with the body characteristics of the offspring. The remaining chromosome can be one of two types, an X chromosome or a *Y chromosome*. Fifty per cent of sperms contain an X chromosome and the other 50 per cent contain a Y chromosome. If a sperm with an X chromosome fertilises an egg, the baby will be a girl. If a sperm containing a Y chromosome fertilises an egg, the baby will be a boy.

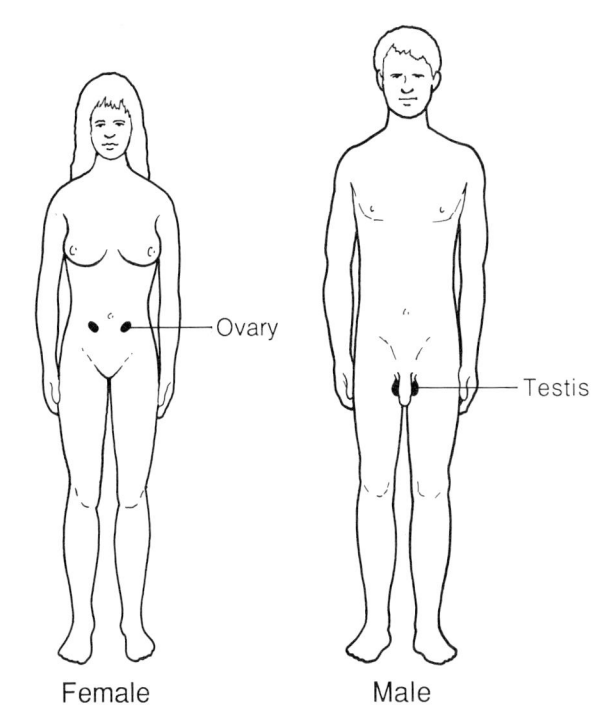

Positions of the sex-cell producing tissues in humans

Chromosome Numbers

Human body cells contain two sets of chromosomes giving 46 chromosomes in each. This number remains the same when cells divide by **mitosis** during growth and repair. In the special tissues where sex cells are made, a type of cell division occurs which produces cells with only one set of 23 chromosomes. This type of cell division is called **meiosis**. In females the sex-cell-producing tissue is called **ovary tissue**. In males the sex-cell-producing tissue is in the **testis**. When a sperm cell fertilises an egg cell, a **zygote** is formed. The zygote contains two sets of chromosomes, one paternal set from the sperm and one maternal set from the egg. The diagram shows the movements of chromosomes during meiosis. For simplicity, only one pair of chromosomes is shown in the parent cell although in humans there are 23 such pairs. You can read more about meiosis on page 161.

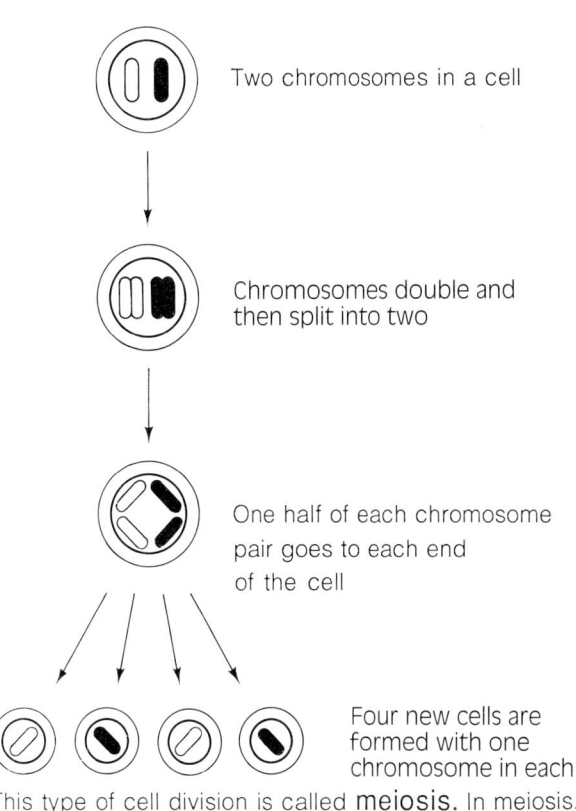

Two chromosomes in a cell

Chromosomes double and then split into two

One half of each chromosome pair goes to each end of the cell

Four new cells are formed with one chromosome in each

This type of cell division is called **meiosis**. In meiosis, the number of chromosomes in each cell is halved.

Meiosis

170 INHERITANCE

Making Female Sex Cells

Human females release eggs from their ovaries once a month from puberty until about the age of 50. Each egg cell contains a maternal set of 23 chromosomes. 22 of these are concerned with the general body characteristics of the offspring. The remaining chromosome is called the X chromosome and it is concerned with the sex of the offspring. All eggs contain an X chromosome.

Making Male Sex Cells

Human males normally produce sperm cells from the age of puberty until their sixtieth year or beyond. Each sperm contains a set of 23 paternal chromosomes. 22 of these chromosomes are concerned with the general body characteristics of the offspring. The remaining chromosome is one of two possible types, an X chromosome or a Y chromosome. Fifty per cent of sperm produced by a male will carry an X chromosome and the other 50% will contain a Y chromosome. The photograph shows an egg cell surrounded by many sperms. If the egg is fertilised by an X-containing sperm then the baby will be a girl. If an egg is fertilised by a Y-containing sperm then the baby will be a boy. It is a matter of pure chance whether an egg is fertilised by an X sperm or a Y sperm. The sperm cell determines the sex of the baby.

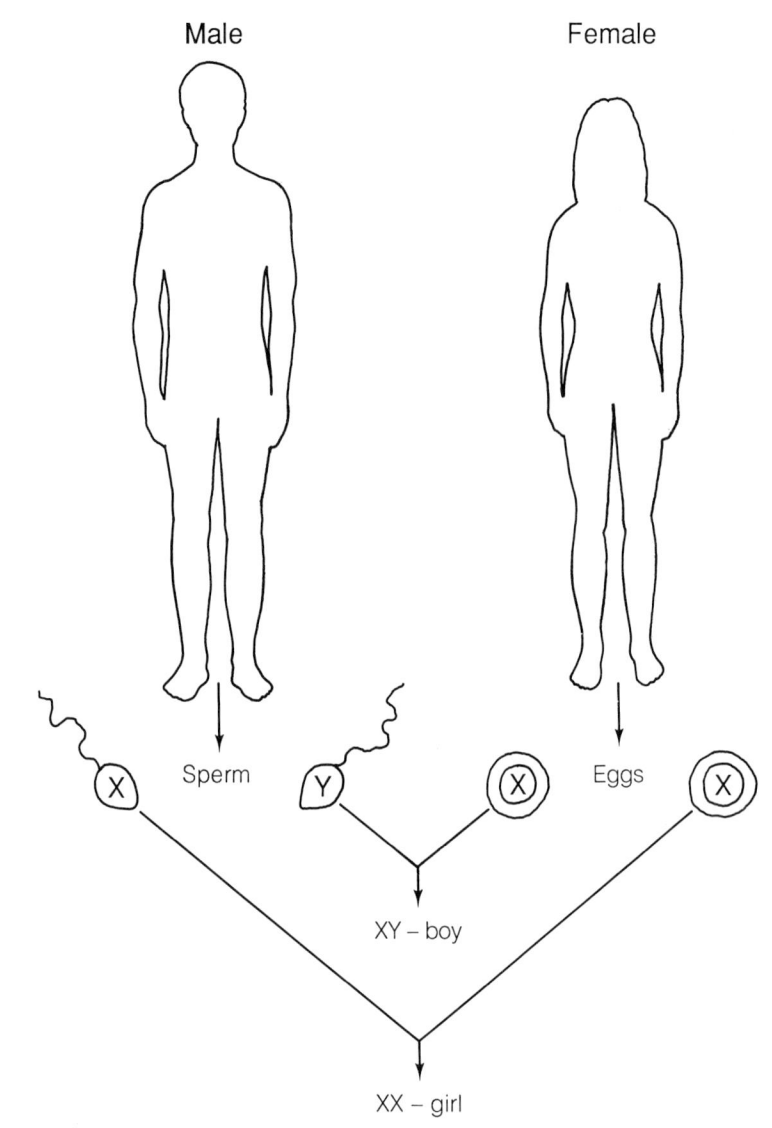

Inheritance of sex in humans

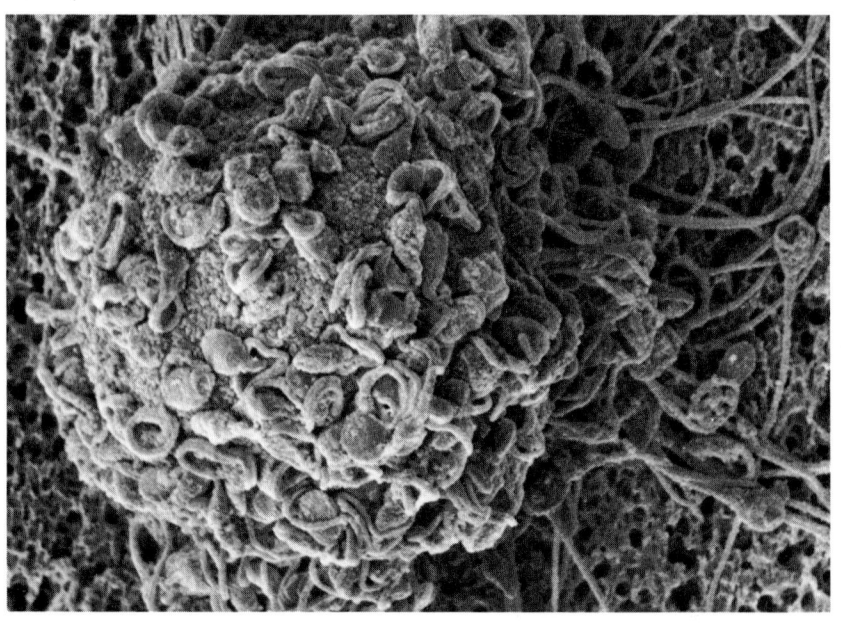

Sperm surrounding an egg cell

Activities

1. How many chromosomes are there in
   (a) a sperm cell
   (b) an egg cell
   (c) a fertilised egg
   (d) a body cell?

2. What will be the sex of a baby formed from a zygote containing two X chromosomes?

3. What will be the sex of a baby formed from a zygote containing an X chromosome and a Y chromosome?

4. The human population as a whole contains half males and half females. Explain why this is so.

5. Mr and Mrs Smith have three sons. Mrs Smith is pregnant. She is convinced that the baby will be a girl because she has already had three boys. Imagine that you are her doctor. Write an account of what you would tell her about the chances of the baby being female.

8 Chromosome Mutations

Key Ideas

Chromosome mutations are errors which alter some aspect of the chromosomes of an organism. An important example of a chromosome mutation is *non-disjunction* which causes the wrong number of chromosomes to appear in cells. In the production of human egg cells non-disjunction can cause eggs to be produced with an extra chromosome. These eggs contain 24 chromosomes instead of 23. If one of these cells is fertilised by a normal sperm then the resulting zygote will contain 47 chromosomes. This can have very serious consequences for the developing baby.

A 24 year old Down's syndrome woman

Non-disjunction

This type of chromosome mutation results in failure of one chromosome pair to move apart during cell division. The photograph shows the results of non-disjunction of one pair of chromosomes during the production of an egg cell compared with a normal division.

Down's Syndrome

If non-disjunction occurs between the pair of human chromosomes known as no. 21, egg cells are produced with either an extra no. 21 or without a no. 21 at all. Cells without this chromosome seldom survive but those with an extra no. 21 sometimes do and can be fertilised in the usual way. The babies produced by this fertilisation develop and are born with a set of differences known as **Down's syndrome.**

Some of the characteristics associated with Down's syndrome are:

1. Folds of skin often develop over the inner angle of the eye.

2. The bridge of the nose is often flat.

3. The baby has a smallish, oval shaped head.

4. The tongue sometimes has a groove in it.

5. There is often a deep crease across the palm of the hand.

6. The baby is mentally retarded to some extent and does not usually develop beyond the mental capacity of a seven-year-old if untreated.

7. There are often whitish specks on the baby's iris.

8. The baby's hands are broad with in-curved little fingers.

9. Down's children are usually cheerful and friendly and sometimes develop appreciation of areas such as music, drama and art well beyond their mental capacity.

10. Recent medical advances in hygiene and nutrition have greatly increased the life span of many Down's children.

Maternal Age

Down's syndrome is more likely to occur as the mother's age increases. This table shows the risk of Down's compared with the mother's age.

Mother's age	Risk
20–30	1 in 1300 births
30–35	1 in 600 births
35–40	1 in 200 births
40–45	1 in 50 births
over 45	1 in 20 births

INHERITANCE 173

Amniocentesis

Nowadays it is possible to find out about the chromosomes of an unborn child while it is still within its mother's uterus. The procedure, invented in the 1950s, is known as **amniocentesis** and can be performed under local anaesthetic after the 14th week of pregnancy.

The general idea is that a sample (about 14 g) of the amniotic fluid surrounding the developing baby is withdrawn using a long hollow needle fitted to a syringe as shown in the diagram. The fluid has been swallowed by the baby and passed out again and it contains cells which have been rubbed off the baby's skin and other organs.

The cells are separated from the fluid in a centrifuge. These cells can be specially stained to show up their chromosomes. When the stained cells are examined by microscope, chromosome abnormalities can often be identified. Also, chemical analysis of the fluid can give information about the baby, such as the detection of **spina bifida**.

If amniocentesis shows up a serious abnormality, the doctors may be able to offer the mother the chance to **terminate** her pregnancy. Amniocentesis is offered to nearly all pregnant women over 35 years old.

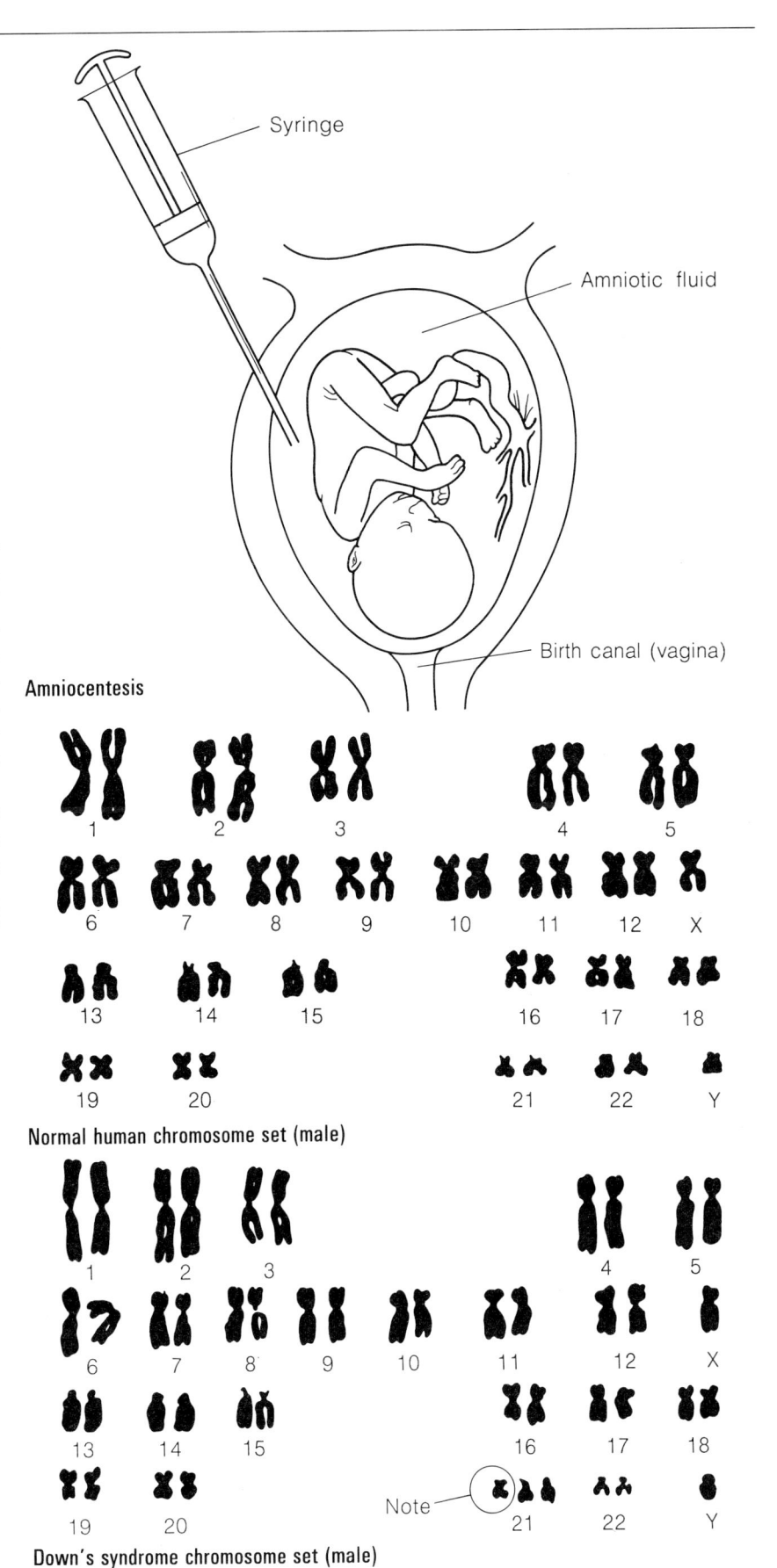

Amniocentesis

Normal human chromosome set (male)

Down's syndrome chromosome set (male)

Activities

1. What is meant by non-disjunction?
2. What effect does non-disjunction have on the number of chromosomes within a cell?
3. Describe the main features of Down's syndrome.
4. Which of the Down's features do you think are most important medically?
5. Draw a bar chart to show how a mother's age increases the risk of Down's syndrome.
6. What is meant by the word amniocentesis?
7. Why do you think that amniocentesis cannot be done safely before 14 weeks of pregnancy?

9 Improving Domestic Animals and Plants

Selective Breeding

Jersey

Ayrshire

Hereford

Aberdeen Angus

Key Ideas

Ever since man learned to domesticate animals and cultivate crops, he has struggled to make them more suitable for his purposes. Stock can be improved by *selective breeding*. This means that the breeder chooses parent organisms with desirable qualities and breeds them together. In plants this involves the use of *hand pollination*, and in animals *artificial insemination* is used.

Another way of improving stock is to use drugs to produce chromosome mutations. Improvements that have been achieved include increased yield, increased resistance to pests and disease, and increased resistance to unfavourable conditions like frost.

The idea of selective breeding is to choose organisms which show desirable characteristics and breed them together in the hope that the offspring will inherit these qualities. This has been successfully done with many domestic plants and animals.

In cattle, for instance, varieties have been developed which give increased yields in milk. These varieties include **Jersey** and **Ayrshire**. Different varieties such as **Hereford** and **Aberdeen Angus** have been selectively bred for meat production.

In crop plants like wheat and barley, selective breeding has increased the yield of grain per hectare by many times and it is reckoned that there are about 12 000 different varieties of these cereals grown worldwide. These have been bred to grow well in such widely differing climates as Canada, Australia and India. They are suitable for different purposes including making macaroni, producing whisky, and making flour to bake bread and biscuits.

Barley varieties

The Story of Wheat

Archaeologists excavating ancient sites in the Holy Land discovered evidence that crops like wheat have been cultivated there for 9000 years. They found flint implements which appear to have been used by ancient peoples for harvesting grain. The wheat grown was a wild plant brought into cultivation. Seeds were collected from the wild and simply planted close to human habitation.

Wild Wheats

The wild ancestral forms of wheat have special features which help them to survive.

1. They have ears which are very brittle and are easily blown off the parent plant. This feature helps them to be dispersed naturally.
2. The grains are covered with a tough coating to protect them from damage.
3. The ears ripen one by one over a fairly long period of time. This ensures a continuous supply of seed through the season.

The yield of these plants would not have been especially high and they would not have produced particularly good flour. Most of the plants which are thought to be the ancestors of modern bread wheat have 14 chromosomes in their cells and are called goat grasses.

Modern bread wheat

Wild wheat

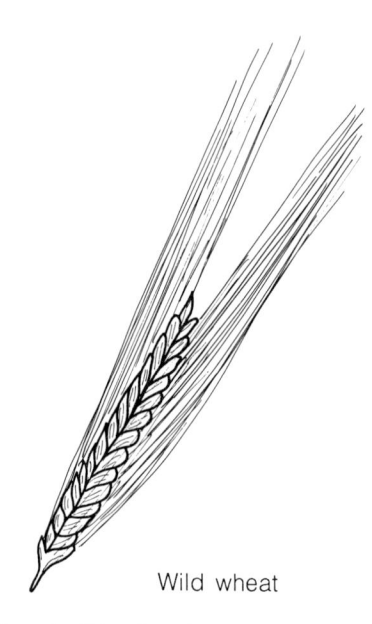

Ears of wild and modern wheat

Modern Wheat

Several thousand years after the cultivation of the wild goat grasses, man bred modern wheat. Modern wheat has characteristics which are desirable in a cultivated plant but which would not be helpful in a wild variety.

1. All the ears ripen at the same time so that a quick, effective harvest is possible.
2. The ears are not brittle and so do not become detached from the parent plant before harvest.
3. The grains are very large, giving high yield.
4. They are not covered with a tough coating and so are easier to thresh.

The chromosome number in the modern wheat varieties is either 28 or 42.

Development of Modern Wheats

By breeding different ancestor plants together, the offspring plants combined the desirable characteristics of their parents. However, the problem with this was that the offspring were usually infertile and did not produce seed at all. Offspring which were fertile were found to have chromosome mutations such as non-disjunction.

In early times, the crossing of parents and the occurrence of mutation happened naturally and by accident. Man has learned to cross parents by selective breeding and to cause mutation by the use of drugs. Thus he has been able to produce new varieties to suit his purposes.

More about Stock Breeding

Improving Corn

Corn or maize plants are grown widely in the USA. There are two main products from the corn plants, corn flour and corn oil. In an experiment, American scientists took one corn strain and selectively bred plants to yield both high oil content corn and also low oil content corn which would be more suitable for extracting flour. The scientists bred selectively for about 50 generations using about 250 plants in each generation. Only plants producing seed nearest to the desirable quality were used as parent plants. The results of this experiment are shown in the graph.

Improving Cattle

One of the reasons for keeping cattle is to produce milk. Selective breeding of dairy cattle over the last 150 years has roughly doubled the yield of milk per cow per year. In the early 1800s, a farmer could only expect about 2000 litres per year from each cow. The table shows the average yield of milk per year from Jersey cattle between 1958 and 1975.

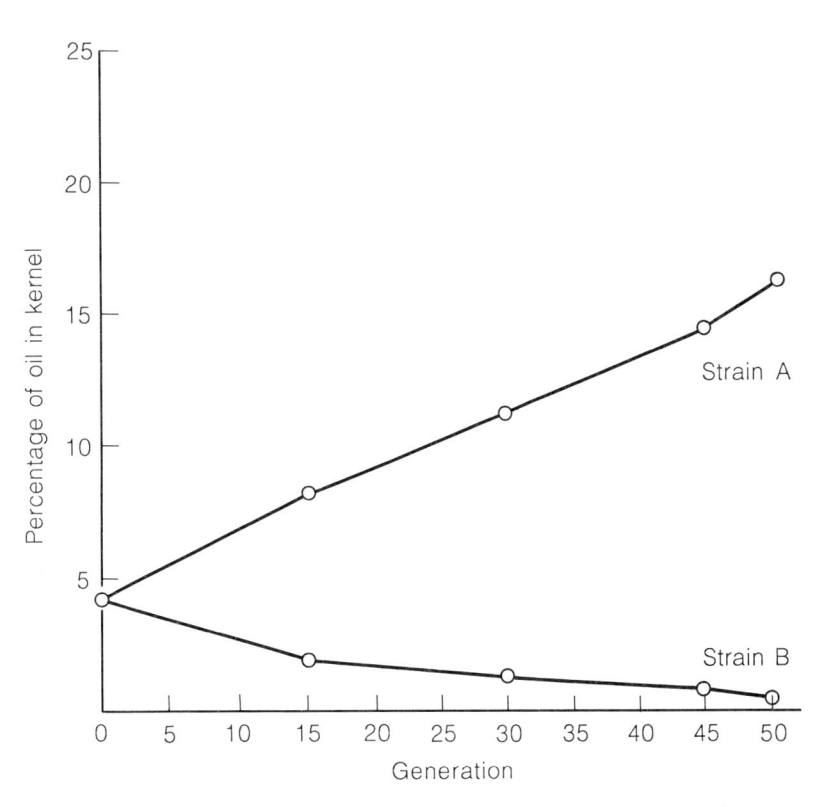

Graph to show oil content of two corn strains derived from one original strain

Year	Average yield per year (l)
1958–59	3280
59–60	3350
60–61	3480
61–62	3550
62–63	3580
63–64	3500
64–65	3550
65–66	3580
66–67	3650
67–68	3700
68–69	3700
69–70	3750
70–71	3900
71–72	4000
72–73	4100
73–74	4050
74–75	4080

Table of average milk yield in Jersey cattle 1958–75

178 INHERITANCE

Mutation Rates

Mutations happen naturally but are rare. They occur in about 1 in 100 000 sex cells. Scientists who want to increase the rate of mutation in an organism can use various procedures. Drugs such as **mustard gas** (which is really an oily liquid) or **colchicine**, and radiation such as **X-rays** and **ultra-violet** light all speed up the rate of mutation and are called **mutagenic agents**.

There is concern nowadays that radiation leaks from nuclear installations such as power stations may increase the chance of serious mutation diseases like **leukaemia** amongst the human population.

Mutation Breeding

Sometimes, useful chromosome mutations can be produced in domestic plants and animals. A good example is of a variety of sugar beet widely grown in Britain today. This variety has an extra set of chromosomes in its cells. The result is that the plants have a much higher yield of sugar than the usual plant variety. About 20 per cent of the British sugar beet crop is of this variety.

Activities

○ 1 What is meant by selective breeding?

○ 2 For each of the following organisms, give *two* different qualities which might be sought by the breeder:
   (a) horses
   (b) pigeons
   (c) sheep

○ 3 List the general qualities which a plant breeder might want in his stock.

● 4 Study the graph on page 177 which shows the oil yield from corn.
   (a) What was the final oil content of strain A?
   (b) What was the final oil content of strain B?
   (c) Find the percentage difference in oil content between the two strains at the 15th generation.
   (d) How much oil would be extracted from 50 kg of seed from the 30th generation of strain A?

● 5 Draw a bar graph of the milk yield in Jersey cattle in the years 1959–60, 1964–65, 1969–70 and 1974–75.

● 6 List four mutagenic agents.

● 7 Find out what is meant by a leukaemia cluster.

1 Introducing Biotechnology

Key Ideas

Biotechnology is a new word. It has been made up from the words biology and technology. It refers to any activities which use the abilities of living things to make products for man or to do work for man. The living things used in biotechnology are usually microorganisms like bacteria. Although the word is new, the activities are not, since man has used microorganisms in the making of *beer, wine, bread* and *cheese* for centuries. However, biotechnology is advancing and developing very rapidly and it is becoming increasingly important in our daily lives.

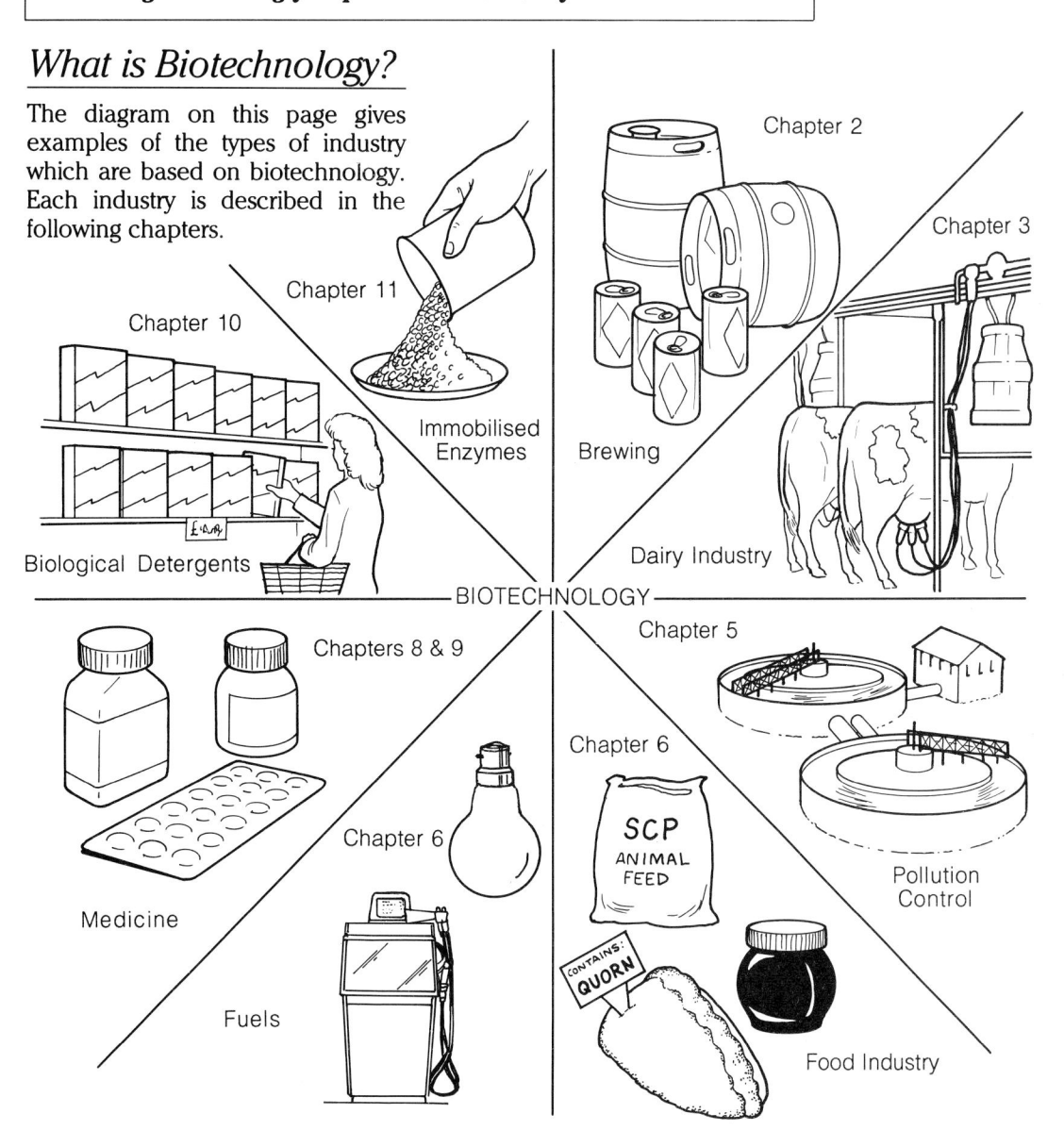

What is Biotechnology?

The diagram on this page gives examples of the types of industry which are based on biotechnology. Each industry is described in the following chapters.

Chapter 2 — Brewing
Chapter 3 — Dairy Industry
Chapter 5 — Pollution Control
Chapter 6 — Food Industry (SCP Animal Feed, Quorn)
Chapter 6 — Fuels
Chapters 8 & 9 — Medicine
Chapter 10 — Biological Detergents
Chapter 11 — Immobilised Enzymes

Biotechnology in industry

BIOTECHNOLOGY

Activities

1 Which activities carried on over 1000 years ago could be described as biotechnology?

2 This table shows the volume of fermentation in some of the biotechnology industries in the UK in 1981.

Industry	Volume (m³)
sewage processing	2 800 000
brewing	128 000
baking	19 000
antibiotics	10 000
dairy (cheese only)	3 000

(a) What is the total capacity in m³ of the industries mentioned in the table?
(b) Name some industries, not mentioned in the table, which are biotechnological activities.
(c) Draw a bar chart to show the figures for brewing, baking and antibiotics.

2 Yeast, Baking and Brewing

Key Ideas

Yeast is a single-celled fungus. It can use glucose sugar as food. When yeast uses glucose as a source of energy it can produce carbon dioxide and alcohol. The commercial use of this process is called *fermentation*. The raising of dough in bread-making and the brewing of beer depend on fermentation by yeast. In beer brewing, the yeast requires ideal growing conditions.

Yeast

Yeast is a fungus. Unlike a mushroom or toadstool, it exists as separate cells only visible under the microscope.

Yeast needs food to grow and usually this food is sugar. It gets its energy from the sugar by **respiration**. If this occurs in the absence of oxygen gas then the process is called anaerobic respiration. This produces carbon dioxide gas and alcohol. It can be summarised by the following word equation:

$$\text{SUGAR} \xrightarrow{\text{yeast}} \text{CARBON DIOXIDE} + \text{ALCOHOL}$$

We use this yeast process commercially to make bread and alcoholic drinks such as wine and beer. This is fermentation.

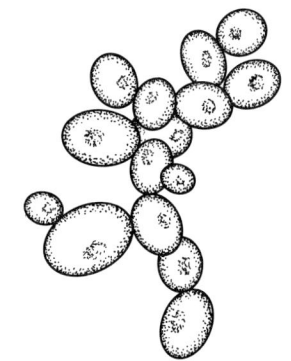

Making Bread

In making bread, flour and water are mixed together to make a **dough**. Yeast is added to the dough. Some of the starch in the flour is broken down into sugar by enzymes. The sugar produced is used by the yeast as a food for energy. The waste products formed from the fermentation process are carbon dioxide and alcohol. The carbon dioxide gas is trapped as bubbles in the bread dough, causing it to rise. When the dough is baked, the yeast is killed and the alcohol which was produced is boiled away. Extra water is evaporated away and a light, spongy loaf of bread is formed.

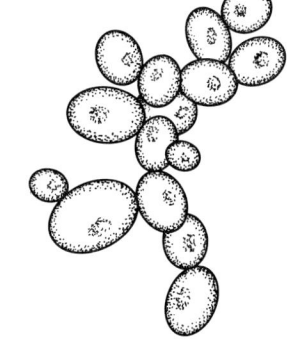

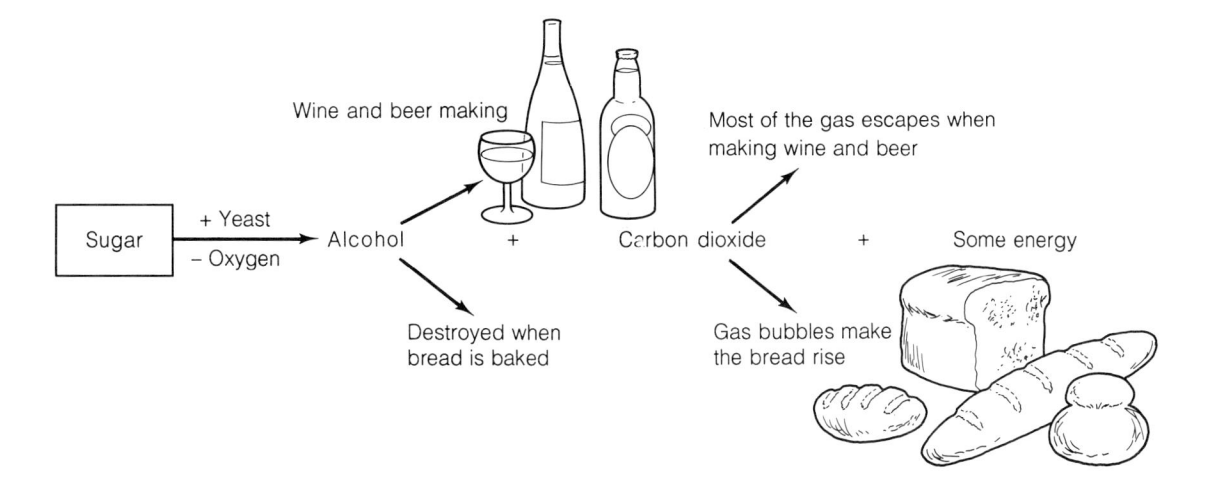

Fermentation of sugar

182 BIOTECHNOLOGY

Wine making

Wine is made when sugars in grape juice are fermented. Carbon dioxide and alcohol are produced.

After the grapes are picked they are crushed, not by people treading them with their feet nowadays, but in large machines which squeeze the juice out of the grapes. This juice is called the **must**. Yeasts that grow on the surface of the grapes will start to ferment the sugars in the grape juice. Sometimes extra yeast is added to speed the process.

It is important that the fermentation takes place at the correct temperature. If it is too hot, the yeast may be killed. If too cold, the fermentation will be slowed down and very little sugar will be turned to alcohol.

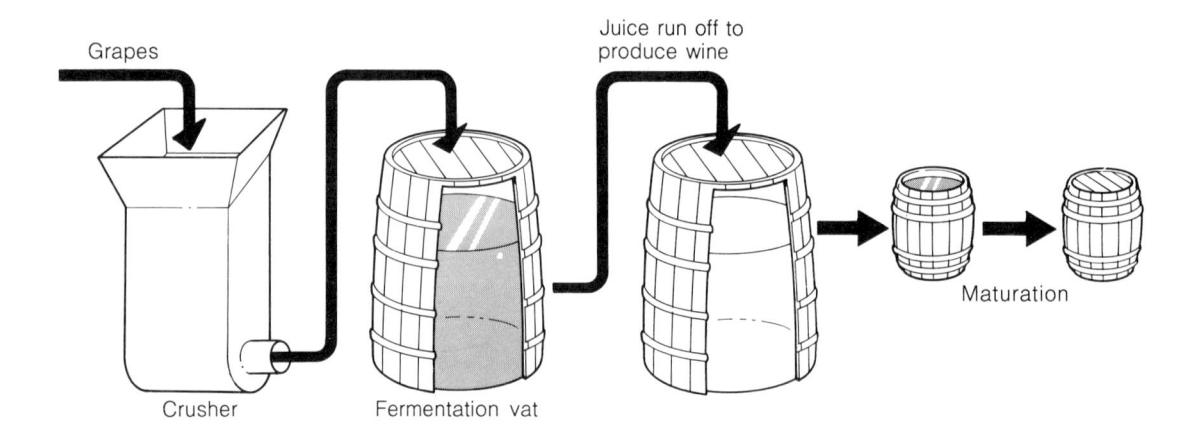

Wine making process

Barley used for malting

Making Beer

Accurate temperature control of the fermentation process is just as important in the brewing of beer. Commercial brewers ensure that temperatures are not allowed to vary. Different temperatures are required at different stages of the brewing process. Sometimes heating will be required, and sometimes controlled cooling, to maintain the correct temperature for each stage.

Yeast is damaged by conditions which are too acidic or too alkaline. Brewers have to ensure that the correct **pH** is maintained at each stage of the process.

Barley grains provide the food for the yeasts used in making beer. Barley grains contain starch. To provide food for the yeast, the starch must first be converted to sugars. This conversion will only take place after the barley grains, which are seeds, are soaked in water. As they start to **germinate** into barley seedlings, enzymes in the barley help to turn the starch into sugars. This stage of brewing is called **malting**.

BIOTECHNOLOGY

The malted grains are then crushed and mixed with hot water to release the sugar. This is called **milling** and **mashing** and produces a liquid called a **wort**.

Next, dried **hops** are added to the mixture and it is boiled to stop the enzymes working and stop any bacteria growing. The hops give flavour to the beer. After boiling the mixture is cooled and the liquid separated off into large fermenting tanks.

Yeast is then added to the mixture and fermentation takes place for about 5 to 8 days. Each brewery may have its own species of yeast, such as *Saccharomyces carlsbergiensis*. The beer can then be put into barrels to mature.

Brewing process

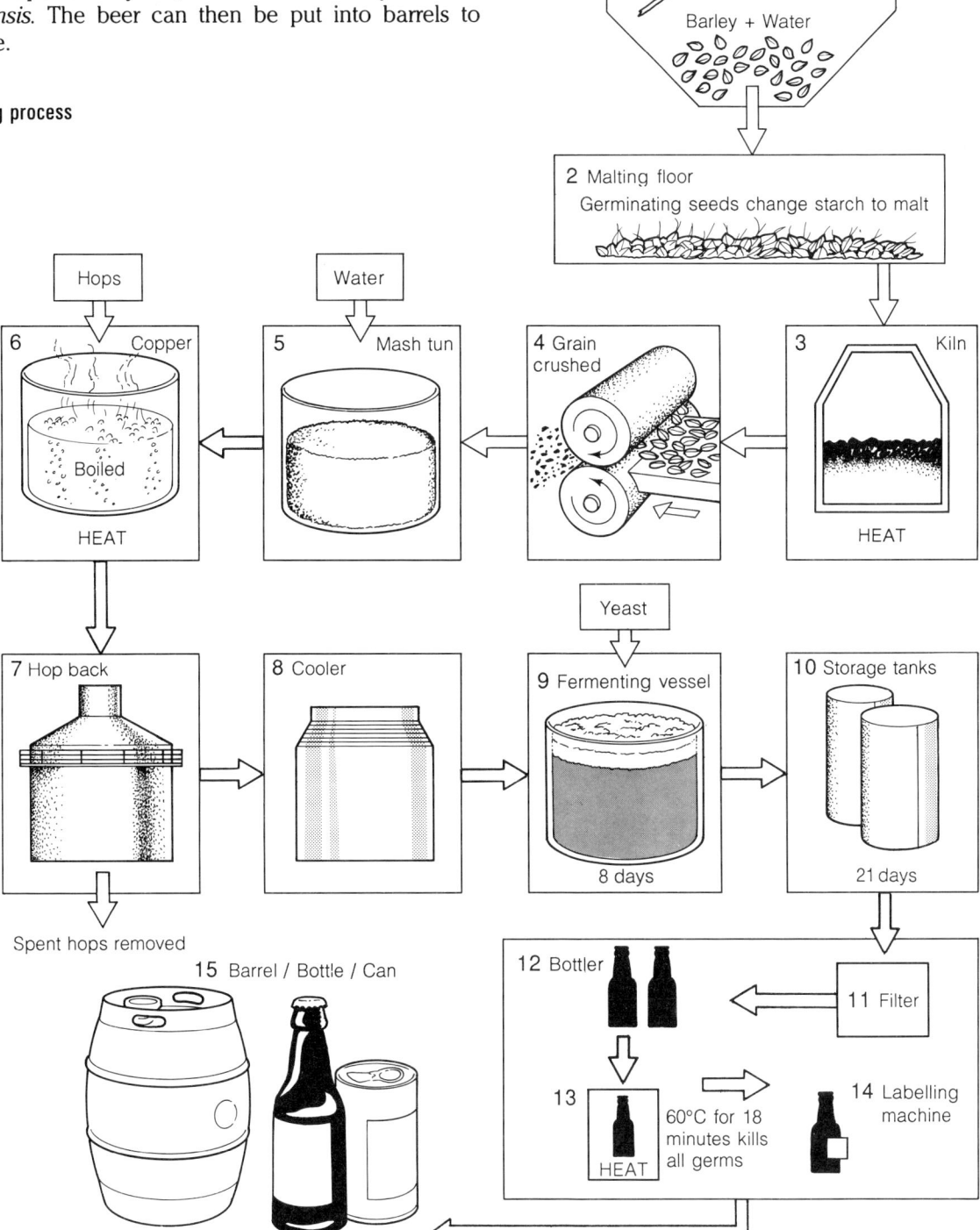

1. Malt house — Barley + Water
2. Malting floor — Germinating seeds change starch to malt
3. Kiln — HEAT
4. Grain crushed
5. Mash tun — Water
6. Copper — Hops — Boiled — HEAT
7. Hop back — Spent hops removed
8. Cooler
9. Fermenting vessel — Yeast — 8 days
10. Storage tanks — 21 days
11. Filter
12. Bottler
13. HEAT — 60°C for 18 minutes kills all germs
14. Labelling machine
15. Barrel / Bottle / Can

Respiration

Respiration takes place in living cells. It releases energy from sugar. There are two types of respiration:

AEROBIC RESPIRATION

This occurs when oxygen is available. It releases a lot of energy from sugar and produces water and carbon dioxide as waste products.

ANAEROBIC RESPIRATION

When all the available oxygen is used up, cells can continue to break down sugars to release energy. This process of anaerobic respiration occurs in fermentation to produce alcohol and carbon dioxide. Less energy is released by anaerobic respiration than by aerobic respiration.

Batch processing

Brewing of beer by the method described in this chapter is an example of **batch processing**. This means that one lot of beer is made, then the fermentation process is stopped. The beer is removed from the fermentation vessel which is then prepared for the next **batch**.

Activities

○ 1 Which commercial products depend on the fermentation of yeast?

○ 2 State the conditions which can affect the fermentation process.

◐ 3 Draw a simple flow diagram to describe the process of making beer.

● 4 Draw a table to compare aerobic and anaerobic respiration. You should describe the differences between the two processes.

3 Dairy Products

Key Ideas

By the 14th century people had learned to make *yoghurt* and *cheese*. Since the 19th century we have understood that it is the activities of various bacteria which convert milk into these dairy products.

Making Yoghurt

In the making of yoghurt, milk is sterilised by heating to about 90 °C for 25 to 30 minutes and then cooled. A starter culture of lactic acid bacteria is added to the milk. It is then **incubated** at 37 °C for 4 to 6 hours.

The bacteria produce acid from part of the milk as they feed on it. The acid then makes the milk curdle and thicken. This gives yoghurt its sharp, slightly sour taste. Flavourings and colourings are added to give the final product.

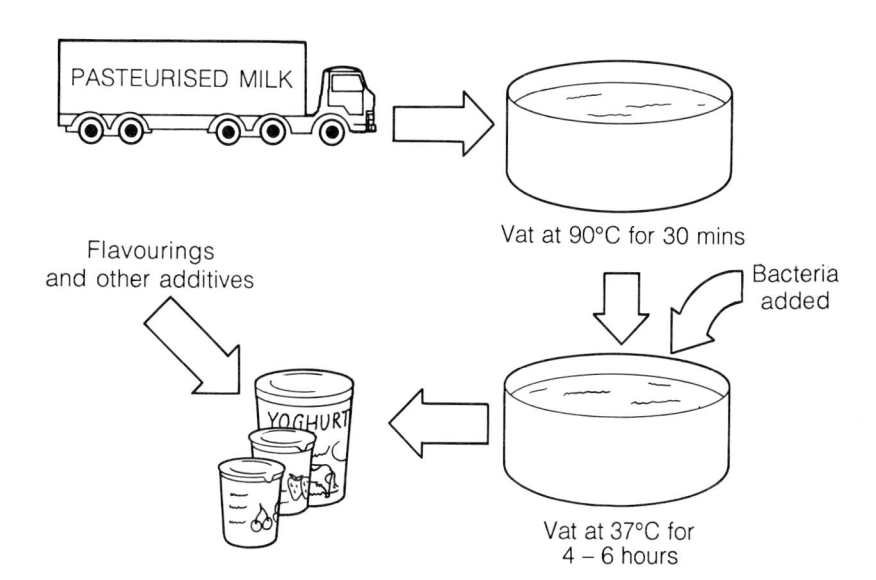

Yoghurt making

Making Cheese

The process of cheese making begins by heating milk with a starter culture of lactic acid bacteria. After a while, **rennet** is added which **coagulates** the milk. The coagulation process produces **curd**. The solid curd is cut into pieces using special knives. The curd is then removed from the liquid **whey**. Next, the curd is ground in a mill and salt is added for preserving and flavouring. The salted curd is pressed into moulds and ripened for up to a year.

Cheese making

BIOTECHNOLOGY

Souring of Milk

Both yoghurt and cheese rely on the souring of milk by bacteria. In the dairy industry this is encouraged by the addition of bacteria to the milk. However, souring is a natural process caused by bacteria already in the milk. The souring is really a kind of fermentation process. The graph shows the changes in the pH of milk going sour over a few days.

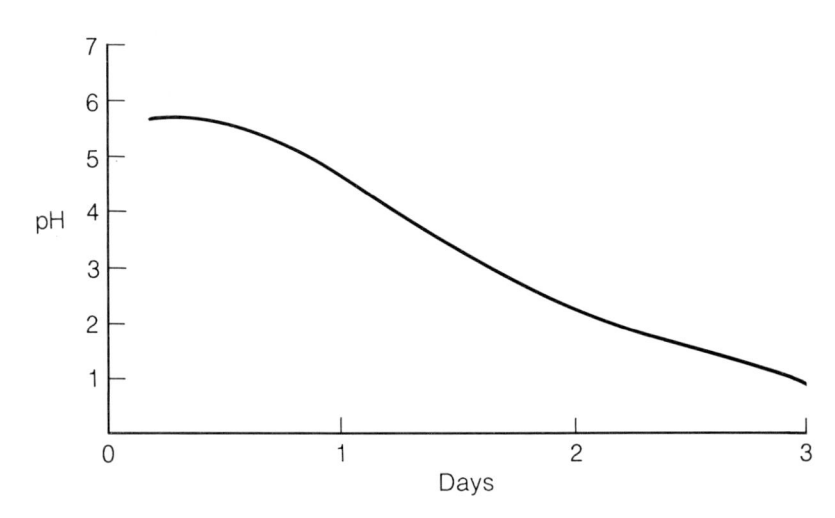

Changing acidity of milk with time

How the Souring Happens

The natural milk sugar called lactose is fermented into lactic acid by the action of the lactic acid bacteria. Lactose is a disaccharide sugar made up of glucose and galactose. It has the formula $C_{12}H_{22}O_{11}$. During fermentation a water molecule is combined with the sugar to produce four lactic acid molecules with the formula $C_3H_6O_3$.

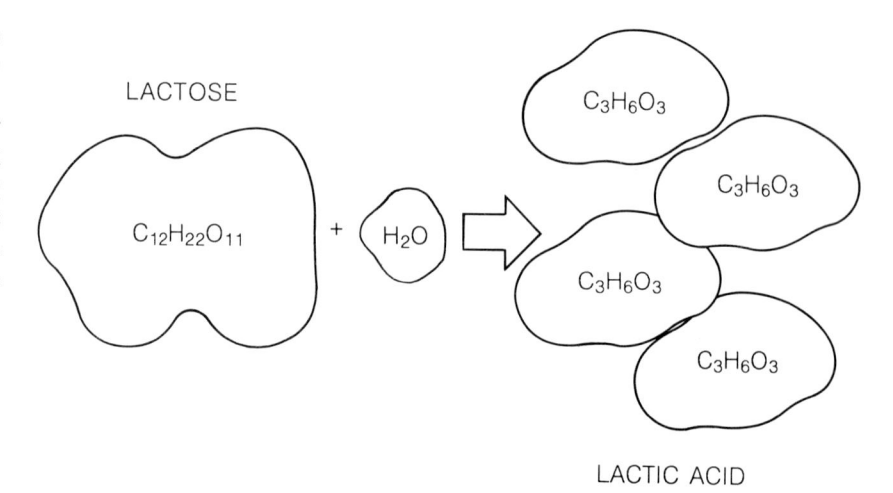

Fermentation of lactose

Activities

1. Why are bacteria important in the dairy industry?
2. Explain why a bottle of milk goes sour.
3. Suggest why milk keeps longer in the winter than in summer.
- 4 Write an equation for the fermentation process in milk.

BIOTECHNOLOGY

4 Growing Microorganisms

Key Ideas

Microorganisms usually grow and reproduce very quickly. If you want to study microorganisms you will usually need to grow large numbers of them. Some of these could cause disease if released. It is important to work safely with microorganisms using sterile procedures.

There are many different types of microorganisms. As individual cells they can only be seen under a microscope. Large numbers of them growing together are known as *colonies*. These can be seen with the naked eye.

Bacteria

There are many types of bacteria. Under high magnifications some look like this:

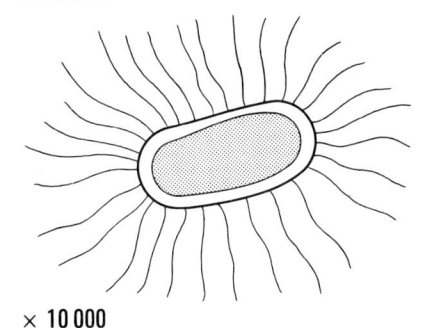

× 10 000

Others look like this:

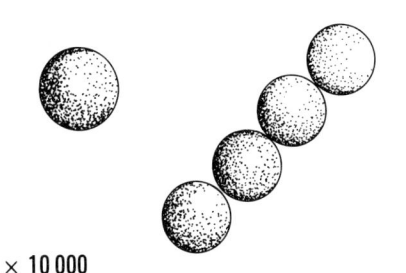

× 10 000

A bacterial colony of about 3 millimetres across may contain over 10 million bacterial cells.

Bacteria reproduce asexually. All of the bacteria in a colony have been produced by mitosis from a single bacterial cell.

Bacterial growth

Some types of bacteria can divide as often as once every 20 minutes. In 12 hours, one single bacterium can form more than 60 000 million new bacteria. In fact, in 4 days one cell could produce a quantity of bacteria greater than the mass of the Earth! Fortunately this does not happen. Like us, bacteria need food to grow and they produce waste products which pollute their surroundings. As a result, many bacteria will die. This serves as a natural control on the number of bacteria.

Fungi

There are many types of fungi. Through a microscope, a colony of fungi may look like this:

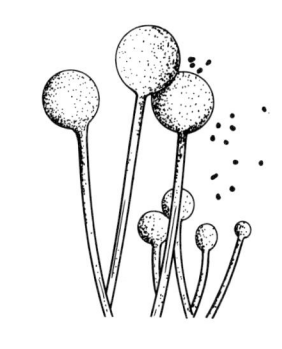

× 50

Yeast is a kind of fungus.

Growing Conditions

Microorganisms need a source of energy (from food), moisture and warmth. With these essentials, microorganisms can be grown on nutrient agar plates, which are petri dishes containing a layer of agar jelly with food added to it.

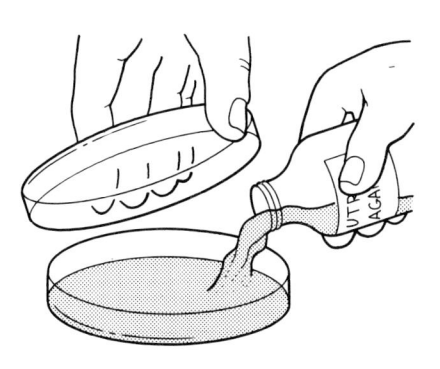

Bacteria and fungi can also be grown in screw-topped McCartney bottles, in a nutrient broth.

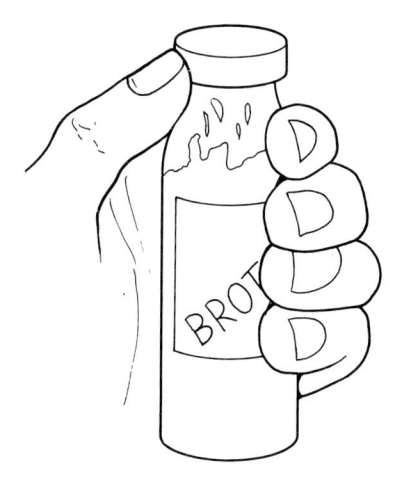

Safe Handling of Microorganisms

The microorganisms supplied for use in schools are considered to be safe. However, disease-causing microorganisms, called **pathogens**, may appear. It is very important therefore that all cultures are treated as if they were pathogenic.

BIOTECHNOLOGY

Aseptic Techniques

Petri dishes and McCartney bottles are transparent and allow the growth of colonies to be seen. The microorganisms are transferred using an inoculating loop.

There are bacterial and fungal spores in the air all around us, on our clothes and bodies and in dust. They must be kept from contaminating cultures of microorganisms by following special procedures. These procedures are also designed to stop microorganisms from the culture reaching the environment, and are generally known as **aseptic** techniques. These techniques should be practised several times before working with cultures, to develop skill in their use.

1. Select an area of bench away from draughts and open windows.
2. Swab the bench top with alcohol or an antiseptic solution.
3. Assemble the apparatus required.

Sterilisation of inoculating loop

This is done by heating the loop to red heat in the flame of a bunsen or spirit burner. It is important not just to heat the tip, but to heat it right back to the end of the handle.

After sterilisation, allow the loop to cool for a few seconds before use. After use, always resterilise the loop and allow it to cool before putting it down.

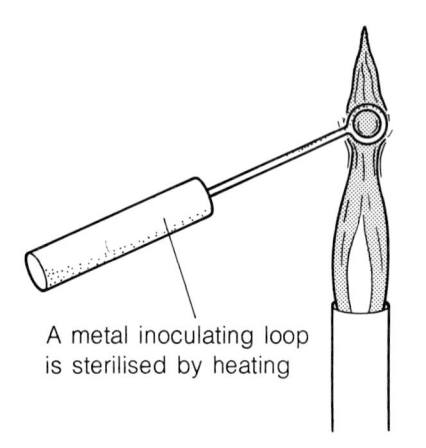

A metal inoculating loop is sterilised by heating

Opening culture bottles

When culture bottles are open there is a risk of contamination from the atmosphere. The following procedure should be followed to decrease contamination.

1. Loosen the cap, but do not remove it.
2. Hold the bottle in the hand you do not write with and remove the cap with the little finger of your other hand.

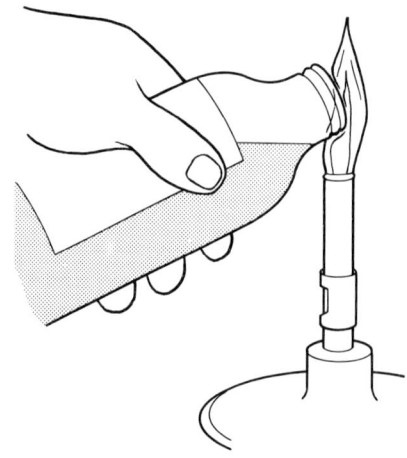

Flaming the neck of a bottle

3. Flame the neck of the bottle by passing it through a burner flame. At this stage, something could be introduced or removed from the culture with an inoculating loop.
4. Flame the neck again as in the previous stage.
5. Replace cap. **Remember:** Do not leave the bottle open any longer than necessary.

Petri dishes

The plastic dishes obtained from suppliers have been sterilised by gamma radiation. Only open a pack when it is needed immediately. When opening the pack, remove only the number of petri dishes you require and reseal the pack with adhesive tape.

The inside of the dish will remain sterile as long as the top is kept on.

It will be necessary to pour medium into dishes and to introduce and remove organisms using the inoculating loop. When this is being done, the lid of the petri dish should be lifted off with the hand you do not write with, and held at an angle over the dish. The loop can then be used with your other hand. Do not completely remove the lid, and replace it immediately the operation is complete.

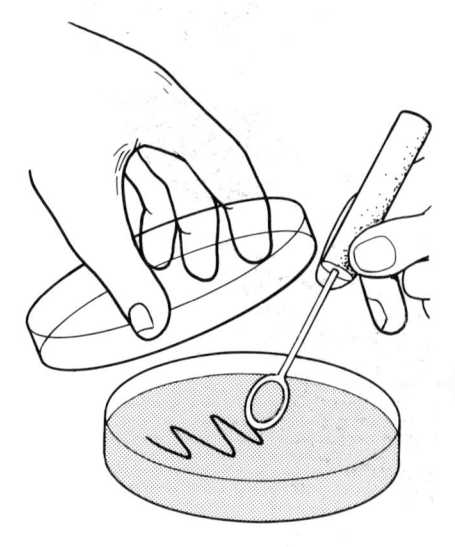

Introducing organisms using an inoculating loop

Before carrying out an experiment with microorganisms, practise all of these techniques.

Manufacturing Processes

For any industrial processes which use microorganisms it is important to make sure that no other microorganisms are allowed to contaminate the process. This could happen through airborne fungal or bacterial spores entering the containers being used.

To prevent this, raw materials and equipment are often sterilised before use. Equipment such as fermenters are sealed off from the atmosphere to prevent spores entering, feeding from the nutrients and multiplying. Sterilisation cannot be ensured by simply boiling or washing equipment with boiling water. This is because some bacterial and fungal spores have been known to survive temperatures in excess of 100°C. Therefore sterilisation may require chemical treatments or irradiation.

Activities

1. Describe what is meant by a bacterial colony.
2. The following table shows the growth of a bacterial colony from a single cell.

Time (mins)	20	40	60	80	100
Numbers	2	4	8	16	32

   (a) How many bacteria will there be after 4 hours?
   (b) Draw a line graph to show the number of bacteria at 20 minute intervals for the first 4 hours.
3. What do microorganisms need in order to live and grow?
4. Describe three precautions you should take to avoid releasing dangerous microorganisms into the atmosphere?

5 Pollution

Key Ideas

Over half the sewage from coastal cities in Europe flows into the sea without being properly treated. Many diseases such as cholera and dysentery can be spread by untreated sewage.

Microorganisms can digest the harmful bacteria in sewage. To do this the microorganisms need a large supply of oxygen. Many different types of microorganisms are needed for the breakdown of the variety of wastes in sewage into harmless waste products.

Decay Microorganisms

When plants or animals die in the wild, their cells and tissues decay. Microorganisms use the dead organisms as a food supply for energy and growth. Microorganisms such as these are called decay or **decomposer** microorganisms.

There are many different types of decomposers. As with other different types of living things, the different decomposers have different diets.

Sewage

Every day each of us uses vast quantities of water:

for washing ourselves	50 litres
for cooking and drinks	5 litres
for washing clothes	10 litres
for washing dishes	15 litres
for flushing toilets	60 litres

The results of a polluted river

Most of this water leaves our houses and workplaces through drainpipes which enter the main sewers of our towns and cities. You can read more about the pollution this causes in The Biosphere.

This waste is what we call sewage. Many towns near the coast simply pump this sewage into the sea without treating it. The sewage is diluted by the vast amount of water in the seas. However, the amount of sewage being pumped untreated into the North Sea is so great that the sea water volume is not sufficient to dilute it enough to make it harmless.

Untreated sewage contains disease-causing pathogens. Humans coming into contact with such polluted water, or drinking water polluted by sewage, can catch many unpleasant diseases, such as cholera, typhoid, and dysentery.

Animal and plant life in rivers and seas can be killed. Untreated sewage pumped into rivers causes rapid growth in the numbers of bacteria which, in turn, use up oxygen dissolved in the water. Lack of oxygen results in the death of many insect larvae and fish.

Recently a fatal disease spread through the seal population of the North Sea which was thought to have been caused by pollution.

Sewage Treatment

In Britain there has been an increase in the amount of sewage carried to sewage treatment works. Here, the sewage is made relatively harmless.

When sewage reaches the treatment works it first passes through a screen which catches large objects such as bits of wood and plastic. It then passes into settling tanks, where solids settle to the bottom. The water from the top of these tanks is usually passed to filter tanks, where it is sprayed over stones. Microorganisms on the surface of the stones break down the remaining sewage particles in the water.

It is important to keep the water circulating through the sprays in the filter tanks. This allows a large amount of oxygen from the air to dissolve in the water, as the microorganisms need oxygen to help break down the sewage.

The sludge from the settling tanks may be pumped into activated sludge tanks, where air is bubbled through the sewage to help the decay microorganisms to break down the solids in the sludge. The remaining sludge can then be used as fertiliser for farmland.

The cleaned water from the filter tanks is passed into final settling tanks where any fine remaining solids settle to the bottom and are removed to the sludge tanks.

The cleaned water, which is regularly tested to ensure that it is safe, is finally pumped out into rivers or the sea. The purified sewage is called **effluent**.

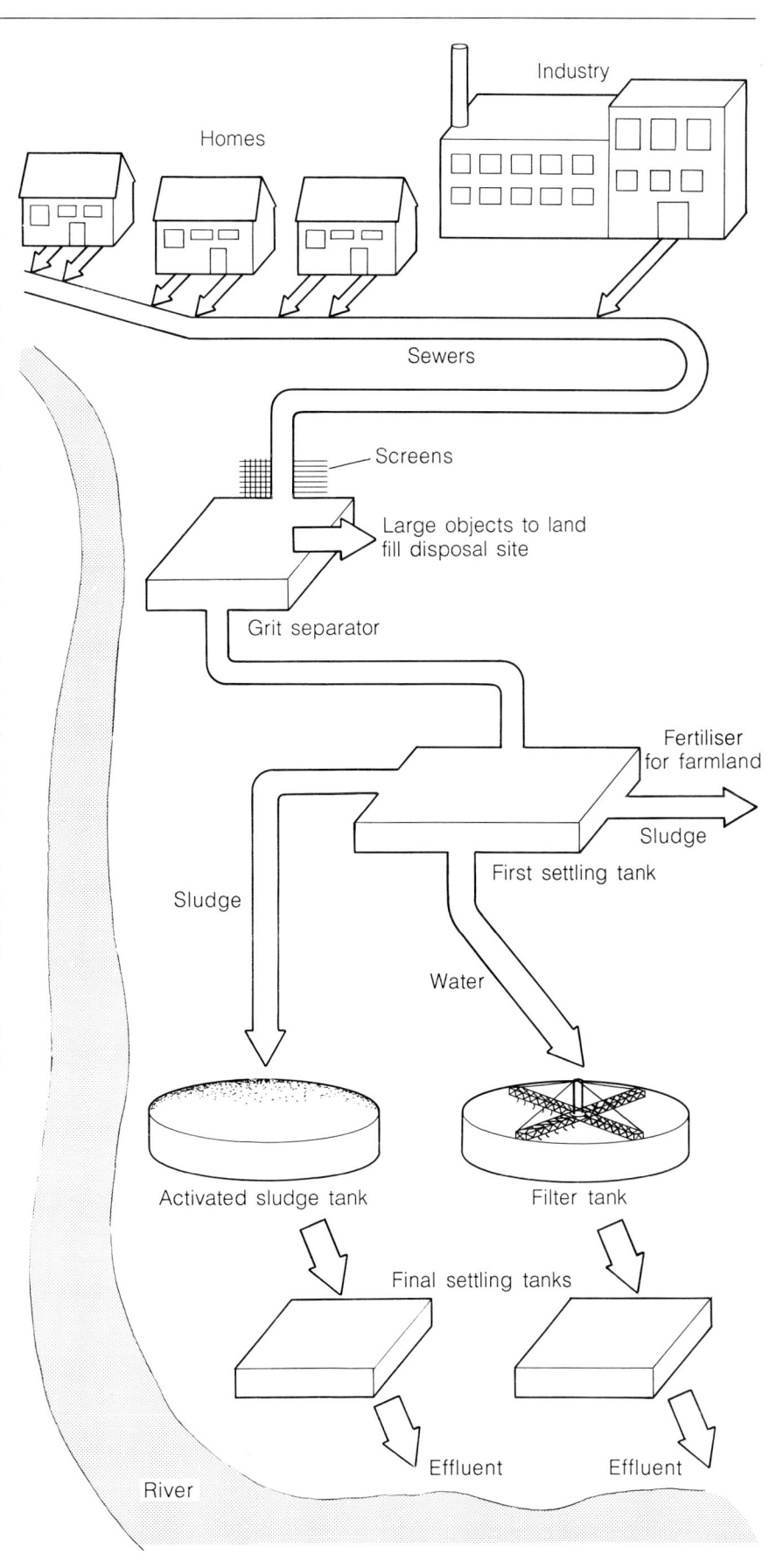

Aerobic Conditions

In the activated sludge treatment of sewage, after the large solids in sewage have settled in a tank, the liquid is pumped into a second tank. Here oxygen is pumped through the liquid. This causes increased growth of the decomposer microorganisms which then clump together with fine solid sewage particles to form floating layers which attract and trap other particles suspended in the liquid. The sewage particles are then broken down by the decomposers and what remains is filtered again.

The liquids are safely passed into rivers or the sea and the solids can be used as fertiliser.

Recycling by Decomposers

Fungi and bacteria live in soil in vast numbers. One millilitre of soil can contain millions of bacteria. As living things, these microorganisms need a food supply. They feed on dead plant and animal material and on wastes from animals. Their feeding and digestion results in the decay of these dead and waste materials.

The products of decay are simpler chemicals than the proteins, fats and carbohydrates making up the original animals and plants. These products are either released into the soil or into the atmosphere. They can then be used by plants growing in the soil or by animals and plants absorbing them as gases from the air. Two chemical elements which are recycled in this way are nitrogen and carbon.

The role of microorganisms in recycling these two chemicals can be seen in the diagrams of the carbon and nitrogen cycles (see The Biosphere, pages 21–22).

Activities

○ 1 Draw a bar graph to show the amount of water you use for different purposes each day.

○ 2 Describe what may have caused the fish to die in the photograph on page 190.

○ 3 List, in the correct order, the main stages of the treatment of sewage.

● 4 Describe how decomposer organisms help in the treatment of sewage.

● 5 Describe one way in which a chemical element is recycled in nature.

6 Food and Fuel from Microbes

Key Ideas

Microorganisms can be used to upgrade waste or to convert surplus materials into more useful products such as food or fuel.

Fermentation by microorganisms produces alcohol and methane gas which may be used as fuels. Microorganisms use the waste products as food and grow very fast. They are very rich in protein.

Protein from these bacteria can be extracted industrially. This *single cell protein*, called *SCP*, can be used to feed animals that provide animal protein for humans.

Biogas

Manure production by farm animals is on the increase, as is the production of sewage from the increasing numbers of humans on our planet.

Many microorganisms are able to produce **methane gas** as a by-product from feeding on sewage or manure. Methane is a fuel which will power electrical generators or even cars, replacing petrol. Sewage and manure are collected in tanks, usually sunk into the ground, where the microorganisms present gradually release methane which is collected in tanks. The remainder of the sewage can be treated, dried and used as fertiliser.

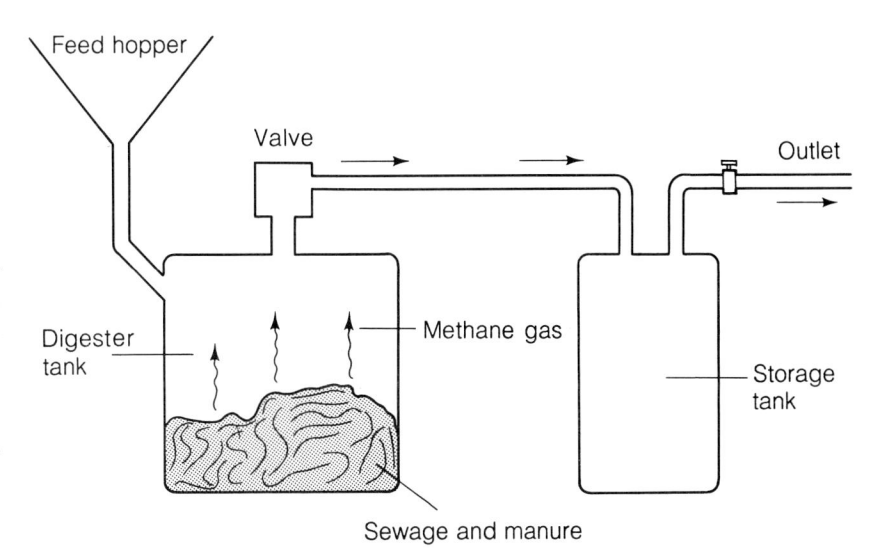

Biogas tank

Single Cell Protein

The cells of some bacteria and yeasts are rich in protein. Bacteria can be grown and then the cells dried to make single cell protein (SCP). Biotechnologists have developed a way of using the waste from paper mills as food for bacteria to produce SCP which is then used as animal feed.

Yeasts thrive on the wastes from food processing. Other bacteria can produce large quantities of protein by feeding on straw stubble which would otherwise be burnt.

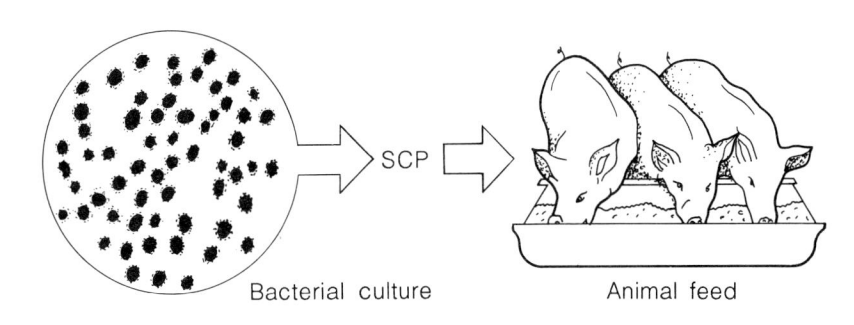

194 BIOTECHNOLOGY

To Waste or Not?

Waste products which are buried in the ground or flushed out to sea cannot be recycled. Waste burning and sea dumping cause pollution. When straw stubble is burnt in fields after the harvest, energy is wasted.

However, growing microorganisms on waste products, to convert them into useful food and fuels, reduces pollution and saves energy. This also provides jobs and profits for industry, and so society benefits from its own waste products.

> **Case Study – Allsorts**
> Waste from the Bassetts sweet factory in England contains quite large amounts of sugar and used to be flushed into the river. As well as being a waste of sugar, it encouraged bacterial growth in the rivers, reducing oxygen levels and killing river life. This meant that Bassetts had to pay increased water rates to help clean up the rivers.
>
> The company decided to find a biotechnological answer to the problem. Scientists from the Tate and Lyle sugar company developed a process to convert the sugar into protein for animal feed using microorganisms. Virtually sugar-free water could then be released into the rivers.

The Need for Protein

We all need protein in our diet for growth and repair. However, people in many parts of the world have far less protein in their diet than they need.

Europe can help by providing surplus food to famine areas, but this is not a long-term solution. SCP could be one answer to some of the food problems of developing countries.

This is not such a new idea. Hundreds of years ago the Aztecs used to harvest a single celled organism, an alga, from lakes. They dried it to eat. It contains up to 70% protein and can produce 500 times more protein per hectare than cattle or sheep.

Region	Total protein in diet (average per day)	
	actual	recommended
East Asia	61 g	74 g
Africa	61 g	75 g
Britain	92 g	79 g

Protein in the diet

BIOTECHNOLOGY

Industrial Production of SCP

A single cell protein product can be produced by growing bacteria on methanol, which can be made from North Sea gas. The bacteria are also provided with mineral salts, air, water, warmth and ammonia as a nitrogen source. The process takes place inside a large **fermenter**, which can produce thousands of tons of SCP every year.

Fermenter (kept warm)

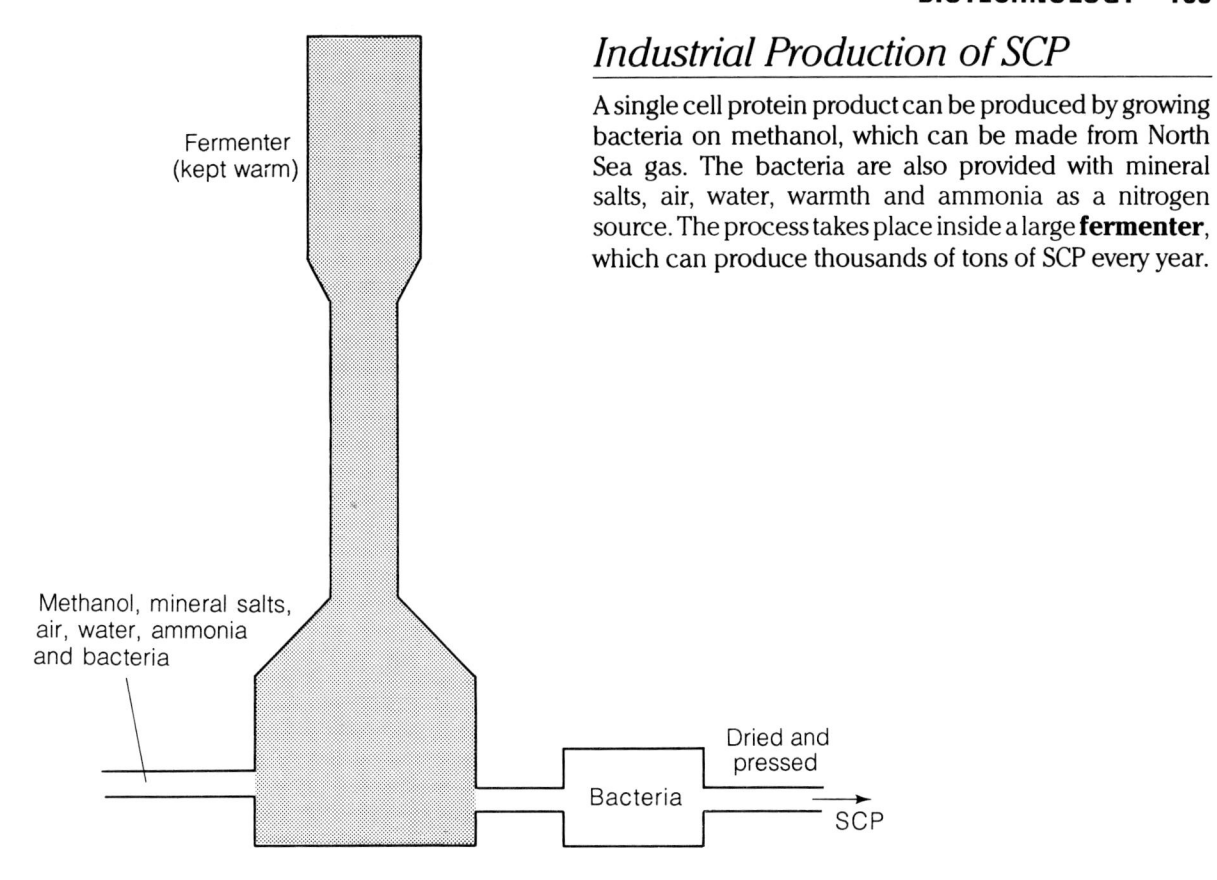

Methanol, mineral salts, air, water, ammonia and bacteria

Bacteria — Dried and pressed → SCP

How the fermenter works

SCP for humans

The company, Rank Hovis McDougall, have developed a process for producing SCP from a fungus. The SCP contains 45% protein, 15% fat and is rich in fibre. The fungus can be grown on wheat, potatoes and other starchy foods. The product extracted from it, called "Quorn", is as nutritious as some types of meat. You may have seen it advertised and you can buy it in products in your local supermarket.

In Britain, brewer's yeast has contributed to our diet for many years, not just in beer making! Extra yeast from the brewing process has been converted into animal feed or to products such as "Marmite".

Gasohol

Fermentation of sugars by yeasts or other microorganisms produces alcohol. As well as alcoholic drinks, fermentation produces alcohol for other purposes. Alcohol can be used as a fuel for cars.

Brazil developed a scheme in the 1970s to produce alcohol from sugar cane. Brazil now produces over 5 billion litres of alcohol fuel, called "Gasohol", per year at half the cost of buying petrol. Alcohol is also environment friendly. It is lead free and when burnt in car engines produces only water and carbon dioxide as waste products. It is virtually pollution free.

As an alternative to petrol, alcohol also has the advantage of reducing the use of fossil fuels. Alcohol is a renewable energy source. Sugar cane can be harvested year after year.

Upgrading Waste

Biotechnology allows us to obtain energy from waste materials which would otherwise be lost. Microorganisms, for example, can convert simple foodstuffs into concentrated protein.

Activities

○ 1 List the different ways in which microorganisms can help to provide us with food or fuel.

○ 2 Why do we need protein in our diet?

○ 3 Describe what is meant by single cell protein (SCP).

○ 4 List three cases of pollution which could be helped by the use of microorganisms. In each case describe how the microorganisms would be used.

○ 5 Many of the processes and ideas for upgrading waste described in this chapter are not used very much. What disadvantages do **you** think are discouraging their use?

What do **you** think should be done to encourage these biotechnological processes?

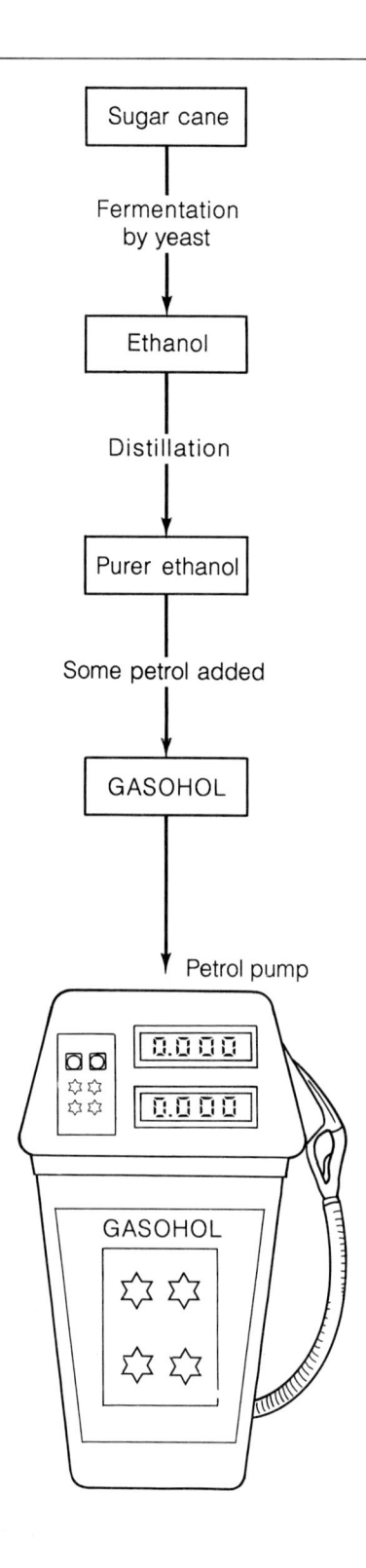

Sugar cane
↓ Fermentation by yeast
Ethanol
↓ Distillation
Purer ethanol
↓ Some petrol added
GASOHOL
↓ Petrol pump

7 Genetic Engineering

Key Ideas

The *chromosomes* of bacterial cells control the activities of the cells. They control what substances the bacteria can make. In *genetic engineering*, a piece of chromosome from another organism may be transferred into bacterial cells. The bacteria may then make a substance normally made by the other organism. By this method, bacteria can be made to produce human insulin.

Nowadays the engineered bacteria are cultured in huge quantities in apparatus called *fermenters*. Large amounts of useful substances made by the bacteria may then be collected from the fermenter.

Bacterial Cells

Bacteria, the organisms normally used in genetic engineering, are **prokaryotic**. This means that they have no real nucleus. Their chromosomes are spread around in the cytoplasm of the cell as small loops called **plasmids**. Each bacterium is surrounded by a membrane and enclosed in a cell wall. Some bacteria have a slimy **capsule** on the outside.

The chromosomes control the cell activities and contain information for making the substances the cell needs.

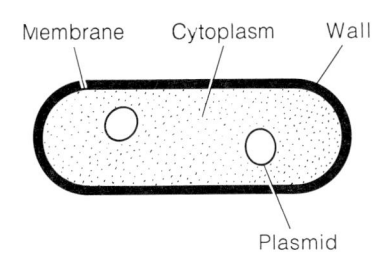

Prokaryote bacterial cell

Fermenters and Sensors

Genetically engineered microbes are grown in containers called fermenters. These are specially designed to produce the best and most economic growth conditions for the microbes being cultured.

The diagram shows a typical laboratory fermenter designed to contain only about 10 litres of culture. Special instruments called sensors monitor conditions such as temperature, oxygen level and pH in the fermenter.

Industrial fermenters like the one in the photograph are designed to handle as much as 200 000 litres of culture.

There are three main problems in scaling up a fermenter to industrial size:

1. The fermenter is so big that it cannot lose enough heat and tends to get too warm.
2. Microorganisms in the middle of the huge fermenter have difficulty in obtaining enough oxygen.
3. It is difficult to prevent contamination by unwanted microorganisms.

Designing and building large fermenters is difficult and very costly.

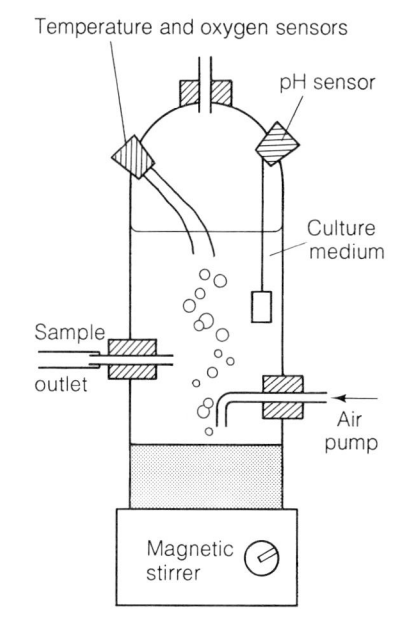

Laboratory fermenter

Industrial fermenter

BIOTECHNOLOGY

Stages in Genetic Engineering

1. The first stage in genetic engineering uses **restriction enzymes** to remove a useful gene from the cells of an organism. These enzymes act like scissors and snip out the useful gene.

2. Next, a bacterial plasmid is cut open with another restriction enzyme.

3. The human gene is then inserted into the bacterial plasmid and joined permanently using an enzyme called a **ligase**.

4. Finally, altered plasmids are mixed with a culture of the bacteria. Some of the plasmids move into the bacterial cells. These cells will then start to make the useful protein.

These stages of genetic engineering are carried out on a small scale in test tubes. The bacteria can then be cultured in huge quantities in a fermenter and large amounts of the useful substance obtained.

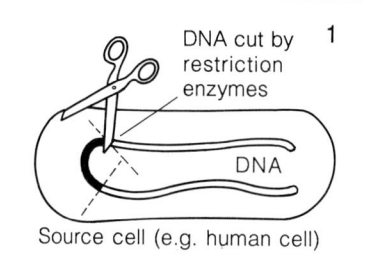

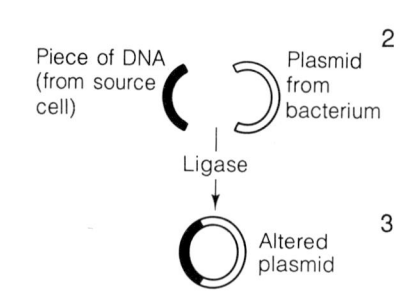

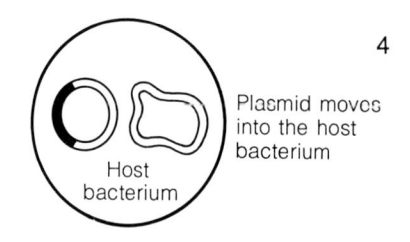

Stages in genetic engineering

Genetic Engineering versus Selective Breeding

Selective breeding has its limits. An animal which has been selectively bred for many generations eventually reaches a point where it cannot be further improved. The animal has reached the limits of its natural variety.

Genetic engineering techniques can sometimes continue the improvement. Drugs have been produced by genetic engineering which can be fed to livestock. When given to a cow, the substance **Bovine Somatotropin (BST)** increases the milk yield by 25%.

Other genetically engineered substances have recently been used as vaccines to protect animals against disease.

Activities

1. Draw a labelled diagram of a bacterial cell.
2. What is the job of the bacterial chromosomes or plasmids?
3. What is meant by the term "genetic engineering"?
4. What are the advantages of industrial fermenters in genetic engineering?
5. What are the following?
   (a) restriction enzymes
   (b) ligases
7. What are the advantages of using genetic engineering to produce new organisms compared with the older method of selective breeding?

8 Genetic Engineering in Medicine

Key Ideas

Many drugs such as insulin are very costly and difficult to produce. There are also problems in making these drugs in sufficient quantitites. The drugs are usually obtained from animal sources and can cause side effects. Genetic engineering provides a way of solving these problems and produces cheaper drugs in large quantities without the use of animal organs.

Insulin

Insulin is a human hormone. Its job is to keep the level of glucose in the blood normal. There should be about 0.1 grams of glucose in every 100 cm^3 of blood.

A gland called the pancreas, found just behind the stomach, makes insulin. If people do not make enough insulin, they cannot control their glucose level and they suffer from **diabetes**. Diabetes can be controlled by injections of insulin. Until recently, insulin for injection was extracted from animals. It was difficult and expensive to produce the insulin this way. Nowadays the hormone can be obtained using genetic engineering.

Other useful substances obtained by genetic engineering include human growth hormone, thyroid stimulating hormone, the anti-viral drug interferon and the anti-haemophilia product factor VIII.

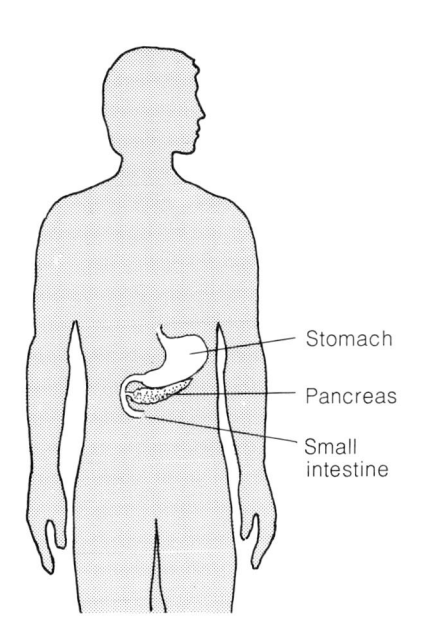

The human pancreas

The Need for Insulin

There is an ever-increasing need for drugs like insulin manufactured by genetic engineering.

1. As the population grows, there is a greater number of diabetics.
2. Better medical care increases the life expectancy of diabetics, and so the demand for insulin grows.
3. Many people don't like the idea of using insulin from animals. This puts more pressure on the genetic engineers to produce insulin from other organisms.

A diabetic receiving an injection of insulin

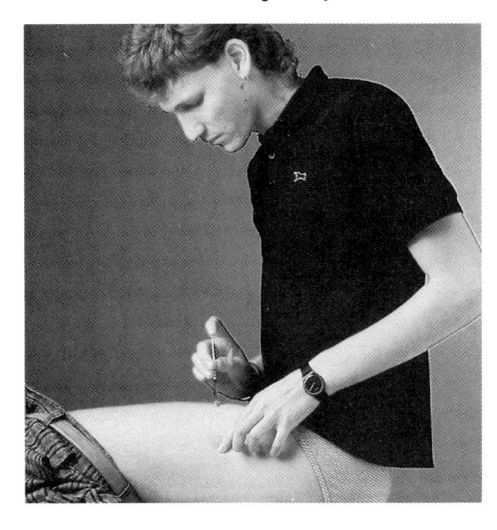

Activities

1. Make up a table of substances produced by genetic engineering and their uses, using two headings, Product and Use.

2. Why is there an ever-increasing demand for insulin produced by biotechnology?

3. John and David are brothers. Unfortunately John was born with a condition in which he lacked enough growth hormone and was not growing at the normal rate. He was given injections of growth hormone which had been made by genetic engineering and now he is the same height as his brother. The following figures show the heights (cm) of the two boys at ages 1–9 years.

Age (years)	1	2	3	4	5	6	7	8	9
JOHN	70	80	83	85	102	108	115	122	130
DAVID	75	85	95	100	105	115	120	125	130

(a) Draw two line graphs of the figures, but plot them both on the same set of axes.
(b) At what age do you think John started to receive his treatment?

9 Antibiotics

Key Ideas

The first antibiotic drug was discovered by Alexander Fleming in 1928. Ten years later, antibiotics were being produced for human use.

The need for large quantities of the drugs to treat infectious diseases during World War Two triggered the start of a huge antibiotics industry. The industry is now a biotechnological one. Many of the drugs are produced by genetically engineered microorganisms in massive fermenters. Many different antibiotic drugs are now used to help cure a wide variety of different bacterial diseases.

Sir Alexander Fleming

What are Antibiotics?

Alexander Fleming discovered the first antibiotic drug by accident. He was growing the bacterium *Staphylococcus aureus* in dishes in his laboratory. One of the dishes accidentally became contaminated by a mould called *Penicillium*. Fleming noticed that the presence of the mould affected the growth of the bacteria. They could not grow in the area around the mould. He correctly assumed that the mould had leaked something into the jelly in the dish and that this substance prevented the bacteria from growing.

The substance was later identified and called penicillin. Penicillin actually works by preventing the bacteria from forming an outer wall. Fleming won the 1945 Nobel prize for his discovery.

Antibiotics and Disease

Penicillin proved to be very effective against diseases such as **pneumonia** and **meningitis**. Unfortunately, it was not able to cure other diseases such as tuberculosis. Penicillin proved to be a **narrow spectrum** antibiotic, only effective against a small range of diseases.

Other antibiotics were discovered which could deal with these other diseases, and today **tuberculosis** is treated with **streptomycin**, a **broad spectrum** antibiotic. There are over 100 different antibiotics in medical use today.

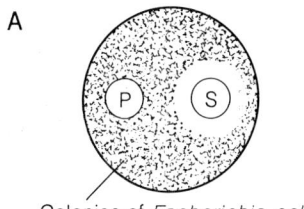

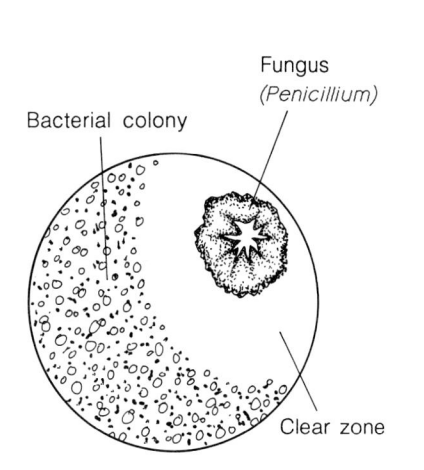

A

Colonies of *Escherichia coli*

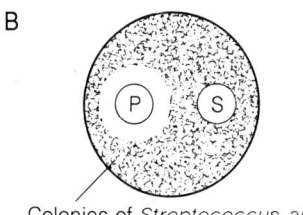

B

Colonies of *Streptococcus alba*

P = penicillin disc
S = streptomycin disc

Culture plates of bacteria with different antibiotics

Fungus (*Penicillium*)
Bacterial colony
Clear zone

Culture plate with moulds

BIOTECHNOLOGY

Activities

1. Who discovered antibiotics?
2. Look at the drawing of the culture plate containing *Penicillium* on page 201. What evidence is there that the mould had leaked an antibiotic into the jelly?
3. What is meant by the terms
    (a) narrow spectrum antibiotic
    (b) broad spectrum antibiotic?
4. Name a disease that penicillin cannot help to cure.
5. The following table shows the approximate number of deaths from diphtheria in England and Wales between 1911 and 1961.

Year	Number of deaths
1911	4900
1921	4700
1931	2600
1941	2600
1951	30
1961	10

   (a) Plot these figures as a line graph.
   (b) Why did the graph show such a fall between 1941 and 1951?
6. Study the drawings of culture plates A and B.
    (a) Which drug is effective against *E. coli*?
    (b) Which drug is effective against *S. alba*?

10 Biological Detergents

Key Ideas

Most detergents are synthetic soap powders made from petroleum. Adding certain enzymes to these powders helps to break down organic and biological stains such as egg, blood and grass. The enzymes allow fabrics to be washed clean at quite low temperatures. This is an advantage since, at low temperatures, fibres do not shrink and dyes do not run. Recently, interest in the environment and pollution has made these washing powders less popular.

Biological Detergents

The idea of biological detergents is not really new. In the first decade of this century a patent was granted for an enzyme based washing powder.

In the 1960s and 1970s, washing powders containing enzymes became very popular. The modern powders contain **proteases** which break down certain biological stains, such as blood, which were otherwise very difficult to remove. The powders have lost their popularity recently, after it was suggested that inhaling enzyme dust was causing respiratory problems in factory workers. Some developed skin allergies after exposing their hands to the washing powders.

The powders have been improved recently by enclosing the enzymes in minute wax beads which swell and burst on contact with water. This prevents the enzyme dust from blowing around in the factory. The manufacturers recommend the use of rubber gloves for hand washing.

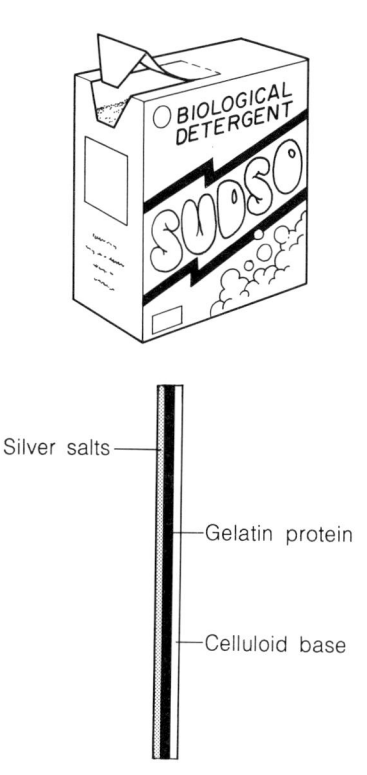

Layers of photographic film

The Action of Biological Detergents

The action of biological detergents can be demonstrated with a simple experiment. Photographic film has silver halide salts dispersed in a film of protein called gelatin. If a protein-digesting enzyme is added to a piece of film, the gelatin will be digested and the silver salts will come off. This will leave the film transparent.

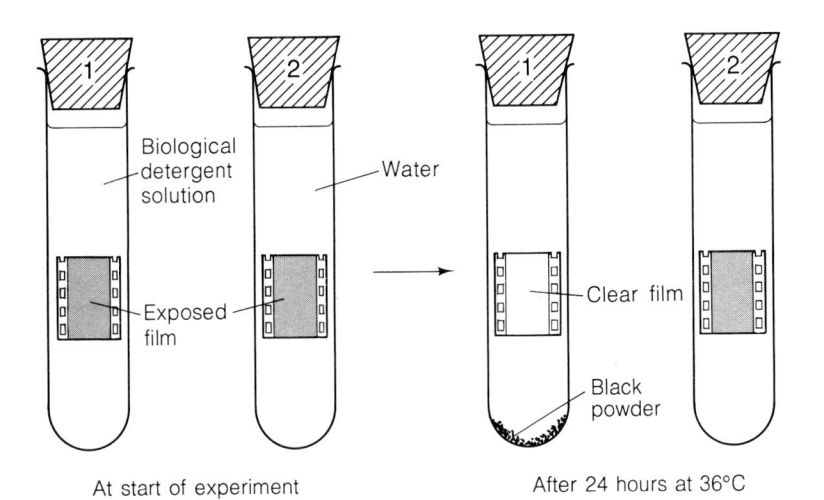

The effect of biological detergent on photographic film

Advantages of Biological Powders

Traditionally, biological stains were removed from fabrics by washing in very hot water, at about 85–90°C. Not only is it expensive to provide the energy to heat the water, but the heat also damages the fabrics. Delicate fabrics tend to shrink, and those which have been dyed tend to lose their colour. As well as shrinking, the fibres of the fabrics may also be damaged.

Biological detergents work well at relatively low temperatures of about 40°C, and so avoid all of these problems.

Activities

1. What is a biological washing powder?
2. How does a biological washing powder work?
3. Study the experiment using photographic film.
   (a) Why is tube 2 included in the set-up?
   (b) Explain what has caused the presence of the black powder in tube 1 after 24 hours.
4. What are the advantages of washing at the low temperatures allowed by biological detergents?

BIOTECHNOLOGY

11 Immobilised Enzymes

Key Ideas

Up until the 1950s, industrial processes such as brewing, which involved enzymes, used whole enzyme-containing cells. Nowadays, many industrial processes use isolated enzymes. Isolated enzymes can be held in place in a thin layer, immobilised, to make them more effective and the process more economic.

Traditional Methods

The whole yeast cells of fermentation use up nutrients and produce a wide variety of substances, not just the desired product. The product must be removed from the mixture before it can be used. Separation can be difficult and costly.

Isolated enzymes are more efficient because they catalyse a single reaction and need only the substrate to make a pure product. Unfortunately, isolating the pure enzyme is an expensive process, and enzymes tend to be unstable.

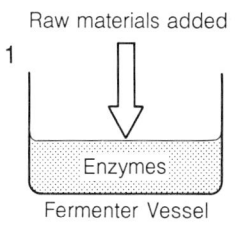

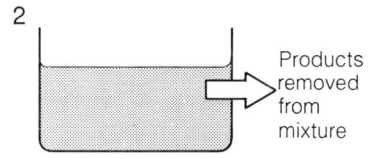

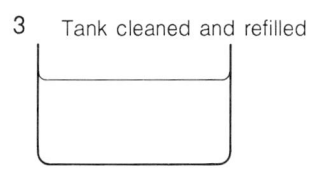

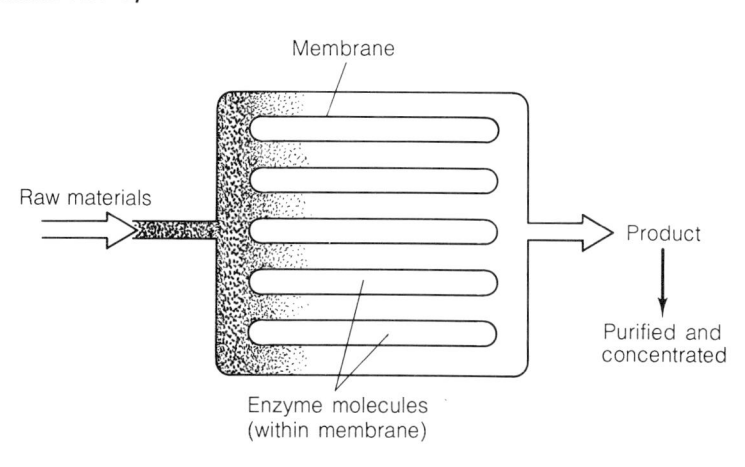

Techniques of enzyme immobilisation have allowed the production of stable enzymes which are easy to collect and reuse after catalysis. Also, the final product is free of enzyme.

Continuous Flow Systems

Immobilised enzyme technology has made it possible to develop fermentation systems which work on a **continuous flow** basis. This means that the substrate enters the fermenter from one end and the product emerges from the other. The enzyme is located within the fermenter. This system has the following advantages over a **batch system**.

1. There is no need to clean out the fermenter as it is in continuous production.
2. Pollution is reduced because there is no waste to dispose of.
3. Continuous processes with more than one enzyme stage are easily designed.
4. The system is more economical to run.

Continuous Flow System

A Batch System

1. Raw materials added — Enzymes — Fermenter Vessel
2. Products removed from mixture
3. Tank cleaned and refilled

Raw materials → Membrane → Product → Purified and concentrated

Enzyme molecules (within membrane)

206 BIOTECHNOLOGY

A Simple Immobilisation Experiment

The enzyme amylase, which digests starch, can be immobilised in a school laboratory. The method is described here:

1. 4 cm³ of amylase is drawn into a syringe along with 6 cm³ of sodium alginate. The syringe is turned to mix the contents.

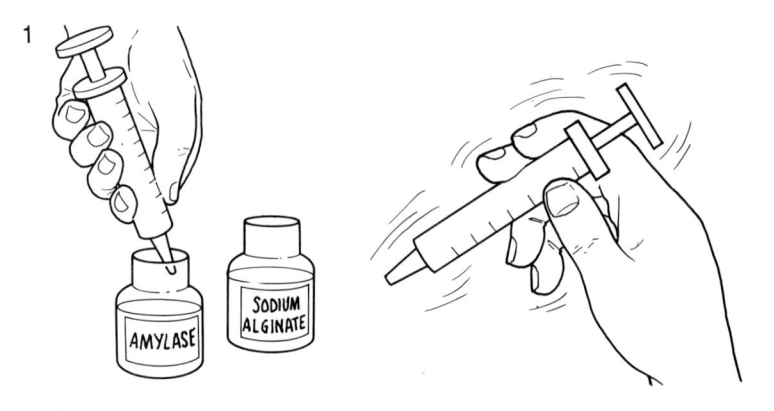

Draw amylase and sodium alginate into a 10 cm³ syringe. Mix the contents

2. The syringe contents are squeezed drop by drop into a beaker of calcium chloride solution. Each drop becomes a solid bead containing the enzyme. The beaker should be gently shaken while this is happening.

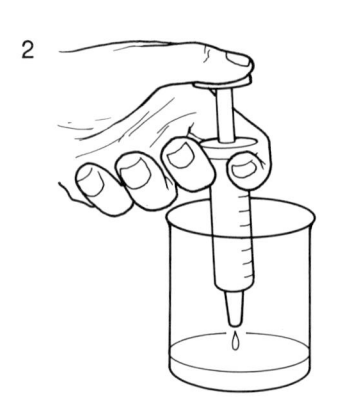

Release dropwise into calcium chloride solution, and then shake beaker

3. The beaker contents are then filtered and rinsed with distilled water. The beads of enzyme can be used in experiments such as the one in activity 3.

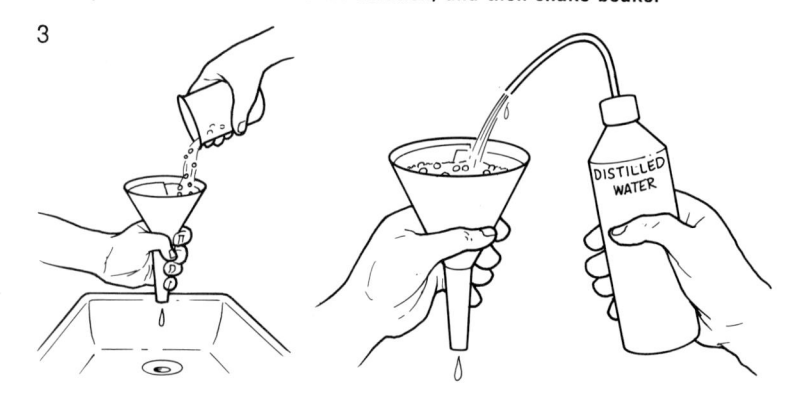

Filter and rinse

4. The beads contain the enzyme in an immobilised form. In industry the beads would be more usually made of glass or cellulose.

Activities

1. What is meant by the term "enzyme immobilisation"?

2. Copy and complete this table to show the advantages of enzyme immobilisation over traditional methods.

Traditional method	Immobilised enzyme method
nutrients used up	
products not pure	
difficult to remove enzyme from fermenter to be reused	
batch system needed	
pollution problems	

3. The following experiment was set up:

Measure 50 cm³ of starch solution into each of two clean beakers labelled A and B.

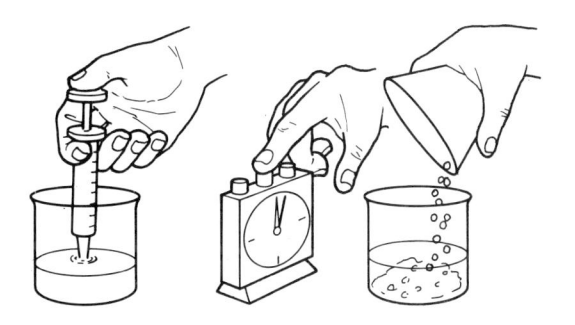

Draw up 4 cm³ of amylase and 6 cm³ of distilled water into the clean syringe. Empty the contents into beaker A. At the same time add beads from the immobilisation procedure on p. 206 to beaker B.

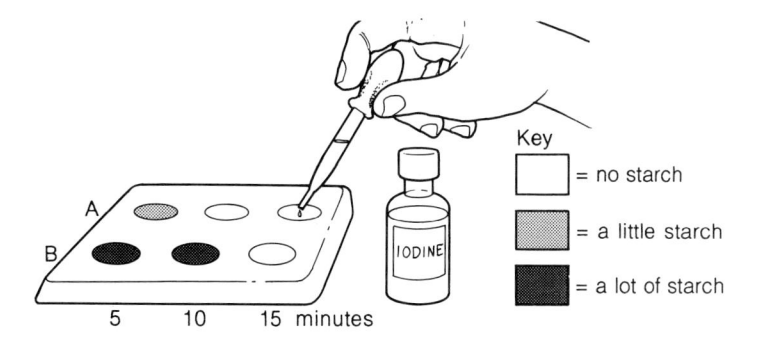

Key
☐ = no starch
▨ = a little starch
■ = a lot of starch

At intervals of 5 minutes the contents of each beaker were tested for starch. A few drops of the liquid were placed in a dimple tile and iodine added as shown.

(a) What is the disadvantage of using the enzyme beads?
(b) What would be the obvious advantages of using the beads?

4. What is meant by continuous flow processes?

5. List the advantages of continuous flow over the traditional batch methods.

GLOSSARY

The definitions of terms included in the glossary are intended to refer to the terms in the context of this book.

abiotic directly relating to the physical (non-living) features of an environment, e.g. temperature (see **biotic**)
absorption the movement of substances from the digestive system into the blood
acetic orcein stain which colours chromosomes dark red
acid rain rain containing sulphuric acid made in the atmosphere from the pollutant gas sulphur dioxide
aerobic using oxygen
aerobic respiration release of energy from foods in a chemical process which takes place in cells using oxygen
aerosol can a container filled with a liquid under pressure. The liquid is forced out as a fine spray
agar carbohydrate extracted from seaweed and used as a growth medium for microorganisms
agriculture farming activities concerned mainly with the production of food
air sac a small air-filled sac found in the lungs and made up of a group of alveoli
alcohol chemical produced by fermentation
alevin a newly hatched fish
alkaline having a pH greater than 7
allele form of a gene occurring at the same position on each of a pair of homologous chromosomes
alveolus a tiny air-filled sac through which oxygen and carbon dioxide diffuse into and out of the blood
amino acids chemical compounds containing the elements oxygen, carbon, hydrogen and nitrogen; proteins are made from long chains of amino acids
amniocentesis medical technique used to diagnose disease in an unborn foetus
amniotic sac fluid-filled 'bag' which surrounds and protects the developing embryos of mammals, reptiles and birds
Amoeba single-celled animal found on the mud of ponds
amylase type of enzyme which speeds up the breakdown of large starch molecules
anaerobic without oxygen
antagonistic the opposing action of two muscles, when the contraction of one is accompanied by the relaxation of the other
anther cluster of pollen sacs in which pollen is made
antibodies proteins made by white blood cells which can counteract bacteria and other foreign materials in the blood
antidiuretic hormone a hormone which stimulates the mammalian kidney to reabsorb water
anus the opening at the end of the digestive system to the outside
anvil a small bone of the middle ear
appendix a short, closed-off tube attached to the start of the large intestine which performs no known function
artery a muscular-walled blood vessel which carries blood away from the heart
artificial selection selective breeding of domesticated animals or plants
atrium one of two upper chambers of the heart which receives blood from either the lungs or the body
auditory nerve a bundle of nerve fibres carrying information from the ear to the brain

bacteria microscopic organisms, usually single-celled and occurring in different shapes
ball and socket joint a type of joint with a wide range of movement and found in the hip or shoulder of animals
barley cereal crop
behaviour response of an organism to internal or external stimuli
bicarbonate indicator a pH indicating chemical which turns red with alkali and yellow with acid. It also can be used to identify carbon dioxide which turns it yellow
biceps a muscle attached to the shoulder and across the elbow joint to the radius. When contracted it bends the arm at the elbow
bicuspid valve a valve allowing blood to flow in one direction only, from the left atrium to the left ventricle of the heart
binocular vision when both eyes have an overlapping field of view which can allow distance and depth to be judged
biological key a set of statements about a group of organisms which is used to identify and name members of the group
biological washing powder washing powder which contains proteases and other enzymes
biotic directly relating to the organisms in an environment, as opposed to its physical features (see **abiotic**)
bladder a 'bag' which collects urine from the kidneys and stores it, later to be released to the outside through the urethra
blind spot an area on the retina of the eye which has no light receptor cells because it is at the position where the optic nerve leaves the eye
blood capillaries tiny blood vessels, with walls only one cell thick, which link arteries to veins
bloodworm an indicator species of polluted water
Bowman's capsule a small, cup-shaped structure in the kidney where soluble substances are filtered out of the blood
brewing the process of making beer
bronchioles small tubes which are branches of the bronchi in the lungs of mammals
bronchus a tube leading from the trachea to a lung
buffer chemicals chemicals which can resist pH changes
bulb composed of underground buds surrounded by fleshy leaves on a flat stem. Method of asexual reproduction

caecum the first part of the large intestine. it has no function in humans
calcium a mineral essential for the formation of strong bones and teeth
calorimeter apparatus used to determine the energy values of foods
canine sharp, pointed tooth found between incisors and molars; used by carnivores to kill and to tear meat from bones
carbohydrate food consisting of compounds of carbon, hydrogen and oxygen; carbohydrates are made in plants by photosynthesis and are a source of energy for plants and animals
carbon cycle the circulation of carbon between the atmosphere and living organisms
carbon dioxide atmospheric gas which green plants absorb during photosynthesis
cardiac muscle muscle tissue which makes up the wall of the heart
carnassial specialised molar teeth, found in carnivores, used for shearing flesh
carnivore an animal (or plant) whose diet consists of meat

carpel female part of a flower

cartilage material covering the ends of bones. It helps to reduce friction in joints

catalase widely distributed enzyme involved in the degradation of hydrogen peroxide into water and oxygen

catalyst substance which increases the rate of a reaction

catalytic cracker chemical plant in which oil is broken down by catalysts to yield products such as petrol

cell unit of life consisting of cytoplasm and a nucleus enclosed by a cell membrane

cell membrane selectively permeable layer which forms the boundary of cells

cell wall cellulose covering of plant cells which give support to plant tissue

cellulose carbohydrate from which cell walls are made

central nervous system the brain and the spinal cord

centrifuge apparatus for separating materials of differing density

cerebellum the part of the brain which coordinates the balance and posture

cerebrum the part of the brain concerned with conscious coordination, memory and learning

CFCs chlorinated fluorocarbons which are used as propellant gases in aerosols and which damage the ozone layer

checklist a list of the names of the organisms expected in a certain habitat which is used to record those actually found

chemical energy energy form stored in foods and fuels

chlorophyll green pigment of plants, essential in photosynthesis

chloroplasts small 'beads' in the cytoplasm of green plant cells; they contain chlorophyll which traps light energy in photosynthesis

chromatid one of the two identical strands which make up a chromosome during cell division

chromosome rod-shaped structure in the nucleus of a cell which is made up of the units of heredity called genes

chromosome mutation error in cell division resulting in cells with abnormal chromosomes

cilia microscopic hair-like structures found on cells, lining the windpipe

clot solid formed from blood where a wound occurs

cochlea a coiled tube in the inner ear which converts sound vibrations into nerve signals which are sent to the brain

colchicine drug obtained from the crocus plant and used to increase the rate of mutation

collecting duct a tube within the kidney which collects urine and passes it into the ureter

colon main part of the large intestine, where water and mineral salts are absorbed

colonisation occupation of an area by living organisms

community all of the organisms sharing a particular habitat

companion cells small cells with nuclei found in plant phloem tissue

competition interaction between members of a community sharing a common, limited resource

concentration the numbers of solute molecules present in a certain volume of solution; usually stated in grams per litre

consumer an organism which eats other organisms

cornea clear protective layer on the front of the eyeball

coronary artery blood vessel which supplies oxygen and food to the heart muscle

cotyledons fleshy starch-filled leaf (or leaves) in seeds

coverslip small square of thin glass used to prevent evaporation of fluid from a microscope preparation

cross-pollination transfer of pollen from the anther of one flower to the stigma of another flower (see **self-pollination**)

cuticle waxy, waterproof non-cellular layer on the surface of plants

cutting small piece cut from a plant capable of growing into another plant

cytoplasm the watery component of cells

deamination process which gets rid of excess amino acids in the liver, producing urea as a waste product

decay the process by which the tissues of dead organisms are broken down by bacteria and fungi

decomposer organism which feeds on dead material and breaks it down into simpler chemicals

degradation enzyme reaction in which large molecules are broken down into smaller ones

dehydrated having lost water, or had it removed

denatured state of proteins such as enzymes which have been damaged by extremes of temperature or pH

denitrifying bacteria bacteria in soil which can break down nitrates into nitrogen and oxygen (see **nitrifying bacteria**)

diaphragm a dome-shaped sheet of muscle and tendon separating the chest cavity from the stomach and intestines. Its movement aids breathing

diastase plant enzyme found in barley grains which converts starch to maltose

diastole the phase of the heart beat when the heart muscle is relaxed and the chambers fill with blood

dicotyledonous describes a seed with two cotyledons (see **monocotyledonous**)

diffusion movement of particles of liquid or gas from areas of high concentration until they are evenly spread

digestion the breakdown of large food molecules into smaller molecules which can be more easily absorbed

digestive system organs of the body through which food passes and where digestion and absorption take place

digitalis drug extracted from the foxglove used to treat heart disease

diploid having two sets of chromosomes in the cells

discontinuous variation variation in which there are clear cut differences between different forms

dislocation when a bone is forced out of its normal position in a joint

dispersal the scattering of fruits and seeds

diurnal active during the day

dominant form of a gene which always shows itself in the phenotype; usually given a capital letter as its symbol

donor a person, living or dead, who gives a part of their body for transplant or transfusion

dormant describes seeds when life processes are suspended before germination

dough mixture of flour and water used to make bread

Down's syndrome inherited human genetic disorder in which the fertilised egg contains an extra chromosome

duodenum first part of the small intestine

eardrum a delicate membrane between the outer and middle ear which passes sound vibrations to the bones of the middle ear

ecology the study of ecosystems

ecosystem usually thought of as being the relationships between members of a community and their habitat

effector an organ or tissue that responds in a particular way to a nerve impulse from a motor neuron

effluent sewage after purification treatment
egg cell see **ovule**
egg yolk food store for the developing embryo of a bird or reptile
embryo first stage of development of an organism after fertilisation
embryo plant young plant found inside a seed
enamel hard outer layer of a tooth
energy the "power" needed to sustain life. Exists in a variety of forms, such as chemical energy in food
environment the particular surroundings of a living organism
enzyme biological catalyst which helps to speed up the rate of chemical reactions in cells
epidermis outermost layer of cells in plants or animal skin
epiglottis small flap of tissue in the throat which can close over the entrance to the trachea to prevent choking during swallowing
epithelium a layer of cells in an animal, usually lining an organ on the inside surface
equator the central plate-shaped area of a spindle
errors (in sampling) defects in data, usually caused by the method of sampling chosen
external fertilisation fertilisation which happens outside the body, usually in water
extinct used to describe a species with no living members
eyepiece lens glass lens at the top of a microscope tube through which the observer looks
F_1 generation first generation of a cross; the number is changed to indicate successive generations ie F_2, F_3 and so on
faeces waste material of digestion which passes out of the body via the anus
fat (oil) high-energy food; oils are liquid at room temperature whereas fats are solid
fats chemical compounds consisting of carbon, hydrogen and oxygen; made up of the smaller units of fatty acids and glycerol. Provide a high-energy food source
fatty acids one of the products of fat digestion
fermentation the process of turning sugars into alcohol and CO_2
fertilisation the process by which male and female gametes join to form a zygote
fertilised egg zygote – (see **fertilisation**)
fibre also known as roughage; indigestible part of plants, made of cellulose, which aids digestion and gives bulk to the faeces
filament stalk on which an anther is supported
fluoride mineral salt which strengthens tooth enamel
focus knob part of a microscope used to vary the distance between the specimen and the objective lens, allowing the image to be brought into sharp focus
foetus stage of development of a mammal prior to birth when the main features become obvious
food chain a sequence of the names of organisms through which energy flows, thus showing which organisms eat which
food web shows what the different organisms in a habitat eat
forestry the techniques of growing and harvesting trees for timber
fossil fuels materials like coal and oil which have been made from ancient remains of animals or plants and which are burned to release energy
fruit part of a plant which holds the seeds and which develops from the flower
fungi members of the Plant Kingdom without chlorophyll which feed on dead or dying organisms

gamete male or female reproductive cell

gas state of matter without fixed volume or shape consisting of particles which are in random, rapid movement
gastric glands found in the lining of the stomach and produce gastric juices
gastric juices digestive fluids secreted by gastric glands, containing hydrochloric acid and the enzyme pepsin
gene part of a chromosome which controls an inherited characteristic
genetics the study of variation and inheritance
genotype the genetic make-up of an organism, usually written as a formula e.g. Tt
genus a group of closely related species
germination the development of a seed into a small plant
glass slide used to mount a specimen for observation through a microscope
glomerular filtrate fluid which passes out of the blood from the glomerulus into the kidney tubules
glomerulus bundle of blood capillaries found inside Bowman's capsule in the kidney
glucose small carbohydrate molecule; final product of starch digestion
glycerol one of the products of fat digestion
glycogen large storage carbohydrate in animals
goblet cells type of cell found in the epithelium which secretes mucus
graft method of artificial propagation in which piece of one plant is fixed on to the root system of another
guard cells bean shaped cells at either side of a stoma

habitat type of place in which specific organisms normally live
haemoglobin red blood pigment containing iron found in red blood cells and responsible for carrying oxygen around the body
hammer a small bone found in the middle ear
hamstring a large muscle at the back of the thigh
haploid having one set of chromosomes in the cells
heavy metal a metal with a large mass number such as lead which can accumulate in the tissue of animals in a food chain
hepatic portal vein large blood vessel carrying products of digestion from the small intestine to the liver
herbivore animal whose diet consists of plant material
heterozygous condition in which an organism has two different alleles of a gene e.g. Tt
hinge joint a joint which can only move in one plane, like a door hinge e.g. knee and elbow
homozygous condition in which an organism has two identical alleles of a gene e.g. TT or tt
hops female fruits of a vine-like plant which give flavour and bitterness to beer
hormone chemical messenger which is carried in the blood in animals and controls certain body processes
hormone rooting powder chemical used to cause root growth in cuttings
horticulture commercial production of plants

ileum main part of the small intestine, where some digestion and most absorption takes place
impermeable does not allow water to pass through
incisor chisel-shaped tooth found at the front of the mouth, used for biting
infertile not capable of reproducing
inheritance transfer of genetic material from one generation to the next

insect pollination pollination carried out by insects (see **wind pollination**)
intercostal muscles a set of muscles connecting adjacent ribs. They are responsible for the breathing movements of the rib cage
internal fertilisation fertilisation which happens inside the female's body
iodine solution red-brown stain used to stain starch black
iris the part of the eye which is coloured and controls the size of the pupil

jawbone bone which provides sockets for the teeth

kidney one of a pair of organs of the body concerned with removing waste products from the blood
kidney tubule narrow tube leading from Bowman's capsule which carries the glomerular filtrate
kilojoule a unit of energy – 4.2 kilojoules is the amount of energy needed to raise the temperature of 1 kilogram of water by 1°C

lacteal small lymphatic vessel found inside a villus in the small intestine; absorbs the products of fat digestion
layer side-branch of a plant which can be rooted artificially to form a new plant
legumes a group of plant species, including peas, beans and clover which have a relationship with nitrogen-fixing bacteria
lens a transparent structure found behind the pupil which focuses light on the retina of the eye
leukaemia type of blood disorder caused by mutation
ligament strong, flexible tissue which holds the ends of bones together across a joint. It encloses the joint
light energy form of energy from the sun, some of which is used in photosynthesis
lipase type of enzyme which aids the breakdown of fats
lipid a fat or oil compound
liquid state of matter with fixed volume but changeable shape consisting of particles which are free to move over each other
liver organ of the body with many chemical functions such as storage of glycogen, production of bile and deamination
lymphatic system system of vessels that transports lymph from body tissues to the blood system
lymphocytes white blood cells with a large nucleus which produce antibodies

magnification number of times larger than actual size that a specimen appears under a microscope
malnutrition the effects on the human body of a diet which is not correctly balanced
malt whole barley grain after germination and drying
malt sugar common name for maltose
maltase enzyme which degrades maltose into glucose and fructose
malting process by which barley is germinated and dried
maltings building in which malting takes place
maltose product of starch digestion
mammal trap a trap and catching box for the live capture of small mammals, such as mice and voles
marrow tissue inside bones from which blood cells are produced
mashing the mixing of crushed malt with hot liquid, when enzymes will convert starch to sugar
maternal chromosome chromosome from the mother
mayflies indicator species of clean, unpolluted water

medulla structure at the base of the brain which controls heart and breathing rates
meiosis type of cell division used in reproduction and leading to gametes with half the chromosome number of the parent cell
menstruation periodic breakdown of the uterus lining and its loss through the vagina
metabolism general term for all of the chemical reactions occurring in cells
methane colourless, inflammable gas, formed by the breakdown of dead plant or animal material
methanol methyl alcohol: a colourless poisonous inflammable organic liquid which can be used as a raw material for chemical processes
micrometre standard international unit of length defined as one thousandth part of a millimetre
microorganisms living things only visible with the aid of a microscope
micropyle tiny hole in an ovule of a flower through which the pollen tube can enter
microscope instrument for looking at very small objects such as cells
migration movement of the members of a species from one area to another which offers better conditions at that time
milling crushing of malt grains before mashing
mirror used to reflect light from a lamp or window through the specimen on a microscope stage
mitosis type of cell division used in growth and leading to cells with the same chromosome number as the parent cell
molar tooth found at the back of the mouth used for chewing and grinding food
monocotyledonous describes a seed with one cotyledon (see **dicotyledonous**)
monoculture in agriculture, the cultivation of a single crop species in huge fields
monohybrid organism which is heterozygous for one pair of alleles
monohybrid cross a cross in which two pure bred parents are crossed to produce heterozygous offspring
motor nerve nerve leading from the central nervous system to a muscle or gland
mucin a sticky fluid which protects the stomach lining
mucus a sticky fluid produced by the goblet cells which line the main breathing tubes
must juice squeezed out of grapes
mustard gas chemical used to increase the rate of mutation

nectar sugary substance produced by flowers and which insects feed on
nephron part of a kidney from Bowman's capsule to ureter
nitrate a form of nitrogen in which it is chemically combined with oxygen
nitrate bacteria a group of bacteria capable of producing nitrate from other forms of nitrogen
nitrifying bacteria a group of soil bacteria which produce nitrates from the decaying remains of dead organisms (see **denitrifying bacteria**)
nitrogen cycle the circulation of nitrogen between the soil, the atmosphere and living organisms
nocturnal active at night
nucleus dark-staining part of a cell which contains the chromosomes; it controls the overall functioning of the cell

GLOSSARY

obesity the effects on the human body of a diet with too much food
objective lens glass lens at the bottom of a microscope tube which is directly above the specimen
oesophagus the tube through which food passes from the mouth to the stomach; also known as the gullet
omnivore an animal whose diet consists of plants and animals
optic nerve nerve leading from the back of the eyeball to the brain
optimum the temperature or pH value at which a particular enzyme works best
Ordnance Survey the organisation which produces accurate maps of the land areas of Great Britain
osmosis movement of water through a selectively permeable membrane from a region of high water concentration to a region of lower water concentration
oval window membrane covered aperture between the middle ear and the inner ear through which vibrations are passed
ovary (1) tissue which produces female gametes
ovary (2) part of the flower where the female sex cells are made
overcrowding the packing of too many organisms into an area
oviduct tube along which eggs pass from an ovary to the uterus and eventually to the outside of the body
ovule female sex cell of flowers
oxygen atmospheric gas which living organisms absorb during respiration
oxyhaemoglobin condition of the red blood pigment when it is carrying oxygen
ozone a combined form of oxygen found in the upper atmosphere which protects life on Earth from damage by ultra-violet radiation

palisade mesophyll main photosynthetic tissue in a leaf
pancreas organ which produces digestive juices
pancreatic juice digestive fluid containing amylase, protease and lipase enzymes
pathogen disease-causing microorganism
pectoral girdle ring of bones at the shoulder level from which the arm bones are hung
pelvic girdle ring of bones at the hip level from which the leg bones are hung
penis the male sexual organ which releases sperm during copulation
pepsin a protease enzyme found in gastric juice; helps break down proteins into peptides
peptide a product of protein digestion
peristalsis wave-like contractions of the muscles surrounding the digestive system which help move material through the system
petal large, brightly coloured, often scented organ of a flower which attracts insects
pH a measure of acidity, neutrality or alkalinity
phagocytes white blood cells with lobed nuclei which engulf bacteria
pharynx region at the back of the mouth containing the windpipe and gullet openings
phenotype the outward appearance of an organism
phloem plant tissue which transports sugars (see **xylem**)
photosynthesis the process in green plants of making organic food from simple materials using sunlight energy
pituitary gland a small gland found at the base of the brain, which secretes horomones
placenta organ through which a developing foetus obtains food and oxygen from its mother and gets rid of waste products to the mother's blood

plaque a sticky film made up of bacteria, saliva and food particles which builds up on teeth
plasma liquid part of the blood in which the cells are carried
plumule shoot of an embryo plant
pollen basket part of the back leg of a honey bee which carries the pollen
pollen grain male sex cell of flower
pollen sac part of the anther which holds the pollen
pollen tube tube through which the male sex cell moves from the stigma to the ovary of a flower
pollination transfer of pollen from anther to stigma
pollution process by which humans add harmful substances to the environment
population collection of individuals of a particular species occupying a specific habitat
potato phosphorylase enzyme which synthesises starch from sugar
potometer device for measuring water loss from leaves
pregnancy the period from implantation of an embryo or embryos in the uterus of a female mammal to birth
primary consumer a herbivorous animal next to the producer in a food chain
producer an organism which comes at the beginning of a food chain sequence and which is capable of synthesising its own food from simpler raw materials
product result of an enzyme catalysed reaction
protease type of enzyme which helps to digest proteins
protein food used for body building and containing the element nitrogen
puberty the stage of development in humans when they become sexually mature
pulse the rhythmic beat of the heart which can be felt in arteries which are near to the skin surface
pupil the hole in front of the eye through which light enters
pure (true) breeding describes homozygous individuals
pyramid of biomass the relationship between the masses of organisms at each stage of food chain. The further the stage from the producer, the less mass present
pyramid of numbers the relationship between the numbers of organisms at each stage in a food chain. The further the stage from the producer, the smaller the numbers present

quadrant a frame, usually a 0.5m^2 metal square, used to sample ground cover of animal or plant species

radicle root of an embryo plant
radio-active waste long-lasting waste material produced in nuclear power stations
reaction time the elapsed time between the body receiving a stimulus and making a response
receptor regions at the ends of sensory nerve cells where stimuli are detected
recessive allele which only shows up in the phenotype when it occurs in the homozygous form; usually given a small letter as its symbol
recovery time the time taken after exercise for the heart rate, breathing rate and levels of lactic acid in the blood to return to normal
rectum the last part of the digestive system in which faeces are stored until they are expelled through the anus
reflex type of response which is controlled by the spinal cord and which does not involve conscious thought eg sneezing

renal artery blood vessel carrying blood to a kidney
renal vein blood vessel taking blood away from a kidney
respiration chemical process by which energy is released from food in cells
respirometer apparatus used to measure the oxygen consumption of organisms during respiration
response action in answer to a stimulus or stimuli
retina light sensitive lining on the back of the eyeball containing cells called rods and cones
root hairs tiny elongated cells which increase the surface area of a root and through which water containing dissolved minerals is absorbed
root nodule an outgrowth on the roots of leguminous plants containing nitrogen-fixing bacteria
roughage fibre in an animal's diet consisting mainly of cellulose
runner special side-branch of a plant capable of rooting and producing new plants

saliva digestive juice produced by the salivary glands
salivary amylase enzyme found in saliva which aids starch digestion
salivary gland found under the tongue; secrets saliva
sample a small representative part of a much greater quantity of organisms or data
scent smell from flowers used to attract insects
scrotum 'bag' of skin containing the testes
scrubbing the process by which waste gases from industry are treated to remove harmful substances before leaving a chimney
secondary consumer a carnivorous animal which eats a primary consumer in a food chain
seed develops from the ovule after fertilisation, and contains embryo plant
selective breeding practice in which parent stock organisms are carefully chosen to pass desirable characteristics onto their offspring
selectively permeable a membrane which allows certain substances to pass through but not others
self-pollination transfer of pollen from an anther to the stigma of the same flower (see **cross-pollination**)
semen liquid in which sperm are transported
semicircular canals set of three tubes in the inner ear which act as balance receptors
semilunar valves valves in the two arteries leaving the heart which stop backflow of blood into the ventricles
sensor nerve nerve which carries an impulse from the receptor into the central nervous system
sepals small green leafy organs covering the flower bud
sewage waste from animals, including humans, consisting of water, urine, faeces and other waste material
sex cell gamete (sperm, egg, pollen or ovule)
sexual reproduction method by which new individuals are brought into existence by the combination of male and female gametes
sieve tubes main conducting cells in phloem tissue
single cell protein protein extracted from single celled organisms which can be fed on waste products, for example, and convert these into protein
small intestine part of the digestive system beyond the stomach, made up of the duodenum and ileum
smog an air pollutant formed when smoke mixes with fog
soda lime mixture of chemicals used for absorbing carbon dioxide from air samples

solid state of matter with a fixed shape and volume consisting of particles which do not move freely
species group of organisms which can interbreed to produce fertile young
specific the property of enzymes which allows them to work on one type of substrate only
specimen object or preparation to be viewed under a microscope
sperm the male sex cell which can move using a small tail
sperm duct tube through which sperm pass from the testes to the penis
spinal cord large bundle of nerves which runs from the base of the brain within the vertebrae to the base of the back
spindle fibres which guide the movements of chromosomes during cell division
spine vertebral column
spongy mesophyll photosynthetic leaf tissue which also exchanges gases with the air
stage part of a microscope on which the specimen is placed
stain coloured dye used to provide contrast in colourless preparations so they are easier to observe
stamens male parts of a flower
starch large carbohydrate food molecule made up of sugar subunits
stigma part of the carpel where pollen lands
stimulant drug which increases body activity
stimulus change in an organism's surroundings which may cause a response
stirrup smallest bone of the body and found in the middle ear
stolon special stem of a potato plant which grows underground and bears potato tubers
stoma(ta) pores on the surface of a leaf through which gases are exchanged
stoneflies indicator species of clean, unpolluted water
stroke when a blood vessel in the brain bursts causing damage to brain tissue
style tissue of the carpel through which the pollen tube grows
substrate substance upon which an enzyme acts
synovial fluid liquid found in moveable joints which lubricates the moving ends of bones
synovial membrane thin membrane which encloses the synovial fluid and which produces new fluid when required
synthesis process by which small molecules are built up into larger ones during an enzyme reaction
systole part of the heartbeat in which the ventricles contract and squeeze blood out of the heart

tendon tough bundle of fibres which connects muscles to bones
termination artificial abortion of very early embryos
territory the area defended by an animal, usually round a breeding site, and which is large enough to meet the needs of the animal, its mate and its young
tertiary consumer a carnivorous animal which eats secondary consumers in a food chain
testa tough outer covering of a seed
testis male reproductive gland where sperm are produced
thrombosis a blood clot which occurs inside a blood vessel
tongue muscular organ inside the mouth, used for tasting, swallowing and speaking
trachea the windpipe or main breathing tube
transect a line or belt crossing a study area along which samples are taken at intervals

transpiration water loss from leaves
transplant to transfer an organ surgically from one body to another
triceps large upper arm muscle responsible for the straightening of the limb
tricuspid valve large heart valve separating the right atrium from the right ventricle and preventing backflow of blood into the atrium
trigger stimulus stimulus which produces a specific response
triploid having three sets of chromosomes in the cells
tuber underground plant storage organ

ultra-violet radiation high-energy radiation from the sun which is potentially harmful to life
urea nitrogen-containing waste product in urine, produced by the deamination of amino acids
ureter tube which carries urine from a kidney to the bladder
urine liquid waste produced by the kidneys; made of a solution of urea and salts
uterus organ where the embryo implants and develops in a female mammal

vacuole sap-filled 'bag' occupying the central part of a mature plant cell
vagina the part of the female reproductive system into which the penis is inserted during copulation
valves structures found in the heart and veins which prevent backflow of blood
variation difference between individuals of a species or differences between species
variegated describes plant varieties which have white or yellow parts on their leaves
variety group of plants of a species which share certain characteristics
vascular bundle cluster of phloem and xylem vessels in a plant

vein (1) a large thin walled blood vessel which returns blood to the heart
vein (2) tiny vascular bundle in a leaf
ventricle one of the lower thick-walled chambers of the heart which pump the blood into the arteries
vertebra one of the bones which make up the vertebral column or backbone
villus a finger-like fold in the lining of the small intestine; it increases the surface area of the intestine and contains lacteals and blood vessels to absorb the products of digestion
vitamins molecules needed in the diet for normal growth and development

wind pollination pollination in which the pollen is carried by wind (see **insect pollination**)
windpipe tube leading from the throat to carry air to and from the lungs (see **trachea**)
word equation statement of the raw materials and products of a chemical reaction in words rather than formulae
wort rich, sugary liquid produced by mashing malt

X chromosome sex chromosome found in pairs in the nuclei of female cells in humans
X-rays type of radiation which can increase mutation rate
xylem water-conducting tissues of plants (see **phloem**)

Y chromosome sex chromosome found only in the nuclei of male cells in humans
yeast type of fungus used in brewing and baking
yolk the food store in the eggs of most mammals, birds and reptiles

zygote a fertilised egg produced from the joining of a male and a female gamete

INDEX

abiotic 2
absorption 65, 70
acetic orcein 95
acid rain 25
activated sludge 191–192
aerobic respiration 184
aerosol can 24
agar 187
air sac 123–124
alcohol 37–38, 181, 196
alevin 76
allele 165
alveolus 123–124
amino acid 61, 62, 68
    absorption of 70
    deamination of 71
amniocentesis 173
amniotic sac 76, 77
Amoeba 100
amylase 206
anaerobic respiration 139, 181
anther 41
antibiotic 201
antibodies 131
antidiuretic hormone 81
anus 62, 66
appendix 66
artery 129
artificial insemination 175
artificial propagation 49–51
aseptic techniques 188
asexual reproduction 47–48
association 147
atrium 128
auditory nerve 144

bacteria 7, 185, 187
balance 145
barley 37, 182
batch process 184, 205
beer 36, 37, 82
behaviour 86
    rhythmical 89
bicarbonate indicator 117, 122
binocular vision 142
biogas 193
biological clock 88
biological key 10
biological washing powder 105, 203–204
biotic 2
bladder 82
blind spot 142
blood 131
bloodworms 27, 28
bone 135
botanic gardens 155
bovine somatotropin 198
Bowman's capsule 82, 83
brain 146
bread 181
breathing 121, 123
    mechanism of 126
    model of 127

brewing 37
bronchioles 123–124
bronchus 123–124
buffer 111
bulb 47

caddisfly larva 10
caecum 66
calcium 135
    chloride 206
calorimeter 114
canine 63
capillaries 82, 83, 129, 130
capsule 197
carbohydrate 52
    digestion of 68
    energy value of 114, 119
    in photosynthesis 61, 62
carbon 20, 61
    cycle 20, 55
carbon dioxide 20, 37
    in breathing 121–122
    in fermentation 181
    in the greenhouse effect 34
    in respiration 116–117
    transport of 131
cardiac muscle 128
carnassial 63
carnivore 12, 63
carpel 41
cartilage 123, 135
catalase 105
catalyst 105
catalytic cracker 105
cell membrane 92–93
    and diffusion 99–100
    and osmosis 102
cell wall 92–93
cellulose 36
central nervous system 141, 146
cerebellum 146
cerebrum 146
CFC 24
characteristics
    acquired 157
    inherited 157
cheese 185
chlorophyll 53, 54
chloroplast 92, 93
chromatid 97
chromosomes 98, 160, 163
    in genetic engineering 197–198
    in mitosis 95–97
    X and Y 169
ciliated cell 125
circadian rhythm 89
clone 50
coagulation 185
cochlea 144
colchicine 178
collecting duct 82, 83
colon 66
colonisation 47, 50

community 1
companion cell 60
competition 17, 45, 50
consumer 52
    primary 12
    secondary 12
continuous flow process 205
co-ordination 141, 147
cornea 142
coronary artery 129
cotyledon 32, 39, 40
curd 185
cuticle 57
cutting 49
cytoplasm 92–93

deamination 71
decay
    microbial 20
    tooth 64
decomposer 13, 190, 192
deforestation 35
degradation 105
denatured 110
denitrifying bacteria 22
diabetes 199
diaphragm 126, 127
diastase 110
diet 63
diffusion 99, 124
digestion 65, 66
digestive juices 65, 68
digestive system 65, 69, 70
digitalis 36
dislocation 138
dispersal 45–46
diurnal 88
dominant 158, 159, 163
dormant 39
dough 181
Down's Syndrome 98, 172
Drosophila 160
duodenum 66

ear drum 144
ecologist 9
ecology 1
ecosystem 1, 30
effector 141, 147
effluent 191
egg cell 72, 73, 74, 76, 78
egg yolk 76
embryo
    animal 76, 77
    plant 39
enamel 64
energy 12, 38, 61, 71
    chemical 52
    light 54, 56
    requirements in diet 119
    value of food 114
environment 1

216 INDEX

enzymes
   digestive 65, 68
   immobilisation of 205
   in biological washing powder 181, 203
   in brewing 37
   in cells 105–109, 110–112
epidermis 56
epiglottis 66
epithelium 125
equator 97
evaporation 57
expiration 126
extinct 3, 34

faeces 66, 80, 82
fats 61, 62, 68, 114, 119
fatty acids 61, 62, 68, 70
feedback control 81
fermentation 181
fermenter 195, 197, 201
fertilisation 41, 43, 160, 161
   external 72, 76
   internal 72, 73, 75, 76, 79
fertiliser 25
fibre 61
flatworm 10
flower 41, 42, 43
fluoride 64
foetus 77
food chain 12, 52
food web 12, 52
forestry 31
fossil fuels 20
fresh-water shrimp 10
fresh-water snail 10
fruit 37, 39
   formation 44
fruit fly 160, 167
fuels 36
fungi 187

gamete 72, 160, 161
gas exchange adaptations 125
gasohol 196
gastric juice 66
gene 160, 163
genetic engineering 197
genetics 150
genotype 163
genus 154, 156
germination 39–40, 182
girdle
   pectoral 134
   pelvic 134
glomerulus 82
glucose 62, 70, 71
glycerol 61, 62, 68, 70
glycogen 71
goblet cell 125
grafting 49
greenhouse effect 34
guard cell 57

habitat 1, 2, 34
haemoglobin 131, 132
Harvard step test 140

heart 128
heavy metal 25
hepatic portal vein 71
herbivore 12, 63
heterozygous 165
homozygous 165
hops 183
hormone 74
   rooting powder 49
hydrogen 20, 38, 52, 61
   peroxide 105
humus 6
hybrid 165

ileum 66, 70
incisor 63
indicator species 27, 28, 29
infertile 18
injuries 138
inspiration 126
insulin 199
intercostal muscles 126
intestine 62, 66, 70
iodine solution 107
iris 142

jawbone 63
jet-lag 89
joint
   ball and socket 135
   hinge 135

kidney 80, 81, 82, 83, 84, 85
kidney tubules 82
kick sampling 8

lacteal 71
lactic acid 139, 186
lactose 186
larynx 125
layering 49
leech 10
legumes 22
lens 142
leukaemia 178
ligament 135
lignin 60
light energy 54, 56
limiting factor 54
lipase 68
lipids 61
liver 71
Longworth mammal trap 8
lungs 121
   cleaning mechanism 125
lymphatic system 71
lymphocytes 131

McCartney bottle 187
magnification 90
malt 37
malting 182
maltose 110
marasmus 120
mashing 183
mayfly 27, 28

mayfly larva 10
medulla 146
meiosis 169
memory 147
meningitis 201
menstruation 74
metabolism 118
methane 38, 193
microorganisms 187, 193, 197
micropyle 43
microscope 90
middle ear bones 144
migrate 18
milling 183
minerals 6, 61, 71
mitosis 75, 76, 95
   stages 97, 169, 187
molar 63
monoculture 30
monohybrid 158, 159
motor nerve 147
mucin 65
mucus 125
muscle 137
   antagonistic 138
must 182
mustard gas 178
mutagenic agent 178
mutation 172, 178

nectar 42
nerve
   impulse 147
   motor 147
   sensory 147
nephron 82
niche 18
nitrate 6
nitrate bacteria 22
nitrifying bacteria 22
nitrite 22
nitrogen cycle 7, 20
nocturnal 88
nodules 22
non-disjunction 172
nuclear fuel 26
nucleus 92–93

obesity 119
oesophagus 66, 67
omnivore 12, 63
optic nerve 142
optimum 111
osmosis 102
ovary 74, 169
oviduct 74, 75, 76
ovulation 74
ovule 41, 43–44
oxygen 6, 34, 36, 61, 77
   in breathing 121–122
   in photosynthesis 52
   in respiration 116
   transport 131, 132
ozone layer 24

pancreas 199

INDEX

pathogens 190
penis 74, 75
pepsin 68
peptide 68
period 74
peristalsis 65, 66, 67
pesticides 25
petal 41–42
pH 182, 186
   and enzymes 111
phagocyte 131
pharynx 123
phloem tube 59
phenotype 157, 158
phosphate 6
photosynthesis 7, 52, 56, 93
pituitary gland 81
placenta 77
plaque 64
plasma 102, 131
plasmid 197
plasmolysed 103
plumule 39
pneumonia 201
pollen 41–42, 43
pollen basket 42
pollen tube 43
pollination 41, 190
   cross 41, 157
   insect 42
   self 41, 157
   wind 42
pollution 7, 190
population 17
potato phosphorylase 106
potometer 57
predation 18
predator 17
pregnancy 77
premolar 63
primary consumer 12
producer 12, 52
product 105
prokaryotic 197
protease 68, 203
protein 61, 62, 114
puberty 74, 75
pulse rate 139
pupil 142
pure bred 158
pyloric sphincter 66
pyramid of biomass 16
pyramid of numbers 16

quadrat 8

radiation 24
radicle 39
radio-active waste 25
rainforest 30, 31, 34
reaction time 139–140
receptor 141
recessive 158, 159, 163
recovery time 139
rectum 66
recycling 20

red blood cells
   and oxygen 124
   structure of 131
reflex action 148
renal artery 82
renal vein 82
rennet 185
respiration 20, 55, 113, 121, 181, 184
respirometer 116
response 86, 141, 147
retina 142
ribs 126–127
root hair 59
roughage 36
runner 47

saliva 65
sample 8
scrotum 75
scrubbing 25
seed 37
   dispersal 45–46
   structure 39–40
selective breeding 50, 175, 198
selectively permeable 93, 104
semen 75
semi-circular canals 145
senses 86
sensor 197
sepal 41
sewage 27, 190
   treatment 24, 191, 193
sexual reproduction 72, 80
sieve tube 60
single cell protein 193, 194, 195
skeleton 133
skull 133
small intestine 66
smog 25
soda lime 116
sodium alginate 206
species 3, 149, 155
sperm 72, 73, 74, 75
sperm duct 74, 75
spina bifida 173
spinal cord 146
spindle 97
stamen 41
starch 37, 52, 61
starvation 119
stigma 41
stimulant 36
stimulus 86, 87, 89, 141
   trigger 88
stolon 48
stoma(ta) 56, 57, 58
stomach 66
stonefly 27, 28
   larva 10
stroke 120
style 43
substrate 105
sugar 52, 61
sweat 80
synovial fluid 136
synovial membrane 136

teeth 63
tendon 137
territory 18
territorial behaviour 18
testa 39
testis 74, 75, 169
tongue 65
trachea 123
training 139–140
transect 9
transpiration 57
transplant 84
tuber 48
tuberculosis 201
Tubifex 10
turgid 103

ultra-violet 24, 178
urea 71, 81, 82, 83, 85
ureter 82
urine 80, 81, 82, 83, 85
uterus 74, 75, 76

vacuole 92–93
vagina 75
valve
   biscuspid 128
   semi-lunar 128
   tricuspid 128
variation
   continuous 149
   discontinuous 149, 157
variegated 53
variety 32
vascular bundle 60
vein
   blood vessel 129
   leaf 59
ventricle 128
villus 66, 70, 71
Visking tubing 62, 99–100
vitamins 61, 71
voluntary action 147

water louse 10
water mite 10
weedkiller 25
wet mount 91
wheat 176
whey 185
white blood cell 131
windpipe 66
wine 182
wort 183

X-rays 178
xylem 59

yeast 37, 181, 205
yoghurt 185
yolk sac 78

zoological gardens 153
zygote 72, 75, 160, 161, 169